The New Industrial Geography

Over the last twenty years the economies of North America and Western Europe have undergone massive industrial–geographical transformations. *The New Industrial Geography* focuses on three of the most important: on the heightened importance of the region as a generator of both technological innovation and economic wealth; on the contingent effects of new local, national and international forms of regulation; and on the emergence of new institutions, and the reworking of old ones.

Drawing on the theoretical resources of institutional economics, *The New Industrial Geography* opens new perspectives in economic geography. In its focus on historical and geographical context, institutional embeddedness, and tacit rules and formal regulations, institutional economics is shown to be the perfect basis for understanding the profound economic and geographical changes of the last two decades, and on which also to build a new kind of industrial geography. Issues covered include: the retheorization of the geography of industrial districts; the analysis of institutional 'thickness', and the economic–geographical effects of institutional ridigity and sclerosis; the economic–geographical consequences of new regulatory bodies and policies; and the geographically situated character of institutions and regulatory frameworks, and the effects of separating them from their originating context; the development of new strategies for achieving more equitable forms of regional development.

This interdisciplinary volume brings together some of the most prominent scholars writing on the topic of contemporary industrial and economic geographical change. They are Ash Amin, Trevor Barnes, John Britton, Susan Christopherson, Philip Cooke, Richard Florida, Meric Gertler, Roger Hayter, John Holmes, Ann Markusen, Kevin Morgan, Mark Samber, Erica Schoenberger, Michael Storper, Nigel Thrift and David Wolfe. It will be of interest to students and researchers of economic and industrial geography, industrial and regional economics, political science, industrial sociology and urban and planning studies.

Trevor J. Barnes is Professor of Geography at the University of British Columbia and **Meric S. Gertler** is Professor of Geography and Planning, University of Toronto. They are the authors of numerous books and articles on economic–industrial geography, industrial and regional economics and urbanism and planning.

Routledge Studies in the Modern World Economy

1 **Interest Rates and Budget Deficits**
A study of the advanced economies
Kanhaya L. Gupta and Bakhtiar Moazzami

2 **World Trade after the Uruguay Round**
Prospects and policy options for the twenty-first century
Edited by Harald Sander and András Inotai

3 **The Flow Analysis of Labour Markets**
Edited by Ronald Schettkat

4 **Inflation and Unemployment**
Contributions to a new macroeconomic approach
Edited by Alvaro Cencini and Mauro Baranzini

5 **Macroeconomic Dimensions of Public Finance**
Essays in honour of Vito Tanzi
Edited by Mario I. Blejer and Teresa M. Ter-Minassian

6 **Fiscal Policy and Economic Reforms**
Essays in honour of Vito Tanzi
Edited by Mario I. Blejer and Teresa M. Ter-Minassian

7 **Competition Policy in the Global Economy**
Modalities for co-operation
Edited by Leonard Waverman, William S. Comanor and Akira Goto

8 **Working in the Macroeconomy**
A study of the US labor market
Martin F. J. Prachowny

9 How Does Privatization Work?
Edited by Anthony Bennett

10 The Economics and Politics of International Trade
Freedom and trade: Volume II
Edited by Gary Cook

11 The Legal and Moral Aspects of International Trade
Freedom and trade: Volume III
Edited by Asif Qureshi, Hillel Steiner and Geraint Parry

12 Capital Markets and Corporate Governance in Japan, Germany and the United States
Organizational response to market inefficiencies
Helmut M. Dietl

13 Competition and Trade Policies
Coherence or conflict
Edited by Einar Hope

14 Rice
The primary commodity
A. J. H. Latham

15 Trade, Theory and Econometrics
Essays in honour of John S. Chipman
Edited by James C. Moore, Raymond Riezman, James R. Melvin

16 Who Benefits from Privatisation?
Edited by Moazzem Hossain and Justin Malbon

17 Towards a Fair Global Labour Market
Avoiding the New Slave Trade
Ozay Mehmet, Errol Mendes and Robert Sinding

18 Models of Futures Markets
Edited by Barry Goss

19 Venture Capital Investment
An agency analysis of UK practice
Gavin C. Reid

20 Macroeconomic Forecasting
A sociological appraisal
Robert Evans

21 Multimedia and Regional Economic Restructuring
Edited by Hans-Joachim Braczyk, Gerhard Fuchs and Hans-Georg Wolf

22 The New Industrial Geography
Regions, regulation and institutions
Edited by Trevor J. Barnes and Meric S. Gertler

The New Industrial Geography

Regions, Regulation and Institutions

Trevor J. Barnes and Meric S. Gertler

London and New York

First published 1999
by Routledge
2 Park Square, Milton Park, Abingdon, Oxon, OX14 4RN

Simultaneously published in the USA and Canada
by Routledge
711 Third Avenue, New York, NY 10017

Routledge is an imprint of the Taylor & Francis Group

First issued in paperback 2011

Typeset in Baskerville by
Prepress Projects, Perth, Scotland

British Library Cataloguing in Publication Data
A catalogue record for this book is available
from the British Library

Library of Congress Cataloging in Publication Data
The new industrial geography : regions, regulations and institutions /
[edited by] Trevor J. Barnes and Meric S. Gertler.
p. cm. – (Routledge studies in the modern world economy : 22)
1. Industrial location. 2. Regional economics. 3. Industrial organization. 4. Regional economic disparities.
I. Barnes, Trevor J. II. Gertler, Meric S. III. Series.
HD58.N48 1999
338.6'042–dc21 99-22501
CIP

ISBN13: 978-0-415-21802-3 (hbk)
ISBN13: 978-0-415-51375-3 (pbk)

Contents

List of illustrations xii
List of contributors xiii
Preface xv
Acknowledgements xxi

1 Industrial geography, institutional economics and Innis 1
TREVOR J. BARNES

Introduction 1
Harold Innis: marginal theorist 2
Institutional economics 6
A new industrial geography? 12
Conclusion 17
Acknowledgement 18
Bibliography 18

PART I
Regions

2 The resurgence of regional economics 23
Ten years later
MICHAEL STORPER

The rediscovery of the region, and its critics 23
Institutions and industrial divides: the ill-fated debate over small firms 25
Industrial organization, transactions, agglomeration: the California School of external economics 28
Innovation, high technology, and regional development 33
Technology, path dependency, and untraded interdependencies 36
From technology to action: the region as a nexus of untraded interdependencies 41
Conclusion 45
Acknowledgements 46
Notes 47
Bibliography 48

3 The co-operative advantage of regions 54
PHILIP COOKE

Introduction 54
The problem: how to achieve regional economic growth? 56
The cluster in theory and practice 57
Co-operative advantage in growth regions 60
Clustering in less favoured regions 63
Conclusion: How to achieve regional economic growth 70
Bibliography 71

4 Reversing attrition? 74
The auto cluster in Baden-Württemberg
KEVIN MORGAN

Introduction 74
Innovation and the collective entrepreneur 75
The chastening of Baden-Württemberg 79
Bibliography 95

5 Sticky places in slippery space 98
A typology of industrial districts
ANN MARKUSEN

The puzzle of stickiness in an increasingly slippery world 98
Identifying and analysing sticky places 99
Marshallian and Italianate industrial districts 106
Hub-and-spoke industrial districts 110
Satellite platforms 112
State-anchored districts 115
Sticky mixes 117
Research and policy implications 119
Acknowledgements 120
Bibliography 121

PART II
Regulation

6 Harnessing the region 127
Changing perspectives on innovation policy in Ontario
DAVID WOLFE

Introduction 127
Paradigm shifts and national systems of innovation 128

The dynamic role of the region 131
The roots of industrial policy in Ontario 135
Towards institutional reflexivity? 140
Rolling back the tide 147
Conclusion 150
Acknowledgements 150
Notes 150
Bibliography 151

7 Rules as resources **155**
How market governance regimes influence firm networks
SUSAN CHRISTOPHERSON

Introduction 155
National systems governing investment and financial markets 156
Alternative solutions to market governance 158
Market rules and firm strategies 164
Conclusion: new parameters for interpreting networks 171
Notes 172
Bibliography 173

8 Continentalism in an era of globalization **176**
A perspective from Canada's resource periphery
ROGER HAYTER AND JOHN HOLMES

Introduction 176
Continentalism and the regulation of Canada's staple industries 179
Principles of continentalism 179
Critics of continentalism from a Canadian perspective 182
After Fordism: the modification of continentalism 183
Continentalism and the Canadian paper industry 187
Powell River and continentalism 193
Conclusion 198
Acknowledgement 198
Bibliography 198

PART III
Institutions

9 The firm in the region and the region in the firm **205**
ERICA SCHOENBERGER

Introduction 205
The firm in the region 206

The region in the firm 210
Examples, exceptions that prove the rule, and possibilities 211
Conclusion 221
Acknowledgements 222
Notes 223
Bibliography 223

10 The production of industrial processes **225**
Regions, nation states and the foundations of regulation
MERIC S. GERTLER

Introduction 225
The transatlantic transfer of advanced manufacturing technology: a case study 227
Interpreting the case: the influence of macroregulatory frameworks 230
The role of national and regional institutions 231
Conclusion 235
Acknowledgement 236
Bibliography 236

11 Does nationality still matter? **238**
The new competition and the foreign ownership question revisited
JOHN N. H. BRITTON

Introduction 238
Models of industrial competition 240
The structure of Canadian trade 242
New technology-based capability 245
A regional perspective on the development of new technology-based industry 252
Conclusion 258
Notes 261
Bibliography 262

12 Capital and creative destruction **265**
Venture capital and regional growth in US industrialization
RICHARD FLORIDA AND MARK SAMBER

Introduction 265
Early venture finance and the rise of New England textiles 267
Financing the second industrial revolution: Andrew Mellon and the Pittsburgh technology complex 270
Venture capital and the high-technology revolution 273
Conclusion and discussion 280
Acknowledgements 282

Notes 282
Bibliography 287

13 Institutional issues for the European regions **292**
From markets and plans to socioeconomics and powers of association
ASH AMIN AND NIGEL THRIFT

Introduction 292
The growing regional divide in Europe 292
The managed economy as an alternative to neo-liberalism 295
A third way 298
Building powers of association 303
From associationism to radical democracy 306
Conclusion 311
Acknowledgements 311
Bibliography 311

Index 315

Illustrations

Tables

5.1	Hypothesized features of new industrial district types	102
5.2	Selected US metropolitan employment growth rates, 1970–90	107
7.1	Network characteristics by market governance regime types	165
8.1	Product mix of the Canadian pulp and paper industry	188
8.2	US pulp and paper tariffs	
8.3	Canadian newsprint production and exports to the US, and US production, 1915–90	189
8.4	Corporate R&D expenditure in the pulp and paper industry in 1986	190
8.5	Estimated geographic distribution of Powell River paper mill's newsprint sales in 1954	194
8.6	Estimated geographic distribution of Powell River paper mill's sales for 1993	195
8.7	Powell River paper mill: employment levels 1974–94	197
11.1	Canada: exports by foreign corporations, 1987	243
11.2	International comparisons R&D/GDP, selected years	246
11.3	R&D expenditures for selected industries in Canada	247
11.4	Foreign and domestic R&D for selected industries in Canada	249
11.5	Canada: R&D expenditures and R&D establishments, selected regions	254
11.6	Technology-intensive manufacturing establishments, Greater Toronto Area, 1995	254
13.1	Examples of intermediate forms of governance	301
13.2	Radicalizing socioeconomics	309

Figures

5.1	Firm size, connections and local versus non-local embeddedness	105
8.1	Powell River paper mill: production 1924–92	193

Contributors

Ash Amin is Professor of Geography at the University of Durham.

Trevor Barnes is Professor of Geography at the University of British Columbia.

John Britton is Professor of Geography at the University of Toronto.

Susan Christopherson is Professor of City and Regional Planning, Cornell University.

Philip Cooke is Professor of City and Regional Planning and Director of the Centre for Advanced Studies in the Social Sciences at the University of Wales, Cardiff.

Richard Florida is the H. John Heinz III Professor of Regional Economic Development in Carnegie Mellon University's Heinz School of Public Policy and Management.

Meric Gertler is Professor of Geography and Co-Director of the Program on Globalization and Regional Innovation Systems in the Centre for International Studies, University of Toronto.

Roger Hayter is Professor of Geography at Simon Fraser University.

John Holmes is Professor and Head of the Department of Geography at Queen's University.

Ann Markusen is Professor and Director of the Project on Regional and Industrial Economics at Rutgers University.

Kevin Morgan is Professor of City and Regional Planning at the University of Wales, Cardiff.

Mark Samber completed his doctorate in history at Carnegie Mellon University and is currently founder of a high-tech startup company.

Erica Schoenberger is Professor of Geography and Environmental Engineering at the Johns Hopkins University.

Michael Storper is Professor of Regional and International Development in the School of Public Policy and Social Research at UCLA.

Nigel Thrift is Professor and Head of the Department of Geography at the University of Bristol.

David Wolfe is Professor of Political Science and Co-Director of the Program on Globalization and Regional Innovation Systems in the Centre for International Studies, University of Toronto.

Preface

The origins of this collection are with a conference that took place in the autumn of 1994 in Toronto to mark the centenary of the birth of Harold Innis (1894–1952), the Canadian economic historian and political economist. The purpose of that conference, though, was not to venerate Innis – he would have been aghast at that idea – but to use his work as a catalyst, a jumping-off point, for thinking about contemporary industrial and economic geographic issues from the wider institutionalist perspective he practised.

In brief, Innis was interested initially in the economic history of his own country and, later, in issues of empire and communications (for more details, see Barnes's opening chapter). In both phases Innis adopted a peculiar methodological stance, captured by his self-applied moniker, 'dirt economist' (Innis 1936: 26). It is an apt description for all kinds of reasons. It reflects the empirically grounded nature of his work, his belief that he was constructing an organic theory of the Canadian economy, his scepticism about the purity of orthodox economic theory, and his disposition towards irony and self-reflection.

As a moniker it is also an apt description of many of the essays found in this collection. For they, too, are empirically grounded, attempt to develop local models of the economy, are frequently distrustful of conventional economic explanations, and often take self-reflection seriously. More generally, many of the contributors to this volume, like Innis, seek some kind of institutionalist 'third way' between the two standard theories of neoclassical economics and classical Marxism. In doing so, many of the contributors, also again like Innis, pursue that third way through incisive social, political and geographical analyses of on-the-ground geographical institutional regulation and change.

That said, half a century – the span of time separating Innis's main corpus of economic work from the essays collected here – clearly makes a difference. Let us note two.

First, in the period since Innis died there has been significant theoretical extension and elaboration of the institutionalist approach that he deployed (and which is reflected in the theoretical disposition of this volume's papers). Institutional economics was formally founded at the turn of the century by the American iconoclast Thorstein Veblen. For the period between the wars (and the time Innis was completing his graduate degrees) it was a small but vibrant intellectual tradition within economics, and best represented by the work of economists such as Commons and Mitchell. After the Second World War, however, with the ascendancy of neoclassical economics, institutionalism was increasingly marginalized. It was viewed by orthodoxy as overly descriptive, analytically woolly, and a little too close to Marxism for comfort. But after suffering several decades in the wilderness, institutional economics re-emerged in the 1980s, and since then has been revivified and substantially developed. Emphasizing among other things institutional practice and transformation, the cultural and social embeddedness of economic action, the processes and consequences of technological change, the contingency of geographical and historical context, and moments of crisis and system shift, contemporary institutional economics is now an eclectic, loose-bound, but powerful body of theoretical ideas and concepts.

Certainly, as a corpus of work it informs many of the chapters contained in this book. In this sense, one principal contribution of this volume is its systematic application of the new institutionalist literature to problems of contemporary industrial change. We are not claiming that this represents a 'paradigm' shift or anything like that. But the institutionalist literature, as several recent reviews have made clear (Hodgson 1994; Samuels 1995; Ingham 1996), is burgeoning and vigorous, and it seems important to explore its application in cognate disciplines such as industrial and economic geography, to see where it might lead. Certainly, the intellectual credentials of institutionalism, with its roots in American pragmatist philosophy, chime well with the so-called recent 'cultural turn' increasingly found and advocated in industrial and economic geography. As Barnes argues in his introductory chapter, institutional economics may be the best theoretical bet for realizing an industrial and economic geography that takes both economy and culture seriously.

Second, the context about which Innis and other old institutional economists were writing is vastly different from the one that preoccupies our contributors. The world has turned. This does not mean that the industrial system operates on entirely different principles: for example, accumulation and profit clearly remain central (Harvey 1989). But its form has undergone massive transformation. In this volume we focus on three such morphological transformations, around regions, regulations and institutions. In turn, we use those three themes as the book's main sections in order to organize the chapters within the collection.

The first section is on the region. In the past, the regional scale was subordinate to the level of the nation state, and typically was only of interest at all because it went hand in hand with another word, 'problem'. Further, that sense of subordination was reinforced by the division of labour within the academy: economists, true scientists, examined the economy as a whole, while regional scientists and geographers, whose qualifications were always a bit suspect, got only part of the economy, the region. Such a view, however, is no longer tenable, if it ever was. More than ever before, the region is recognized as providing the fundamental basis for national, and even international, economic wealth, growth and trade. Regions provide the wherewithal for firms to compete successfully at all geographical scales. Industrial and economic geographers, of course, have long recognized the geographical foundations of economic activity, but within the last ten years they have gone further and sought to demonstrate how the region inheres in the very process of industrialization itself. Furthermore, this recognition is now increasingly visible academically as non-geographers such as the economists Paul Krugman and Laura Tyson, management theorists such as Michael Porter and Rosabeth Moss Kanter, and political scientists such as Charles Sabel and Robert Putnam also recognize the power of the region. Although there are sometimes sharp differences among these different writers, all agree that geography matters, and that both space and place need to be included at the very outset of analysis rather than tacked on as background.

Michael Storper's essay that begins the section on the region provides a compelling overview. He concludes that the region occupies an increasingly central position in dynamic capitalist economies because innovative production now relies more and more upon the ability of firms to develop what he calls 'untraded interdependencies' with one another, and which are available only at the level of the region. Interdependencies in the form of close linkages among spatially proximate firms are further explored in Phil Cooke's chapter that follows. Arguing for what he calls 'network-based development', Cooke uses his case studies of three European less favoured regions, the Ruhr Valley, Wales and Valencia, to argue for the importance of a co-operative ethic among firms in promoting regional competitiveness. Kevin Morgan's chapter is also concerned with a European region, Germany's Baden-Württemberg, which was recognized as a success story for much of the post-war period. However, because of the region's fall from grace in the early 1990s, Morgan's chapter is principally concerned with the recent strategies by the local government to encourage, as Cooke suggests in his paper, greater collaboration and linkages among the region's Mittelstand firms in order to revive its ailing economy. The final chapter in the section, by Ann Markusen, examines the various regional forms taken by industrial districts. Her point is that there is no single regional economic mould – typically taken in the literature as the 'Marshallian district' – but a variety of them, and each a consequence of a particular set of contingent institutional and regulatory relationships found at a given place.

The second section takes up Markusen's theme of place-bound regulatory relationships. There is often an underlying supposition in standard economic theorizing, of both the right and the left, that industrial economies are somehow above social and political regulation; that they have an inner dynamic or momentum that is unsullied by society and politics. If this was ever true, all of the papers in this section now give lie to that supposition. They argue that at every geographical scale – regional, national and international – institutions of regulation enter in at the ground level to affect outcomes. Regulation is not background scenery, but part of the fray itself.

This is certainly evident in David Wolfe's chapter that starts the section. Examining the attempt by the Ontario NDP (social democratic) government to implement an industrial policy in the early 1990s based upon precisely the kinds of precepts for new institutional collaboration discussed by Storper, Cooke and Morgan, Wolfe shows how difficult this task can be because of institutional rigidity and entrenchment. Christopherson's chapter that follows in part explains the kind of obstreperous institutional rigidity that Wolfe finds. Christopherson's argument is that local institutional rules and regulations are reflective of wider national political and social structures. Here, as she persuasively argues, there is a clear division between countries such as the United States, dominated by a 'thin' regulatory structure which discourages institutional collaboration, and countries such as Germany where that structure is thicker and promotes the kind of co-operation and flexibility that Wolfe (and the NDP) would like to have seen develop in Ontario. The last paper, by Hayter and Holmes, uses the case study of the single-industry town of Powell River, British Columbia, to examine the profound effects of global regulation that are found even on this 'periphery of a periphery'. The point is that often 'the global' is used to connote a universal, placeless and purely economic process. But as Hayter and Holmes make clear, globalization is intimately shaped and directed by regulations of concrete, place-bound institutions.

The book's last section turns to the nature of those institutions. Veblen defined institutions as 'settled habits of thought', and by that he meant the way institutions embody a particular attitude to the world, which then shapes their actions within it. But those 'settled thoughts' don't emerge out of the blue: instead, they are related to wider social and cultural sentiments of the particular times and places in which institutions are formed and develop. Through the vehicle of the institution, then, economic institutionalists provide the possibility of a contextual and culturally sensitive account. It is an account in which the actions of institutions are not reducible to the universal rational calculations of individuals found within them, but are embedded within, and constrained by, a local institutional culture of social relations, tacit rules and formal regulations.

One problem that institutions often face is adjusting their 'settled habits of thought' to changing external circumstances. This is the issue addressed by Erica Schoenberger in her study of corporate decision-making that leads off this section. Following the institutionalist line, she portrays the corporation as anything but the all-seeing, all-knowing colossus that figures so prominently in popular narratives about globalization and the like. Instead it is an organization riven by internal discord, tension and a diversity of world-views; that is, by a peculiar institutional culture. The limitations of that institutional corporate culture are explored further by Meric Gertler, who in his chapter uses the example of the international machine tool industry to argue that the national level remains a critical scale for shaping institutional corporate norms and expectations. He shows this by detailing the various problems that unfold when machinery designed in Germany, with the German workplace and worker in mind, is transferred to an American setting. Some of these same themes raised by Gertler return in a different form in the following chapter, where John Britton considers the implications of a shift in the nature of capitalist competition for national economies already strongly penetrated by foreign direct investment. Using as his case study the Toronto region, Britton argues that the institutional inclination of foreign-owned firms is to import technology-intensive inputs from their home base, thereby stifling a potentially important source of economic development for both the Toronto region and Canada as a whole. Just how important high-technology firms can be for national economic growth is picked up by Richard Florida and Mark Samber in their chapter on the changing institutional forms of venture capital over the course of US industrial history. Following Schumpeter they argue that capitalism is characterized by a process of discontinuous evolution driven by an uneven process of technological change (Schumpeter's 'gales of creative destruction'). Critical, though, to those all-important innovations is an appropriate institutional form of venture capital which makes them possible, and as the form of capitalism changes historically so must that institutional form. The concluding chapter of the book by Amin and Thrift in many ways returns to the issues discussed in the first one by Barnes. Concerned substantively with problems of regionalism in the European Union, their essay is also a theoretical rumination about the very nature of institutions and their relation to the economy. It is also a blueprint for progressive political action which for them involves mobilizing new institutions.

David Harvey (1982) uses the metaphor of the 'whirligig' – a carousel or roundabout – to characterize the continually changing form of capitalism. Always in motion, always becoming rather than being, the profit-seeking imperative drives capitalism if not upwards then certainly onwards to take on continuous new guises. While the process of change is certainly temporal, it is also resolutely geographical. As all of the contributors to this volume argue, geography over the last two decades has become increasingly complex, requiring new forms of analysis and theoretical vocabulary. While there are differences in the precise form of the analysis and vocabulary that is applied by the different contributors, all of them recognize the pivotal relationship between regions, institutions and forms of regulation. This is not the region as an abstract geometry, or institutions as rational agents, or regulation as an obstacle to the functioning of the market. Rather, it is all more complex, contingent and contextual, which is why an institutionalist theoretical perspective is so important. In many ways this returns us to Innis. Not that he had all the answers even for his time, let alone our own. But he did pose the right kinds of questions which turned around issues of the role of the region, institutional variability, regulatory milieu, and the appropriate theoretical framework. Those questions are precisely the same ones asked by the writers gathered here.

Trevor Barnes and Meric Gertler

Bibliography

Harvey, D. (1982) *The Limits to Capital*, Oxford: Blackwell.

—— (1989) *The Condition of Postmodernity*, Oxford: Blackwell.

Hodgson, G.M. (1994) 'The return of institutional economics', in N.J. Smelser and R. Swedberg (eds) *The Handbook of Economic Sociology*, Princeton, NJ: Princeton University Press.

Ingham, G. (1996) 'Some recent changes in the relationship between economics and sociology', *Cambridge Journal of Economics* 20: 243–75.

Innis, H.A. (1936) 'Approaches to Canadian economic history', *Commerce Journal* 26: 24–30.

Samuels, W.J. (1995) 'The present state of institutional economics', *Cambridge Journal of Economics* 19: 569–90.

Acknowledgements

For all kinds of reasons this book took much longer, required much more labour, and caused much more anguish than we initially anticipated. That it has been completed at all is a consequence first and foremost of the patience, good will and understanding of the contributors as well as those who might have been contributors. We thank them all.

We also have some very specific acknowledgements to make. John Browne (Principal of Innis College, University of Toronto) and Daniel Drache were instrumental in initiating the round of conferences associated with the Innis centennial celebrations, of which ours was one. Funding for the initial preparations for the conference came from Innis College. Monies for staging the conference were provided by the Social Sciences and Humanities Research Council of Canada, the Canada–US Fulbright Program, the British Council and the Innis Centenary Celebration Committee (through York University). At the University of Toronto, support came from the offices of the Vice-President and Provost, the Vice-President for Research and International Relations, the Faculty of Arts and Science, the Department of Geography and University College (which generously hosted this event). We thank them all.

The book manuscript has undergone a variety of forms in its long life, but we would particularly like to thank Betsy Donald for her editorial assistance in producing the final version. We would also like to thank Alison Kirk and Andreja Zivkovic at Routledge for supporting our project even though we ourselves sometimes despaired of it.

Harold Innis said that one needed a sense of humour to be a social scientist in Canada. Certainly we needed it for this project, and here we thank our families and especially our children – Michael and Claire, Isabel and Miles – for making us smile.

The editors and publisher are also grateful to the following for permission to reproduce material: Michael Storper for Chapter 2; Clark University and Ann Markusen for Chapter 5, which appeared originally as 'Sticky places in slippery space: a typology of industrial districts', *Economic Geography* (1976, 72: 293–313); and Ash Amin and Nigel Thrift for Chapter 13, an earlier version of which appeared as 'Institutional issues for the European regions: from markets and plans to socioeconomics and the powers of association', *Economy and Society* (1995, 24: 41–66).

1 Industrial geography, institutional economics and Innis

Trevor J. Barnes

Introduction

When seeing Niagara Falls for the first time, Oscar Wilde made two quips: 'It would be more impressive if it ran the other way' and 'It is the second disappointment of the honeymoon.' Both judgements could equally be made about the relationship between industrial geography and the work of Harold Innis, the original impetus for this collection of essays. Industrial geography would have been more impressive if it had significantly contributed to the development of Harold Innis's work, but it was not to be. Likewise, although Innis initially recognized the allure of geography – he even adopted the title of Associate Professor of Economic Geography for a short period – he quickly became disappointed, concluding that much of the work in the discipline was just 'bad descriptive economics.'

Innis would likely also have been disappointed by industrial geography's subsequent turn to the universal models of spatial science during the 1960s, and its later shift to various forms of Marxism during the 1970s and 1980s. He thought universal models were based upon a colonial conceit, one in which, as Carey (1975: 28) puts it, 'imperial powers seek to create not only economic and political clients but intellectual clients as well.' And while sometimes sympathetic to Marx's writings, Innis thought that they provided only a theory of metropolitan powers, whereas what was required for Canada were 'fresh interpretations and not the same interpretations' (letter to Irene Spry, quoted in Parker 1983: 148). To achieve fresh interpretations Innis thought it necessary for him to be a 'dirt economist' (Innis 1936: 26); to practice an economics that was grounded in the nitty-gritty of the institutions, technology and ecology of particular places.

In pursuing dirt economics, Innis was also in effect forging a distinctively Canadian brand of economics that was attuned to the specific institutional structure, including regulatory frameworks, norms and conventions, of the place in which he lived. Intellectually his project shared a number of characteristics with Thorstein Veblen's work, and the school of American institutional economics that Veblen pioneered. In both cases, all-encompassing theories of economic and social life, such as neoclassical economics or Marxism, were eschewed for a third way that emphasized the importance of local knowledge, institutional embeddedness, historical specificity, technological dynamism, and critical reflexivity.

It is exactly these sorts of features that since the early 1990s have been picked up within industrial and, more broadly, economic geography. The purpose of this chapter is to plot the points of inflection between both Innis's and Veblen's institutionalist economic perspective and that of current industrial and economic geography, and in so doing draw them into the circle of current industrial and economic geographical discussion. That inclusion might not be as dramatic as reversing either the flow of Niagara Falls, or the disappointment of honeymooners, but after sixty years of virtually no relationship, any relation between industrial and economic geography and institutionalist scholarship would be impressive, if not miraculous.

The chapter is divided into three sections. First, I review briefly Innis's two main theoretical contributions, the staples model and his theory of communications, and set them within the context of his wider institutionalist project. Second, I relate Innis's work to Veblen's, and in doing so delineate some of the broader characteristics of the institutionalist school. I also review some contemporary variants of institutionalism, including socioeconomics and evolutionary economics. Finally, I link the various elements of Innis's and Veblen's schemes to some recent works in industrial and economic geography. My argument will be that these works, including chapters found in this book, by insisting on the importance of space and place have the potential to benefit institutionalist scholarship as much as that scholarship has the potential to benefit industrial geographers.

Harold Innis: marginal theorist

To understand Innis's work one must embed it in the circumstances of his life, one of a colonial intellectual (Watson 1981). Growing up on a small southern Ontario farm at the turn of the century, Innis's intention was to become a Baptist minister, and to that end he entered McMaster University in 1912. Completing his studies in 1916, but also driven by fierce patriotic beliefs, he postponed entering the church to enlist in the Canadian infantry and fight in World War I. It was a pivotal decision: 'he went to war as a Christian and a colonial … [but] came back an agnostic and a Canadian' (Watson 1981: 24). In particular, the horrific experience of trench warfare, especially at the battle of Vimy Ridge where he was severely wounded, convinced Innis first that there was no beneficent caring God and, second, that, given the callousness and pure stupidity of British high command to which Canadian troops were subject, there was no beneficent, caring empire of King and country either. It was his conversion to a secular nationalism made on the battlefields of Belgium and France that was to infuse his life's work.

That work began immediately Innis returned home to Canada in 1917. Still recuperating from his wounds, Innis completed an MA at McMaster

University, and then in 1918 entered the University of Chicago to study for a PhD in economics. Although Thorstein Veblen, the American institutional economist, had long left the Chicago economics department, his intellectual legacy remained potent. Certainly, Innis's own brand of secular nationalist economics was later to draw heavily upon that legacy. The completion of Innis's doctoral thesis at Chicago on the history of the Canadian Pacific Railway led in 1920 to his appointment at the University of Toronto, a post he held until his death in 1952.

Innis's more than thirty years of work at the University of Toronto can be divided roughly into two related phases: the first was the elaboration of the staples thesis, and the second, beginning in the latter part of the 1930s, was centred on communication studies. Both projects were an attempt to develop a native Canadian view untainted by the intellectual biases of empire. He pursued this project first with respect to the writing of his country's own history, and later and more generally with respect to understanding the relationship between knowledge, power and empire.

The staples thesis

Innis's home-grown theory of Canadian history is found in his writings on staples. The central thesis is that in analysing Canadian economy and society one must begin with its export to metropolitan powers of a series of minimally processed primary resources, staples. In this scheme staples function as the leading sector of the economy, and set the pace for economic growth (Watkins 1963: 144). That growth, though, is continually frustrated, and never comes to fruition in the form of equilibrium development. For a staples economy is eventually ensnared in a staples trap where industrial diversification is thwarted. The result, to use Innis's terminology, is that staples-producing regions become hinterland economies, the fates of which are strongly tied to events in more powerful foreign metropoles. Of course, this is not a conclusion that neoclassical orthodox economic theory would ever draw. It would say that staples nations, such as Canada, through the free workings of the market would eventually achieve equilibrium industrial development by initially specializing and trading in those commodities in which it possesses a comparative advantage, primary resources. It was this view, however, that Innis (1956: 3) dubbed 'a new form of exploitation with dangerous consequences.'

To avoid those consequences, Innis developed his theory of staples accumulation in such a way that it was peculiarly suited to the local Canadian context. That theory brought together three concerns: geographical, institutional and technological. In turn, this triad became the basis for Innis's theory of staples accumulation.

By geography, the first leg of the triad, Innis has at least two things in mind: first, the 'natural' environment of an area; and second, broad spatial relationships. Specifically, each type of staple is associated with a particular space–time 'bias' towards either geographical centralization or decentralization, making the Canadian economic landscape a patchwork quilt of different staples' geographies. Such biases are not innocent, but give shape to the very nature of regionalism within Canada: the lumber economy of British Columbia, the oil patch of Alberta, Prairie wheat growers, Quebec pulp and paper producers, and Atlantic Provinces' fishers.

Technology, the second component, has been seen by some as the most important. Watkins (1963: 141), for example, concludes that 'methodologically, Innis's staples approach was more technological history writ large than a theory of economic growth in the conventional sense.' In Innis's model the dominant technology affects both how (and if) staples are produced, and, through its manifestation in the form of transportation, the very space–time biases inherent in each resource commodity. Nonetheless, Watkins's claim seems exaggerated. Geography and technology work hand-in-glove, and furthermore, this interaction occurs only provided that the third leg of the triad is also present, an appropriate institutional structure.

Investing in staples production in the periphery requires large amounts of capital expenditure because of the high 'minimum indivisible cost[s] that must be met if production is to be undertaken at all' (Spry 1981: 155–6). Only two institutional forms are capable of raising sufficient funds to cover such costs: the state, that provides basic infrastructure, and large corporations, often foreign owned, that meet the immediate costs of plant and capital equipment.

When the right geography finally comes together with the right technology and the right institutional structure the result is accumulation of 'cyclonic' frenzy. In this way virgin resource regions are transformed and enveloped within the produced spaces of the capitalist periphery. Such intense accumulation never lasts, though, and, because of the very instabilities of staples production, sooner rather than later investment shifts to yet other places, leaving in its wake abandoned resource sites and communities.

Knowledge, power and empire

At some point during the late 1930s Innis abandoned his hitherto successful work on staples, and began pursuing a different line of enquiry, communications, that attempted to address the second of the intellectual problems he sought to unravel, the relationship between knowledge, power and empire. The cause of the switch has never been completely clear, but a number of commentators suggest that a principal catalyst was Innis's planned study of the pulp and paper sector (Parker 1977; Watson 1981). Originally an investigation of yet another staples industry, because of its linkages to the newspaper business it prompted Innis to think about communications and knowledge more generally, and their media of transmission. From that point on Innis moved away from the staples of empire to their media of communication and knowledge; a move from fur, fish and forestry, to papyrus, paper and printing.

The main thesis in the communication studies is that the 'medium of communication has an important influence on the dissemination of knowledge over space and time' (Innis 1951: 33). This is justified, following Carey (1967: 8), on the grounds that such media 'influence the kinds of human associations that can develop in any period' and thus the way humans think and what they think about. Indeed for Carey (1967: 7/8) 'consciousness is built on these human associations' and in this sense 'communication media are literally extensions of the mind.'

That term 'human associations' does not mean just physical interaction among individuals. Rather, the argument is that through the influence of the media of communication on institutional structures, themselves structures of power in which human associations are formed, particular kinds of knowledge are legitimated and given authority. Putting it in Innis's terms, the media of communications facilitate 'monopolies of knowledge.' 'Innis wanted to know what, in general, determines the location of ultimate authority in society and what will be recognized as authoritative knowledge. His answer was this: That media of communication ... confer monopolies of authority and knowledge' (Carey 1967: 12). By using that term monopoly, Innis indicates that there is a politics to knowledge. That those who control communications also have control over 'both consciousness and social organization' (Carey 1967: 8). The media of communications are not simply neutral carriers of the message, but deeply imbricated in a wider system of knowledge and power.

Specifically, Innis recognized historically two broad types of communication media, each associated with a particular set of institutional forms that, in turn, control distinctive monopolies of knowledge. 'Light communications', such as paper and later the wireless, because of the ease of transmission across large distances facilitate spatially expansive empires defined by a hierarchical organization and instrumental knowledge. By contrast, 'heavy communications', such as stone and clay tablets, because of the difficulty of their transportation foster spatially restricted monopolies of knowledge defined by an emphasis on a single source of power and historical and religious authority.

On staples and communications

Given these skeletal accounts of the two phases of Innis's work – the one on staples, the other on communications – how do they compare? I will discuss the wider methodological similarities which stem from an institutionalist perspective in the next section, but let me note at least two common related substantive emphases. First, there is the attention to empire itself, a consequence, I would argue, of Innis's own acutely felt situation. That emphasis is clearly central to his communications studies, but it is also a major if sometimes understated theme in his staples work. The argument, following Watson (1981: 234), is that 'Innis never used the staple as anything more than a *focusing point* about which to examine the interplay of cultures and empires' (original emphasis). The staple is a crystallization point for both a set of external forces of economic colonization and a set of internal forces of cultural formation. If for Blake the world is seen in a grain of sand, then for Innis the colonial status of Canada can be seen in the staple be it codfish, beaver pelt, or the 2" × 4". The study of each good is not an end in itself, but an entry point for a wider discussion.

Second, in both phases of his work Innis recognized that empires were above all geographical and historical entities; they could not treated in the abstract, as ghostly phenomena, but necessarily took on spatial and temporal extension. Here he seems to have used his staples model as a template for his discussions of communication. Just as the production of a particular staples commodity engenders a distinctive set of spatial and temporal trading relations within the production system of colonialism, so too does the communication system produce a particular set of space and time biases of knowledge within the cultural and social system of empire. Given this similarity, the change in Innis's work from staples to communications perhaps is best interpreted as a movement in degree rather than in kind. Certainly, this is Marshall McLuhan's interpretation. In his obituary for Innis, McLuhan (1953: 385) wrote that in making the move to communication studies Innis 'shifted his attention from the trade routes of the external world to the trade routes of the mind.' It is the common geographical metaphor that is critical.

Trying to make sense of Innis's life and works is a difficult task. Even Innis 'looked upon his life as a puzzle to be solved' (Watson 1981: 2). To come even close to solving that riddle it is necessary to keep Innis's life and works together, always remembering that he was a colonial intellectual living on the margins of empire. It is for this reason that while there are certainly differences between Innis's early and later writings, there are also significant continuities that revolve around institutions, power, technology, geography and history. Another continuity, as I will now argue, are certain core methodological emphases that derive from Thorstein Veblen's institutionalist influence on Innis, and to which I will now turn.

Institutional economics

Veblen and Innis

Innis's theoretical ideas did not emerge out of the blue, with no past or antecedent. There were a number of important intellectual influences of which the most important was the founder of institutional economics, Thorstein Veblen (Watson 1981: 268; Barager 1996). In fact, in many ways Innis is the Canadian counterpart to Veblen: both were iconoclasts, at odds with their time, critics of orthodoxy, and major contributors to the development of distinctively national schools of economics, respectively Canadian political economy and American institutionalism.

Always a maverick, Veblen's work was both a reaction against the American importation of European neoclassical theory, with its celebration of *homo economicus* (parodied by Veblen (1919: 73) as a 'homogeneous globule of desire'), and a domestic industrial system that spawned massive inequalities in levels of wealth and consumption. Veblen's response was a made-in-America theory of his own time and place, institutional economics. Just as Innis constructed a local theory of his own place, so did Veblen. In both cases, however, because of their restless temperaments, sometimes opaque writing styles, and their suspicion towards 'symmetry and system making' (Veblen 1919: 68), their theories emerged in bits and pieces rather than as seamless wholes. To use Bernstein's (1991: 8) phrase, Veblen's and Innis's respective theories form a 'constellation' rather than a single, coherent scheme; that is, 'a juxtaposed rather than integrated cluster of changing elements that resist reduction to a common denominator, essential core, or generative first principle.'

That said, some elements are more important than others. Within Veblen's work, and from the review above of both parts of Innis's writings, three stand out as especially influential in defining institutionalist economics.

First, and perhaps most basic, there is the pivotal place of institutions, defined by Veblen (1919: 239) as 'settled habits of thought.' In turn, those institutions influence behaviour. Veblen (1919: 242–3) writes, 'The wants and desires, the end and aim, the ways and means, the amplitude and drift of the individual's conduct are functions of an institutional variable that is of a highly complex and wholly unstable character.' Individuals, then, are always institutionally situated, where institutions 'act upon men's historical view of things, ... altering or fortifying a point of view or a mental attitude handed down from the past' (Veblen 1953: 190–1).

Similarly, Innis in both phases of his work keenly emphasized the power of institutions in shaping action and belief. More broadly, both men sought some form of cultural economics, where culture was defined by the prevailing set of institutions and associated norms and conventions. This also explains why they both heaped so much scorn on the *homo-economicus* postulate: it assumed a world of behaviour outside of culture.

The second element turns on dynamism and change, which was often conceived as dramatic, producing uneven effects. In Veblen's case this theoretical sensibility stems from his evolutionary framework; indeed, he called his approach 'post-Darwinian economics.' Veblen assumed that institutions were subject to a process of evolutionary selection. As the environment changes, often through abrupt technological shifts, some institutions fall by the wayside, while others thrive and prosper, and by passing on their good habits, the 'genotype' of surviving institutions influences the next generation. The result, though, is not some final end point of equilibrium, but only 'a continuity of cause and effect. It is a scheme of blindly cumulative causation in which there is no trend, no final term, no consummation' (Veblen 1919: 436).

That term 'cumulative causation' is particularly important. By it Veblen meant the self-reinforcing effect (the 'virtuous circle') of institutional behaviour: initial beliefs embodied in an institutional form result in more people holding those beliefs, thereby strengthening further the institution. The problem, though, is that when external change occurs, as it must, and which is incompatible with those beliefs and associated institutional forms, the resulting crash is that much bigger.

Innis's work is similarly informed by historical change and rupture. Both empires and staples by their very nature are transient, subject to flux and vicissitude. Certainly there are powerful self-reinforcing institutional forces that maintain them, sometimes for long periods, but inevitably even they buckle under intense external change. The kind of historically unstable boom and bust economy associated with staples production is a paragon case.

Third, there is the importance of technology. For Veblen technology was the most important factor promoting institutional change. Because of 'idle curiosity', as he called it, humans were always coming up with new ways to solve old problems. The resulting technological change, and carried out under the auspices of 'the engineer', was for Veblen the very basis of productive business. The problem, though, was that productiveness was continually inhibited by the bridle of surrounding institutions, attitudes and people (such as 'captains of industry'). They put a brake on innovation by emphasizing profits and prices over 'workmanship' and productive efficiency. The consequence for Veblen was a consistent tension between the 'pecuniary culture' of industry based upon making money, and the creativity and efficiency of business based upon making things.

Innis, too, made technology one of the pivots of his scheme. But it was conceived neither as deterministic nor Promethean. Technology was, as Innis put it, 'dialectically related' to existing social structures of institutional power and knowledge. It was inseparable from the social, and its instantiated relations of power. Stemming from this recognition that technology is politically coloured, Innis was less optimistic about the effects of technology than Veblen. Pressed into the service of metropoles and empire, Innis thought technology could take on a life of its own, and frequently careen out of control intervening in irrecoverable ways in the intellectual and material life of dependent societies and regions. Technology might be the basis of good, productive business, but it could also be the basis of a lot of bad, unproductive relations between metropoles and hinterlands, empires and their satellite peoples.

Contemporary institutional economics

The institutional economics based on these three elements (and others too; see Hodgson 1994; Samuels 1995) historically never enjoyed much of the limelight within economics; in fact, Keynes once spoke of institutionalism as inhabiting the disciplinary 'underworld'. Over the last fifteen years or so, however, the movement has slowly made its way upward into the daylight of respectability. There are several reasons.

- A dissatisfaction with the perceived social irrelevancy and methodological abstruseness of one of institutionalism's two main rivals, neoclassical economics, and the school that more than any other pushed institutional economics into the underworld in the first place.
- A similar discontent with its other rival, Marxism, at least in its classical form, increasingly viewed as theoretically rigid, closed and economistic, and more generally, since the fall of Eastern European communism, politically unviable.
- A move within the social sciences towards more contextually based explanations grounded upon cultural and historical contingency.

Institutionalism is well placed to contribute to this movement in two ways. First, by its very conception Veblen's and Innis's emphasis on historically situated institutions and their power was a cultural and socially sensitive approach to the economy. Second, institutionalism from its founding was linked to the philosophy of American pragmatism which has consistently emphasized historically situated practice and knowledge (Mirowski 1987; Bernstein 1991: appendix). Originally found in the turn-of-the-century writings of John Dewey and William James, pragmatism has been recently revived through the writings of Richard Rorty (1982) and Richard Bernstein (1991), perhaps the two best-known contemporary American philosophers of the 'cultural turn'. Given this intellectual pedigree, institutional economics, of the three mainstream schools of economics, is easily the most amenable to working with, and contributing to, the new demands for contextually sensitive explanation (Martin 1994; Sunley 1996).

The resulting resurgence of institutional economics since the early 1980s is now manifest in at least three contemporary forms, all of which have the potential to influence to different degrees industrial geography. Before I review them, however, one clarification of terminology is necessary. The term 'the new institutional economics' was coined in the 1970s, and is closely associated with Oscar Williamson's (1975) work on the transactional firm (and in industrial geography found in Allen Scott's (1988) 'neo-Weberian' location theory). But as a number of commentators have argued, Williamson's 'new institutionalism' has very little connection with the old institutional economics of Veblen and Innis (Granovetter 1985; Hodgson 1994; Ingham 1996: 262–5). By assuming that firms treated as institutions organize themselves, and their external transactions, in the most efficient, economically rational way, Williamson has intellectually aligned himself to neoclassicism. By contrast, the three contemporary forms of institutional economics I will review here maintain close affiliations with 'old institutionalism', and distance themselves at almost every point, and certainly on the issue of rationality, from Williamson's essentially neoclassical view.

The first variant of contemporary institutional economics is associated with writers who have stayed closest to Veblen's texts. Two important authors are Geoff Hodgson (1993, 1994), a former acolyte of the mathematically recondite, Sraffa-inspired neo-Ricardian school of economics, and Philip Mirowski (1989, 1990), a historian of economic thought, and strongly influenced by writers within science studies. Hodgson has been concerned with the representation of markets, and Mirowski with economic value. In both cases, they argue, neither markets nor value are spectral manifestations, the result respectively of an 'invisible hand' or an abstract *n*-dimensional consumer preference map. Instead, they are a consequence of human institutions and their instantiated powers.

Specifically, Hodgson argues that any market activity is predicated upon a range of institutional norms, expectations and conventions, which are set within a historically and geographically specific regulatory apparatus, and series of internal organizational hierarchies and structures. Together they affect what and how much consumers buy, the quantity firms produce and their methods of production, and the final set of prices charged. Portraying markets in terms of homogeneous supply and demand functions, therefore, misses all that is institutionally important. Furthermore, the institutional norms and frameworks critical to the workings of markets are neither the precipitates of a more fundamental economic rationality, nor mere background atmospherics. Rather, they are its very basis, its very constitution. Take them away, and nothing would remain.

Similarly, Mirowski (1990) pursues an institutionalist value theory in which the very definition of such entities as commodity and price are set by a set of overlapping, but geographically and historically contingent, networks of institutions. Like Hodgson, Mirowski is keen to stress that there is no final, fundamental, universal entity such as rationality that determines the end result. As he puts it, 'the entire system is like an Escher print, where stairs, and pillars mutually buttress an elaborate and interconnected edifice, but no part of the edifice ever touches the ground' (Mirowski 1990: 716). The system is intricately connected, but has neither a single beginning nor end; institutions interleave with other institutions, creating stability and order, but without an overarching plan, or conformance to universal design principles.

A second form taken by contemporary institutionalism is evolutionary economics which begins from, and elaborates on, Darwin's influence on Veblen. There are several variants, but in one way or another they all begin with technological choice and its consequences. Nelson and Winter's (1982) work was the first, and defined firms as profit-satisficing institutions characterized by a stable set of decision-making routines for choosing a production technology. Provided those routines enable the firm to meet the threshold of profitability, they will be repeated (passed on through inheritance) in the future. When the threshold of profitability is not met, however, firms must 'mutate' if they are to survive. There are two strategies: imitating routines of successful firms, or creatively designing new routines. In either case, suggest Nelson and Winter, firms behave like evolving biological organisms (as Veblen suggested for institutions more generally).

Nelson and Winter's work was subsequently elaborated within evolutionary economics using the two ideas of 'path dependency' and 'lock in'. By path dependency is meant the notion that past decisions about technology will shape future ones, thus establishing a particular trajectory of development. That trajectory, though, need not be optimal. A classic example is the use of the QWERTY keyboard originally chosen to slow down typists rather than to maximize their speed. Once selected as the industry norm for key placement, though, it locked in typewriter and keyboard manufacturers to a specific pathway of development, however irrational (David 1985). For evolutionary economists, then, the past always weighs on the present, as it did in Veblen's and Innis's theories.

'Lock in' occurs when a decision made about technology becomes irreversible. Typically the forces making it irreversible take the form of strong positive feedback effects that reinforce the initial choice ('cumulative causation' in Veblen's terms). Specifically, once, say, a technological advantage emerges, because of such factors as externalities, spillovers and 'untraded interdependencies' (Storper 1997), that advantage is made more advantageous over time. The important corollary, as Storper (1997: chapter 1) argues, is an altogether different conception of competition and development. In traditional theory, competition is based upon a firm's skill in rationally allocating its resources. Evolutionary economists, in contrast, by emphasizing positive feedback are suggesting that most competitive advantage derives from a dynamic and interdependent process of technological choice. Once a firm makes that choice no matter how much re-allocation goes on at the margin, a competitor will never catch up. That superiority will be challenged only by some future, abrupt technological change that brings with it its own endogenous processes of cumulative causation.

A final contemporary variant of institutionalism is economic sociology, or as Amin and Thrift (Chapter 13, this volume) call it, socioeconomics (and clearly comprising more than just Veblen's work; see Ingham's (1996) useful review). There is a long history of economic sociology, but within the last ten to fifteen years the field has enjoyed a renaissance (Smelser and Swedberg 1994). A key catalyst was Mark Granovetter's (1985) paper on social embeddedness, an idea he took from Karl Polanyi's (1944) book *The Great Transformation*. Polanyi argued that historically all economies up to capitalism were 'embedded' in a social and cultural structure. With capitalism, however, that changed: the market became autonomous, 'disembedded' from its wider context, creating all kinds of problems.

While Granovetter thinks that Polanyi's substantive conclusion about capitalism is wrong, he is eager to use his conceptual idea of 'embeddedness', by which he means that all action (including 'economic') takes place 'in concrete, ongoing systems of social relations' (Granovetter 1985: 487). In turn, those relations are conceived as networks of interpersonal contacts and attachments. While Granovetter thinks of those networks as comprising primarily personal interactions, one can also think of them occurring at a distance, and involving a variety of intervening media. To understand economic activity, one must therefore embed it within the networks of social relations that both constitute it and give it meaning.

The consequence, and again in line with Veblen and Innis, is a view of human behaviour that rejects any single, uniform explanation of action such as provided by the rationality postulate. As McDowell (1997: 119) puts it: 'rationality is rejected like all social interactions, economic decisions are as much affected by tradition, historical precedent, class and gender interests and other social factors as by consideration of efficiency and profit.' Furthermore, just as human action is institutionally embedded, so are markets. This last conclusion is especially important because it points to the possibility of institutional manipulation in order to achieve certain social and even geographical goals. Amin and Thrift's discussion (this volume) of 'institutional thickness' for achieving regional development derives directly from this perspective (and elaborated below).

In summary, there is a third strand of economic theorizing, institutional economics, that lies between the formal abstruseness of orthodox economic theory with its celebration of individual rationality and the propriety of the market, and a *sometimes* rigid Marxism with its emphasis on structural economic determination and theoretical self-righteousness. Institutionalism clearly owes much to Veblen's original formulations, but as I've argued, by its very design it is an open body of theory, and people like Innis, and more recently Hodgson and Mirowski, and also writers within evolutionary and socioeconomics, have both taken and contributed ideas. The same increasingly holds for industrial and economic geographers as I will now argue.

A new industrial geography?

Even if industrial geographers had read Veblen's writings, and even more improbably, Innis's, it is unlikely that they could have changed the discipline until at least recently. During much of the postwar era, at least, the adoption of the scientific method and then various forms of Marxism meant that most industrial geographers strove for an often unreflective, universal certainty that both Veblen and Innis would have found anathema (see Barnes 1996: chapters 1 and 4). Times change, however, and because of an increasingly different methodological sensibility, one tending towards more contextually sensitive accounts emphasizing geographical and historical situatedness, and because of a changed world, one where space, technology, institutional power and knowledge seem to be colliding in new and important ways, there exists the possibility of a mutually constructive exchange between industrial and economic geography and some kind of institutionalist approach (Barnes 1996: chapter 1; Martin 1994).

In making such a suggestion, I don't intend to provide yet another methodological agenda for economic geographers to follow. Apart from the practical reason that such programmatic statements are rarely, if ever, taken up, the very notion of a set agenda would be foreign to both Innis and Veblen. More importantly, it would undermine the contextual position that both offer by supposing that ideas from their time and place can be unproblematically transposed to our own. Rather, my purpose is briefly to juxtapose five elements taken from the discussion above – local and reflexive knowledge, institutional analysis, embeddedness and networks, cultural norms and conventions, and path dependency and 'lock ins' – with some work from contemporary industrial geographers to assess potential connections; to assess if there is the basis for 'conversation', to use one of the key metaphors of philosophical pragmatism (Rorty 1982).

The first potential point of intersection is the emphasis on local knowledge and reflexivity. Both Innis and Veblen were attempting to work out local models of their own place; ones that shunned supposedly universal principles, and were open to geographical and historical specificity. One consequence of that quest was a scrutiny by both men of their own local knowledge; that is, reflections on their own reflections: reflexivity. For once one eschews the universal certainty found in such universal models as neoclassicism or classical Marxism, it is then critical to understand the basis of one's own (local) knowledge through critical self-reflection and analysis. It was for this reason that Innis explicitly called for 'a sociology or a philosophy of the social sciences, an economic history of knowledge or an economic history of economic history' (Innis 1946: 83), and that Veblen structured his work such that by its very design it embodied reflexivity (Samuels 1990).

Within industrial geography ever since Massey's (1984) work there have been explicit attempts to devise theories or models that are sensitive to the local context; indeed, it has defined the research agenda of industrial geography since the mid-1980s. It includes the CURS locality project (Cooke 1990), and also research carried out examining flexible production and the 'politics of place' within a given territorial complex (Scott and Storper 1992). It also surfaces in the works of regulationists, especially those concerned with representing local modes of regulation (e.g. Tickell and Peck 1996). And most recently it is found in industrial geography's 'cultural turn' (Thrift and Olds 1996; Sunley 1996) in which economic activities as varied as work practices (McDowell 1997), choice of production technology (Gertler 1997, and Chapter 10, this volume) and corporate strategy making (Schoenberger 1997, and Chapter 9, this volume) are situated within specific local cultural contexts.

What these different industrial geographers add to institutionalism's concern for local knowledge is an acute geographical sensitivity and detailed, empirical knowledge. In addition, although this is a double-edge sword, industrial geographers are typically much better than Innis or Veblen in providing an explicit methodology and theory for studying and representing the local. If the qualification to be a 'dirt economist' is to be a genius then it is not useful.

Where industrial geographers might benefit from Veblen and Innis, though, is in reflecting on the localness of their own formulations, and not being carried away by what seem to be ineluctable procedures and irresistible general theories. Related is often a lack of theoretical reflexivity on the part of industrial geographers. It is true that reflexivity as a concept has been recently discussed, for example, by Storper (1997) who speaks of organizational reflexivity, and Amin (1998) who makes use of reflexive rationality. In both cases, though, reflexivity is taken as a characteristic of the objects of study (i.e. organizations and individuals), and not a strategy to be used by the authors themselves for understanding their own works. Not that this is a mistake, but one of the compelling features of both Innis's and Veblen's works was recognizing the importance of both studying the local *and* reflecting on how it entered into their own formulations of it. It is that second step that is often absent in the work of industrial geographers.

A second potential articulation between industrial and economic geography and institutionalism is with respect to institutions and their power. There was always an underground interest in institutions in industrial geography, found, for example, in the geography of enterprise literature (Hayter and Watts 1983), and segmented labour markets (Danson 1982). With the shift in emphasis during the last decade towards more contextual, and less universally deterministic, accounts, the explanatory weight accorded to institutions has increased substantially.

Perhaps the most important contribution industrial geographers have added here is their recognition of the geographical constitution of institutions; that institutions are not cut from the same template, but are actively constructed in particular kinds of places and spaces, and therefore are quite different from one another, producing varied effects. For example, Saxenian (1994: 8) contrasts the form and function of the various regional institutions ('universities, business associations, local governments, as well as the many less formal hobbyist clubs, professional societies and other forums') operating to make both Silicon Valley and Route 128 what they are, which is quite different. Or, Gertler (1997: 53), using the case study of German machine manufacturers supplying equipment to Canadian firms, illustrates the sharp difference in national 'institutions which regulate capital markets and business finances, labour markets, labour relations and the employment relations of user firms.' Because of those institutional differences, Gertler argues, suppliers and users are consistently at odds with one another resulting in mutual misunderstanding and failed expectations.

Gertler (1997) also argues there are policy imperatives stemming from his findings. At the most basic level, they show that the types of economic activities found in a place, or a region, or a nation, are necessarily restricted by the kinds of institutional structures found there. Fostering new kinds of economic activity, say, for regional development purposes, will therefore require crafting geographically appropriate institutions, designing them for the local context at hand. Here the work of Amin and Thrift (Chapter 13, this volume; 1997; Amin 1998) on 'institutional thickness' is important. Briefly, they argue for the establishment of regionally specific institutional structures which are open, interlinked ('associationist'), reflexive, and grounded in a given territory. As a result, they would be able to give a 'voice' to a place, as well as allowing transfers of appropriate knowledge and information to enhance economic performance. Such a strategy for Amin and Thrift represents 'a third way' between the anarchy of market liberalism, and the contextual insensitivity of central planning.

Third, the contribution of industrial and economic geographers to Granovetter's ideas of embeddedness and networks is their recognition that both are profoundly shaped by the places and spaces in which they occur. There are two important points here. First, that embeddedness and networks operate differently at different geographical scales. McDowell (1997), for example, in her work on female merchant bankers in the City of London, is concerned with embeddedness at the level of the individual work place, and as a result examines those social relations that revolve around institutions of class and gender. Mitchell (1995), in contrast, is interested in embeddedness at the global level, and in her specific case study works out how 'extended family networking, business trust, and the importance of socio-cultural connections in the use of credit and information' have been used by Hong Kong Chinese entrepreneurs, such as Li Ka-shing, not only to be successful at home, but also to effect restructuring around the Pacific Rim (Mitchell 1995: 379). More broadly, social and cultural embeddedness is not fixed at one spatial scale, but is finely variegated and nested, varying in meaning and consequence.

The second important point here is that embeddedness when joined with a geographical sensibility becomes a potent conceptual combination for understanding new forms of business organization, especially associated with the high-technology sector. The argument is that some kinds of industrial activities require more geographical embedding than others, where geographical embedding means spatial proximity among firms; or, as Gertler (1995) puts it, the importance of 'being there.' Specifically, for those industrial sectors relying on specialized information or skill or rapidly changing innovations, spatial proximity among firms facilitates the frequent interaction, both formal and informal, that engenders the trust, cooperation and exchange of information (tacit and explicit) necessary for success. Embeddedness of these industrial sectors is necessarily geographical; place and space enter into the very constitution of the industry.

Fourth, the importance of conventions and norms was always implicit in behavioural approaches to industrial and economic geography, but they have taken on increasing significance with the institutionalist turn. Conventions and norms are so important because, as Veblen realized, they lie behind the key decisions made within an economy; that make an industrial economy what it is. Storper (Chapter 2, this volume; 1997; Storper and Salais 1997) has provided the most systematic analysis of conventions from an industrial geographical perspective. His argument is that in order to participate in a capitalist economy, which is subject to complexity, uncertainty and transactions with others, one must have the expectation that one's actions will have the anticipated outcome. In order to achieve that end, actors collectively construct conventions. They allow mutually interdependent activity under conditions of uncertainty to occur. As Storper and Salais (1997: 16) write: 'Conventions resemble hypotheses formulated by persons with respect to their relationship between their actions and the actions of those on whom they must depend to realize a goal.' The important geographical point of Storper's work, and illustrated empirically in a range of case studies carried out by him, is that such conventions are forged in specific places and spaces, resulting in differential 'worlds of production.' So while Veblen and Innis were correct in their insight that different norms produce different kinds of economic cultures, for example, 'pecuniary' or 'workmanship', they never enquired about the geographical constitution of those norms and their variability. This is Storper's insight.

In addition, Schoenberger (1997) also effectively draws on ideas of conventions and norms in understanding the corporate restructuring of the last two decades, especially the movement from mass to flexible production. Her thesis, and again resonating with Veblen's work, is that the conventions and norms guiding large institutions, such as big industrial corporations, quickly become ossified, which then creates all kinds of problems when the external environment changes. This was the case when, among other things, new technology led to the possibility of flexible production systems and organizations. As she shows (Chapter 9, this volume), some of the largest US corporations, because of an old, inappropriate set of norms and conventions held by their upper management, experienced extreme difficulties in coping with the change. Again there is a geographical dimension here. Divisions of the corporation farthest away from the head office were better able to respond to change because they were less in the grip of the old conventions and norms (Schoenberger, Chapter 9, this volume).

Finally, the technological 'path dependency' and 'lock in' discussed by evolutionary economists was initially only couched in temporal terms. But it is now clear that there is an important geographical dimension. This has been recognized even by economists, for example Krugman (1995). Couched in terms of regional specialization and trade, Krugman's theoretical work, based upon combining models of imperfect competition and increasing returns to scale, represents a formal explanation of how space enters into a given regional economic trajectory. In particular, locally based increasing returns to scale ensure that the original regional specialization which brought initial success is maintained. But this is only a formal explanation. More suggestive has been less formal theorizing, and often worked out in the context of specific industrial geographical case studies.

Storper's (1997, and Chapter 2, this volume) work again has been formative. The gist is that new technology development requires a set of self-reinforcing, place-based 'relational assets' or 'untraded interdependencies'. Those 'assets' or 'interdependencies' operate cumulatively over time, continually bolstering the initial technology selected, making it increasingly competitive. As a result, such places become locked in to a particular specialization, with their future trajectory determined by a set of past decisions. Storper's work also clearly links to the research discussed above on the high-technology sector. Many of the 'relational assets' and 'untraded interdependencies' that maintain a particular economic specialization in place are possible because of spatial proximity.

Note that while Veblen and Innis never used the terms 'lock in' and 'path dependency', they are implicit in both men's work. In this sense, Storper's writings elaborate on an already existing intellectual tradition. For example, Innis coined the term 'staples trap' which he used as a shorthand to represent the varied forces that both resulted in particular regions in Canada specializing in staples production, and maintained their hinterland status, while Veblen made use of the term 'cumulative causation'. While the substantive details are very different, Storper and Innis and Veblen are making the same basic point: that powerful, geographically based, and self-reinforcing forces are always shaping the direction of the economy.

Conclusion

Industrial geography has always been a bell weather sub-discipline reflecting methodological changes within economic geography, and the discipline at large. It was the site for the first forays into spatial science and location theory in the late 1950s, behavioural theories of the firm in the late 1960s, and structural Marxism and critical realism in the 1970s and 1980s. That same opportunity for methodological innovation is present now.

Within the last decade or so a number of social sciences, including human geography, have moved towards explanatory accounts that emphasize cultural and social context. Such accounts necessarily are messier, more local, and less deterministic and elegant than those that they replace. They emphasize complexity, contingency and conjunction rather than simplicity, necessity and uni-causality. The basic explanatory categories are around social power, cultural identity and institutional situatedness rather than economic ownership, universal definitions and individual agency.

These new contextual accounts come in various shapes and sizes. I would argue that the institutionalist approach reviewed here is one of them, and as such offers a vehicle for meeting the new methodological imperatives that turn on social and cultural context. Indeed, a number of industrial and economic geographers have come to the same conclusion, and already have added to the institutionalist tradition by demonstrating both theoretically and empirically the ways in which geography matters. This is the significance of many of the contributions gathered in this volume. As a result, our contributors as well as other industrial and economic geographers elsewhere may finally redeem Innis's initial faith in the discipline.

Acknowledgement

I would like to acknowledge John Watson's (1981) doctoral thesis on which I've relied heavily in writing the first section of the chapter.

Bibliography

Amin, A. (1998) 'Institutionalist perspective on regional economic development', paper presented at the OECD conference on regional development, Boras, Sweden, January 1998.

Amin, A. and Thrift, N.J. (1997) 'Globalization, socioeconomics, territoriality', in R. Lee and J. Wills (eds) *Geographies of Economies*, London: Arnold.

Barager, F. (1996) The influence of Thorstein Veblen on the economics of Harold Innis. *Journal of Economic Issues* 30: 667–83.

Barnes, T.J. (1996) *Logics of Dislocation: Models, Metaphors and Meanings of Economic Spaces*, New York: Guilford Press.

Bernstein, R.J. (1991) *The New Constellation: The Ethical–Political Horizons of Modernity/Postmodernity*, Cambridge: Polity Press.

Carey, J.W. (1967) 'Harold Adams Innis and Marshall McLuhan', *The Antioch Review* 27: 5–39.

—— (1975) 'Canadian communication theory: extensions and interpretations of Harold Innis', in G. Robinson and D.F. Theall (eds) *Studies in Canadian Communications*, Montreal: McGill University Press.

Cooke, P. (1990) *Back to the Future: Modernity, Postmodernity and Locality*, London: Unwin Hyman.

Danson, M. (1982) 'The industrial structure and labour market segmentation: urban and regional implications', *Regional Studies* 4: 255–66.

David, P.A. (1985) 'Understanding the economics of QWERTY', *American Economic Review (Papers and Proceedings)* 75: 332–7.

Gertler, M.S. (1995) ' "Being there": proximity, organization, and culture in the development and adoption of advanced manufacturing technologies', *Economic Geography* 71: 1–26.

—— (1997) 'The invention of regional culture', in R. Lee and J. Wills (eds) *Geographies of Economies*, London: Arnold.

Granovetter, M. (1985) 'Economic action and social structure: the problem of embeddedness', *American Journal of Sociology* 91: 481–510.

Hayter, R. and Watts, H.D. (1983) 'The geography of enterprise: a reappraisal', *Progress in Human Geography* 7: 158–81.

Hodgson, G.M. (1993) *Economics and Evolution: Bringing Life Back into Economics*, Cambridge: Polity Press.

—— (1994) 'The return of institutional economics', in N.J. Smelser and R. Swedberg (eds) *The Handbook of Economic Sociology*, Princeton, NJ: Princeton University Press.

Ingham, G. (1996) 'Some recent changes in the relationship between economics and sociology', *Cambridge Journal of Economics* 20: 243–75.

Innis, H.A. (1936) 'Approaches to Canadian economic history', *Commerce Journal* 26: 24–30.

—— (1946) *Political Economy and the Modern State*, Toronto: Ryerson.

—— (1951) *The Bias of Communication*, Toronto: University of Toronto Press.

—— (1956) 'The teaching of economic history in Canada', in M.Q. Innis (ed.) *Essays in Canadian Economic History*, Toronto: University of Toronto Press.

Krugman, P. (1995) *Development, Geography and Economic Theory*, Cambridge, MA: MIT Press.

Massey, D. (1984) *Spatial Divisions of Labour: Social Structures and the Geography of Production*, London: Macmillan.

McDowell, L. (1997) 'A tale of two cities? Embedded organizations and embodied workers in the City of London', in R. Lee and J. Wills (eds) *Geographies of Economies*, London: Arnold.

McLuhan, M. (1953) 'The later Innis', *Queen's Quarterly* 60: 386–94.

Martin, R.L. (1994) 'Economic theory and human geography', in D. Gregory, R. Martin and G. Smith (eds) *Human Geography: Society, Space and Social Science*, Basingstoke: Macmillan.

Mirowski, P. (1987) 'The philosophical foundations of institutionalist economics', *Journal of Economic Issues* 21: 1001–38.

—— (1989) *More Heat than Light. Economics as Social Physics, Physics as Nature's Economics*, Cambridge: Cambridge University Press.

—— (1990) 'Learning the meaning of a dollar: conservation principles and the social meaning of value in economic theory', *Social Research* 57: 689–717.

Mitchell, K. (1995) 'Flexible circulation in the Pacific Rim: capitalisms in context', *Economic Geography* 71: 364–82.

Nelson, R. and Winter, S. (1982) *An Evolutionary Theory of Economic Change*, Cambridge, MA: Harvard University Press.

Parker, I. (1977) 'Harold Innis, Karl Marx and Canadian political economy', *Queen's Quarterly* 84: 545–63.

—— (1983) ' "Commodity fetishism" and "vulgar Marxism": On "Rethinking Canadian political economy" ', *Studies in Political Economy* 6: 143–72'.

Polanyi, K. (1944) *The Great Transformation*, Boston, MA: Beacon Hill Press.

Rorty, R. (1982) *Consequences of Pragmatism*, Minneapolis, MN: University of Minnesota Press.

Samuels, W.J. (1990) 'The self-referentiality of Thorstein Veblen's theory of the preconceptions of economic science', *Journal of Economic Issues* 24: 695–718.

—— (1995) 'The present state of institutional economics', *Cambridge Journal of Economics* 19: 569–90.

Saxenian, A.L. (1994) *Regional Advantage: Culture and Competition in Silicon Valley and Route 128*, Cambridge, MA: Harvard University Press.

Schoenberger, E. (1997) *The Cultural Crisis of the Firm*, Oxford: Blackwell.

Scott, A.J. (1988) *Metropolis: From the Division of Labor to Urban Form*, Los Angeles, CA: University of California Press.

Scott, A.J. and Storper, M. (1992) 'Regional development reconsidered', in H. Ernste and V. Meier (eds) *Regional Development and Contemporary Industrial Response: Extending Flexible Specialization*, London and New York: Belhaven Press.

Smelser, N.J. and Swedberg, R. (eds) (1994) *The Handbook of Economic Sociology*, Princeton, NJ: Princeton University Press.

Spry, I.M. (1981) 'Overhead costs, rigidities of productive capacity and the price system', in W.H. Melody, L. Salter and P. Heyer (eds) *Culture, Communication and Dependency: The Tradition of H. A. Innis*, Norwood, NJ: Ablex.

Storper, M. (1997) *The Regional World: Territorial Development in a Global Economy*, New York: Guilford Press.

Storper, M. and Salais, R. (1997) *Worlds of Production: The Action Frameworks of the Economy*, Cambridge, MA: Harvard University Press.

Sunley, P. (1996) 'Context in economic geography: the relevance of pragmatism', *Progress in Human Geography* 20: 338–55.

Thrift, N.J. and Olds, K. (1996) 'Reconfiguring the economic in economic geography', *Progress in Human Geography* 20: 311–37.

Tickell, A. and Peck, J. (1996) 'The return of Manchester Men: men's words and men's deeds in the remaking of the local state', *Transactions of the Institute of British Geographers* 21: 595–616.

Veblen, T.B. (1919) *The Place of Science in Modern Civilization and other Essays*, New York: B.W. Huebsch.

—— (1953) *The Theory of the Leisure Class: An Economic Study of Institutions*, New York: New American Library.

Watkins, M.H. (1963) 'A staple theory of economic growth', *The Canadian Journal of Economics and Political Science* 29: 141–58.

Watson, A.J. (1981) 'Marginal man: Harold Innis's communications works in context', unpublished PhD thesis, Department of Political Science, University of Toronto.

Williamson, O. (1975) *Markets and Hierarchies*, New York: Free Press.

Part I
Regions

2 The resurgence of regional economics

Ten years later

Michael Storper

The rediscovery of the region, and its critics

Something funny happened in the early 1980s. The region, long considered an interesting topic to historians and geographers, but not considered to have any interest for mainstream western social science, was rediscovered by a group of heterodox political economists, sociologists, political scientists and geographers. Not that no attention had been paid to regions by social scientists before that: in regional economics, development economics, and economic geography, regional growth and decline, patterns of location of economic activity, and regional economic structure were well-developed domains of inquiry. But such work treated the region as an outcome of deeper political economic processes, not as a fundamental unit of social life in contemporary capitalism equivalent to, say, market states or families, nor a fundamental process in social life, such as technology, stratification, or interest-seeking behavior. Economic geography was a second-order empirical topic for social science.

In the early 1980s, in contrast, it was asserted that the region might be a fundamental basis of economic and social life 'after mass production.' That is, since new successful forms of production different from the canonical mass production systems of the post-war period were emerging in some regions and not others, and since they seemed to involve both localization and regional differences and specificities (institutional, technological), it followed that there might be something fundamental which linked late twentieth-century capitalism, regionalism, and regionalization.

Certain images piqued the interest of social scientists: the dense vertically disintegrated industrial districts of Northeast-Central Italy; Toyota City; Silicon Valley; Orange County; Route 128; the *cité scientifique* of Paris; Toulouse; Baden-Württemberg and Bavaria; and even such lesser-known and less high-tech cases as the London and New York financial districts; Los Angeles' garment district; Hollywood; Jutland; the metalcutters of the Haute Savoie; Sakaki; and hundreds of others. All of these were said to be manifestations of a resurgence of the region as the center of 'post-Fordist', 'flexible', 'learning-based', production systems – the emerging face of capitalist industry in this *fin de siècle*. At a larger scale, it became evident that even with increasing intensity of global trade and investment flows, national specificities in terms of products traded and technologies produced were increasing: in certain respects, integration was not bringing similarity, but specialization, a form of regionalization.

But how important is regionalization? Is the region somehow a necessary source of the dynamism of these production systems and, hence, of the developmental dynamics of contemporary capitalism itself? Or is regionalization merely an expression of, another interesting empirical dimension of, technological and organizational changes in successful production systems?

Surprisingly, a fairly large number of social scientists, and not just those whose professional specialty is the region, began to respond in the early 1980s that regionalization was very important, and that it might be more than merely another localization pattern: it might actually be central to the coordination of the most advanced forms of economic life today (see *inter alia* Sabel 1988; Becattini 1987; Bellandi 1989). And so a lively debate was joined. Over a period of more than ten years, the initial propositions have been re-examined theoretically and empirically, and new propositions have emerged. There has been the usual spate of hair-splitting articles, but the debate over regionalization in contemporary capitalism continues to generate fascinating propositions, and for the first time has been taken seriously by social scientists interested in such central topics as technological and organizational innovation and national competitive advantage in a world economy. It is also increasingly regarded as a level of economic policymaking for these reasons and not simply as a way to buy political calm, the traditional reason in much of Europe for regional policy (Bianchi 1992; Bianchi *et al.* 1988; Lassini 1985; Tolomelli 1993). The stakes of these debates are big in both theoretical and practical terms.

Three main 'schools' have participated in the debate: those interested in institutions; those focusing on industrial organization and transactions; and those who concentrate their attention on technological change and learning. Each has made strong claims about the bases of the new competition and the role of the region, and each has inspired empirical research and theoretical critique. I propose a reprise of the debate – but not an exhaustive literature review – in order to claim that there is good reason for including the region as an essential level of economic coordination in capitalism. But, I shall argue, none of the main schools in the resurgence of regional economies debate has come up with the correct formulation of why this is the case. The critics of each of these schools, while in no way dismantling the case for regional economies, have shown their attempts at formulating the basis for the resurgence of regional economies to be partial, although often very rich in insight. The general, and necessary, role of the region is as the locus of what economists are beginning to call 'untraded interdependencies'[1] between actors; these untraded interdependencies generate region-specific material and non-material assets in production. These assets are the central form of scarcity in contemporary capitalism, with its fantastic capacity for production of standardized outputs, essentially because they are not standardized. All three of the most important recent schools of debate have something important to contribute to our understanding of these interdependencies, but none of them has yet got the formulation right. The region, in this analysis, is important as an underpinning for these interdependencies, which allow actors to generate technological and organizational change; hence, the region is a key source of *becoming* – of development – in capitalism.

Such an analysis, I shall argue, involves something different from the hard 'production systems' (especially input–output relations) orientation of most regional economics, as well as of most of the economics of industrial organization and technological change. It also has major implications for how we think about the problem of regional and industrial policies, both for certain kinds of 'motor' regions and for those in development. In illustrating this point I shall conclude by making some remarks about regional policy in contemporary North America and Europe.

Institutions and industrial divides: the ill-fated debate over small firms

From the mid-1970s, Italian scholars called attention to the different development model which characterized the Northeast-Center of their country, dubbed the 'Third Italy' by Bagnasco (1977). In the English-speaking world, the industrial systems of that region were made famous in 1984 by Piore and Sabel (1984; see also Sabel and Zeitlin 1985), who were the first to capture within a general model the twin characteristics of flexibility and specialization. Generalizing from Italy to certain other cases (notably German ones), they then placed the success of such forms of production in macroeconomic and historical context and postulated the possibility of an 'industrial divide' separating a putative era of flexible specialization from that of post-war mass production.

Their account was both empirically rich and theoretically powerful. It incited a debate which centered mostly on the empirical material they adduced to support the theory. Yet it was the theory, and at that the elements, which were least picked up in the subsequent debate that makes, in my view, the lasting contribution to our understanding of capitalist development in general and the status of the region in particular. Piore and Sabel echoed and paralleled the work which had been going on in Florence under the direction of Giacomo Becattini, who had become one of the major contemporary students of Alfred Marshall, in seeking the analogy between what was happening in Italy and Marshall's notion of 'industrial districts' in late nineteenth century England. Becattini's Florentine group engaged in a systematic elaboration of the concept of a 'Marshallian industrial district', turning both on its economic characteristic (externalities lodged in a division of labor) and on the socio-cultural supports to inter-firm interaction within an industrial district. This latter account was achieved both through theoretical work and through very detailed studies of the history and structure of Tuscan industrial districts, especially that of Prato, the woolmaking district next to Florence (Becattini, 1991; Balestri, 1982).

The critics of the empirical account centered on the lessons of the 'Third Italy'. The critical literature which emerged in response to this Italian work is vast and too large to discuss in detailed fashion here (see Storper 1995 for a more complete review). However, in my view, the critics gave disproportionate attention to the problems of whether the empirical versions of flexibility, a deepening division of labor, and regionalization were adequate or not, and insufficient attention to the fundamental contributions of the Italian School, Piore and Sabel, and others to the study of contemporary capitalist development. These contributions, it seems to me, consist in four points which remain unchallenged.

First, technologies of production and divisions of labor in production are not dictated by a movement toward a globally optimal, foreseeable 'best practice' for each sector. They are, rather, the outcomes of institutional pressures and choices made at critical points in the histories of products and their markets, and the direction of development is thus not necessarily toward greater scale and integration, but can be the reverse.[2] It is, moreover, possible that radically different forms of organization will coexist in the same sector, in that efficiency can be composed of different factors. Production is politicized not just in the sense of distributional relations, but at its very heart, in the sense of defining what is made and how it is made, even within a world of market competition, which has a less powerful convergence effect than is imagined by orthodox theory (Sabel and Zeitlin 1985; Nelson and Winter 1982; Storper 1985a).

Second, the flexible specialization school got something basically right in identifying flexibility and specialization as fundamental alternatives to mass production. It is less important that their definitions were not sufficiently wide or precise to accommodate the many different ways that flexibility (internal, external, static, dynamic, products, processes, adjustment, etc.) can take form, or the many different ways that specialization can be organized (production units, firms, etc.). From IBM to Modena, these principles have not been challenged, though we are learning that the precise ways they are organized into industrial systems frequently take us far from the ideal types of Italy and southern Germany. A consequence of both these observations is that the 'industrial divide' postulated by Piore and Sabel has probably been crossed, in the sense that the post-war mass production economy is being replaced by one characterized by greater flexibility and specialization, but the imagery which associated that crossing with Italy and southern Germany, or even with Japan, was much too restrictive. The strength of the analytical insight regarding flexibility-plus-specialization is testified to the fact that it has made its way into virtually every important theory of the firm and the production system in 'post-Fordism', including the high-volume, lean production models of Japan (Aoki 1988; Dosi *et al.* 1988; Dore 1987; Cohendet and Llerena 1989; Best 1990; Porter 1990; Powell 1987; Thorelli 1986; Illeris 1990; Mariti and Smiley 1983), and the language of flexibility-plus-specialization is now employed openly by corporate managers themselves when they restructure (as in the case of IBM).

Third, though the original examples of regionalism were much too pure, it seems clear that some of the dynamic forces in contemporary capitalist development are both localized and territorially specific. This insight, too, has become common currency not just among regionalists, but also among economists (Krugman 1992; Dosi *et al.* 1990; Porter 1990; Amendola *et al.* 1992) and students of technology and trade. The contribution of the flexible specialization school was to assert that this seemed to have something to do with regionalized and territorially specific institutions, though this was not stated as clearly as would have been desired ten years ago.

Fourth, the key texts of this school emphasize that appropriately institutionalized networks are essential to successful ongoing adaptation of a regional economy in the face of uncertainty (technological, market, etc.). This adaptive capacity is not available to other forms of industrial organization (such as canonical mass production); but neither is it available to regional economies based on networks which lack appropriate institutional forms of coordination, which is the key to survival of the economy as a whole. As we shall see later on, the flexible specialization school's analysis of networks of firms differs in very critical ways from the use of the network paradigm in much business and organizational analysis. Something approaching a new orthodoxy has arisen in the academic business economics and management literature in recent years, a network paradigm for organizing production systems. Participation in such networks is akin to a new best business practice, in much of this literature, much in the way that mass production was best practice three decades ago. There are now detailed microeconomic analytics for such a production paradigm, from single firms to whole *filières*. They differ essentially from the main points of the flexible specialization schools, where little emphasis on a single best practice or on the notion of optimum has figured to date; the latter is explicitly about economically imperfect but politically supple and strong forms of industrial adjustment in the face of uncertainty.

Having said this, however, and as noted above, the flexible specialization school itself did not develop an analytical language about ongoing industrial adjustment – or what is now called 'learning' – sufficient to capture in a generalizable way the nature of flexible and specialized industrial systems that have long-term survival capacity without wage-price reductions from those which do not. It is precisely to this critical underdeveloped analysis that we will return later in this chapter.

Industrial organization, transactions, agglomeration: the California School of external economics

What we might call, for lack of a better term, the 'California School' came at the problem of new production paradigms and the region from the perspective of different industries, and a different political–institutional setting, than those described above; as such, it is not surprising that they also chose a different theoretical route. In the early 1980s, Allen Scott was already theorizing about the relationship between the division of labor, transactions costs, and agglomeration, in his initial studies of the women's clothing industry in Los Angeles (see Scott 1988a). Just shortly thereafter, with no real prior theoretical disposition, Susan Christopherson and I, in studying Hollywood's film and television industries, observed a strong process of vertical disintegration (Christopherson and Storper 1986; Storper and Christopherson 1987). Piore and Sabel's book appeared while we were interpreting our empirical results. Other investigations, many carried out by Scott and his students, followed, and both Scott and I continued this work with our own investigations in France and Italy in the mid- and late 1980s (Scott 1988b; Scott 1986; Scott and Angel 1987; Scott and Storper 1987; Scott and Kwok 1989; Scott 1991; De Vet 1990; Storper and Salais 1997). Other geographers and regionalists, such as John Holmes, took an interest in the division of labor as well (Scott and Storper 1986; Holmes 1986).

The argument that emerged rooted flexibility in the division of labor in production, and linked that to agglomeration via an analysis of the transactions costs associated with inter-firm linkages. In essence, it took what seemed to be fact in the Italian cases and created an economic model of the agglomeration process (Scott 1988a; Scott 1993). It assumed that certain exogenous or endogenous market conditions gave rise to uncertainty – shifts in market conditions, or movements along a technological trajectory, for example. This uncertainty is met by deepening the division of labor, in one case to minimize exposure to risks of overcapacity (both production and labor force hoarding), in another to maximize the benefits of specialization and minimize the danger of technological lock-in.

In turn, disintegration of production, *ceteris paribus*, raises the transactions costs of input–output (I–O) relations. There are more transactions external to the firm, and these transactions are, in a number of the empirical circumstances identified, more frequent, less predictable, and more complex. This raises their costs with geographical distance, and the feasibility of carrying out substantively complex transactions drops for certain kinds of complexity (especially non-codifiable or tacit knowledge or where trust is required and full contingent contracting impossible). So agglomeration is an outcome of the minimization of these transactions costs, where such minimization outweighs other geographically dependent production cost differentials.

This organization and cost-related explanation holds that agglomeration is one element in the external economies which attach to interdependent production systems; under the circumstances specified above, those external economies are maximized in the presence of agglomeration, for without agglomeration, the advantages of interdependence – flexibility, risk minimization, specialization – are reduced (or, in the extreme case, overwhelmed) by the costs or difficulties of the intensified transacting. External economies themselves have to do with the way flexibility lowers input costs (by minimizing factor hoarding) and increases throughput to each firm because a greater number of external input–output interconnections raises the probability of successful sale or purchase, all other things being equal.

This analysis thus partakes of a major trend in the business economics literature, shared also by much economic sociology: the economics of network forms of production (Powell 1990; Aoki 1988; Foray 1990; Johansen and Mattson 1987; Lecoq 1989). It seemed to have several advantages over the institutionally inspired flexible specialization school. First, it did not seem to depend on thick and historical institutional contexts. Indeed, one of the main claims we made had to do with the establishment of new industrial spaces. We argued that new industries – those which emerge after technological branching points – have input structures which are independent of older industries – and hence enjoy what we labeled 'windows of locational opportunity,' in the sense that they are not attached to old stocks of external economies (Scott and Storper 1987). But once a group of firms begins to get ahead, the proliferation of external linkages gives them advantages which rapidly attract new entrants and hence only a few major new agglomerations can form in a given new industry. So we offered an explanation for new flexible production agglomerations such as Silicon Valley.

Second, we argued that older industries, analogous to those found in the European cases, could be accounted for via the process of externalization and interlinkage of firms – the story of Hollywood, going from its own version of 'mass' production and toward spatial diffusion toward vertical disintegration and re-agglomeration, was a case in point. We averred that there could be many reasons for such switches in the organizational and geographical pathways of development – in Hollywood, it was regulatory and technological changes which set the process in motion (Storper 1989); in the Third Italy, it was a combination of long-standing civic cultures and the events of the post-war period (Becattini 1978; Brusco 1982; Cappecchi 1990a, 1990b; Ritaine 1989); in the Los Angeles fashion industry, it was endogenous changes in fashion and the possibility of making distribution more attentive to consumer demand, by increasing the number of collections per year (Pitman 1992). Another major case would be consumer durables industries, where technological changes in production and distribution made possible more rapid changeovers; once these possibilities were realized by the Japanese, all world competitors had to follow suit. The list could go on, *ad infinitum*.

The coverage of the model, in other words, was meant to be greater than the initial version of the flexible specialization model, in that it allowed any mix of firm sizes, any sector, any mixture of interlinkages. Indeed, we defined the model around three groups of sectors found to account for increasing proportions of employment, output, and value added in industry – high technology, revitalized craft production, and producer and financial services – thus extending our reach.

As the debate proceeded, however, we realized that the linkage–transactions cost model was incomplete. Toward the end of the 1980s, we became more sensitive to the possibility that the agglomeration was a source of industrial dynamics. We held that agglomerations, once in place, constituted industrial communities where endogenous dynamics of knowledge and technology development occurred, drawing on the example of technology development in Sassuolo documented by Russo (1986), and extending this to our own Californian cases (Cooke and Morgan 1990; Storper and Scott 1989; Scott and Storper 1991). This account of technological innovation turns explicitly on user–producer relations – i.e. on information transactions in an input–output system – and holds that localization and appropriate communication rules are important to innovation in some industries.

This latter brought us to the question of institutions. Though agglomerations could be theoretically accounted for as the way that potential external economies were realized, there was no assurance that markets alone, nor even various forms of contracts, could successfully coordinate the nexus of transactions in an industrial agglomeration. Such transactions – in labor markets, in inter-firm relations, in innovation and knowledge development – tended to have points of failure in the absence of appropriate institutions. In these two respects – evolution and institutions – we attempted to go beyond the initial Williamsonian framework to argue that the 'institutional arrangements' of agglomerations (Cooke and Morgan 1990; Storper and Scott 1989; Scott and Storper 1991) – i.e. the nexus of transactions and their economic performance – were themselves outcomes of broader institutional environments, and themselves generators of future choices for pathways of development. So we came 'full circle' to rejoin the initial authors of the flexible specialization thesis (and the Marshallian theme of 'atmosphere'), albeit with a somewhat different point of entry and without quite the same perspective on the role of institutions in development as a whole. And, as we shall see shortly, we came to realize the central importance of the new economics of technological change and its core notions of evolution and path dependency, for our problem of the role of the region in post-Fordist capitalism.

As with the flexible specialization school, notwithstanding some spurious criticisms, serious critiques did eventually emerge. It seems as if the California School's analysis does apply to certain modernized craft or traditional industries as well as certain labor-intensive manufacturing and service sectors: in clothing, furniture, jewelry, cinema and television, some financial services and banking industries, as well as certain segments of the mechanical engineering industries, the density of local linkages is consistent with the account of agglomeration. In other words, the Californian School's successfully analyzed cases overlap very strongly with those of the flexible specialization school. The critique does not attempt to deny the existence of agglomerations, nor of their recent growth, in other industries, but observes that dense local input–output relations are not present in them in sufficient quantity to account for the existence of the agglomeration. Though, it must be admitted, the critics have not carried out much systematic, rigorous measurement of the geographical extent and density of linkages in flexible production systems, they can be given the benefit of the doubt: it seems as if, in many industries – including some that we claimed as examples of our input–output agglomerations – the direct local I–O relationships between firms are not dense enough to account either for the size of the agglomeration or for a high proportion of what goes on in the sector. The examples where this seems most applicable are parts of high technology and certain parts of supplier-intensive sectors such as mechanical engineering – that is the capital-intensive, high-wage examples of flexible production (Gordon 1990; Veltz 1993).

The critics have attempted a sort of counter theory, which has as its point of departure not the input–output system, but the *firm* (Aoki 1988; Dosi *et al.* 1988; Dore 1987; Cohendet and Llerena 1989; Best 1990; Porter 1990; Powell 1987; Thorelli 1986; Illeris 1990; Mariti and Smiley 1983). The post-Fordist firm is, for them, a nexus for the management of vast flows of resources, the principal node in a set of shifting property and production networks. The means for the firm to manage these networks is a mixture of ownership, contract, and alliance (Badaracco 1988; Mytelka 1990; Mowery 1988; Cooke and Morgan 1991) and in general, this new flexibility of networks carries out all the functions that disintegration does in the flexible production school's analysis. Rather than an economy of direct cost reduction, even for the most innovative activities, we are in an 'economy of organization', where scale, over long distances, can reduce the time and cost of flexible adjustments of capacity and shifts in product mix. Flexibility is retained as a key, but now linked to scale and geographical dispersion. Much of the causality of the flexible production school's analysis with respect to regions is reversed.

Their description of the large firm as a nexus of shifting relations, and of the industrial system as a nexus of nexuses, is at the heart of much of the contemporary empirical economics of the firm (Hakansson 1987). It is not clear, however, that this stands in as an explanation of innovation, agglomeration, or the geography of input–output systems. If the flexible economy were really contained in such dispersed large-firm networks, for example, why would such firms allow significant parts of their activity to be 'trapped' in specific countries and regions? Pavitt and Patel (1991) and Dunning (1988) all show empirically that the core technological activities of the biggest firms are principally rooted in their home countries. Why, indeed, would a firm like IBM bother with the cost and inconvenience of Silicon Valley at all? Here, the economy of organizations school responds that big urban areas are general 'basing points' for advanced (knowledge-intensive) activities with high levels of risk (Veltz 1993). We are back to urbanization economies. There are two problems with this. The first is that such an explanation of big firm–big city interdependence is necessarily a transactions-based explanation, insofar as the reason invoked for big-city location is proximity to factor markets due to the need for high levels of factor (read: labor) turnover in the presence of uncertainty. In countries with primate urban systems, such as France and Japan, what appear in the form of urbanization economies cannot be distinguished from multiple and overlapping localization economies in, say, Paris and Tokyo. The two ways of interpreting the problem would lead to radically different policy prescriptions. The second is that the economies of even the biggest of the big cities, but especially middle-sized cities, are not only urbanized, but have strong sectoral specificities. So urbanization economies are underpinned by localization. This localization involves *parts* of firms, those which are in certain technological or economic 'spaces', in the sense defined by Perroux (1950).

One suspects that the model of the firm they have evolved is applicable to the flexibilization of rather routine productive activities – precisely those where market uncertainty is manageable (e.g. in the mass segments of clothing) or those where innovation is also gradual and manageable: this is the spatially extended economy of organization. The *parts* of these *same* big firms which are involved in those productive activities are *not* free of agglomeration *nor* free of uncertainty in the relevant parts of their input–output chains, and it seems unlikely that transportation, telecommunications, and formal institutional arrangements (i.e. strategic alliances and contracts) are sufficient to obviate the need for proximity in these cases.

In any case, the problem staked out by the flexible production school remains: what are the sufficient conditions for the existence of the observed agglomerations of productive activity, which grew so strongly in the 1980s? The California School came up with an explanation, but it was partial, and it sensitized us as to the importance, complexity, and geography of input–output relations. But the localization of such I–O relations, i.e. the localization of traded interdependencies, is inadequate to the task of explaining the link between flexible production and the resurgence of regional economies in contemporary capitalism.

The California School's explanation also suffered from the same problem as that of the flexible specialization school: the central aspects of its theory could not distinguish between 'good' agglomerations and 'bad' ones. Vertical disintegration, high transactions costs, and agglomeration could be found both in high-wage, technologically dynamic industries and in low-wage technologically stagnant ones. Adding in institutions helps, in the case of traditional industries, to distinguish good versions from bad. But in technologically dynamic industries, agglomerations are often found without overwhelmingly dense local I–O linkages and without the kinds of explicit institutional coordination found in many European industrial districts. A different explanation was needed.

Innovation, high technology, and regional development

The subject of innovation is prefigured in the schools of thought reviewed above, though innovation is seen in both as a consequence of the institutional or organizational frameworks of production. From the late 1970s on, students of regional development investigated the regionally uneven distribution of high-technology industries and the apparently better propensity of some regions than others to develop 'high-tech' economic bases (Malecki 1984; Breheny and McQuaid 1988; Glasmeier 1986; Tödtling 1992). Defined as such, their problem was not the same as that of the two schools of thought reviewed above: rather than a broad problem of a change in production paradigms – flexibility and its consequences – they defined their subject as that of the incidence of industries based on new technologies. The empirical subject matter nonetheless overlapped with the preceding schools in certain cases; Saxenian's work on Silicon Valley falls securely into the institutionalist flexible specialization school (Saxenian 1988, 1994) and Scott and Storper and others argued that high-technology development could be understood from the standpoint of their theory of agglomeration and the division of labor (Scott and Storper 1987). What distinguishes the work reviewed here is that their point of departure was technology, mostly high technology, and regional development.

In using high technology as a point of departure, they attempted to isolate cases of 'advanced' regional development. They assumed that by studying areas that had become centers of production for advanced technologies, there would be lessons for policymaking (how to imitate these places), and – for some of these scholars – there would be lessons about advanced economic development in general, and the role of the region in those forms of development. Much of this, it must be said, was not apparent in the early literature on high technology and regional development; the research was motivated straightforwardly by the high rates of growth in places such as California and Massachusetts and the desire to figure out how to get a part of the action. Little was said, initially, about the qualities of that growth or its possible broader significance in contemporary capitalism. A second concern of the literature is Schumpeterian: what occurs to economic activities affected by waves of radical technological change?

Two branches of this work can be reviewed here. The American school of high-technology regional development sought the conditions for growth in Silicon Valley and Route 128 (Markusen *et al.* 1986). What was it that had set off and sustained growth in these places? The work identified many different factors said to have contributed to these processes, among which the single most discussed is the research university spin-off process. Drawing on the American interest in entrepreneurship (and a strongly American reading of Schumpeter), and on the key experiences of Stanford University–Silicon Valley, MIT–Route 128, an abundant literature on R&D and regional development was generated. To this was added a list of secondary factors said to be present in successful high-tech regions, among which were a 'high quality of life', good infrastructure, even climate (although how Boston could figure there is a mystery). It does appear, from the American historical record, that there were decisive links between universities and founders of firms in the Massachusetts and California cases. The problems come when this is taken to be a universal logic of new technology-based infant industry development. The logic works only when innovation is strongly formal-science based, as in the early years of semiconductors. It was not true, for example, in the case of airplanes in the 1920s and 1930s, where no research universities were strongly present in the leap forward of Los Angeles (Gauthier 1993; Scott 1991; Storper 1982). To this the high-tech school responds: 'that was then, this is now,' for organized science has become more and more important in the development of new technologies (Storper 1985b). So they predict that the university–production link will be critical in future technology-based industries, such as biotechnology.

Assume (for the sake of argument) that this is the case. The question is how to theorize what it is, specifically, that leads from research to the establishment of a regional production base. For there are many research universities, and even many which have generated lots of knowledge in semiconductors, but there is a much smaller number of Silicon Valleys and Route 128s. So there is something untheorized about what actually makes the interaction virtuous. The Californian School discussed above offered a partial response to this, by noting that what distinguishes nascent agglomerations from other early centers is the rate at which their external economies grow due to the proliferation of input–output linkages. But this observation, while essential, is insufficient: it does not plug the gap in knowing what it is about the kind of knowledge or its transfer to producers that makes R&D presence effective sometimes and not effective at other times and places.

A second branch of the American school is what we might call the 'regional politics' approach (Markusen 1985; Markusen *et al.* 1986, 1991). It holds that regional coalitions secure resources that push for the transfer of high-technology resources: thus, Silicon Valley got ahead partially because of the Stanford connection, but also because its early industrialists were clever enough to commandeer resources from the military–industrial complex. Indeed, much of the 'gunbelt' developed because of politics, especially its key complexes in New England and southern California. Here again there are interesting observations, but they fall far short of a coherent theory. For one, the southern California aerospace complex was in place well before the growth of the military–industrial complex: its roots were in the success of Douglas Aircraft's DC3 in the 1930s. The military followed that installed technological competence; it did not place it there in Los Angeles. For another, there are lots of places where politically motivated investments have taken place (Texas, Georgia, Toulouse, Nice) but nothing approaching a diverse and dynamic high-technology agglomeration has been created. Politics alone doesn't do the trick.

The problem, then, is that the American school has not come up with a theory of high-technology development or any necessary link to regional development. No underlying logic of these processes has emerged from its considerable, and interesting, body of empirical work.

An alternative, European, approach has been developed by the GREMI group (*Groupe de Recherche Européen sur les Milieux Innovateurs*), principally Franco-Italian-Swiss regional economists. Their central theoretical notion is that of the *milieu*. There are many different branches of this approach, many of them very rich; I shall attempt simply to summarize what I see as the central theme which encompasses them all, with apologies to those who feel that their work is inadequately distinguished from the whole (Aydalot 1986; Aydalot and Keeble 1988; Camagni 1991; Maillat and Perrin 1992; Maillat *et al.*, 1993; Maillat *et al.* 1990; Camagni, 1992).

The milieu is essentially a context for development, which empowers and guides innovative agents to be able to innovate and to coordinate with other innovating agents. The milieu is something like a territorial version of what the American economic sociologist Mark Granovetter labeled the 'embeddedness' of social and economic processes (Granovetter 1985). The milieu is described, variously, as a system of regional institutions, rules, and practices which lead to innovation. Many of the milieu theorists use the 'network' as their principal organizational metaphor. For some, the milieu is itself a network of actors: producers, researchers, politicians, and so on, in a region. For others, the network concerns the input–output system, and it is this network which is embedded in a milieu, and the milieu provides members of the network with what they need for coordination, adjustment, and successful innovation.

Milieu is suggestive of something interesting, which rejoins a key theme of the Marshallian school: that there is something intangible, 'in the air' as Marshall would have it, which permits innovativeness to proceed in some places and not in others (Marshall 1919). The GREMI group, however, has never been able to identify the economic logic by which milieu fosters innovation. There is a circularity: innovation occurs because of a milieu, and a milieu is what exists in regions where there is innovation. The following definition is exemplary, not exceptional:

> A territory is not a defined space of resources. It is the mode of establishment of a group, in the natural environment, which through the organization and localization of activities, generates prevalent conditions of communication-language and collective learning (the forms of cooperation which create technological and organizational rationalities).
>
> The milieu appears as the socio-economic formation which, at one and the same time, generates the economic dynamic and constitutes itself in setting this dynamic into motion. In other words, milieux take form in organizing themselves and they do so even better insofar as they are

> territorialized. The emergence of organizational dynamism is correlative to the dynamism of local milieux.[3]

The milieux school returns, again and again, to the properties of milieux, but they do not specify the potential mechanisms and processes by which such milieux function, nor precisely what the economic logic of a milieu would be – why localization and territorial specificity should make technological and organizational dynamics better. Thus, though they attempt to go beyond the input–output-based models of the Californian School, they cannot seem to specify the logic or content of the intangible they are after. As such, they do not reveal what it is about regions in innovation that is essential to contemporary capitalist development.

Nonetheless, the GREMI group, and in particular the work of Perrin (1993), has successfully reformulated the problem of what regional 'science' should be all about, in calling for an abandonment of regional analysis based on the two fundamental precepts of neoclassical economic science, i.e. comparative statics (equilibrium), and the rational action paradigm for human behavior. Instead, they argue, the economic process is fundamentally about creation of knowledge and resources, and this 'Schumpeterian' (and Marxian as well) process cannot be derived from the calculations of the rational actor on the margin. How economic actors reason and interact is, they argue, in large part a product of their context, and this context is likely to have – at least in part – territorial boundaries and specificities. So the process of economic creation by such actors should depend on their milieu.

How, then, to get beyond this impasse to define, in the context of capitalism, what generates the dynamic of becoming, that is organizational and technological creation?

Technology, path dependency, and untraded interdependencies

It was left to a group of non-orthodox economists and sympathizers in other disciplines – a group which was not principally interested in territoriality or regions, nor even really in post-Fordism *per se* – to develop the analytical tools which, appropriately adapted, now permit us to identify (at least theoretically, if not empirically) the intangible aspect of a territorial or regional economy that underlies innovative, flexible agglomerations, of both the high- and the low-tech variety.

The first insight came from the evolutionary economics pioneered by Nelson and Winter (1982), and refined for the case of technology by Dosi, Arthur, Soete and others (Dosi 1987; Dosi and Orsenigo 1985; Dosi *et al.* 1990; Arthur 1989). They claimed, essentially, that technologies develop along pathways or trajectories, which describe choice sets that are totally different from those of orthodox economics. In contrast to the standard model's key mechanisms of substitutability and reversibility in choice, where investments and returns can always be adjusted well to each other, they show that choices are characterized by strong irreversibilities and by non-ergodicities (the shape of the function's curve is not convex); as a result, and unlike the orthodox model, it is virtually impossible to predict outcomes from a starting point, even if actors are rational, and the outcomes reflect no single optimum, but – at best – optima which are continually redefined as choices are made and other choices are foreclosed. So the relationship between starting point and ending point is no longer clear, no longer highly predictable, no longer amenable to the same claims about efficient resource allocation made in orthodox economics. In evolutionary economics, what we do is path dependent, i.e. truly historical; it is not the result of a series of actions on spot markets, where the long term can be reduced to a series of disconnected instants.

All this is the case because technologies are the products of *interdependent* choices, and interdependency means *uncertainty*, since we cannot determine exactly what others, upon whom our choices are dependent, will do. Technologies, for one thing, are subject to a variety of user–producer and user–user interactions: every technology made by a producer must have a user, and as the number of users of a given technology rises, it tends to cut off the possibility of different patterns of use (and hence production) for other users. This is, very simply, an external economy which benefits those who follow suit in both cost and feasibility terms (the story invoked by Arthur about why we all drive on either the right or the left, even though there's no efficiency reason, is because everybody else does and it would be costly and hazardous to change (Arthur 1989); or David's (1975) story of why we use the inferior QWERTY keyboard – because it got ahead of other models early).

Beyond these external economies-as-accidents-of-history, there are reasons why producers tend to follow certain pathways. There are significant *technological spillovers* in the economy: knowing how to do one thing is frequently consequent upon knowing how to do another, or key to doing certain other things (Romer 1990). This idea draws on the seminal work of François Perroux in the 1950s, who noted that an economy consists of 'spaces' or fields of endeavor, in part having to do with the density of non-traded technological connections between them (e.g. common types of knowledge or similar types of machines, or knowledge of how to work similar types of basic materials or inputs) (Perroux 1950). In some cases, these non-traded connections overlap with traded input–output relations, i.e. using similar inputs such as raw materials or capital goods; but often – and this is critical – the connections are untraded. The new economics of technological change has suggested, in the 1980s, that there are knowledge or 'common practice' spillovers such that technological excellence comes in packages or ensembles (Lundvall 1990b; Lundvall and Johnson 1992; Beije 1991). Since such excellence relies frequently on knowledge or practices which are not fully codifiable, the particular firms who master it are tied into various kinds of networks with other firms, both through formal exchanges and through untraded interdependencies. The latter include labor markets, public institutions, and locally or nationally derived rules of action, customs, understandings, and values (Dosi and Orsenigo 1985). Technological trajectories, in certain cases, are parallel or complementary with other technologies. Firms thus become dependent on decisions made outside their borders by other firms or decision-makers in the technological space (Storper 1989; Young 1928; Kaldor 1972). When things are going well, external economies – interdependent production functions and imperfect relationships of investment to return – are strongly positive for the ensemble of interdependent actors traveling down these pathways (and there is, in technical terms, no ambiguity about these effects being defined as true external economies).

The evolutionary economists point out that such a framework necessitates a change in focus of attention in economics generally. Essentially, they acknowledge two forms of competition – allocational, which is the basis for comparative advantages – and technological, which is the basis for absolute advantages. Orthodox economics is mainly concerned with the way the market allocates resources and assumes that structural change and development follow from either the additive forces of this allocational process or from exogenous influences such as technological or demographic change. Evolutionary economics holds that technological change is an endogenous property of economic systems and that it is not principally the result of allocational adjustments but of interdependent actions in which the signaling, knowledge development and doing the best one can are central (Dosi *et al.* 1990).

The evolutionists reinterpret the effects of competition in capitalism via this distinction. Comparative advantages are had when a firm or a group of interdependent firms in a nation or region finds a more favorable location along a given production price frontier: they are allocational. This is familiar to everyone who has ever taken an economics class. But, claim the evolutionists, this isn't what drives the distribution of market shares or the composition of economic activities in many cases. Absolute advantages exist when a firm, nation, or region possesses superior technologies such that virtually no set of alternative factor prices (production costs, in essence) would serve to effectuate a redistribution of shares or activities. And this, they claim, is an aspect of the dynamic of capitalist competition wholly overlooked by the orthodox theory of competition-as-allocation.

So what does all this have to do with the themes of post-Fordism, flexibility, and the resurgence of regional economies? The evolutionary economics presented thus far is in the realm of basic theory, but it can be applied to a reinterpretation of the mass production–post-Fordism question. In the system of mass production, absolute advantages certainly were held by certain major firms. And in the post-war period, many of these firms were American. In the early post-war period, indeed, American firms had such technological advantages that their higher factor costs (wages, especially) were of little consequence (Chandler 1966, 1977; Aglietta 1976). But ultimately those firms ceased to make rapid technological progress within the mass production paradigm, for a variety of reasons which we cannot discuss here. Their technologies became imitatable, and the absolute advantage disappeared. A race for comparative advantages was set in motion, both between the US and Europe and via reallocation of production activity from the northern to the southern countries, in search of lower costs *within* a technological paradigm, which is the linchpin of Ricardian comparative advantage.

Ultimately, however, the struggle for world markets began to take another form. From a variety of places – Japan in consumer durables, Italy in non-durables, Germany in mechanical engineering, and so on – new forms of production, not based on mass production methods but instead oriented again toward the *technological learning* which had once characterized competition within mass production, began to emerge as competitive standards on world markets.[4] And so, technological trajectories were 're-opened', and the western world was once again, and still is, a vast 'learning economy', in the felicitous phrase of Lundvall (see Lundvall and Johnson 1992; Lundvall 1990a, 1990b, 1992). The particular contours of this learning economy are much as described by the new business economics and the various schools of flexibility. But what is important is the notion that it is not flexibility *per se* that is the central theoretical element of the current age, but flexibility (and many other features of contemporary production systems) as a means to technological learning and the absolute advantages it is generating for learners. We learned then (in post-war mass production) and we learn now; but we are learning within different meta-paradigms, with different basic technological capacities, at a different point in history.

The evolutionary economists working on technological change, not surprisingly, discovered territory – nations and regions. In theoretical terms, they began to reason that the technological spillovers and their untraded interdependencies would be territorialized under certain conditions, notably where the technological trajectories were particularly open, i.e. had wide margins of potential variation, thus increasing the uncodifiability and tacitness of knowledge development and the importance of communicational clarity and common interpretation in understanding information (Lundvall 1990b, 1992).

In other words, the territorial agglomeration of certain untraded interdependencies and spillovers, or the territorial differentiation of the same, by permitting actors to travel along superior technological trajectories (or to do so more rapidly than others) can confer on them absolute advantages which shelter them, at least temporarily, from Ricardian competition. This would show up as territorial specialization and differentiation in trade, whether between regions or at the international level (Patel and Pavitt 1992).[5] And the more learning going on in the world economy as a whole, the more we should expect, *ceteris paribus*, such territorial agglomeration or differentiation.

The argument can be summarized now, as the following:

- Technological change is *path dependent*.

- It is path dependent because it involves interdependencies between choices made over time – choices are sequenced in time, not simultaneous, and often irreversible.
- These choices have a spatial dimension, which is closely tied into their temporal uncertainty and interdependence; some inter-organizational dependencies within the division of labor, i.e. input–output or network relations, involve some degree of territorialization. But in *all* the cases where organizations cluster together in territorial space in order to travel along a technological trajectory, they have interdependencies which are *untraded*, including labor markets, and 'conventions', or common languages and rules for developing, communicating, and interpreting knowledge (though direct input–output relations may also play a role here).

There are counter-forces to the territorialization process, of course. Among them are technological imitation, and the ongoing effort to transcend geographical distance in both the untraded interdependencies and input–output relations which are critical to technological learning. But those forces are very far from triumphing, or so it would appear from the empirical evidence. Virtually all the systematic empirical investigations of the technological performance of nations suggest that high, and increasing, differentiation or specialization have characterized the western economies since the late 1970s. The main studies include Dosi *et al.*'s study of international trade (1990); Pavitt and Patel (1991); Amendola *et al.*'s (1992) interpretation of OECD statistics, and Dunning's (1988) study of multinational firms. Both Dunning and Pavitt and Patel note, in contrast to the prevailing assumption that multinational firms are indifferent to territory or to local context, that the major multinational firms of the world locate virtually all their most advanced technological capacities in their home countries and that where there are exceptions, they are almost always explained by investment in a technological core capacity of the host country, i.e. they are attracted to the local technological tissue of another country. Jaffe, in the USA, has shown empirically that technological overspills correspond strongly to the patenting activities of a firm (Jaffe 1986); and Antonelli in Italy has indicated, in a very preliminary way, that overspills are often geographically bounded (although the measurement problems remain considerable) (Antonelli 1987; see also Tödtling 1992).

I began to use the evolutionary paradigm in two published papers in 1985 and 1986 to explain technological branching points and the appearance of new high-technology centers (Storper 1985b, 1986). I believe these were among the first uses of this reasoning to account dynamically for processes of regional development. Subsequently, I developed it – drawing on Allyn Young – to try and explain the 'industrial divide' crossed in the film industry, as a path-dependent phenomenon (Storper 1989). Scott and I, later, tried to marry some of the evolutionary insights to the transactional theory of agglomeration, as noted earlier in this chapter, where we observed that, once in place, agglomerations as nexuses of transactions had their own evolutionary dynamics (Scott and Storper 1991). More recently, I tried to show that specialization in international trade corresponds to regional concentrations of industries – what I called their 'technology districts' – and thus that globalization of economic activity was linked to regionalization, through the mechanism of localized technological learning (although my theoretical explanation relied too heavily on input–output relations at that time) (Storper 1992).

But it should be noted that the evolutionary approach is, if not incompatible with the transactions cost approach to agglomeration, then at least wedded to fundamentally different theoretical commitments about dynamic processes of capitalist development. For the transactions cost-based theory of the California School is about allocation through cost minimization, with evolutionary path-dependent phenomena an afterthought (Scott 1988a) and this is because transactions cost economics is about traded input–output relations. The evolutionary approach is about much more than allocation and is fundamentally not about cost minimization; it is about the forces that allow the parameters of cost minimization to be altered and which get in the way of optimizing (Dosi *et al.* 1990; Johansen and Mattson 1987). And in terms of mechanism, as we have noted, evolutionary economics opens up the field of untraded interdependencies which does not figure in transactions-based approaches. Even though one can argue that untraded interdependencies are rooted in transactions – though perhaps not *input–output transactions* and market or contract exchanges – the analysis of such transactions cannot be easily accommodated within transactions *cost*-based theories.

As we shall see, this does not mean that the two approaches are incompatible at an empirical level; but their fundamental theoretical commitments are undeniably quite different.

From technology to action: the region as a nexus of untraded interdependencies

The evolutionary school of technological change opened up the question of economic development as one of learning, or *becoming*, and of untraded interdependencies as a major feature of this process. But certain limitations remained. As a number of observers have pointed out, the notion of trajectory was too narrow, in the sense that pre-established 'technological fields' defined the trajectories and the question then became merely where firms positioned themselves along it (Piore 1989). But what defines the trajectory? And can trajectories themselves be developed and redefined through actions which fall outside of an existing possibility set? It is too easy to relegate this kind of creative action to major technological 'breakthroughs' or 'ruptures' in the trajectory, as when basic science opens up a major new field of endeavor; new possibilities seem to emerge from much more mundane, incremental modification of products and processes and from new, not formerly envisaged applications of basic knowledge. New 'branches' on evolutionary 'trees' are part of the evolutionary process, not merely the choice of which branch to jump on to.

And why limit trajectory to 'technology'? Surely the evolutionary properties of production systems involve more than hardware. The definition of technology may be stretched to include 'soft' dimensions of technology such as know-how and organizational rationalities, and this widens the scope of what may be considered a technological trajectory. Learning certainly concerns all of these dimensions of production: the design of products, processes, know-how, and the evolution of organizational skills, i.e. of the 'science' of organization in capitalism.[6]

But perhaps even this does not go far enough. There are other dimensions of the evolution of production systems which cannot easily be captured via the word 'technology'. All production systems involve uncertainty, in the sense that there is no configuration of markets and firms which involves zero levels of interdependency on other actors. Even in a hypothetical case of a single firm where all inputs were produced internally and outputs resulted, there would still be market uncertainty to face. In reality, virtually all production systems involve uncertainties of several kinds: between producers in the input–output chain; between producers and workers, in securing the labor desired at the price paid; between producers and consumers, especially over time. All markets involve uncertainties and fluctuations of some sort. The main way that such uncertainty is resolved is through *conventions*, which are taken-for-granted rules and routines between the partners in different kinds of relations defined by uncertainty.[7] There are different combinations of such uncertainty, giving rise to different possible conventions so that producers attempt to structure production so as to cope successfully with it. These constitute 'frameworks of economic action', and different frameworks are possible for different kinds of products, markets, and kinds of labor: these are 'possible worlds of production', defined by the ensemble of their conventions.[8] Such conventions are always different for fundamentally different kinds of products; but they are also often different for similar kinds of products, from region to region and especially from nation to nation, according to the particular way that actors resolve uncertainty so as to enter into the form of collective action known as production. Some such 'real worlds of production' are more successful than others in competition, of course, as reflected by their market shares and profit levels. But in any case, the evolution of these production systems is strongly dependent on the worlds of production, rooted in their underlying conventions, constructed in given times and places, and to which producers, workers, and consumers are subject. Industrial evolution concerns these conventions, for they affect the ensemble of dimensions of innovation and change we have noted above. We might think then about 'trajectories of conventions', 'trajectories of worlds of production', or organizational trajectories, as the appropriate object of dynamic analysis of production systems.

Michael Piore made a similar critique, in a somewhat different vein, in a (to my knowledge) unpublished paper several years ago. He claimed that the notion of external economies as contained in Marshall was actually incompatible with the Marshall who brilliantly observed that 'secrets of industry were ... in the air.' External economies in Marshall were simply the external economies of scale, due to the external scope of a set of producers tied together by input–output relations. The real effect of 'in the air' as untraded interdependencies was not captured, and could not be captured, by the term external economies as employed by most economists. Without using the term untraded interdependencies, Piore called our attention to the collective and interdependent character of work in industrial districts as a particular, historically and geographically defined *form of action*; a framework of action defined by a community of persons which enables them to produce successfully in a certain way.

This definition of the problem incorporates a wider range of the resurgent regional economies identified by recent scholarship than any of the preceding perspectives on regionalism and post-Fordism, and does so in a dynamic manner.[9] We may say that, in technological or organizational spaces, there are moments when economic assets are more general and others when they are more specific. For example, an old, well-developed, highly codifiable, and standardized technology rests on both knowledge and physical inputs that are widely diffused, but highly specific to the technology. The elaboration of the technology over time, its differentiation into many different products and using more and more differentiated inputs, makes the assets of the industry often highly specific to its firms and products. In the late 1940s and early 1950s, product and process technologies were quite specific for vacuum-tube-based electronic products, in what was then an old technology which had little development left in it.[10] But then miniaturization came along to replace the vacuum tube, first via the transistor, and then via the silicon-based semiconductor. When new, these technologies had few established inputs that were specific to them; they had to 'invent' their own input chains, and the knowledge going into them, which had not yet become highly applications-specific. In other words, they began as generic assets which, over time, evolved into more specific assets. This is one reason why the semiconductor industry was not attached, geographically, to its parent industry – radio and television equipment – on the East Coast, and instead found its center in Silicon Valley.[11] It had to reinvent its own input chain, thus creating assets specific to the emerging technological space. It also had to convert generic electronic engineers into labor which had skills specific to semiconductors – labor which, by definition, could not have existed prior to the invention of the semiconductor. As a technology develops and both its inputs and applications become more differentiated, the technological spillovers we mentioned earlier come into existence, when technologically cognate fields of knowledge elaborate their parameters. In three ways the labor market, the input–output system, and the knowledge system – there is a process of becoming specific.

But these three levels are, in my view, not the deepest levels at which this analysis can be formulated. All three, I would propose, evolve from generality to specificity on a foundation of conventions which make possible communication, interpretation, and coordination among the actors who are making them become specific. In other words, frameworks of action which govern the production system start from a position of generality and move to specificity, as they are sedimented into conventions, practiced by actors, and sometimes embodied in formal institutions and rules. Think of this with respect to the semiconductor industry. The hagiographies written in the 1970s and 1980s (with titles such as *Silicon Valley Fever* or *Life in the High Tech Fast Lane*) can be reinterpreted in a serious analytical way. They are trying to grasp the emergence of a nexus of conventions – frameworks of action – which are specific to an emerging industry and also highly regionalized. Certain dimensions of this culture have diffused, globally; but there is only one Silicon Valley if one wants to be 'in the know' for the most advanced innovations in semiconductor technology. Diffusion of these frameworks of action is highly imperfect and partial.

We know that input–output relations alone have costs associated with uncertainty in infant industries that are high enough to bring agglomerations into existence in the early days of existence of many industries – the strong point of the California School's transactions cost analysis. Yet, as we have pointed out, such geographical input–output constraints disappear rapidly in many industries, including high-technology industries, as some inputs become more standardized and are produced at higher output levels; for these cases, linkage-based models predict that geographical diffusion should be possible. And much diffusion does take place, as in the movement of semiconductor production to Southeast Asia and areas other than Silicon Valley in the USA. But in many cases, less such decentralization (often associated today with 'globalization') takes place than would seem possible from the standpoint of these geographical linkage costs. Silicon Valley continues to hold much direct productive activity and, as an agglomeration, to show essentially *no* sign of weakening even to this day. Might this be the case because *the geographical constraints on untraded interdependencies outlive the geographical constraints on input–output linkages*? And could this especially be the case when there are actual or expected high levels of technological or organizational learning, whether in basic or incremental form? Here, the rules of action that permit participants in the production system to develop, communicate and interpret information, as well as to develop knowledge, and to develop the people who develop and interpret knowledge, may have greater geographical constraints than the process of trading inputs and outputs. The conventions to which I refer, in other words, underlie the *capacities for action* of the actors who carry out the collective activity known as learning.

These conventions are a principal form of untraded interdependency, along with labor markets. Thus, regional economies constitute nexuses of untraded interdependencies which emerge and become, themselves, specific but public assets of production communities (assets of coordination, i.e. frameworks of collective action), and which underpin the production and reproduction of other specific assets such as labor and hardware.

We can now propose that an answer to the principal dilemma of contemporary economic geography – the resurgence of regional economies, and of territorial specialization in an age of increasing ease in transportation and communication of inputs and outputs and of increasingly scientific organizational rationalities of managing complex systems of inputs and outputs – must be sought in two lines of reasoning. One is the tension between respecialization and destandardization of inputs and outputs which, *ceteris paribus*, raises the transactions costs associated with them.[12] The other is the association of organizational and technological learning with agglomeration, which in turn has two roots. The first, and more limited case, is that of localized input–output relations, which constitute webs of user–producer relations essential to information development and exchange, hence to learning (Lundvall 1990b; Russo 1986; von Hippel 1987). The other, and more general case, is the untraded interdependencies which attach to the process of economic and organizational learning and coordination. Where these I–O relations or untraded interdependencies are localized, and this is – as we have suggested – quite frequent in cases of technological or organizational dynamism, then we can say that the region is a key, necessary element in the 'supply architecture' for learning and innovation. It can now be seen that theoretical predictions that globalization means the end to economies of proximity have been exaggerated by many analysts because they have deduced them only from I–O analysis.

Conclusion

The purpose of this chapter has been to identify, in theoretical terms, why regions keep emerging as centers for new rounds of growth even as our capacities for transcending the frictions of space continue to improve. The logic identified here is intended to apply to the recent re-emergence of regional economies as centers of technological and economic spaces, in spite of the historical trend to transcend the limitations of raw distance in the transport and communication of goods, people, capital, and information. We have made a proposition that the region has a central theoretical status in the process of capitalist development which must be located in its untraded interdependencies.

The assertion that the central theoretical status of regions in capitalist development is as a locus of untraded interdependencies means, simply, that these interdependencies are necessary to capitalist development and that they are, under certain conditions, necessarily regionalized. But this does not mean that, on the ground, there are not other reasons for regional economies to exist or to grow; politics, for example, may decide which regions grow. Established regions, especially those of a certain size, have strong auto-reproducing Keynesian dynamics which have little to do with the logic elaborated here, for example. And the dynamics of a global division of labor and the national or global shifting of productive activity continue, and require analytical tools other than those outlined in this paper. Thus, the proposition made here is not intended to stand in for a complete theory of regional development. But these other reasons, however empirically and politically interesting, do not tell us whether there is a necessary role for regions in the economic process in capitalism.

Having stated that the theoretical status of the region in capitalism is as a nexus of untraded interdependencies, we can now recognize that our claim is something of a banality: in some respects, it might be seen as not so different from what practitioners of the *histoire-géographie* tradition on the Continent, or of regional geography in the USA, wanted to identify. But they were incapable of getting out of the trap of regional uniqueness (of 'idiographic' analysis, as it was then called); lacking an analytical, scientific language for what they recounted, they could neither compare nor generalize, and hence could not contribute (at least in the eyes of other social scientists) anything to the general body of emerging social scientific theory. The purpose of developing an analytical language for the region is precisely to re-state one central issue implicit in those schools in a way which might now be able to contribute something essential to a general understanding of the economic processes under capitalism, i.e. its developmental dynamic based in learning.

The task of researching untraded interdependencies as the basis of the ongoing resurgence of regional economies, patterns of regional growth, regional differentiation in development, trade, and technology accumulation, is an enormous and exciting multidisciplinary project. It actually is not strictly a regionalist project either, for everything that we have said about untraded interdependencies applies more generally to the mysteries of a 'learning economy', and to the mysteries of why some economies do not develop.

Acknowledgements

An extended version of this paper was originally published in *European Urban and Regional Studies* 2: 191–221 (1995). The paper was written while the author was a visiting scholar at the Institut de Recherches sur les Societes Contemporaines (IRESCO), within two of its research units, the Centre de Sociologie Urbaine and the Groupement de Recherches 'Institutions, Emploi et Politique Economique', supported by the PIR-Villes Program of the French CNRS. I wish to thank, in particular, Francis Godard, Edmond Preteceille, Robert Salais, and Christian Topalov for their sponsorship of this visit.

Notes

1 I first became aware of this term in the work of Dosi and that of Lundvall, although there are echoes of it in the writings of François Perroux and Tibor Scitovsky in the 1950s.
2 Even proponents of the thesis of a revival of certain principles of mass production, in the context of 'lean production', readily admit that this is a lesson of recent industrial history; see, for example, Coriat (1991), or much of the neo-evolutionist work coming out of the Regulationist School; the best statements, in my opinion, are Dosi (1987) and Dosi and Orsenigo (1985).
3 Both quotes are from an excellent paper by Perrin (1993). My translations attempt to get the sense of the message. They read, in the original, a bit differently. For another sophisticated treatment, see Dupuy and Gilly (1992).
4 I am not sure who was the first to make this point, but it is now the stock-in-trade of many evolutionary economists and business economists.
5 As noted in Porter (1990); Amendola *et al.* (1992); and Storper (1992).
6 This is now well incorporated into recent work within the evolutionary paradigm, for example as in Lundvall (1992).
7 From the French school of *économie des conventions*. References include: Eymard-Duvernay (1987); Thevenot (1986); *Révue Economique* (1989); Salais and Storper (1992); and Storper and Salais (1997). This is by no means a complete list, as many branches of this school have now come into being.
8 A brief account of these worlds is found in Salais and Storper (1992) and a detailed treatment is in Storper and Salais (1997). See also, for a more traditional institutionalist approach, Tolliday and Zeitlin (1988).
9 In the following discussion of general and specific assets, I owe much to Steve Bass and Ahmed Enany (doctoral students at UCLA), and in particular Bass (1993). See also Gaffard (1990). The concept of specificity in relations is brought out in Asanuma (1991). This notion of agglomerations as action systems where particular kinds of agglomeration-specific rationalities are produced and constitute secrets of how the production system works is to be found in, for example, Lecoq (1993) and Amin and Thrift (1993).
10 This is exactly opposite to what Williamson (1985) says about assets, where specificity is a function of the numbers of owners/deployers of assets and, hence, their reproducibility. An older industry thus has non-specific assets, frequently, because they are widely diffused and can be purchased from large numbers of potential suppliers. The purchaser cannot be held hostage. One could call these assets specific in the sense of dedicated to the purposes of the consuming industry, the result of specialization of such assets to these purposes, choices which are now irreversible. In any case, this reveals the fundamental ambiguity of this terminology.
11 Scott and I made a similar argument in 1987, but did not distinguish between input–output-induced behavior and the untraded interdependencies I am emphasizing here.
12 Scott and I also argued that the ongoing process of product differentiation in capitalism destandardizes outputs (and hence inputs); this means that new inputs become necessary. The uncertainty attached to these new input–output relationships re-creates the need for proximity in input–output transactions. We used the recent growth of financial services agglomerations as an example, that is an industry where transport costs for the 'product' are practically zero.

Bibliography

Aglietta, M. (1976) *A Theory of Capitalist Regulation*, London: New Left Books.

Amendola, G., Guerrieri, P. and Padoan, P.C. (1992) 'International patterns of technological accumulation and trade', *Journal of International and Comparative Economics* 1: 173–97.

Amin, A. and Thrift, N. (1993) 'Globalization, institutional thickness and local prospects', *Révue d'Economie Régionale et Urbaine* 3: 405–30.

Antonelli, C. (1987) 'L'impresa reti: cambiamento tecnologico, internalizazzione, e appropriazione di quasi-rendite', *Annali di Storia dell Impresa* 3: 79–119.

Aoki, M. (1988) *Information, Incentives, and Bargaining in the Japanese Economy*, Stanford: Stanford University Press.

Arthur, B. (1989) 'Competing technologies, increasing returns and lock-in by historical events', *The Economic Journal* 99: 116–31.

Asanuma, B. (1991) 'Manufacturer–supplier relationships and the concept of relation-specific skill', *Journal of Japanese and International Economics* 3: 1–30.

Aydalot, P. (ed.) (1986) *Milieux Innovatuers en Europe*, Paris: CEE.

Aydalot, P. and Keeble, D. (eds) (1988) *High Technology Industries and Innovative Environments: The European Experience*, London: Routledge.

Badaracco, J., Jr (1988) 'The changing form of the corporation', in J. Meyer and J. Gustafson (eds) *The U.S. Business Corporation: An Institution in Transition*, Cambridge: Ballinger.

Bagnasco, A. (1977) *Tre Italie*, Bologna: Il Mulino.

Balestri, A. (1982) 'Industrial organization in the manufacture of fashion goods: Prato, 1950–1980', MA thesis in Economics, University of Lancaster.

Bass, S. (1993) 'Growth pole theory and the technopolis: prelude to a study of Japan's Technopolis Program', PhD dissertation proposal, University of California at Los Angeles.

Becattini, G. (1978) 'The development of light industry in Tuscany: an interpretation', *Economic Notes, Monte dei Paschi di Siena* 7(2–3): 107–23.

—— (ed.) (1987) *Mercato e Forze Locali*, Bologna: Il Mulino.

—— (1991) 'Per una lettura sistematica dei distretti industriali Marshalliani', Florence: University of Florence, Department of Economics, Paper.

Beije, P. (1991) 'The economic arena for management of innovation networks', paper presented at the international seminar 'New Frontiers in Science and Engineering in a European Perspective', Paris, 27–29 May.

Bellandi, M. (1989) 'Capacitá innovativa diffusa e distretti industriali', Florence: Universita degli Studi di Firenze, Department of Economics, Marshallian Studies Series.

Best, M. (1990) *The New Competition: Institutions of Industrial Restructuring*, Cambridge: Polity Press.

Bianchi, P. (1992) 'Levels of policy and the nature of post-Fordist competition', in M. Storper and A.J. Scott (eds) *Pathways to Industrialization and Regional Development*, London: Routledge.

Bianchi, P., Giordano, M.G. and Pasquini, F. (1988) 'Industrial policy in Italy at a local level', paper presented to the Regional Science Association 28th Regional Congress, Stockholm, August.

Breheny, M.J. and McQuaid, R. (1988) *The Development of High Technology Industries: An International Survey*, London: Routledge.

Brusco, S. (1982) 'The Emilian model: productive decentralization and social integration', *Cambridge Journal of Economics* 6: 167–84.

Camagni, R. (ed.) (1991) *Innovation Networks: Spatial Perspectives*, London: Belhaven Press.

—— (1992) *Innovation Networks: The Spatial Perspective*, London: Belhaven/ Frances Pinter.

Cappecchi, V. (1990a) 'L'industrializzazione a Bologna nel novecento: dagli inizi del secolo alla fine della seconda guerra mondiale', *Storia Illustrata di Bologna* 18(V): 341–60.

—— (1990b) 'L'industrializzazione a Bologna nel novecento: dal secondo dopoguerra ad oggi', *Storia Illustrata di Bologna* 9(V): 161–80.

Chandler, A. (1966) *Strategy and Structure: Chapters in the History of the Industrial Enterprise*, Cambridge, MA: MIT Press.

—— (1977) *The Visible Hand: The Managerial Revolution in American Business*, Cambridge, MA: Harvard University Press.

Christopherson, S. and Storper, M. (1986) 'The city as studio; the world as back lot: the impacts of vertical disintegration on the motion picture industry', *Society and Space* 3: 305–20.

Cohendet, P. and Llerena, P. (eds) (1989) *Flexibilité, Information, et Décision*, Paris: Economica.

Cooke, P. and Morgan, K. (1990) *Learning through Networking: Regional Innovation and the Lessons of Baden-Württemberg*, Cardiff: University of Wales.

—— (1991) 'The network paradigm: new departures in corporate and regional development', paper presented at an international conference on Europe after Maastricht, Lemnos, Greece, 2–5 September.

Coriat, B. (1991) *Penser à l'Envers*, Paris: C. Bourgois.

David, P.A. (1975) *Technical Choice, Innovation, and Economic Growth*, London: Cambridge University Press.

De Vet, J.M. (1990) 'Innovation and new firm formation in southern California's medical device industry', MA thesis, UCLA, Department of Geography.

Dore, R. (1987) *Taking Japan Seriously*, Stanford: Stanford University Press.

Dosi, G. (1987) 'Institutions and markets in a dynamic world', Brighton: SPRU Discussion Paper No. 32.

Dosi, G. and Orsenigo, L. (1985) 'Order and change: an exploration of markets, institutions and technology in industrial dynamics', Brighton: SPRU Discussion Paper No. 22.

Dosi, G., Freeman, C., Silverberg, G. and Soete, L. (eds) (1988) *Technical Change and Economic Theory*, London: Pinter.

Dosi, G., Pavitt, K. and Soete, L. (1990) *The Economics of Technical Change and International Trade*, New York: NYU Press.

Dunning, J.H. (1988) *Multinationals, Technology, and Competitiveness*, London: Unwin Hyman.

Dupuy, C. and Gilly, J.P. (eds) (1992) *'Dynamique Industrielle, Dynamique Territoriale, et Stratégies des Groupes'*, Toulouse: Institut d'Economie Régionale de Toulouse.

Eymard-Duvernay, F. (1987) 'Les entreprises et leurs modèles', *Cahiers du Centre d'Etudes de l'Emploi* 30: 5–27.

Foray, D. (1990) 'The secrets of industry are in the air: eléments pour un cadre d'analyse du phenomène du réseau d'innovateurs', *Research Policy* 20(5): 393–405.

Gaffard, J.L. (1990) 'Sunk costs and the creation of technology', paper presented to the OECD/TEP Conference on Technology and Competitiveness, Paris/La Villette, 27–29 June.

Gauthier, D. (1993) 'The aerospace industry in southern California between the Wars', MA thesis, UCLA, Los Angeles.

Glasmeier, A. (1986) 'The structure, location and role of high technology industries in U.S. regional development', PhD dissertation, Department of City and Regional Planning, Berkeley.

Gordon, R. (1990) 'Systèmes de production, réseaux industriel, et régions: les transformations dans l'organisation sociale et spatiale de l'innovation', *Révue d'Economie Industrielle* 51: 304–39.

Granovetter, M. (1985) 'Economic action and social structure: the problem of embeddedness', *American Journal of Sociology* 93(3): 481–510.

Hakansson, H. (ed.) (1987) *Industrial Technological Development: A Network Approach*, London: Croom Helm.

von Hippel, E. (1987) 'Cooperation between rivals: informal know-how trading', *Research Policy* 16: 291–302.

Holmes, J. (1986) 'The organization and locational structure of production subcontracting', in A.J. Scott and M. Storper (eds) *Production, Work, Territory*, Boston and London: Unwin Hyman.

Illeris, S. (ed.) (1990) *Networks and Regional Development*, Copenhagen: NordREFO.

Jaffe, A. (1986) 'Technological opportunity and spillovers of R&D: evidence from firms' patents, profits and market value', *American Economic Review* 76: 984–1001.

Johansen, J. and Mattson, L.G. (1987) 'Interorganizational relations in industrial systems: a network approach compared with the transaction cost approach', *International Studies of Management and Organization* XVII(1): 34–48.

Kaldor, N. (1972) 'The irrelevance of equilibrium economics', *The Economic Journal* 82: 1237–55.

Krugman, P. (1992) *Geography and Trade*, Cambridge, MA: MIT Press.

Lassini, A. (1985) *Gli Interventi Regionali per i Servizi alle Imprese*, Milan: FrancoAngeli.

Lecoq, B. (1989) 'Réseaux et système productif regional: contenu, portée, et fondèments théoriques du concept de réseau', Neuchatel, Switzerland: Dossiers, Université de Neuchatel.

—— (1993) 'Proximité et rationalité economique', *Révue d'Economie Régionale et Urbaine* 3: 469–88.

Lundvall, B.A. (1990a) 'From technology as a productive factor to innovation as an interactive process', *Research Policy* 20: 5.

—— (1990b) 'User–producer interactions and technological change', paper presented to the OECD-TEP Conference, Paris/La Villette, June.

—— (ed.) (1992) *National Systems of Innovation: Toward a Theory of Innovation and Interactive Learning*, London: Frances Pinter.

Lundvall, B.A. and Johnson, B. (1992) 'The Learning Economy', paper presented to the European Association for Evolutionary Political Economy Conference, Paris, 4–6 November.

Maillat, D. and Perrin, J.C. (1992) *Entreprises Innovantes et Developpement Territorial*, Neuchatel: EDES.

Maillat, D., Crevoisier, O. and Lecoq, B. (1990) 'Innovation and territorial dynamism', paper for workshop 'Flexible Specialisation in Europe', Zurich, 25–26 October.

Maillat, D., Quevit, M. and Senn, L. (eds) (1993) *Milieux Innovateurs et Réseaux d'Innovation: Un Défi pour le Developpement Regional*, Neuchatel: EDES.

Malecki, E.J. (1984) 'Technology and regional development: a survey', *Journal of the American Planning Association* 50(3): 262–6.

Mariti, P. and Smiley, R.H. (1983) 'Cooperative agreements and the organization of industry', *Journal of Industrial Economics* XXXI(4): 437–51.

Markusen, A. (1985) *Profit Cycles, Oligopoly and Regional Development*, Cambridge, MA: MIT Press.

Markusen, A., Hall, P. and Glasmeier, A. (1986) *High Tech America: The What, How, Where and Why of the Sunrise Industries*, Boston: Allen and Unwin.

Markusen, A., Hall, P., Campbell, S. and Deitrick, S. (1991) *The Rise of the Gunbelt: The Military Remapping of Industrial America*, New York: Oxford University Press.

Marshall, A. (1919) *Industry and Trade*, London: Macmillan.

Mowery, D. (ed.) (1988) *International Collaborative Ventures in Manufacturing*, Cambridge: Ballinger.

Mytelka, L. (1990) *Strategic Partnerships and the World Economy*, London: Frances Pinter.

Nelson, R. and Winter, S. (1982) *An Evolutionary Theory of Economic Change*, Cambridge, MA: Harvard University Press.

Patel, P. and Pavitt, K. (1992) 'Europe's technological performance', Brighton: SPRU, University of Sussex, Paper.

Pavitt, K. and Patel, P. (1991) 'Large firms in the production of the world's technology: an important case of non-globalization', *Journal of International Business Studies* First Quarter: 1–21.

Perrin, J.C. (1993) 'Pour une révision de la science régionale: l'approche en termes de milieu', Centre D'economie Régionale, University of Aix-Marseille, Aix-en-Provence, Paper 148(3).

Perroux, F. (1950) 'Economic space: theory and applications', *Quarterly Journal of Economics* 64(1): 89–104.

Piore, M. (1989) 'Some further notes on technological trajectories', paper for colloquium 'Reversibilities et irreversibilities dans les modes de croissance: institutions, techniques, et economie', Paris, 21–23 June.

Piore, M. and Sabel, C. (1984) *The Second Industrial Divide*, New York: Basic Books.

Pitman, B. (1992) 'Fashion figures: configurations of woman and modernity in geography, planning and design', PhD thesis in Urban Planning, UCLA, Los Angeles.

Porter, M. (1990) *The Competitive Advantage of Nations*, London: Macmillan.

Powell, W.W. (1987) 'Hybrid organizational arrangements: new form or transitional arrangement?', *California Management Review* 30: 67–87.

—— (1990) 'Neither market nor hierarchy: networks forms of organization', *Research in Organizational Behavior* 12: 295–336.

Révue Economique (1989) 'L'Économie des Conventions: numéro spécial', 40(2) (March).

Ritaine, E. (1989) 'La Modernité Localisée? Léçons Italiennes sur le Developpement Régional', *Revue Française de Science Politique* 39(2): 155–77.

Romer, P. (1990) 'Endogenous technological change', *Journal of Political Economy* 98(5): S71–S101.

Russo, M. (1986) 'Technical change and the industrial district: the role of inter-firm relations in the growth and transformation of ceramic tile production in Italy', *Research Policy* 14: 329–43.

Sabel, C. (1988) 'Flexible specialisation and the re-emergence of regional economies', in P. Hirst and J. Zeitlin (eds) *Reversing Industrial Decline?*, Oxford: Berg, pp. 17–78.

Sabel, C. and Zeitlin, J. (1985) 'Historical alternatives to mass production: politics, markets and technology in nineteenth century industrialization', *Past and Present* 108: 133–76.

Salais, R. and Storper, M. (1992) 'The four worlds of contemporary industry', *Cambridge Journal of Economics* 16: 169–93.

Saxenian, A. (1988) 'Regional networks and the resurgence of Silicon Valley', Berkeley: Institute of Urban and Regional Development, Working Paper #508.

—— (1994) *Regional Advantage: Culture and Competition in Silicon Valley and Route 128*, Cambridge, MA: Harvard University Press.

Scott, A.J. (1986) 'High technology industry and territorial development: the rise of the Orange County complex, 1955–1984', *Urban Geography* 7: 3–45.

—— (1988a) *Metropolis*, Berkeley: University of California Press.

—— (1988b) *New Industrial Spaces*, London: Pion.

—— (1991) 'The aerospace–electronics industrial complex in California: the formative years, 1940–1960', *Research Policy* 20(5): 439–56.

—— (1993) *Technopolis: High Technology Industry and Regional Development in Southern California*, Berkeley and Los Angeles: University of California Press.

Scott, A.J. and Angel, D.P. (1987) 'The U.S. semiconductor industry: a locational analysis', *Environment and Planning A* 19: 875–912.

Scott, A.J. and Kwok, E.C. (1989) 'Interfirm subcontracting and locational agglomeration: a case study of the printed circuits industry in Southern California', *Regional Studies* 23(5): 405–16.

Scott, A.J. and Storper, M. (eds) (1986) *Production, Work, Territory*, London: Allen and Unwin.

—— (1987) 'High technology industry and regional development: a theoretical critique and reconstruction', *International Social Science Journal* 112: 215–32.

—— (1991) 'Regional development reconsidered', in H. Ernste and V. Meier (eds) *Regional Development and Contemporary Industrial Response: Expanding Flexible Specialisation*, London: Belhaven.

Storper, M. (1982) 'The spatial division of labor: technology, the labor process, and the location of industries', PhD dissertation, University of California, Berkeley, Department of Geography.

—— (1985a) 'Oligopoly and the product cycle', *Economic Geography* 61(3): 260–82.

—— (1985b) 'Technology and spatial production relations: disequilibrium, inter-industry relationships, and industrial evolution', in M. Castells (ed.) *High Technology, Space and Society*, Beverly Hills: Sage.

—— (1986) 'Technology and new regional growth complexes: the economics of discontinuous spatial development', in P. Nijkamp (ed.) *Technological Change and Employment: Urban and Regional Dimensions*, Berlin: Springer.

—— (1989) 'The transition to flexible specialization in the U.S. film industry: external economies, the division of labor, and the crossing of industrial divides', *Cambridge Journal of Economics* 13: 273–305.

—— (1992) 'The limits to globalization: technology districts and international trade', *Economic Geography* 68(1): 60–93.

—— (1995) 'The resurgence of regional economies, ten years later', *European Urban and Regional Studies* 2: 191–221.

Storper, M. and Christopherson, S. (1987) 'Flexible specialization and regional industrial agglomerations', *Annals of the Association of American Geographers* 77: 104–17.

Storper, M. and Salais, R. (1997) *Worlds of Production: The Action Frameworks of the Economy*, Cambridge, MA: Harvard University Press.

Storper, M. and Scott, A.J. (1989) 'The geographical foundations and social regulation of flexible production complexes', in J. Wolch and M. Dear (eds) *The Power of Geography; How Territory Shapes Social Life*, London and Boston: Unwin Hyman.

Thevenot, L. (1986) 'Economie et formes conventionnelles', in R. Salais and L. Thevenot (eds) *Le Travail: Marchés, Regles, Conventions*, Paris: Economica.

Thorelli, H.B. (1986) 'Networks: between markets and hierarchies', *Strategic Management Journal* 7: 37–51.

Tödtling, F. (1992) 'the uneven landscape of innovation poles: local embeddedness and global networks', University of Vienna: IIR, 46.

Tolliday, S. and Zeitlin, J. (1988) 'Between Fordism and flexibility: the automobile industry and its workers, past, present and future', *Archiv für Social Geschichte* XXCIII: 153–71.

Tolomelli, C. (ed.) (1993) *Le Politiche Industriale Regionali: Experienze, Soggetti, Modelli*, Bologna: CLUEB.

Veltz, P. (1993) 'De l'economie des coûts à l'economie de l'organisation', Paris: Ecole des Ponts Chaussées, LATTS, Working Paper.

Williamson, O. (1985) *The Economic Institutions of Capitalism*, New York: Basic Books.

Young, A. (1928) 'Increasing returns and economic progress', *The Economic Journal* 38: 527–42.

3 The co-operative advantage of regions

Philip Cooke

Introduction

If, as seems likely, *global monetarism* has temporarily triumphed over interventionary economic policies at the level of national economies worldwide, then the future for industrial policy looks bleak. The logic of this assertion is underpinned by an interesting analysis of the decline of Swedish social democracy offered recently by Hutton (1994).

> Why, then, did the [Swedish] system have to move right in the '80s and finally, in 1990, abandon the obligation placed upon the Central Bank of Sweden for full employment? The answer is international financial deregulation ... the new breed of Swedish finance house was getting off the ground and was borrowing from the Kronor Unit Market and lending aggressively to Swedish consumers; there was a mini Swedish credit boom going on. Once you had that cancer in the system it became unmanageable because demand began to grow at higher levels than the whole system could absorb. It was impractical and that led to inflation being higher than the system had required. That led to downward pressure on the Kronor and upward pressure on Swedish interest rates.
>
> (Hutton 1994: 6–7)

There in a nutshell is the dilemma posed for all would-be interventionary governments by the freeing up of financial controls on private investment.

This is now a frame condition for economic policy. More than that, it massively constrains the manoeuvrability of national economic policy instruments and severely weakens the capacity of the contemporary nation-state to behave as an economic policy actor. Rather, it increasingly reduces the state to a function as economic backstop, preventing the monetary objective from going out of bounds and leaving too much scope for accumulation to the players in the game. In a context where many of the largest national economies are members of Free Trade Areas such as the European Union, NAFTA or ASEAN this is merely one more factor helping to reduce the economic sovereignty of national parliaments. This, when into account are taken the contemporary limitations on national influence over trade, competition, industrial subsidization, monetary and even fiscal policies consequent upon membership of supra-national communities or agreements, strongly suggests the days of national economic sovereignty are numbered, even in terminal decline.

Some influential authors welcome this. A case in point is Kenichi Ohmae (1985, 1990, 1993). Following his work on 'triad power', where he was early in identifying the continental importance of North America, Europe and Asia as the key global economic entities of the future, and his subsequent identification of its corollary in a 'borderless world', Ohmae recently turned his attention to the sub-global level. In a widely cited article he argues that, at least in economic terms, *the nation-state has become dysfunctional*. This is because, he argues:

> It represents no genuine, shared community of economic interests; it defines no meaningful flows of economic activity. In fact, it overlooks the true linkages and synergies that exist among often disparate populations by combining important measures of human activity *at the wrong level of analysis*.
>
> (Ohmae 1993: 78; emphasis added)

He goes on to suggest that on the world economic map the frontiers that count are those identifying what Ohmae refers to as 'region-states'.

These region-states are the subject of this contribution, not because Ohmae has selected a terminology, but because there are good, logical reasons for believing, as, for example, Harvie (1994) does, that there is indeed a rise of the *regional* in lockstep with the rise of the *global*. Why should this be? What is that logic? As we have seen, at least in brief, there are compelling reasons for thinking that *economic* sovereignty has long gone from national parliaments. This is because of the demise of the Keynesian state and the rise of a privatistic ethic, most clearly associated with the New Right. Its predilections for a minimal state, deregulation, liberalization and wholesale privatization now occupy the middle ground in most major economies, certainly the G8, with Italy merely the latest – enforced – convert.

However, and this is especially clear in Europe, the forces of globalization can theoretically be met by the unified action of states such as Britain, France, Germany and Italy (more than half of G8) operating together in the European Union. That they have never yet been met in this way is a sign of the system's nation-state-led futility. In North America, where Federalism has a far longer pedigree, the notion that some things are best left to the largest economic entity is unquestioned. Equally so is the tradition that other things are best dealt with much closer to home at state or provincial level. In most European Union countries that idea has taken root, Britain, until New Labour were elected in 1997, being the exception. In real time, the European Union needs policy delivery systems which are reasonably proficient and legitimate to implement its grand strategies. It often cannot achieve this acting through national parliaments that have their own distributional and developmental agendas, not to say pork-barrels. So it looks beneath and finds a common interest with the *regions*, also looking to grow in influence and hamstrung often by the common enemy, the historic nation-state, in decline but still powerful.

A study by de Vet (1993) shows that such an economic logic is well under way. He examined seven OECD countries to see if the hypothesis that greater globalization was accompanied by greater regionalization of economic organization, identity and activity was sustainable. Remarkably, and with considerable consistency, he found the proposition to be true. He found that globalization, in terms of foreign trade and foreign direct investment, had grown significantly in these countries. In particular, he found that as regional economies received enhanced business support, especially technical, promotional and marketing, so the tendency to become more economically specialized and competitive grew. This, in turn, eventually led foreign direct investment in such specialized sectors to seek out the excellent economic regions as destinations for the export of capital. Thus *globalization* reinforces *regionalization*.

The apparent losers from such Ricardian comparative advantage policy outcomes are the less favoured regions of the world. In this chapter, an attempt will be made to show how some of these are seeking to forge new *network* relationships both internally and externally to the region and vertically as well as laterally with larger and smaller enterprises. To exemplify the argument, case examples from Germany and the UK as well as from southern Europe will be provided to show the difficulties as well as the accomplishments of efforts to build new, networked clusters of economic activity along the lines earlier investigated by Cooke and Morgan (1993).

The problem: how to achieve regional economic growth?

If Hutton, Ohmae and de Vet are broadly correct, and the rise of global monetarism has dealt a lethal blow to the capacity of nation-states to secure the diminution of major regional disparities, by pursuing Keynesian interventionary policies, as seen to be successful in the 1960s, what is left? Begg and Mayes (1993) in a wide-ranging study of European industrial policy in the 1980s and 1990s, confirmed the sense that nation-states have everywhere reduced responsibility for regional and industrial policy in favour of seeking balanced budgets and controlled monetary growth targets. They, too, look to the sub-central level of government as the most potentially interesting and perhaps appropriate one at which an industrial policy relevant to the next century may operate. That is, in an era when Fordist mass production is in retreat as an organizational paradigm for industry, to be replaced by lean production *à la* Toyota, with its predilection for outsourcing to families of sub-contractors, what, other than ensuring that regulations governing minimum wages remain relaxed, is left for the nation-state to do?

Increasingly, policies appropriate to this changed set of parameters for industrial organization have to be couched in terms of both regional–local and industrial specificities. No longer can a magisterial nation-state simply decree that regional problems can be dealt with by the designation of areas within which tax reliefs and capital grants are available to inward investors. That approach produced branch-plant economies. And even branch-plants are now demanding more authority to embed themselves in their regional host economies (Glasmeier 1988; Cooke *et al.* 1994; Cooke and Morgan 1998). Industrial support policies have now to be more sophisticated, involving fine-tuning of financial, skills and technical requirements. Often these adjustments have implications for local networks of small-firm supply companies, creating problems insoluble at nation-state level but tractable sub-centrally.

During the recession years of the early 1990s, even some of the most successful instances of regional economic growth have been plunged into difficulty, occasioned by globalization and the pervasive erosion of competitive advantage that it often entails. In the following sub-sections of this paper, after a discussion and elaboration of theoretical points concerning the requirements of *clustering*, as presented by Porter (1990) and exemplified by Boekholt (1994), information will be presented on the difficulties assailing two of Europe's stronger growth regions of the 1980s, Baden-Württemberg and Emilia-Romagna, to show both the scope and the limitations of judicious sub-central government intervention. This will act as a prelude to presentations of three examples of less favoured regions each pursuing a different route towards revitalization under the umbrella of European Commission programme support and specific regional interpretation of the opportunities and threats posed by heightened global competition.

The cluster in theory and practice

Porter's (1990) notion of the cluster has its intellectual origin in the Marshallian concept of the *industrial district* (Marshall 1919). By way of reprise, Marshall's empirically derived concept has the following key elements:

- specialization by many firms in different aspects of the production of a single product range, firms engaging in complementary business activities, forming clusters of sub-contractors in a localized area in the same industry;
- communication, both formal and, importantly, informal, being especially rapid and efficient because of the localized, common basis of understanding and knowledge between firms, employees and the community;
- skilled labour, in those days apprenticeship-trained, readily available in the district because of the dominant industrial specialization.

But Marshall noted something extra about these industrial districts, shared by the South Wales tinplate industry, Manchester for cotton goods and Sheffield for cutlery. The feature he referred to was 'industrial atmosphere', and it is for this as much as for anything else he identified that his work is remembered today.

The work of neo-Marshallians such as Becattini (1990) and Brusco (1992) contributed to a modernization and clarification of the vague Marshallian notion of 'atmosphere'. The more recent work of Dei Ottati (1994) shows how the Prato atmosphere is made up of a further, even more complex layer, of what has been referred to previously as 'soft infrastructure'. This is composed of inter-personal relationships of:

1 co-operation through reciprocal agreements;
2 co-operation based on custom;
3 co-operation sustained by reputation;
4 co-operation provoked by competition;
5 co-operation integrated by trust.

These are kinds of economic co-ordination parallel to, and sometimes intertwined with, the alternatives of *market* co-ordination and co-ordination through the *hierarchy* of the firm.

Now, the fundamental criticism of the work of Porter (1990), in the light of the argument to be developed in this paper, is that his model of the cluster has been somewhat distorted to underplay these co-operative aspects of economic co-ordination in favour of those which stress, as revealed in the title of the book of the same name (Porter 1985), the sources of *competitive advantage*. Hence, this paper is a tentative effort to correct the imbalance created by Porter's version of the cluster concept with an analysis that highlights the co-operative dimension without ignoring the obviously important competitive dimension too.

Before developing this, I want to briefly highlight five equivalent features of competitive economic co-ordination implicit also in Dei Ottati's (1994) study. Constructing an argument based upon neo-institutionalism, Dei Ottati suggests that, even in contemporary industrial districts such as Prato, there must be, to varying degrees, both competition and co-operation for economic co-ordination to be efficient. A version of this approach is that of Langlois (1993) who developed the idea of *economics as a process*, key elements of co-ordination through competition being as follows:

1 competition through rational comparison of costs and benefits;
2 competition through substitution of production factors;
3 non-price competition, e.g. quality or innovation increments;
4 competition enhanced by collaboration;
5 competition extended by customer involvement (after-sales etc.).

Now, if we focus on the Porterian 'diamond' of factors of advantage (Porter 1990: 72) it is clear that, although reference is made to 'links', 'clusters' and 'co-operation', more is made of 'rivalry', 'demanding buyers', 'markets' and 'leadership', and the whole tenor of the approach is, as we would expect, competition-enhancing. What is interesting in Porter's approach is that competitiveness rests on as many co-operative ingredients as it does. This, at least, saves Porter from one dimension of the critique that his work is a mere apology for neo-classical economics. Moreover, it could be argued that, far from being an equilibrium theorization, it is a profoundly disequilibriating conception of economic practice. Once a firm or region has achieved competitive advantage of the kind described, it presumably has a major destabilizing effect on other firms or regions in the market. It is this, and the fact that the diamond describes successful settings where the 'act' has been 'got together', that is of concern, and this is, of course, a product of the reverence for competition explicit in the approach.

That the diamond describes leading-edge economic entities is borne out by reference to the interesting application carried out by Boekholt (1994) for the Dutch flower industry. This is widely accepted as the global leader by a long distance. Located in a cluster of glasshouses around Schiphol airport, Amsterdam, and horticulturally and logistically sophisticated enough to be capable of delivering fresh gardenias for Californian hotel breakfast tables every day of the year, it is a living embodiment of the Porterian cluster. However, two questions are begged: first, can it conceivably be emulated?; and, second, if it were emulated, could it survive?

This is the ultimate weakness of Porter's analysis, for it is a zero-sum prospectus. This is why it fails, in the end, to relate to reality in other than a few, leading-edge instances. The Dutch cut-flower industry has competitive advantage because, in what it does, it is unique in the world. It is a 'global player' because it has a virtual monopoly in terms of quality, deliverability innovativeness, supply-chain linkages, fierce rivalry, elements of co-operation, price and non-price competitive advantage. In this industry, every other cluster of firms or region which specializes in global cut-flower distribution is less favoured, some greatly so.

Having made some critical points about these effects of Porterian thinking, derived as they are from an undue emphasis upon *competitive* behaviour, I do not want to lurch too far in the other policy direction. By this I mean it is equally possible to put the argument in reverse and say, as, for example, Amin and Tomaney (1994) do, that:

> ... strategies of tight monetary control, fiscal stringency, the removal of controls on corporate behaviour (for instance liberal competition laws) and reduced subsidies to industry will remove many of the policy instruments that have provided a 'protective' framework for less competitive firms in the LFRs to develop and grow. Such policies expose the LFRs to market forces working in favour of the most powerful or

> most competitive firms in the national and international economy and are to the detriment of weaker forms of entrepreneurship ...
>
> (Amin and Tomaney 1994: 5)

They thereby draw the conclusion that less favoured regions (LFRs) can only be helped by their nation-state, preferably *collaborating* with other – in this case European Union – member-states but with nation-states leading the Union. While such a situation might, as noted earlier, be welcome, it conveniently overlooks the fact that all LFRs became so under the aegis of the nation-state system. Moreover, it forgets that *global monetarism* within the EU is a product of concerted nation-state pressure through the Council of Ministers. In addition, it assumes that protection and subsidy of firms and regions by nation-states is always going to be possible in the way it once was, given the tenor of the times which, after GATT, are distinctly free trade and liberal. More realistic is the direction advocated by Fritz Scharpf (1991), namely one which he calls a *social democratic supply side* approach. This captures, equally, elements of both the competitive and co-operative dimensions of the process of economic co-ordination discussed earlier.

Co-operative advantage in growth regions

Emilia-Romagna

This is one of Italy's richest regions in terms of gross domestic product per capita (1986–8 GDP per capita 127, cf. EU mean of 100; CEC 1991). It is well known among regional scientists as the home of many industrial districts producing clothing, ceramics, food, process machinery, furniture, shoes and automotives. The network nature of the sub-contracting relationships between firms in the districts has been anatomized by Brusco (1982, 1992) and he, more than any, has shown how the vapid notion of 'atmosphere' takes on a more concrete, institutional meaning, in part through the 'real services' that the public sector provides in collaboration with private firms, in support of businesses in the districts. Indeed, the academic re-discovery of the importance of co-operative modes of economic co-ordination owes more than a little to the findings of Brusco and others concerning the contemporary industrial districts of this region.

However, many writers, and indeed the regional government itself, perceive the Emilian districts to be in crisis. For sure, Italy has, only in 1994, emerged from the lengthy economic recession induced by membership of a European exchange rate mechanism which, driven by the Deutschmark and an over-valued exchange rate, consequent upon high German interest rates, created economic havoc until Italy, like Spain and the UK, departed from it, belatedly, in 1993. Added to this, Italy has experienced political turmoil which, in any other country, would have been described as a revolution, and a not particularly velvet one at that. Although the Emilia-Romagna regional government survived relatively unscathed by the accusations of and indictments for massive fraudulence and corruption that hastened the demise of all the country's post-war governing parties, this former stronghold of the Italian Communist Party (PCI, now PDS) has had to come to terms with new political realities.

Foremost among these was the new right-wing and neo-fascist coalition government of Berlusconi quickly succeeded by the centre-left coalition headed by Romano Prodi. Italy thus experienced a bout of privatizations and neo-liberal economic policies sceptical of notions like 'real services', seen as distortions to the market. As a consequence, the PDS, back in control of the region after an interlude of coalition government, spent a good four years re-thinking the system of public–private business support to small and medium enterprises (SMEs)that they pioneered. The regional development agency, ERVET, author of policy innovations such as CITER, which allowed artisans to acquire access to sophisticated CAD-CAM for clothing design, for example, was at one stage in danger of being closed, but has survived. The price has been a re-alignment of the mode of financial support to business by the public sector.

Whereas during the 1980s support took the form of business innovation centres in the districts, able to provide specialist training or technology transfer support, help mobilize finance and supply business information to a homogeneous, geographically localized industry sector, in the 1990s funding has had to be placed on a *project*-based footing. Private consultancy firms, noticeable by their absence in the 1980s, have pressured the Right to do away with these public subventions. This is not least because they saw them, correctly, as also political subventions, aimed at continuing a political project of collective enterprise and decentralist socialism simultaneously. Now, less than effective real service centres will be closed, whether those in the districts, as many are, or those with a lateral, cross-industry remit, and the private sector may have the opportunity, if it deems the risk worthwhile, of entering markets created by public initiative.

Despite the gloom, however, research commissioned by the region (Franchi 1994) gave cause for hope for the districts, even in the face of authoritative prognostications of decline by experts such as Harrison (1994). Franchi showed that firms in districts outperformed their sector during the recession of 1994. They lost fewer employees and managed to pay better wages than the sectoral norm. Vertical integration, seen as terminal by Harrison (1994), was seen to have taken place, but not to a significant extent and without serious impact upon intra-district interaction where it had. Small firms had been bonding together in groups much more during the recession than before. Although it was perceived to be a useful survival strategy and more attractive, as well as pronounced, than acquisition by outsiders, it had enabled firms to re-organize co-operatively, the better to re-position themselves to compete in the market.

Baden-Württemberg

This traditionally Christian Democrat region of south-west Germany only in late 1994 began to show signs of emerging from its greatest post-war economic crisis. The home of Mercedes-Benz, Porsche, Robert Bosch and a host of world-leader machine-building and machine-tool firms still has an unheard-of 10% unemployment rate, to dent its image as one of Germany's most prosperous and high GDP-earning economies (1986–8 per capita 120, cf. EU mean of 100; CEC 1991). Some 300,000 jobs were lost in engineering, although 100,000 new jobs were found between 1991 and 1993 by those made redundant, a sign that even in recession there is dynamism in an economy whose crisis was very unevenly spread sectorally.

Nevertheless, the Land government of the outgoing CDU party set up a Future Commission to report on the region's prospects for *Economy 2000*. The results made sombre reading. The regional cluster of automotive, machinery and electronics firms face heightened competition from Japan and other East Asian economies. For lower-end market products, Central European countries such as the Czech and Slovak republics are being widely sourced for components supply and targeted for foreign investment by Baden-Württemberg firms. The Land's firms suffer innovation deficits, especially in IT, and an overemphasis on excellence in medium-tech products which are being replaced by IT and electronics (e.g. machine control systems, sensors, lasers, etc.). Finally, production costs became astronomic because of the high value of the Deutschmark, high land and labour costs and production inefficiencies (outdated inventory systems, for example) (Braczyk *et al.* 1998).

The Future Commission recommended that measures should be taken to improve *competitiveness* (this in a regional economy which is the epitome if not a model for Porter's diamond of competitive advantage!). Innovation measures included establishing a Technology Foresight Board (now established with 45 members, yet described by one member as a 'talking shop'). Furthermore, production costs needed to be reduced by stimulating productivity gains amongst firms, encouraging the introduction of new technologies, even new industries, such as biotechnology, engaging in more globalized economic activity (Mercedes-Benz opened a new plant at Tuscaloosa, Alabama, following BMW at Spartanburg, South Carolina, and in 1998 Daimler-Benz merged with Chrysler Corporation of the USA), and getting real wage costs down (Cooke and Morgan 1998).

The Baden-Württemberg Ministry of Economics has a good reputation for the kind of judicious steering of regional industrial policy described earlier. However, one of its initiatives, introduced carefully, at the behest of industry, seems to be less effective than first thought. To help SMEs deal with their innovation deficits in the face of out-sourcing squeezes by the likes of Mercedes, the Ministry set up 'model projects' for collaborative innovation with an incentive scheme and support from the prestigious contract research organization, the Fraunhofer Institute. Anecdotally, however, it seems that these projects have been slow to get off the ground and relatively few firms have been induced to join in, suggesting that, in what some perceive as the home of collaborative competition, wariness about losing know-how is a serious barrier to co-operating where it hurts (Braczyk *et al.* 1993).

Despite this, an interesting sidelight is thrown on the economic development process by local examples of small-firm restructuring, some of which is quasi-public and collaborative, some of which is private but with co-operative implications.

1 In Gosheim, a rural enclave of the Black Forest, a group of twelve or so lathe manufacturers pressed for the establishment of a collective technology transfer centre in state-of-the-art lathe-making. The Steinbeis Foundation (technology transfer) was persuaded to help establish it and the area is now one of Germany's leading turning machine-tool districts. Subsequently a new quality centre has been added (Pyke 1994).
2 In Albstadt, even deeper in Schwarzwald, a small company called Mettler-Toledo, manufacturer of weighing machines, owned by Ciba-Geigy, has caused ripples by dramatic restructuring based on co-operative principles. The inventory system was revolutionized, Taylorism outlawed, and modern marketing introduced, all at the behest of the new twelve-person management team which replaced a five-layer hierarchy (in a 200-employee firm). In five years, turnover trebled, stocks declined by a tenth and outsourcing increased dramatically. The firm is out of debt and profitable (Cooke 1994).
3 In Rosenberg, the firm of Getrag tells a similar story. A key supplier to BMW, it introduced product optimization, teamwork, retraining and self-management principles under the tutelage of its main customer. Employment has increased and turnover has been restored following a 30% reduction in 1991–3. Closer networking with customers and suppliers has been a key element in the transformation (Cooke 1994).

These experiences suggest that the function of regional industrial policy is constrained to fitting in sensibly with what firms say they need when they do in fact have stated needs. It does not mean government trying to lead in identifying solutions to business problems in periods of crisis. Firms are not necessarily very good at crisis management, but they have a direct incentive to survive whereas governments have only an indirect interest in their survival. In more stable periods firms' requirements and the public or quasi-public infrastructure of business support come into reasonable synchronization, but this is only a temporary condition. If firms find solutions, governments and others may have a useful role in disseminating best practice and even giving incentives to others to engage in it.

Clustering in less favoured regions

Against those who prophesy the immutability of underdevelopment in less favoured regions, this last main section will show that in such settings, in the European Union context, new clustering activities and policies are not only possible but can demonstrably bear fruit. In each case, the emergence of a co-operative ethic, or re-discovery of one where it was lost, is part of the network-based development of competitive robustness. The examples can be taken as emblematic of three kinds of regional restructuring strategy, none of which is contextuated only by regional factors, each of which is conditioned by national, supra-national and global factors at least as much.

The three strategies are summarized below:

1 *internal diversification* – this is where firms in a regional economy clearly identified with a specific, perhaps narrow, industrial base (e.g. shipbuilding) diversify out of traditional into new sectors;
2 *external diversification* – where the firms associated with a particular regional industrial specialization (e.g. coal or steel) either disappear completely or shrink and new industries and firms come to dominate;
3 *upgrading specialization* – where firms in specific industrial sectors exist but are backward despite sectoral market potential (e.g. clothing). New firms and/or upgraded existing firms give competitive edge to the economy.

Each category will be exemplified by a specific, recent, European regional experience, respectively: North Rhine Westphalia (particularly the Ruhr); Wales; and the Valencia region in Spain.

Internal diversification – North Rhine Westphalia

The Ruhr district is the traditional industrial heart of North Rhine Westphalia (NRW) and Germany. However, something of a crossroads has been reached in the 1990s. The long-established coal and steel industries on which that economic strength was built may finally have entered terminal decline. If so, this is only an inevitable result of a long-delayed process of industrial restructuring and rationalization that has affected all older industrial economies based on these industries. But for special reasons the Ruhrgebiet has, until now, been able to withstand these pressures better than most of Germany's maturer competitor countries. Special factors having to do with politics, reconstruction in the post-war years, and government intervention and subsidies explain this.

The key to understanding the development of the NRW economy – in which that of the Ruhrgebiet is central – is to think in terms of *production clusters*.

Phase 1, 1830–1950: the Ruhrgebiet's large coal deposits suited the technological revolution of the early nineteenth century. This, combined with its proximity to the Rhine and related waterways, acted as the key location factor for the iron and steel industry. Westphalia was a Prussian province and state commissions created the necessary demands for armaments, railway, shipbuilding and bridge construction. Investors moved into the Ruhr from many parts of Europe, as did the workforce. Interlocking ownership of coal and steel companies developed. By 1902 power generation had been integrated, with steelmakers Stinnes and Thyssen taking 86% of the shares of RWE, the regional power generation and distribution company. By-products of the coal and steel industries such as sulphur then became feedstocks for the chemical industry. Hence, the early expansion of Ruhr industry was based on groups of firms and consortia as business developers. Services such as banking and technical consultancy grew in Düsseldorf on the Rhine, and metal processing expanded in the outlier, handwork areas such as the Siegerland and Bergischland. Between 1850 and 1914, coal-mining employment grew from 12,000 to 400,000, then productivity increases saw coal employment decline to 200,000 by 1929. The Nazi period of autarky in coal and steel boosted these industries in the 1930s and, after the Second World War, reconstruction led to renewed expansion, thus delaying the processes of rationalization experienced elsewhere in heavy industry.

Phase 2, 1950–84: from the mid-1950s onwards, the heavy industrial production cluster centred upon firms such as coal company Ruhrkohle AG (established in the 1960s) and Krupp, Thyssen, Klöckner, Hoesch and Mannesmann in steel began to disintegrate as its economic weight declined. The chemical, plastics and machine-tools industries became more important and were joined by automotive assembly (Ford at Cologne; Opel at Bochum), which in turn gave stimulus to mechanical engineering, microelectronics and new materials industries. However, these industries were most commonly found growing fastest in southern Germany (Baden-Württemberg, Bavaria). New energy sources such as oil, gas and nuclear destroyed the Ruhrgebiet's locational advantage in energy. The response of Ruhr industry was threefold:

1 *globalization* – investment in and plant design for less developed countries;
2 *diversification* – steel firms bought mechanical engineering, plant construction, automotive supply and shipbuilding firms. Also some coal and chemical firms developed into new sectors, such as biotechnology, but located these outside NRW;
3 *sectoral exit* – steel firms, e.g. Mannesmann and Gutehoffnungshütte, ceased production and moved into further processing or electromechanical engineering. Gutehoffnungshütte, for example, merged with the Munich-based MAN automotive group. Also, with the establishment of Ruhrkohle AG, integrated coal and steel firms de-merged.

Thus, by the mid-1980s, the Ruhr-based industrial cluster, though still present, was weaker than hitherto and had been joined by other, new industries. From 1970 to 1987 the share of coal, steel and iron in the Ruhrgebiet's overall employment decreased from 20.3% to 12.6%.

Employment growth in the Ruhr occurred only in agriculture, communications, financial and most other services.

Phase 3, 1984–: this post-war era of restructuring cost the Ruhrgebiet 500,000 industrial jobs (300,000 in mining). These losses were spread among eight of the thirteen administrative areas of the Ruhrgebiet. By 1987 overall employment decreased 3.7% compared with a 4.8% rise in NRW employment and a 10.5% increase in the Federal Republic of Germany.

The growing industries of the 1980s included mechanical and electrical engineering, motor, plastics and secondary chemicals production. Faster-growing sectors included consumer-related industries such as wood, paper, printing, food and, especially, textiles, which doubled its employment between 1984 and 1990. These industries also grew in NRW generally, though at a slower rate. Textile growth includes large expansion of single enterprises such as Steilmann-Gruppe as well as growth in textile handling and finishing at the huge inland port (Germany's fifth largest) at Duisburg.

One of the most significant growth areas has been linked to the desire of the Ruhrgebiet authorities to escape the industrial dereliction of the past, and the rising tide of demands for environmentally sensitive economic development. An example of this has been the commitment to integrating economic, social, political and ecological objectives in the Emscher Park International Building Exhibition (IBA), a 50-kilometre land reclamation and development project at the heart of the Ruhrgebiet. As important has been the development of new markets for environmental technologies. Approximately 1,000 firms employing 100,000 people have developed specialization in various aspects of environmental technology during the 1980s and a new production cluster in this field has emerged. Of great significance is the industry's relative immunity from business cycles, its high R&D intensity, considerable inter-firm co-operation and the dominance of SME growth in the industry. Major centres with this specialization are Münster (52 firms), Essen (97 firms), Düsseldorf (120 firms) and Cologne (82 firms). Dortmund, Duisburg, Bielefeld, Aachen and Wuppertal have 30–40 firms each. NRW has 47% of Germany's investment in the industry. Key activities are: waste and waste water management, air purification, noise abatement, energy and environmental improvement, control and measurement, and environmental services.

Finally, the possibility of the development of a production cluster in automotive components and microelectronics in NRW is seen as credible. There are two opposite trends. First, existing suppliers to the automotive industry have been squeezed by cost-conscious customers (e.g. Opel under Lopez Arriortua – later appointed European purchasing manager of VW). Yet steel companies have made downstream acquisitions into automotive components supply (e.g. Hoesch bought RAFI (auto-electronics) and Camford Pressings and already owned Drauz, an automotive machine-tools firm; now Krupp have acquired Hoesch). At present, the automotive suppliers tend to be concentrated in the Bergischland, to the south of the Ruhr, between NRW's two main automotive assembly firms, Ford of Cologne and Opel at Bochum.

By the 1990s NRW had 49 higher education establishments (with 480,000 students), three major research centres, 11 Max-Planck Institutes, six Fraunhofer Institutes, and 33 technology centres and parks. In 1991 they had a budget of 7 billion DM (an increase of 8.75% on 1990). The three major research institutes are the Forschungszentrum Juelich (KFA), the Gesellschaft für Mathematik und Datenverarbeitung (GMD) in St Augustin, and the Deutsche Forschungsanstalt für Luftund Raumfahr (DLR). The Fraunhofer Institutes are: environmental chemicals and ecological toxicology in Schmallenberg-Graftschaft; trend analyses in the natural sciences in Euskirchen; production technology in Aachen; transport technology and distribution in Dortmund; microelectronic switches and systems in Duisburg; laser technology in Aachen. The Max-Planck Institutes include coal research in Mülheim-an-der-Ruhr, breeding research in Cologne-Vogelsang; and iron research in Düsseldorf. Other research institutes include the Institute for Spectrochemicals and Applied Spectrometry in Dortmund; the Institute for Labour Physiology and Safety in Dortmund; the Helmholz Institute for Biomedical Technology in Aachen; the German Wool Research Institute in Aachen; the Institute for Inland Ship-Building in Duisburg; Coal-Mining Research in Essen; German Textile Research Centre for the North West in Krefeld; and the Research Institute for Rationalisation in Aachen. Much of this investment began only in the 1980s in support of the emergent, diversifying clusters.

External diversification – Wales

Wales has experienced significant economic restructuring since 1980. The two main traditional industries of coal and steel have reduced manpower by some 60,000 and while the steel industry is now competitive, the coal industry has virtually disappeared. Wales is fortunate, in the UK context, in having both a regional department of government, the Welsh Office, and an economic promotion body, the Welsh Development Agency (WDA), the main tasks of which have been to modernize the Welsh economy. While there remain pockets of severe unemployment in the former coalfield areas, these organizations have been remarkably successful in helping to introduce new businesses, many from overseas, and to develop innovative business practices amongst indigenous firms. A recent policy development has been to stimulate partnership between regional and local governments, and networking between firms, supported by innovation policies and functions from government bodies.

Building on traditional regional development institutions and programmes such as selective regional grants and tax reliefs, with an aggressive programme from the WDA to attract innovative foreign direct investment, Wales has now built a new industrial platform. For example, some 30,000 workers are now employed in over 100 automotive firms such as Toyota, Ford, Bosch, Valeo and Lucas. Over 40 Japanese electronics and related businesses employ a further 20,000. Now these firms are looking for suppliers and finding them, especially among the 20 or so new supplier 'clubs' or networks now in existence. On this platform are being constructed several innovative regional technological programmes. Amongst the most important of these are:

- RTP – the Regional Technology Plan; a technology strategy for Wales;
- the South Wales Regional Technopole; an innovation network;
- attraction of the UK National Patent Office, established in 1991;
- establishment of EU Relay Centre; technology exploitation network;
- opening of Engineering Centre; promotion of advanced engineering;
- opening of two mechatronics centres;
- establishment of Imperial College Science Park at Cardiff;
- consolidation of six sub-regional technology and innovation centres.

In numerous ways these initiatives interact with and build upon or replace existing programmes, many of which are aimed at supporting SME development.

One indicator of the relative success of creating an innovative milieu consisting of

1 *innovative foreign firms*, especially Japanese and German, and
2 an *innovation architecture* of business support

is that the success of Welsh SME performance in winning both UK government and EU innovation grants is higher than its GDP, population or manufacturing share of the UK total. The latter are all approximately 5% whereas the Welsh shares of UK SMART (SME Merit Awards in Research & Technology) awards ranged between 9% and 14% from 1989 to 1993, while Welsh SMEs secured 7% of the UK shares of EU Third Framework (Science & Technology) funding between 1987 and 1991. Since 1990 Wales has been a partner of Baden-Württemberg, Lombardy, Rhône-Alpes, Catalonia (and now Ontario) in what was the Four Motors of Europe partnership, but has now grown to 'Six Motors of the Transatlantic'.

In response to this situation further initiatives have been taken by the WDA in partnership with firms and institutions to assist innovation:

- A redoubling of the WDA and Welsh Office foreign direct investment programme which has attracted up to 15% of UK inward investment since 1980. The total amount of inward investment and reinvestment in 1992 was over £1 billion. Many of these firms are themselves innovative.
- Now, in order to balance this success, a Supplier Development Programme, which links 'clubs' of medium-sized firms vertically to large firms in a supply chain, has been established . Twenty supplier clubs now exist in Wales.
- To help to improve the skills of workers and management in supplier firms, Innovative Training initiatives, aimed at improving the *quality* of products and processes, are in place. These are managed in partnership

between the WDA, training and enterprise councils, enterprise agencies and higher education institutes.

- Technology and innovation centres, where new start-up firms are housed or applied technology services are supplied to firms, have been set up in six locations. The Relay Centre, enabling firms to exploit EU science and technology programme results, links to these centres.
- The WDA manages *Eurolink*, a programme linking innovative small firms in Wales to firms in partner regions such as Baden-Württemberg, Lombardy, Catalonia and Rhône-Alpes. These firms exchange technologies and marketing networks.
- A Danish Network scheme (also deployed in Valencia; see below) has been adopted for SME networking at training and enterprise council and enterprise agency level in south, north and west Wales.

The next step, soon to be taken, is to develop the Regional Technology Plan as a series of projects to improve business access to services in demand by encouraging firms to work in networks. One such arrangement has been pioneered as the Cardiff University Innovation Networking scheme involving a large number of South Wales SMEs.

Upgrading specialization – Valencia

The Valencia region is widely perceived within Spain as being the most successful in terms of pursuing a strategic developmental programme in support of its indigenous SMEs. As an Objective 1 region it is very close to the definitional limit of that category with a GDP per head of 75.3 (European Community mean 100) 1986–8, placing the region 37th lowest, between Corsica and Sardinia. On unemployment, Valencia was placed eighteenth poorest with an index number of 174.3 compared with the EU average of 100. This was marginally higher than Catalonia but lower than Northern Ireland during the period 1988–90. Valencia has a rather above-average (for Spain and EU) industrial employment share at 36.3%, and a correspondingly lower (marginally so for Spain) share (52.5%) of services employment.

The higher-than-average industrial labour force may echo a point made in Benton's (1992) study of the region: industrial growth in this region has consistently outpaced development in the rest of Spain since the 1960s. In many respects this Spanish region has the most in common with the manufacturing region of central Italy: a strong export orientation; an emphasis on light consumer manufactures; a symbiotic relationship to agriculture in the early stages of industrial growth; a spatial pattern of specialized industry concentrated in particular towns or clusters of towns; and the dominance of small and medium-sized firms, many of them family businesses (Benton 1992: 69).

Benton's analysis of the reasons for success (e.g. in the Castellon ceramics industry) and relative failure (Alicante shoe industry) of specific industrial districts is interesting for the exclusive emphasis she places on voluntaristic, albeit co-operative or collectively oriented, entrepreneurial activity. Firms have a familial origin, managers have little training, they prefer to invest in real estate rather than R&D and there is a great deal of informalization of economic relations. What appears to differentiate ceramics from footwear is that in the former industry the sector trade association acted institutionally to stimulate diversification and technological upgrading. This did not happen in the Alicante shoe industry which failed to move up-market, and remains cheap and informalized.

A different and much more thorough picture is provided by Pyke (1994). He stresses the crucial role played by the regional government and its regional development agency IMPIVA, in first, networking Valencia with best practice regions such as Baden-Württemberg and Emilia-Romagna and countries such as Denmark, to learn the conditions for successful SME networking and innovation. Pyke then goes on to identify the key role played by technological institutes providing 'real services' such as technological advice, marketing services, and so on, as well as leadership and co-ordination in upgrading and stimulating innovation on a sectoral basis.

Networks operate in spheres such as distribution, sales and promotion, exports, joint purchasing, new products and services, and advanced technology. Most are in the more standard business services, few are in the technology field. In their own terms the technological institutes, business information centres and IMPIVA activities are successful if judged in terms of growth of client base. The centres have often doubled their staff in two years and more than doubled their business in the same period. Clearly, the services being provided are in growing demand. Yet firms face real difficulties in keeping up with technological change while few of the interactions between firms are of a technological nature. This suggests they are inordinately (and unhealthily?) dependent upon the technological institutes as conduits of innovation. It is, of course, much easier to collaborate on such activities as sales and purchasing and it is notable that in the most advanced of the indigenous industries – ceramics – attempts at collaboration to develop production machinery as a substitute for Italian imports from Sassuolo have failed (Benton 1992).

All in all, and given the relatively modest beginnings of the industrial districts of Valencia, it can be concluded that a northern/central EU regional networking model has been implanted and taken up with gusto. Valencia is seen by other Spanish regions (and, in ceramics, even the Emilians) as a success story but the shoe and furniture industries are still in deep crisis, and it is evident that the level of expertise between the technological institutes is highly variable.

Conclusion: How to achieve regional economic growth

The subtitle of these concluding remarks is a paraphrase of a very recent innovation initiative introduced in North Rhine Westphalia, called PlaNet Ruhr, as described by Körfer and Latniak (1994). PlaNet Ruhr is a Land-funded, planned network of science and research organizations, consultants, chambers of industry and commerce and consulting bureaus of the trade unions, operating in the Ruhr area. It is tasked with, first, disseminating restructuring process know-how, and second, funding 10 projects in firms by re-engineering teams from the VDI (Association of German Engineers) and IDW (Research Centre of the German Employers Association). PlaNet Ruhr had a difficult start because of time constraints on members, lack of familiarity with co-operative working, high turnover of network members, lack of commitment, lack of fit between network skills and the needs of firms for vocational training. Why these problems? First, training centres were ill-attuned to the time constraints on SMEs; most courses are designed for large firms. Second, integrated social and technical retraining did not exist, each being split into specialist training centre curricula. Third, firms feared losing know-how by talking to their network partners.

How are the problems solved? By dialogue, problem identification and action. The consultants focused on the integration problem and firms' needs. The network management was taken over by a professional training centre to maintain continuity. It has survived because, as the authors put it: 'a regional co-operation strategy is only interesting for firms if the other alternatives are not' (Körfer and Latniak 1994: 319).

This is the key conclusion of this paper too. Co-operative solutions to problems of industrial organization and economic co-ordination are not necessarily or always superior to competitive ones. But the co-operative approach is not infrequently the only solution to intractable problems posed by globalization, lean production or flexibilization. Such can be the strangeness of co-operative approaches that firms, especially, can find it an unhinging experience. Their response is often a tortoise-like retreat into their shells. This can be terminal for networks, but it need not be, as the PlaNet Ruhr example showed. This is particularly true where competition can be seen to be likely to lead to a 'tragedy of the commons' type of outcome, leaving foreign competitors to take over the market. The *region* is a most appropriate economic and administrative entity around which to plan networking approaches (on this, see also Wolfe 1993). Europe in the 1990s is buying into the approach in big and interesting ways. In the process Europeans are learning the lessons of co-operative advantage.

Bibliography

Amin, A. and Tomaney, J. (1994) 'The regional dilemma in a neo-liberal Europe', paper to conference on 'The Evolution of Rules for a Single European Market', Exeter, September.

Becattini, G. (1990) 'The Marshallian industrial district as a socio-economic notion', in F. Pyke, G. Becattini and W. Sengenberger (eds) *Industrial Districts and Inter-firm Co-operation in Italy*, Geneva: International Institute for Labour Studies.

Begg, I. and Mayes, D. (1993) 'Regional restructuring: the case of decentralised industrial policy', paper to Regional Science Association Annual Conference, Nottingham.

Benton, L. (1992) 'The emergence of industrial districts in Spain: industrial restructuring and diverging regional responses', in F. Pyke and W. Sengenberger (eds) *Industrial Districts and Local Economic Regeneration*, Geneva: International Institute for Labour Studies.

Boekholt, P. (1994) 'Methodology to identify regional clusters of firms and their needs', paper to SPRINT-RITTS Workshop, Luxembourg.

Braczyk, H., Cooke, P. and Heidenreich, M. (1998) *Regional Innovation Systems: The Role of Governances in a Globalized World*, London: UCL Press.

Braczyk, H-J., Schienstock, G. and Steffensen, B. (1993) Baden-Württemberg: still a story of success?, mimeo, Stuttgart: Akademie für Technikfolgenab-schätzung in Baden-Württemberg.

Brusco, S. (1982) 'The Emilian model: productive decentralisation and social integration', *Cambridge Journal of Economics* 5: 167–84.

—— (1992) 'Small firms and the provision of real services', in F. Pyke and W. Sengenberger (eds) *Industrial Districts and Local Economic Development*, Geneva: International Institute for Labour Studies.

Cooke, P. (1994) 'The Baden-Württemberg machine tool industry: regional responses to global threats', paper to workshop on 'Explaining Regional Competitiveness and the Capability to Innovate: The case of Baden-Württemberg', Center for Technology Assessment, Stuttgart.

Cooke, P. and Morgan, K. (1993) 'The network paradigm: new departures in corporate and regional development', *Society & Space* 7: 543–64.

Cooke, P. and Morgan, K. (1998) *The Associational Economy, Firms, Regions and Innovation*, Oxford: Oxford University Press.

Cooke, P., Price, A. and Morgan, K. (1994) *The Welsh Renaissance: Inward Investment and Industrial Innovation*, Cardiff : CASS-UWCC.

Dei Ottati, G. (1994) 'Co-operation and competition in the industrial district as an organisation model', *European Planning Studies* 2: 463–84.

Franchi, M. (1994) 'Developments in the districts of Emilia-Romagna', paper to conference on 'Industrial Districts and Local Economic Development in Italy: Challenges and Policy Perspective', Bologna.

Glasmeier, A. (1988) 'Factors governing the development of high tech industry agglomerations: a tale of three cities', *Regional Studies* 22: 287–301.

Harrison, B. (1994) 'The Italian industrial districts and the crisis of the cooperative form: Part I', *European Planning Studies* 2: 3–22.

Harvie, C. (1994) *The Rise of Regional Europe*, London: Routledge.

Hutton, W. (1994) *Global Markets, Regional Clusters and Liberal Democracy*, Centre for Advanced Studies Occasional Paper No. 2, Cardiff: CASS.

Körfer, H. and Latniak, E. (1994) 'Approaches to technology policy and regional milieux – experiences of programmes and projects in North Rhine-Westphalia', *European Planning Studies* 2: 303–20.

Langlois, R. (ed.) (1993) *Economics as a Process*, Cambridge: Cambridge University Press.

Marshall, A. (1919) *Industry and Trade*, London: Macmillan.

Ohmae, K. (1985) *Triad Power: The Coming Shape of Global Competition*, New York: Harper.

—— (1990) *The Borderless World*, New York: Harper.

—— (1993) 'The rise of the region state', *Foreign Affairs* 72: 78–81.

Porter, M. (1985) *Competitive Advantage*, New York: The Free Press.

—— (1990) *The Competitive Advantage of Nations*, New York: The Free Press.

Pyke, F. (1994) *Small Firms, Technical Services and Inter-firm Co-operation*, Geneva: International Institute for Labour Studies.

Scharpf, F. (1991) *Crisis and Choice in European Social Democracy*, Ithaca: Cornell University Press.

de Vet, J. (1993) 'Globalisation and local and regional competitiveness', *STI Review*.

Wolfe, D. (1993) 'The wealth of regions: rethinking industrial policy', paper presented to the Annual Meeting of the Canadian Political Science Association, Carleton University, Ottawa.

4 Reversing attrition?

The auto cluster in Baden-Württemberg

Kevin Morgan

Introduction

Debates on regional economic development in Europe and North America in recent years have been dominated by the twin themes of 'globalization' and 'localization'. At the risk of caricaturing the situation we might say that the vast corpus of literature on the first theme allots a prominent role to multinational companies, markets and competition, while in the second theme pride of place goes to the role of small firms, networks and collaboration. Cross-fertilization has of course occurred, but there is still a sense in which these themes have been addressed as separate furrows, with the result that the devotees of each theme remain, to a surprising degree, insulated from each other. For a whole series of reasons, however, this intellectual division of labour is no longer sustainable, not least because the 'industrial district' model of economic development – which was the main focus of the 'localization' school of thought – is being transformed under the combined weight of endogenous and exogenous forces.

If the 1980s saw the celebration of the 'industrial district' model, the 1990s seems set to deliver a more sceptical view on account of the fact that many of these local agglomerations are, to say the least, under duress. But let us be clear at the outset: the key features of these distinctive agglomerations or clusters do not have to be abandoned from a policy standpoint simply because of current problems – indeed, I shall argue here that these features, suitably modified, could play a seminal role in helping these areas to renew themselves in the future. The fate of these areas has a wider significance. Because the 'industrial districts' have inspired policy-makers throughout Europe and North America to re-think the ways in which they design and deliver regional policies (and to consider the potential of endogenous over exogenous development, innovation-related networks, public–private orchestration, decentralized governance structures, a skilled and versatile workforce, etc.), it would be a tragic mistake to jettison such advances simply because these districts are experiencing economic difficulties which are common to western economies in general.

It is surely worth reminding ourselves that even mainstream economic development thinking has conceded that the neo-liberal economic agenda –

with its emphasis on deregulation, competition and individualism, etc. – is not of itself a viable recipe for successful technological innovation and regional development in the 1990s (OECD 1993). More specifically, the member states of the European Union are being enjoined to promote better forms of networking – which among other things involves the disposition to collaborate to achieve mutually beneficial ends – if they are to overcome one of the key problems of the European economy, namely, that compared with Japan, for example, the European Union has a poor record of transferring knowledge from laboratory to industry, from firm to firm and from sector to sector (Commission of the European Communities 1993). In this context the debate on the 'industrial districts' may have something to offer to a wider audience.

Indeed, one of the underlying arguments of this paper is that even if the 'industrial district' model is under duress at this point in time, many of the practices and policies which it embodies – like the stress on collective entrepreneurship for example – are beginning to resonate way beyond the districts themselves and are consistent with the more robust theories of technological innovation and regional development. To examine these issues in more detail the following section looks at two innovative forms of economic development: 'the Japanese firm' and the 'industrial district', while the final section focuses on the problems and possibilities in Baden-Württemberg's automotive cluster.

Innovation and the collective entrepreneur

However we choose to characterize the era in which we live – be it 'post-Fordism', 'flexible specialization', 'lean production' or whatever – there would seem to be general agreement that it departs in significant ways from what is generally understood to be the traditional Fordist era. Among other things the latter was correlated with vertically integrated and departmentally segmented firms, standardized products for mass markets, fairly predictable commercial and technical environments, rigid separation of conception and execution within the workplace and relatively undemanding quality standards with respect to both process and product. As we shall see in more detail in the next section, the new competitive era marks a radical departure from many of these Fordist practices. What is perhaps most conspicuous about the new competitive era is the accelerating pace and escalating costs of technological innovation, the globalization and differentiation of markets, the abbreviation of product life-cycles, vertical disintegration and the associated growth of outsourcing, deeper buyer–supplier relationships, the revival of small and medium-sized production units, the diffusion of exacting quality standards and the re-integration of conception and execution within the workplace.

Of itself, scale is no guarantee of success, indeed it may even be part of the problem given the premium that is now attached to rapid and reliable knowledge transfer within and between organizations. Faced with a more demanding and less predictable environment we should not be surprised to learn that even the largest firms – like General Motors, IBM, Philips, etc. – have encountered immense difficulties in negotiating the transition to this new competitive era. However, it is too simplistic, and not a little ethnocentric, to portray the new competitive era as a crisis of mass production because, as Sayer reminds us, this system 'is alive and well in Japan' (Sayer 1989). Instructively, Sayer also argues that the analysis of the new competitive era should eschew binary histories – mass producers versus batch producers, large versus small firms, etc. – because this creates the misleading impression that each side of the dualism is subject to its own peculiar dynamics, when in fact they are all subject to very similar pressures, a point which has been painfully demonstrated by the trials and tribulations of large and small firms alike in Baden-Württemberg today.

From a corporate perspective the key point to make about this new competitive era is that innovation is finally being recognized for what it really is, namely, an ever more collective social endeavour. In other words the role of the heroic individual entrepreneur, so beloved of both the early Schumpeter and neo-liberal ideology, is fast being superseded by what we might call the collective entrepreneur. This is a short-hand way of signalling the crucial significance of the collaborative ethic in the innovation process, especially as between management and labour within the firm, between firms in the supply chain and between companies and their local milieux (Cooke and Morgan 1998). The notion of collective entrepreneurship applies as much to the leading Japanese firms, and their associated lean supply networks, as it does to the local agglomerations of small firms which constitute 'industrial districts' (Best 1990).

The practices pioneered by the leading Japanese firms, practices which are being emulated with highly variable results by western firms, are nowadays subsumed under the label of lean production. At the enterprise level three key features of collective entrepreneurship in 'the Japanese firm' should be mentioned here:

1 The first concerns the extraordinarily high level of horizontal integration within the firm as between R&D, production and marketing functions, a feature which expedites the transfer of information throughout the organization, aiding and abetting the learning capacity of the firm as a whole.
2 The second distinctive feature concerns the deep and enduring vertical linkages between the leading firms and their key suppliers, a system which allows the former to reap the benefits of *de facto* vertical integration without the costs, the result being that the large firms are able to tap the expertise of a corporate constituency which is much wider than in the west.
3 The third notable feature is the high priority accorded to shopfloor expertise: with production organized on a flow-based system, with 'fragile'

levels of inventory to expose bottlenecks, shopfloor teams are actively encouraged to use their hard-won expertise, hence they grow accustomed to the idea of 'using the factory as a laboratory', one of the key sources of incremental innovation in the Japanese firm and a resource denied to the Fordist firm because of its commitment to Tayloristic shopfloor principles.

These three features help to explain the awesome reputation which Japanese firms have acquired, especially with respect to cost containment, short product development cycles and high-quality mass production processes (Dore 1986; Aoki and Rosenberg 1987; Freeman 1988; Sayer 1989). Indeed, this Japanese model appears to be an exemplary illustration of recent theories of technical change which stress the essentially interactive character of the innovation process and the significance of multiple learning channels, including shopfloor workers, suppliers, customers, technical institutes, etc. (Lundvall 1988). These innovative features of 'the Japanese firm' have not been devalued by the current crisis of 'the Japanese model'.

If Japanese lean production is the most successful example of collective entrepreneurship in the large firm sector, much the same is claimed for 'industrial districts' on behalf of the small firm sector. What is important here, of course, is not so much the firm, but the territorially based production network, which at a minimum embraces inter-dependent, specialized firms and a panoply of intermediate institutions engaged in the provision of common services – credit, training, research, quality control, export promotion and market forecasting, etc. – most of which would be beyond the financial reach of a single firm acting alone (Sabel 1989; Pyke and Sengenberger 1992; Pyke 1994). Although dozens of these districts are said to exist in Europe and North America, most of the international debate tends to focus on the canonical districts of the Third Italy and Baden-Württemberg. Before we look at the current reality in these regions let us stay with the stylized facts of the 'industrial district' model to illustrate one of the key challenges, namely, regulation.

Even though large firms are having to grapple anew with the problems of regulating their affairs – how far to devolve control to local business units, how to resolve the make or buy dilemma, how to forge high-trust partnerships with suppliers, etc. – these regulatory problems are much more acute in the looser federation of firms which constitute the 'industrial district'. One of the perennial regulatory problems in this model is how to strike a sustainable balance between competition and collaboration. In other words what mechanisms are available for conflict resolution when the district has none of the command structures, none of the control mechanisms and none of the centralized authority on which the large firm can draw – not always successfully it has to be said – to settle internal disputes?

One painfully condensed answer from the pro-district fraternity is that the districts draw not on the hierarchical rules of command and control systems but, rather, on their stock of social capital, which consists of high-trust relations, norms of reciprocity and networks of civic engagement (Sabel 1992; Putnam 1993a). That is to say, the burden of regulation is carried by an unwritten social constitution which encourages firms, their associations and local public bodies to realize their interests through joint solutions to common problems, with the result that the districts avoid the cut-throat form of competition which is so prevalent in the Anglo-American environment by competing on quality, technique and design, etc. This would seem to be a fair summary of the pro-district position.

Without wishing to deny that social capital is a fundamentally important resource for regional development – a resource that is too often ignored by both market-based and state-led recipes for regional renewal – we have to ask what is the current situation in the key districts today? In the case of Emilia-Romagna, for example, the small firm networks are being destabilized by external takeover in the food packaging sector, by the growth of sub-contracting to lower-cost regions and countries in the knitwear sector and by fears that the fragmentation of the local machine tool industry may be a weakness, necessitating mergers in the future (Cooke and Morgan 1998). Others go further, and suggest that what we are seeing is 'the crisis of the cooperative form' in the Italian industrial districts, as new corporate hierarchies begin to displace the traditional collaborative ethic among hitherto symmetrically powerful firms (Harrison 1993, 1994).

Turning to Baden-Württemberg we must begin by asking whether this case actually corresponds to the 'industrial district' model in any strict sense? At a simple empirical level it is clear that the auto industry, one of the key industries in the regional economy, is dominated by very large firms, admittedly supported by a flotilla of small and medium-sized firms. While these supply-chain networks were admittedly close by traditional western auto standards, they were not nearly as effective and as innovative as comparable networks in Japan, one of the reasons for the plight of the region's auto industry today.

If the region's cluster of small machine tool firms more closely approximates the 'industrial district' model there is room for debate as to how far these firms actually engage in the kind of collaborative practices that are the hallmark of district-based firms. Equally significant, to what extent can we say that the collective institutions of the machine tool industry – the Verein Deutscher Werkzeugmaschinen (VDW) and the Verband Deutscher Maschinen- und Anlagenbau (VDMA) – have been able to steer firms so that they avoid competition and pursue collaborative projects? Herrigel's influential work suggests that the collaborative ethic is very pronounced in this sector (Herrigel 1989, 1993, 1994). Our own work, based on information from industry leaders like Trumpf and the regional office of the VDMA, suggests the need for a more sceptical view (Cooke and Morgan 1998).

In both Emilia-Romagna and Baden-Württemberg the small and medium-sized firm clusters are confronting a problem which has been thoroughly underplayed by the pro-district literature, namely, price competition. Because these firms are said to be niche-based, specialized producers, competing on quality, technique and design, etc., one is left with the impression that they are somehow impervious to price competition. If this were ever true in the past, it is certainly not the case today. A similarly under-explored problem for the district-based firms concerns 'globalization'. Traditionally, the internal coherence of the districts – in the shape of deeply embedded and heavily localized inter-firm transactions – was partly predicated on the fact that foreign markets could be served through exports. Now, however, there are growing pressures to have a local presence in one's main markets and this creates a new set of problems for regions dependent on small firm clusters.

To look at some of these issues in more detail let us turn to consider the problems of Baden-Württemberg's auto cluster – a term which is less loaded than the concept of the 'industrial district' – and inquire whether the region's existing stock of social capital and other resources are sufficient for it to reclaim the high ground in economic development terms.

The chastening of Baden-Württemberg

Impossible as it is to know in advance what the future holds for Baden-Württemberg (BW), perhaps this is the place to raise an issue which has fascinated scholars since time immemorial. Why do immensely successful enterprises – whether they be empires or nations, firms or regions – grow, peak and then decline, as if beholden to some ineluctable natural process? Like Hegel's owl of Minerva, a metaphor for philosophy as the wisdom of ripeness, we can only fully comprehend the process when it is over. When we are in the eye of an economic storm, for example, it is difficult to know whether we are dealing with a system which is under duress or in terminal crisis, a judgement we must leave to future historians. What we can say with some confidence is that BW has reached a critical point in its history. In this section the aims are twofold: first, to outline some disturbing trends in the regional economy and second, to highlight the problems in the auto cluster.

The allure begins to fade

Few regions have exerted such a pervasive influence on regional economic development thinking on both sides of the Atlantic as BW. Being one of the premier regional economies in what by any standard is one of the world's strongest national economies, BW's economic success has attracted a great deal of international attention. To explain this success story – which is not my aim here – researchers have cited such things as:

- a concentration of sectors – autos, machine tools and electrical engineering – each of which enjoyed strong growth trajectories over the post-war period;

- a hard core of large firms – like Mercedes-Benz, Bosch and SEL – all of which have highly localized supply bases;
- dynamic small and medium-sized firms (the fabled Mittelstand) operating in high-value-added export markets;
- a robust vocational education and training system which underwrites a skilled and versatile labour force;
- a formidable technology transfer infrastructure which embraces both basic research facilities and, through the Steinbeis Stiftung, caters for the near-market development needs of small firms;
- a wide array of governance mechanisms, public, private and hybrid, including the Land government itself, the well-equipped chambers of industry and commerce (IHK), and strong regional offices of the trade associations (like the VDMA);
- a strong stock of social capital in the form of norms of reciprocity, networks of civic engagement and high-trust relations, which informs the interactions at many different levels of economy, state and civil society in the region (Sabel *et al.* 1987; Herrigel 1989; Hassink 1992; Schmitz 1992; Semlinger 1993; Cooke and Morgan 1994).

Notwithstanding all these positive attributes the fact remains that the regional economy now finds itself in the deepest crisis since the state was founded in 1952. The most palpable signs of this crisis – a term which is freely employed within the region's political and industrial circles – is the growth of unemployment, which increased by 50% between 1992 and 1993, and the growing proportion of short-time workers, up by 282% over the same period (Brujmann *et al.* 1993). Furthermore, in 1991 the GDP growth rate in BW (2.8%) was lower than the Federal average (3.4%) for the first time since 1978, placing it in last-but-one position, just ahead of Rheinland-Pfalz. Other danger signals have been evident over a longer period: in the Stuttgart region, for example, the auto industry began to stagnate during the second half of the 1980s, with output down by 5.6% and employment almost static, compared with increases of 21% and 4.1% respectively in the FRG as a whole (Gaebele 1992). Having grown accustomed to better than average economic performance, BW began to be discussed in terms that would have been unthinkable in the 1980s. Typical of this new mood is the view that:

> ... Baden-Württemberg is no longer the best, and the Stuttgart region no longer the motor of South-Western progress. ... The realization that the region is threatened with a crisis is difficult to accept. The belief that with Daimler-Benz, Bosch and IBM behind us nothing untoward can happen is too deep-rooted. This is nonsense. The powerful supporting pillars of the regional economy are still a long way from tottering; the earth, however, is quaking.
>
> (Richter 1992)

Sentiments such as these might be dismissed as traditional German Untergangsstimmung – the tendency to magnify the slightest local difficulty into something of almost apocalyptic proportions – if a growing body of public officials and leading industrialists was not so ready to concur. For instance, Berthold Leibinger, the head of Trumpf and one of the chairmen of the Zukunftskommission, argued that the recent downturn in the region's prospects was the first real hard evidence of what many in the regional business community had been claiming for some time: that the advantages conferred by the Land's education and economic infrastructure, though still impressive by international standards, could no longer compensate for the high costs associated with location in BW (Richter 1992).

By common consent the cyclical downturn of the early 1990s exposed structural weaknesses in the regional economy, including the belated adjustment to lean production methods on the one hand and to global markets on the other; a weak profile in new technologies (such as information technology, biotechnology, new materials, etc.); high labour costs; inflexible work patterns (associated with the problem of machine running times which are reckoned to be 20% lower than the European average in hourly terms); and problems converting R&D into commercial products (Zukunftskommission Wirtschaft 2000 1993; Cooke and Morgan 1998).

Another issue which deserves to be mentioned – though this requires far more research – is how far BW suffers from what, in the context of the Ruhrgebiet, has been called the 'weakness of strong ties' (Grabher 1993). Conceptually, this involves local actors – firms, associations and public bodies – in a series of lock-ins which erode a region's capacity to change course when danger signals first appear. Functional lock-in, which refers to close buyer–supplier relations, becomes a major problem when suppliers fail to invest in their own boundary-spanning functions (that is, the multiple learning channels noted earlier), so that they become dependent on the antennae of their customer. Cognitive lock-in, which stems from long-standing personal ties and common conventions, etc., runs the risk of degenerating into rigid 'groupthink'. Finally, political lock-in refers to the way in which public bodies, through aid programmes to traditional industry and alliances with local industrialists, can often reinforce the past at the expense of the future.

It would be surprising if some of these problems were not applicable to the BW case. Indeed, we know that in the auto industry, for example, BW firms were very late to recognize the Japanese challenge and this is partly attributable to the widely shared notion ('groupthink') that the 'Made in Germany' label in the luxury car market was more or less invulnerable to price competition (Cooke *et al.* 1993). Furthermore, local experts speak of a political lock-in, in the sense that the economic and technology policy of the Land government has been heavily biased towards 'modernisation within the core branches' (Braczyk *et al.* 1994).

The 'weakness of strong ties' may help us to explain some of the current problems of belated adjustment in BW, but this thesis can be carried too far:

strong ties may have been part of the problem in the past but, suitably modified, they are most certainly part of the solution.

The metamorphosis of the auto cluster

Along with mechanical and electrical engineering the auto industry is one of the three 'classical industries' which have together underwritten the post-war success of the BW economy. In employment terms the auto industry peaked with 240,000 employees in 1991, equivalent to roughly 25% of the German total. Within BW the auto industry, defined as manufacturers and suppliers, is heavily concentrated in the Middle Neckar (the Stuttgart region). In and around Stuttgart – in towns like Boblingen, Esslingen, Ludwigsberg, Sindelfingen and Gǫppingen – is where we find the territorial heart of the auto cluster, a region where one in every seven jobs was directly or indirectly dependent on autos in 1990 (Bohm *et al.* 1992).

In corporate terms the cluster revolves around a number of large firms, the biggest of which is Mercedes-Benz, which had over 79,000 employees in the region in 1990, with nearly 46,000 concentrated at Sindelfingen alone. The other key firms are Audi, with nearly a half of its 37,000 employees at Neckarsulm, north of Stuttgart; Porsche, with some 8,000 employees in 1992, mostly spread between its R&D centre in Weissach and its production base in Zuffenhausen; and Bosch, which had 57 sites and over 113,000 employees in Germany in 1992, a hard core of which are in the Stuttgart region. With at least 250 additional supplier firms, the Stuttgart region hosts the largest, thickest and most powerful auto cluster in Europe.

Whatever the strengths of a cluster, the restructuring problems are that much more pronounced during a crisis because of the negative multiplier effect. Like the rest of the German auto industry, BW's auto firms are being forced to adapt to a new, leaner industrial paradigm. The scale of this challenge was highlighted when the Verband der Automobilindustrie (VDA) announced that the German auto industry would have to shed a minimum of 100,000 jobs during the 1990s if it was to remain internationally competitive. Indeed, on a number of different indicators – labour costs, productivity, working hours and absenteeism – the German auto industry has lost ground to its competitors, European as well as Japanese, in the past six years. On labour costs, for example, the total hourly wage cost in Germany is almost double the UK level (Morgan 1994). In terms of productivity Japan's lead over Germany stems from four different but partially linked sources: longer working hours, lower total pay, better machine time utilization and better work process design.

Goaded by the deepest post-war recession, and conscious of the need to make structural changes that were considered impossible prior to 1991, the auto industry is striving to make up the lost ground: in BW, for example, over 33,000 auto jobs have been lost since 1991.

Restructuring is never uniformly painful: the large firms, such as Mercedes,

Audi, Porsche and Bosch, clearly have the capacity, the resources and the options to see it through successfully. Smaller suppliers are far more vulnerable, and auto workers, from the shopfloor to middle management, are the most vulnerable of all. However, since the large firms have effectively steered the auto cluster – by setting their own in-house standards and by tutoring suppliers on quality, price and organizational competence – they must carry the main burden of responsibility for the current state of affairs. To appreciate the problems and possibilities in the large firm sector let us focus on Mercedes-Benz (MB), the dominant firm in the auto cluster. Like the other large firms MB is belatedly pursuing a leaner industrial paradigm: it is restructuring its internal operations, diversifying into new market segments, re-fashioning its supply base and shifting production to lower-cost locations, all of which have enormous implications for the local auto cluster.

The key to MB's failures in recent years is that it took too long to realize that its niche status did not insulate the company against competitive pressures in the world auto industry: the premium which MB had been able to charge was steadily eroded during the later 1980s. The final ignominy came in 1993, when Daimler-Benz announced a record DM1.8 billion net loss. In every year since 1985 MB's new car registrations performed worse than the German auto market as a whole. In productivity terms it fell behind a number of its key competitors, including its arch rival BMW, proving that only part of MB's cost disadvantage on a global scale could be attributed to Germany as a high-cost location. What helped to trigger the cultural revolution at MB was the successful US launch of the Lexus in 1989, demonstrating that Toyota could produce much cheaper luxury saloons without sacrificing (perceived) quality. Aside from the problems with its traditional three product lines, MB is also paying a price for failing to react soon enough to new car concepts and rapidly growing market segments.

The cultural revolution at MB was very much associated with Helmut Werner, who assumed the chairmanship in 1993, although some of the new practices had emerged prior to this time. Taking full advantage of a new start, Werner frankly conceded that MB's products were over-engineered and over-priced, and that the company had a significant productivity gap to bridge in the 1990s. To overcome these problems MB aimed to increase throughput by between 20 and 30%, lower the break-even point for new models to less than 60,000 cars, increase productivity by a minimum of 30%, halve new development costs, reduce material costs by 20% within four years and lower the costs for quality control by up to 40%. Let us look at some of the ways through which MB hopes to achieve this ambitious new strategy:

- *A new management structure*: a leaner, flatter and more devolved management structure was implemented, beginning in January 1993, when MB reduced its six managerial layers to four. New profit centres are being created throughout the company, the aim being to give plant managers much more control. This reverses the traditional situation where plant managers were responsible for about 85% of their costs, but had direct influence on no more than 20% of these costs. Despite its image as a niche producer, MB has clearly been labouring under a management structure which was closer to the traditional Fordist firm.

- *A new product development vocation*: belatedly MB has moved away from a cost-plus pricing system to the more cost-effective system of target-pricing which was pioneered by the Japanese. MB claims that it was this new approach which enabled the company to price its newly introduced C-class in exactly the same range as the 190 predecessor, rather than at a premium, which was the traditional approach. Overall, the key aim is to reduce the development cycle of new models (beginning with the C-class, which was 44 months instead of the normal 57 months), and to be able to offer product differentiation at low cost. However, MB has a long way to go before it can claim to have mastered the process-oriented, cross-functional approach to product development which holds sway in Japan, and which BMW seems to have pioneered in Germany at the Forschungs und Ingenieurzentrum (FIZ) in Munich. By German standards the FIZ heralds an unprecedented degree of inter-mingling of product development, purchasing and manufacturing personnel.
- *A new approach to production*: late in the day MB has begun to experiment with new production concepts at home and abroad. In 1993 MB estimated that its cost disadvantage with the Japanese was roughly 35%, and it believes it will have closed most of this gap by the late 1990s, in part through the introduction of new, leaner work practices. MB introduced these new work practices in 1993 as part of the brief for the new generation of V6/V8 engines, which it decided to build at Unterturkheim, near Stuttgart. This location was chosen after an agreement with IG Metall, which is expected to reduce costs through better utilization of capital equipment and new streamlined working procedures, including a new emphasis on work groups, fewer breaks, a more flexible shift system and the incorporation of an output-related bonus in a new payment system. Alongside the reorganization of the traditional plants MB has pinned its greatest hopes on Rastatt, its wholly new plant which opened in 1992.

Rastatt is designed to be far more than just another factory: MB sees it as a test-bed for the company's German manufacturing strategy, pioneering a local version of lean production, logistics and personnel policy. Devoid of a conventional assembly line, production at Rastatt largely revolves around teams which are responsible for each stage of assembly and, in contrast to Sindelfingen (where some 10% of the 45,000-odd workforce is engaged in quality control and end-of-line repairs), the line worker and the quality controller are designed to be one and the same person. Although MB insists that this model is not copied from the Japanese, it is predicated on the same idea, namely, that shopfloor workers, when suitably motivated and secure, often know best how to raise productivity on their own turf.

While one must hope that this more human-centred approach to production succeeds, some auto experts have their doubts. For example, US commentators have seized on the fact that Rastatt will use 5,500 employees to assemble 360 cars a day, which is well below Toyota's Tahara plant, where a workforce of 2,500 has a daily output of 1,500, and it also compares unfavourably with BMW's new US plant, in Spartanburg, where 2,000 employees will produce 300 cars a day (McElroy 1992).

Aside from reorganizing its domestic plants MB is placing a new emphasis on overseas production: the 400E and 500SEL models are now being assembled in Mexico, new ventures are planned with SYMC in Korea, the new people carrier will be produced in Spain, and Alabama in the US has been chosen for the new four-wheel-drive leisure car. MB intends to use these foreign plants as learning laboratories. At the US plant, for example, where 1,500 employees will produce 60,000 vehicles a year, MB intends to make just 30% of the value of the vehicle in-house, a lower proportion than any other MB facility. Moreover this plant is to serve as a model for all future plants and act as a 'centre of competence' for the group as a whole.

Daimler-Benz has also entered an alliance with the Swiss watchmaking group, SMH, to produce the Smart minicar at Hambach in eastern France. This joint venture, known as Micro Compact Car (MCC), is said to be the most revolutionary experiment ever undertaken in modular production, not least because MCC and its on-site suppliers, dubbed 'system partners' to signal the co-makership philosophy, have abolished all distinctions between their respective employees in the 'Smart Ville' complex. Less dramatic forms of reverse learning are under way at Daimler's new US auto plant in Alabama, which has been designated a 'centre of competence' for the group as a whole (Simonian 1998).

- *A new supplier strategy*: conscious of the fact that the supply base constitutes a major, and growing, role in the competitive position of frontline auto firms, MB is desperately seeking to streamline its overgrown and unwieldy supply base in an effort to harness the full potential of its key suppliers. Through the 1980s MB's internal procurement costs increased three times as quickly as external suppliers' prices and, among other things, this rendered outsourcing more attractive. It is generally agreed that MB's level of in-house manufacturing is higher than the German average and the latter is itself high by the standards of most other auto firms, especially the Japanese. In 1990 MB's procurement budget was valued at over DM30 billion, of which nearly 90% by value was spent in Germany and, of this, some 50% was reckoned to be spent in BW. The total number of direct suppliers is estimated to be between 1,600 and 1,800 in all, and MB intends to reduce the number to an upper range of 500 system suppliers (Bohm *et al.* 1992). In addition, it intends to reduce its procurement spend on German-based suppliers from 90% to below 70% to gain the benefits of lower-cost locations and, overall, the aim is to lower purchasing costs. In the discourse of the auto manager, MB intends to realize this strategy through more global, modular and single sourcing, all of which requires a more open and more iterative relationship between buyer and supplier, especially at the design stage.

If these are the main elements of MB's renewal strategy, what are its prospects? Let us mention just one of the key problems that will have to resolved. MB typifies the engineering-driven culture of many German firms and, while this has been a source of strength in the past, some analysts believe that this asset has become a weakness in the era of the lean enterprise. More generally, some authors go so far as to say that the key weakness of the 'German tradition', with its organizational hierarchies and its rigidly defined functional specialisms, is its 'hostility to cross-functional cooperation' (Womack and Jones 1994). Whatever the truth of these larger claims we can certainly say that the power and prestige of the engineers created a problem for MB in two ways. First, in their search for excellence, the engineering fraternity was wont to subordinate commercial factors to technical factors in the design and development process. Second, there was the problem of parochialism in what was more generally a very Stuttgart-centric firm. According to one senior MB manager, 'the engineers prefer to phone a Swabian and they will often say why go to Lucas when we know Bosch'. These deeply embedded norms made it difficult for the purchasing department to forge links with new suppliers. Indeed, the engineers would even make side-deals with their own preferred suppliers without the knowledge of the purchasers!

Furthermore, outsourcing was often opposed by an alliance of senior engineers and the trade union (Morgan *et al.* 1992). If these cross-functional problems are not resolved MB will find it difficult if not impossible to realize its aim of becoming a lean enterprise. In short, MB's traditional premium pricing culture, which could absorb these productivity bottlenecks, is no longer sustainable.

The most dramatic move which MB has made to transform itself came in May 1998, when Daimler-Benz announced that it was to merge with Chrysler of the US to form a new company called Daimler-Chrysler AG. In terms of products and geography the merger was said to be 'made in heaven' because the overlap between the two companies, in terms of both geography and products, was minimal. If the German company has been somewhat pedestrian in recent years, Chrysler has been the most dynamic of the US carmakers. Although it has roughly similar revenues to Daimler, Chrysler has twice the income, more than twice the number of vehicles sold and fewer than half the employees. In other words, the German company has much to learn from Chrysler, not least how to manage the engineering process to get a wider variety of cars to market more quickly (Martin 1998). Nothing in MB's history is likely to have as big an impact on the culture of the company as this merger because it will expose the German operations not just to US design and engineering practices but, more significantly, to US standards of corporate performance.

If MB is over the worst the same cannot be said of the auto suppliers, most of whom have been cast in the role of unwilling shock absorbers to an industry in crisis. While the larger suppliers – like Bosch, ZF, ITT and Mahle – clearly have the capacity to adapt to the new pressures, many small suppliers will either go to the wall or become absorbed by larger rivals unless they are able to forge common cause with like-minded firms.

Some 25% of Germany's 3,000-odd auto suppliers are reckoned to be based in BW and their plight is inscribed in the unforgiving data on pricing and profitability. Between 1980 and 1991, for example, parts' prices rose by only 8%, compared with a 24% increase in the price of the final product. In contrast to Japan, suppliers in BW face comparable labour costs to their customers: consequently, they have experienced a massive fall in profits as annual wage increases outstripped price increases by just under 3% during this period. A recent study by the Stuttgart office of Deutsche Bank showed that BW supplier firms' profits ranged between 1.1% and 3.4%, much lower than was originally thought (Gaebele 1992). As well as having to absorb lower prices these firms are also being asked to take on new tasks, like value analysis, electronic data interchange (EDI) networking, zero defects and greater logistical responsibility, etc. In principle the trend towards more outsourcing promises new opportunities for local suppliers but, in practice, many simply do not have the financial capacity to exploit it, as the recent spate of takeovers attests.

The drive towards single and modular sourcing means that only large firms have much chance of surviving as direct suppliers, so that firms with fewer than 500 employees may have to accept second or third tier status. In BW, though, 63% of auto suppliers have fewer than 100 employees, with 75% of the business going to the top 150 supplier firms (Cooke *et al.* 1993). A report commissioned by the Ministry of Economics identified a number of other key problems in the auto supplier industry:

- global sourcing is used only to a limited degree by supplier firms and too few of them are able or willing to invest in overseas production capacity;
- EDI networking between suppliers and manufacturers is still in its infancy, partly because suppliers fear that their customers will pass sensitive information on to their rivals;
- the organization of production in many supplier firms is too inflexible: set-up times are too long and managerial thinking is too compartmentalized;
- suppliers, depending on their size and their capacity, need to do more to position themselves in the appropriate tier of the industry (Little 1992).

To add to the gloom, a grim analysis from Price Waterhouse came to the conclusion that of Germany's 3,000-odd supplier firms, only 500 would survive as viable businesses and, of these, perhaps only 100 had the capacity to become genuine first-tier suppliers (Parkes 1993). Whatever the future holds, we can be sure of one thing: the structure of the auto supply industry in BW, as in Germany as a whole, is going to be far more concentrated when the dust settles. As the Deutsche Bank noted:

> The pressure of the automobile industry on profit margins and innovation demand a greater capital capacity than most suppliers possess. ... Any small and medium-sized firm in this hitherto overwhelmingly Mittelstand-oriented sector that does not wish to be taken over, must itself set about looking for cooperation partners ... [but] for several small and medium-sized supplier firms the possibility of fusion or a cooperation deal is surprisingly considered to be of little relevance. ... We therefore expect that a number of firms will not survive.
>
> (Gaebele 1992)

To anyone familiar with the Mittelstand, however, it is not at all surprising that these firms recoil from losing their autonomous status: the hallmarks of the owner-managers are pride in their craft, civic standing in their community and, most important of all, independence. Even so, local experts insist that:

> ... the supplier industry will have to strengthen itself through greater cooperation and give up the facade of independence that so many smaller firms have treasured for so long. The car manufacturers will have to do likewise. It's ridiculous that every German manufacturer has its own 6 cylinder and its own 8 cylinder because the development costs are enormous. Without greater cooperation, even between manufacturers, we simply won't be able to withstand worldwide competition.
>
> (Riester 1992)

In the future, the first-tier suppliers will be obliged to take on a whole series of new responsibilities, like organizing the supply chain on behalf of the car manufacturer and providing the latter with a wide array of support at home and abroad. In the lean supply chain model the car manufacturer becomes the chief systems integrator, leaving the detailed work to the first-tier supplier and its lower tiers (Sabel *et al.* 1989; Lamming 1993).

Bosch, the biggest and most innovative auto supplier in Germany, is generally thought to be well equipped to perform these new tasks. Commentators are impressed by the fact that Bosch has been operating a local supplier network since 1970 in which the company acts 'like a technical university' for its suppliers (Sabel *et al.* 1987). Looking back, however, Bosch feels that this network may have benefited the suppliers, but it did not deliver the two-way benefits which accrue from today's lean supply chain networks, based as they are on continuous improvement techniques and joint learning procedures. Big as it is, Bosch is having to learn new skills: indeed, the main reason why it opened a new plant in Wales was to interact with the Japanese car manufacturers in the UK – the fact that total labour costs were 50% lower in Wales than in BW was an additional, but secondary, attraction (Morgan 1994).

Finally, what are the prospects for the auto cluster as a whole? The strengths of the past are not necessarily assets for the future. Supply chain theorists claim that there is no evidence to suggest that close spatial proximity is a requisite part of lean supply because several companies, in Japan, Europe and the US, are achieving just-in-time deliveries over considerable distances: what matters, they argue, is 'not the distance but the travel time between supplier and customer' (Lamming 1993). In other words the density of the local supply networks in BW looks like being substantially reduced in the future as a result of single sourcing, which reduces the number of suppliers, and global sourcing, which substitutes global for regional linkages (Schamp 1991). If it is becoming less dense in quantitative terms (fewer firms, fewer functions and fewer jobs) this does not mean that it is becoming less significant in a strategic sense.

In qualitative terms the character of the cluster seems set to change. The traditional cluster, which spanned the entire spectrum of corporate activities, will probably undergo a deep metamorphosis: the simpler, labour-intensive functions look like being shipped out to lower-cost regions in Europe, leaving in their wake a smaller, high-value-added cluster focused around research, design, development, smart production and systems integration functions (Morgan 1994). This scenario is wholly consistent with what MB is doing today: diversifying abroad whilst at the same time making new local commitments, like the smart production plant at Rastatt and the new R&D facility in the Stuttgart region. One of the key challenges for the large car manufacturers will be to act out in practice what they know to be true in theory, namely, that to be effective in the era of the lean enterprise, the customer has to learn to relinquish control over the process as a whole and share the value-added spoils with its key suppliers. These local inter-firm linkages seem set to become ever more important in the future.

If this scenario offers a solution to the larger firms, customers and suppliers alike, it does nothing to alleviate the problems of the smaller suppliers and the swollen ranks of unemployed auto workers. Although the emerging auto cluster will continue to be a key pillar of the regional economy, we can no longer say that the interests of the large auto firms are wholly synonymous with the fortunes of the Stuttgart region.

Seeds of hope: the collaborative route to renewal

By its own very high standards BW is undergoing something of a crisis. But, if the key test of a system is how well it responds to pressure, then the response in BW provides grounds for hope: the regional authorities are clearly not resigned to BW becoming 'the Ruhrgebiet of the twenty-first century'. If anything, the crisis mentality has induced a new mood in the region – in government, industry and the trade unions especially – which makes them more alert to the problems of the past, more receptive to the need to innovate, in a whole series of different ways, to secure the future. In other words the regional authorities seem to be fully aware that social and institutional innovation are as necessary as technical innovation, indeed that they reinforce each other. Chastened as it is, BW can at least draw upon a fairly robust stock of social capital – the networks, norms and trust which underpin the disposition to collaborate to achieve mutually beneficial ends. Social capital, we must remember:

> ... is not a substitute for effective public policy but rather a prerequisite for it and, in part, a consequence of it. Social capital works through states and markets, not in place of them.
>
> (Putnam 1993b)

If the stock of social capital in BW has been exaggerated, as we saw in the Mittelstand's response to collaboration, it remains formidable by the standards of most European regions. That being said, I want to suggest in this final section that BW's stock of social capital needs to be more consciously nurtured because it is not some immutable construct, impervious to the bruising battles of everyday life. In the auto industry, for example, the traditional norms of reciprocity and trust between buyers and suppliers have been battered beyond recognition, so much so that the prevailing mood among the smaller firms today is one of cynicism and bitterness, attitudes which have a profoundly corrosive effect on social capital in the region. Repairing the damage, by finding joint solutions to common problems, is essential if the regional renewal strategy is to succeed.

The Land government now appears to be committed to what it calls a 'dialogue-oriented market-based industrial policy', a policy which seeks to involve all the main economic parties. Far from being a luxury that BW can ill-afford in a crisis, cooperation is rather seen as a vital part of the solution: in other words, the process (collaboration) is perceived to be integral to the product (competitive renewal). The novelty of this approach should not be exaggerated, indeed its key feature is continuity-in-change. That is to say, the schemes may be novel but the strategy embodies two principles which have a longer lineage in the region.

The first concerns the role of the state. Although it may be fashionable to denigrate him today, it was Lothar Spaeth, the former Minister President, who was primarily responsible for propagating the vision of the regional state as animateur of technological change and regional renewal. Unencumbered by the sterile ideological debate about 'state versus market', Spaeth was sufficiently pragmatic to appreciate that the regional state had a positive role to play in promoting innovation, especially with respect to small medium enterprises (SMEs), technology transfer, education and training. Whatever else has changed since Spaeth's downfall, this vision of the regional state continues to exist, most clearly in the recommendations of the Future Commission, which embody a view of the state as the 'innovative enquirer', organizing and guiding a future-oriented dialogue in both the classical industries and the emerging new technology sectors.

The new strategy is also predicated on Selbstverwaltung – the deeply ingrained and highly regarded principle of self-governing organizations. Although the regional state has begun to assume a much more active role in the process of industrial renewal it is at pains to emphasize that it is not trying to substitute its own role for those of self-governing groups (e.g. firms, trade associations, chambers of commerce, trade unions, etc.). In short, it is not adopting a French-style dirigiste approach to the use of state power. What distinguishes this approach from the Spaeth era, however, is that the regional government is now obliged to strike a better balance between competition and collaboration in the corporate sector. While it continues to respect the sovereignty of the firm, it is trying to encourage Mittelstand firms to recognize the limits of autonomous action because, as we have seen, this is no longer a viable option for many of these firms. To this end the regional government is offering new incentives for smaller firms to collaborate amongst themselves, with their suppliers and with the region's technology transfer institutions.

So, while the Economics Minister presents the strategy as a 'new economic consensus' between government, industry and the trade unions in BW, and as a 'new model' for Germany as a whole, we must remember that, however innovative, it builds on some long-established traditions within the region (Spoeri 1993).

To the extent that the Future Commission's report is an index of government policy in BW we can say that the strategy has two fundamental aims: to regenerate the classical industries and to promote new technology-based industries in which the regional economy is deemed to be weak (e.g. information technology, new materials, etc.). With respect to the classical industries – the focus of this paper – the Future Commission frankly concedes that firms will have to exploit the international division of labour to a much greater extent than hitherto if they are to remain globally competitive. As the Commission puts it:

> Concerns in the advanced industrial nations with their high wage levels move simple, labour-intensive products into low-wage countries. This allows them to remain competitive and to keep in their own country those parts of production that are associated with high value creation: R&D, design, assembly and construction of complex parts. ... With the opening of Eastern Europe we now have low-wage countries on our doorstep. We should not see these countries only as new competitors. Rather we should take the chance of cooperating and increase our international competivity by a strategy of distributing production, particularly to Central and Eastern Europe. This is a concept similar to what our Japanese competitors have put into effect in South-East Asia.
>
> (Zukunftskommission Wirtschaft 2000 1993)

In other words, the scenario which was discussed earlier – with respect to the metamorphosis of the auto cluster – now seems to be part of a more general message for the classical industries. In the longer term, the Commission sees the need to pioneer new product markets, like computer-based traffic-control systems and electric cars for example, which could open up a wide array of new product markets for the auto and auto component firms (Cooke and Morgan 1998).

Shorter term, the strategy stresses the need for new forms of collaboration at home. To this end the government has launched a series of sectorally focused Joint Initiatives, the delivery mechanisms for the long-term strategy contained in the Future Commission's report. The government claims that the key point about these Joint Initiatives is that they are more than mere talking shops: rather, they seek to win binding agreement on concrete measures from government, industry and trade unions in each of the sectors concerned. Through the medium of the 'model project', in which a small number of firms are invited to collaborate in a well-defined problem area under the moderating role of an intermediary institute, it is hoped that the transfer of know-how can be rapidly disseminated beyond the actual participants since the results must be made available to other firms in the sector.

The first of these Joint Initiatives was launched in 1992 in the auto components industry. This sectoral working group (which included representatives of Mercedes-Benz, Bosch, the Industrie- und Handelskammern (IHK) and IG Metall) agreed the following types of project:

- *Better information flows*: studies of the supply industry have shown that the effects of structural change are still not sufficiently appreciated by many firms, hence the need for better information, especially from government and the car manufacturers, and supplier firms are being encouraged to make greater use of the Land's research and advisory institutes. Informal discussion circles in the Economics Ministry and in the IHK will also be used to propagate new solutions.
- *Focused consultations*: the government has given the Steinbeis Foundation a new fund of DM4.5 million to address the special problems of small supplier firms, especially with respect to new production and management techniques.
- *Technology-oriented projects*: ten joint research projects led by the relevant research institute, and supported by the Ministry, are focusing on key areas, including quality assurance in computer-assisted production, small firms' cooperative in casting technology, technical software for engineering users and design for manufacturing techniques. On completion of these projects a Land-wide process of dissemination is to be organized under the auspices of the IHK.
- *Lean production management*: these projects focus on more flexible and less costly modes of organization, including the introduction of teamwork in

production, the need for flatter hierarchies and the creation of profit centres and factors which regulate machine running times, etc. Among other things the Fraunhofer Institute für Arbeitswirtschaft und Organisation has been allotted a key role in this sphere and it is to house a newly created Supplier Management Centre, which will act as an ambassador for best practice in lean supply chain management.
- *Strategic alliances*: because the market is perceived to be 'enforcing cooperation', the Ministry is intent on fostering this process in both the vertical sense (between manufacturers and their suppliers) and in the horizontal sense (among suppliers themselves). Hence the Ministry is supporting model 'cooperation agreements' in supply-chain management in the former category and in joint product development in the latter category (Wirtschaftsministerium Baden-Württemberg 1993).

It is still too early to evaluate the effects of this strategy. In design terms, for sure, it is difficult to see what else could have been done to induce more judicious forms of collaboration within the auto industry. As we have seen, the key problem for many a Mittelstand firm was that it felt unable or unwilling to forge stronger inter-firm ties for fear of losing control over its own fate. The burgeoning crisis, carrying as it does the spectre of bankruptcy, may of course make these firms better disposed to finding joint solutions to common problems. But one cannot be sure of this, not least because the Mittelstand sector is as much a cultural as an economic phenomenon.

On the institutional front, where BW is generally thought to be well endowed, the intermediate institutions have been given a heavy responsibility for brokering the collaboration process and disseminating the results to a wider population of firms. But these institutions – the IHK, the Fraunhofer Institutes and the Steinbeis Foundation, etc. – were never as well networked as the conventional image would have us believe. The pressure to earn revenue induced a great deal of rivalry and this in turn rendered them somewhat proprietorial, with the result that small firm clients did not always receive impartial advice or the most appropriate forms of assistance (Cooke *et al.* 1993). More generally it seems that the role of these intermediary institutions has been greatly exaggerated. The fact that so many intermediary institutions exist in the region should not lead us to assume that they are all equally effective. Indeed, much more research is needed to establish their precise contribution to technological and organizational innovation in the Land. Such problems will clearly have to be resolved if these intermediary institutions are to be equal to the tasks assigned to them under the Joint Initiative programme.

Another pillar of BW's economy – the dual training system – will also have to adjust to the new era. Throughout Germany there are growing fears that this system, geared as it is to the provision of highly specific occupational skills, may be too rigid to cater for the 'polyvalent worker' of the 1990s (Geissler 1991). As we have seen, the trend towards cross-functional working practices sets a high premium on hybrid skills, and the dual training system will have to be re-fashioned to take account of this trend. Equally important, a better balance needs to be struck between traditional and emerging skill requirements: at present the three most popular occupations for male trainees are motor vehicle mechanic, electrician and machine fitter, all of which are in decline relative to IT-based skills for example. More generally the Stuttgart region of the IHK argues that:

> Unemployment of skilled workers is spreading. Even before the structural crisis hit the companies, a great number of skilled workers did not find a working place corresponding with their qualification. We have to cope with a mismatch between qualification and organization of working places.
>
> (Breitmeier 1993)

Many of these fears are said to be unfounded. Some labour market experts argue that there is no evidence of a relative increase in unemployment among skilled workers and that the dual training system, far from being antiquated, 'constitutes institutional capital that justifies optimism' (Schmid 1992). Clearly, these divergent views as to the viability of the dual training system need to be resolved.

Finally, dramatic changes are sweeping through the region's industrial relations system, which was often seen as the pacesetter for terms and conditions throughout Germany. Large employers have begun to re-assert their 'right to manage' because they believe that the consensual nature of German industry prevented firms from making the radical reforms they knew were needed to restore competitiveness. Edzard Reuter, the former chairman of Daimler-Benz, argued that large firms in the region 'got used to giving in to the unions despite knowing this would lead to a very serious situation' (Gow 1993). A combination of redundancies and threats to move abroad have coerced the unions into accepting cuts in pay and bonuses, longer working hours, more flexible shift-patterns and greater management autonomy at plant level. Indeed, the plant has become the real theatre where a new industrial relations script is being rehearsed.

The modernizers within IG Metall freely concede that the union has to be more pragmatic, more flexible, if it is to survive as a social force. As one of the key modernizers puts it:

> Traditionally, the unions have concerned themselves with collective agreements, which didn't allow much room for individual requirements. But this will have to change. As with the Mittelstand, if the unions can adapt, and I think IG Metall has good prospects, then they will emerge far stronger than before. But we must get down to it.
>
> (Riester 1992)

However, there are elements within IG Metall which continue to believe that the lynch-pin of the German industrial relations system is not a common point of view between both sides but, rather, 'the relative balance of strength between the negotiating parties', a balance which helps to keep management on an innovative footing. Even so, echoing the large firm mentality prior to the recession, this view maintains that the competitive edge of German industry 'is not to be found in low prices or in simplified production methods, but rather in more highly developed product engineering, high quality production etc.' (Roth 1992). While much of this is true, of course, the fatal error here is the supposition that low prices and high quality are mutually exclusive. Having lost so many members in the 1990s, IG Metall will have to address itself more forcefully to the plant-level concerns of its members (many of whom are embroiled in cost-reduction issues to preserve jobs) if it wants to remain a relevant force in the engineering industry.

By way of a conclusion it is clear that each of the key elements of the regional economy – large firms, the Mittelstand sector, intermediary institutions, the dual training system and the unions – is under unprecedented pressure. If the problems are clear, the possibilities for renewal remain uncertain. What we can say is that few regions in Europe are as well endowed as BW with respect to technical resources and institutional assets. While these institutional assets were not enough to forestall a crisis of the classical industries – indeed they may even have contributed through a 'lock-in' effect which induced a complacent and parochial attitude to the region's competitive status – they nevertheless constitute seeds of hope, the means through which BW can secure a more innovative vocation for itself in the future. As always, however, much will depend on how well these key institutions orchestrate their efforts, how well they collaborate to achieve mutually beneficial ends – in short, how well they function as a 'collective entrepreneur', spreading the costs and the benefits of technical innovation and social adjustment throughout the region.

Bibliography

Aoki, M. and Rosenberg, N. (1987) *The Japanese Firm as an Innovative Institution*, Palo Alto, CA: Stanford University Press.

Best, M. (1990) *The New Competition*, Cambridge, MA: Harvard University Press.

Bohm, D. *et al.* (1992) *Report on the Automotive Industry: Its Importance and Development in the Stuttgart Region*, Tübingen: IAW.

Braczyk, H.J., Schienstock, G. and Steffensen, B. (1994) *Baden-Württemberg: Still a Story of Success?*, Stuttgart: Akademie für Technikfolgenabschatzung in Baden-Württemberg.

Breitmeier, H. (1993) Head of Vocational Training, IHK, Stuttgart Region, *Interview*, 17 December.

Brujmann, R. *et al.* (1993) *Die Industrierezession in Baden-Württemberg und ihre Folgen für den Arbeitsmarkt*, Stuttgart: ABF.

Commission of the European Communities (1993) *White Paper on Growth, Competitiveness, Employment*, Brussels.

Cooke, P. and Morgan, K. (1994) 'The regional innovation system in Baden-Württemberg', *International Journal of Technology Management* 9(3/4): 394–429.

Cooke, P. and Morgan, K. (1998) *The Associational Economy: Firms, Regions and Innovation*, Oxford: Oxford University Press.

Cooke, P. and Morgan, K. (forthcoming)

Cooke, P., Morgan, K. and Price, A. (1993) *The Future of the Mittelstand: Collaboration versus Competition*, RIR Report No. 13, Cardiff: University of Wales.

Dore, R. (1986) *Flexible Rigidities*, London: Athlone Press.

Freeman, C. (1988) *Technology Policy and Economic Performance: Lessons from Japan*, London: Pinter.

Gaebele, M. (1992) *Expose zur Lage der KfZ-Zulieferindustrie im Bezirk Stuttgart*, Stuttgart: Deutsche Bank.

Geissler, K.A. (1991) 'Das Duale System der industriellen Berufsausbildung hat keine Zukunft', *Leviathan* 19(1): 68–77.

Gow, D. (1993) 'Optimistic dispatch from defiant Reuter', *Guardian*, 18 December.

Grabher, G. (1993) 'The weakness of strong ties: the lock-in of regional development in the Ruhr area', in G. Grabher (ed.) *The Embedded Firm*, London: Routledge.

Harrison, B. (1993) 'The Italian industrial districts and the crisis of the cooperative form', *European Planning Studies* 2(1): 3–22.

—— (1994) *Lean and Mean: The Changing Landscape of Corporate Power in the Age of Flexibility*, New York: Basic Books.

Hassink, R. (1992) 'Regional innovation policy: case studies from the Ruhr, Baden-Württemberg and north east England', PhD thesis, University of Utrecht.

Herrigel, G. (1989) 'Industrial order and the politics of industrial change', in P. Katzenstein (ed.) *Industry and Politics in West Germany*, Ithaca, NY: Cornell University Press.

—— (1993) 'Industry as a form of order', in J. Hollingsworth *et al.* (eds) *Governing Capitalist Societies*, Oxford: Oxford University Press.

—— (1994) *Reconceptualising the Sources of German Industrial Power*, Cambridge: Cambridge University Press.

Lamming, R. (1993) *Beyond Partnership: Strategies for Innovation and Lean Supply*, Englewood Cliffs, NJ: Prentice Hall.

Little, A.D. (1992) *Foerderungsmassnahmen zur Wettbewerbsfaehigkeit von Automobilzulieferen in BW*, Wiesbaden: ADL.

Lundvall, B.A. (1988) 'Innovation as an interactive process', in G. Dosi *et al.* (eds) *Technical Change and Economic Theory*, London: Pinter.

McElroy, J. (1992) 'Why can't Germany compete?', *Automotive Industries*, August.

Martin, P. (1998) 'The new model Chrysler-Benz', *Financial Times*, 7 May.

Morgan, K. (1994) 'The effect of restructuring on the regions', paper presented to the European Commission/European Parliament's 'Forum on the European Automobile Industry', Palais des Congres, Brussels, 1 March.

Morgan, K., Cooke, P. and Price, A. (1992) *The Challenge of Lean Production in German Industry*, RIR Report No. 12, Cardiff: University of Wales.

OECD (1993) *Territorial Development and Structural Change: A New Perspective on Adjustment and Reform*, Paris.

Parkes, C. (1993) 'German producers in turmoil', *Financial Times* Survey on World Automotive Suppliers, 28 June.

Pyke, F. (1994) *Small Firms, Technical Services and Inter-firm Cooperation*, Geneva: International Institute for Labour Studies.

Pyke, F. and Sengenberger, W. (1992) *Industrial Districts and Local Economic Regeneration*, Geneva: International Institute for Labour Studies.

Putnam, R. (1993a) *Making Democracy Work: Civic Traditions in Modern Italy*, Princeton, NJ: Princeton University Press.

—— (1993b) 'The prosperous community: social capital and public life', *The American Prospect* 13 (Spring).

Richter, A. (1992) 'Krisen-Region?', *Stuttgarter-Zeitung*, 10 July.

Riester, W. (1992) Stuttgart District Leader, IG Metall, *Interview*, 6 July.

Roth, S. (1992) *Japanisation or Going Our Own Way?: New 'Lean Production' Concepts in the German Automobile Industry*, Frankfurt: IG Metall.

Sabel, C. (1987) *Regional Prosperities Compared: Massachusetts and Baden-Württemberg in the 1980s*, Discussion Paper IIM/LMP87-10b, Berlin: WZB.

—— (1989) 'Flexible specialisation and the re-emergence of regional economies', in P. Hirst and J. Zeitlin (eds) *Reversing Industrial Decline?*, Oxford: Berg.

—— (1992) 'Studied trust: building new forms of cooperation in a volatile economy', in F. Pyke and W. Sengenberger (eds) *Industrial Districts and Local Economic Regeneration*, Geneva: International Institute for Labour Studies.

Sabel, C., Kern, H. and Herrigel, G. (1989) *Collaborative Manufacturing: New Supplier Relations in the Automobile Industry and the Re-definition of the Industrial Corporation*, Cambridge, MA: MIT.

Sayer, A. (1989) 'Post-Fordism in question', *International Journal of Urban and Regional Research* 13(4): 666–95.

Schamp, E. (1991) 'Towards a spatial reorganisation of the German car industry?', in G. Benko and M. Dunford (eds) *Industrial Change and Regional Development*, London: Belhaven Press.

Schmid, G. (1992) 'Flexible coordination: the future of the dual system from a labour market policy angle', *Vocational Training* No. 1, Cedefop.

Schmitz, H. (1992) 'Industrial districts: model and reality in Baden-Württemberg', in F. Pyke and W. Sengenberger (eds) *Industrial Districts and Local Economics Regeneration*, Geneva: International Institute for Labour Studies.

Semlinger, K. (1993) 'Economic development and industrial policy in Baden-Württemberg: small firms in a benevolent environment', *European Planning Studies* 1(4): 435–63.

Simonian, H. (1998) 'Micro compact car: smart work for partners', *Financial Times*, 23 February.

Spaeth, L. (1985) *Wende in die Zukunft*, Stuttgart.

Spoeri, D. (1993) 'Ein Weg aus der Krise', *Gemeinschaftsinitiative Wirtschaft und Politik*, Wirtschaftsministerium Baden-Württemberg.

Wirtschaftsministerium Baden-Württemberg (1993) *Gemeinschaftsinitiative Wirtschaft und Politik: Ein Modell für Deutschland*, Stuttgart.

Womack, J. and Jones, D. (1994) 'From lean production to the lean enterprise', *Harvard Business Review* March/April: 93–103.

Zukunftskommission Wirtschaft 2000 (1993) *Aufbruch aus der Krise*, Stuttgart.

5 Sticky places in slippery space

A typology of industrial districts

Ann Markusen

The puzzle of stickiness in an increasingly slippery world

In a world of dramatically improved communications systems and increasingly internationally mobile corporations, it is puzzling why certain places are able to sustain their attractiveness to both capital and labour. Movement is, of course, costly and disruptive to both. David Harvey's (1982) work on capital's need for 'spatial fix' and Storper and Walker's (1989) work on labour and reproduction suggest generic reasons why hyper-mobility cannot completely obliterate production ensembles in space. But neither account explains why certain places manage to anchor productive activity while others do not.

The problem is most acute in advanced capitalist countries, where wage levels and standards of living are substantially higher than newly incorporated labour-rich and increasingly technically competent countries (Howes and Markusen 1993). Production space in these countries has become increasingly 'slippery', as the ease to capital of moving plants grows and as new competing lines are set up in lower-cost regions elsewhere. Often the only alternative for the region of exit or any other aspirant appears to be matching local production conditions to those in the competitor place, lowering wages and reproduction costs to the lower common denominator. Much of the stress on improving local 'business climates' in a country like the United States in the past two decades has been driven by the belief that localities have no other options.

Alarmed by the welfare implications of such a strategy, economists, geographers and economic development planners have sought for over a decade for alternative models of development that combine sustaining or transforming existing activities in ways that maintain relatively high wage levels, social wages and quality of life. They have done so largely with inductive methods, searching for the exceptions to the rule and examining the structure and operation of such 'sticky places'. One extensively researched formulation is that of the 'flexibly, specialized' or 'new industrial district' (NID), based on the phenomenon of successful expansion of mature industries in the Emilia-Romagna region of Italy (Best 1990; Goodman and Bamford 1989; Piore and Sabel 1984; Scott 1988a, 1988b; Storper 1989). NIDs owe their stickiness to the role of small, innovative firms, embedded within a regionally cooperative system of industrial governance which enables them to adopt and flourish despite globalizing tendencies.

In this paper, I argue that there are at least three other types of industrial districts, or 'sticky places', which have demonstrated resiliency in the postwar period in advanced industrialized countries. Stickiness connotes both ability to attract as well as to keep, like fly tape, and thus it applies to both new and established regions. Based on an inductive analysis of the more successful metropolitan regions in the United States, I show that structures and dynamic paths quite different from those captured in the NIDs formulation have enabled both relatively mature and up-and-coming regions to weather heightened capital mobility. Contrary to the emphasis on small firms in the NIDs formulation, these alternative models demonstrate the continued power of the state and/or multinational corporations under certain circumstances to shape and anchor industrial districts, providing the glue that makes it difficult for smaller firms to leave, encouraging them to stay and expand, and attracting newcomers into the region. They exhibit greater propensities for networking across district lines, rather than within, and a much greater tendency to be exogenously driven and thus focused on external policy issues than do NIDs. From a welfare point of view, the four types perform quite differently with regard to income distribution, permissiveness towards labour organization, short to medium-term cyclicality and longer-run vulnerability to secular change.

Identifying and analysing sticky places

The three alternative models of sticky places developed in this paper were constructed through a process of inductive inquiry similar to that used in researching NIDs. For the latter, extensive research on particular cases, sometimes comparing across several, has been used to identify causal forces and structural configurations. Piore and Sabel (1984) and Sabel (1989) studied the Third Italy intensively in developing their notions of flexible specialization and industrial districts. In the US, Christopherson and Storper's work on the film industry in Los Angeles (1986), Scott (1986) and Scott and Paul's work on Orange County (1990), and Saxenian's work on Silicon Valley (1990, 1991a, 1991b, 1994) enabled them to derive propositions on how secular changes in technology and markets enabled and rewarded new forms of regional industrial organization. Vigorous debate on the accuracy and applicability of the NIDs formulation ensued, enlivening the economic geography literature for the better part of a decade (e.g. Amin and Robins 1990; Amin and Thrift 1992; Ettlinger 1992; Florida and Kenney 1990; Gertler 1988; Glasmeier 1988; Harrison 1992; Lovering 1990, 1991; Malecki 1987; Markusen 1991; Pollert 1988; Schoenberger 1988).

The research summarized here had its origins in a larger research project to determine the extent to which the NIDs model could explain the durability and flourishing of regional economies in the United States, Japan, Korea and Brazil as adequately as it appeared to do so in the Third Italy. Empirical testing of the NIDs model has been surprisingly thin. Few attempts have been made to determine whether existing agglomerations are 'flexibly specialized' – an exception is Feldman's (1993) remarkable study of US industrial agglomeration – or to determine whether major industries are well characterized by this post-Fordist formulation (see Luria (1990) for an excellent investigation of the auto industry in this regard). No author has rigorously set out the features of new industrial districts in ways that permit easy assessment of their incidence and growth across space and time. The limits of the flexibly specialized new industrial district as an emergent paradigmatic form (a claim made by Scott 1988a, 1988b) are best established by demonstrating that other industrial district profiles are both theoretically plausible and empirically demonstrable.

In each country studied in our larger project, it was clear that certain mature as well as newer agglomerations exhibited an ability to weather the levelling effect of accelerated world market integration and the global search for profitability, attributes which make space 'slippery'. But most of these enclaves did not match the features of the flexibly specialized industrial district of the NIDs literature. Just as deindustrializing regions are quite remarkably distinguishable from each other, as Massey and Meegan have deftly shown (Massey and Meegan 1982; Massey 1984), regions hosting rapid growth and/or escaping industrial decline exhibit quite distinctly different structures. Through inductive research, we were able to identify three alternative patterns.

Our method involved a two-stage process. First, we surveyed metropolitan growth since 1970 for each of the four countries, identifying the universe of those who posted growth rates significantly higher than the national average (tables showing each of these regional sets can be found in Markusen 1995). We then chose a subset of each of these for further case study research, relying on both disaggregated data on industrial structure and expert opinion on industrial organization. For each country, we selected at least one case with apparent conformity to the NIDs formulation, and three to five others whose industrial structure and organization appeared to be quite different. We used techniques pioneered in social science case study research (Yin 1984) and leaned heavily upon interviews with business firms, trade associations, trade unions and regional economy watchers, incorporating and adding to the literature on enterprise studies and corporate interviews as a method for studying regions (Healey and Rawlinson 1993; Krumme 1969; McNee 1960; Markusen 1994; Schoenberger 1985, 1991).

Conceptually, we inquired into the presence or absence of features specified in the NIDs formulation – firm size distribution, up and downstream industrial linkages, degree of vertical disintegration, networks among district firms, district-wide governance structures, innovative capabilities, the organization of production. In addition, we explored a number of features not generally incorporated into NIDs studies (Park and Markusen 1994). First, we examined the role of the state at both the national and the regional/local level as rule maker, as producer and consumer of goods and services and as underwriter of innovation, with consequences for the distribution and anchoring of employment within and across regions (Christopherson 1993, 1994; Linge and Rich 1991; Markusen *et al.* 1991; Markusen and Park 1993; Saxenian 1994). Second, we scrutinized the role of large firms, especially those with internal and external market power, in industrial agglomerations (Amin and Robins 1990; Dicken 1992; Gereffi and Korzeniewicz 1994; Harrison 1994; Sayer 1989). Third, we examined the embeddedness of firms both within their districts and in non-local networks extending across national and international space (Granovetter 1985; Linge 1991; Markusen 1994; Storper and Harrison 1991). Fourth, since sources of profitability vary over the course of an industry's maturation and are linked to changing forms of competition, organizational structures, occupational characteristics and locational tendencies (Markusen 1985), we investigated the longer-term developmental dynamic of major industries and their constituents present in the district, to determine their resiliency and/or vulnerability to longer-term atrophy. Fifth, we assessed the long-term dynamic potential of each region, including the likely trajectory and future competitiveness of its existing industrial ensemble and the ability of the latter to release locally anchored resources, human and physical, into new, unrelated, specialized sectors. Finally, we searched for connections between district structure and operation and a number of social welfare metrics, including employment growth rates over time, cyclical stability, associated income and wealth distribution, trade union presence and political diversity.

A bit more can be said about this final component of the research. Evaluation of the welfare implications of each type of sticky place is a complex task and one rarely undertaken. Scholars of the NIDs literature have generally written in a normatively favourable if implicit way about the virtues of NIDs as providers of good jobs and long-term stability and dynamism – this is especially palpable in the treatments of Piore and Sabel (1984), Best (1990) and Saxenian (1994). A sticky place is 'better' in our normative view if it (1) ensures average or better than average growth for a region as a whole over time; (2) insulates a region from the job loss and firm failures of short- to intermediate-term business or political spending cycles; (3) provides relatively good jobs, ameliorates tendencies towards income duality, and prevents undue concentration of wealth and ownership; (4) fosters worker representation and participation in firm decision-making; and (5) encourages participation and tolerates contestation in regional politics.

Our research findings enabled us to develop several schematic alternatives to NIDs. Like Storper and Harrison (1991), we opt for an expansive connotation of industrial district, which does not confine it to the most common usage, called here the Marshallian (or Italianate variant) district. Elsewhere, we offer the following definition: an industrial district is a sizeable and spatially delimited area of new trade-oriented economic activity which has a distinctive economic specialization, be it resource-related, manufacturing or services (Park and Markusen 1994).

In what follows, I present four distinctive industrial spatial types: (1) the Marshallian NID, with its recent Italianate variety; (2) the hub-and-spoke district, where regional structure revolves around one or several major corporations in one or a few industries; (3) the satellite industrial platform, comprising chiefly branch plants of absent multinational corporations – this type of district may take either a high-tech, branch-plant form or consist chiefly of low-wage, low-tax, publicly subsidized development; and (4) the state-centred district, a more eclectic category, where a major government tenant anchors the regional economy (a capital city, key military or research facility, public corporation). The hypothesized features of each are summarized in Table 5.1. Schematic visual models of each of the first three, showing relative firm size and interfirm connections, both inside and outside the district, are offered in Figure 5.1. Here, firm relationships within the region are depicted inside the circle versus those outside it – suppliers to the left, customers to the right. A real world district may be an amalgam of one or more types, and over time, districts may mutate from one type to another. This conceptualization complements the geographical industrialization schema of Storper and Walker (1989: figure 3.1). While theirs is process-centred, the one offered here is region-centred, with a focus on firm size, interconnections and internal versus external orientations.

Table 5.1 Hypothesized features of new industrial district types

Marshallian industrial districts

- Business structure dominated by small, locally owned firms
- Scale economies relatively low
- Substantial intra-district trade among buyers and suppliers
- Key investment decisions made locally
- Long-term contracts and commitments between local buyers and suppliers
- Low degree of cooperation or linkage with firms external to the district
- Labour market internal to the district, highly flexible
- Workers committed to district, rather than to firms
- High rates of labour in-migration, lower levels of out-migration
- Evolution of unique local cultural identity, bonds
- Specialized sources of finance, technical expertise, business services available in district outside of firms
- Existence of 'patient capital' within district
- Turmoil, but good long-term prospects for growth and employment

Italianate variant (in addition to the above)

- High incidence of exchanges of personnel between customers and suppliers
- High degree of cooperation among competitor firms to share risk, stabilize market, share innovation
- Disproportionate share of workers engaged in design, innovation
- Strong trade associations that provide shared infrastructure – management,

training, marketing, technical or financial help, i.e. mechanisms for risk sharing and stabilization
- Strong local government role in regulating and promoting core industries

Hub-and-spoke districts
- Business structure dominated by one or several large, vertically integrated firms surrounded by suppliers
- Core firms embedded non-locally, with substantial links to suppliers and competitors outside the district
- Scale economies relatively high
- Low rates of turnover of local business except in third tier
- Substantial intra-district trade among dominant firms and suppliers
- Key investment decisions made locally, but spread out globally
- Long-term contracts and commitments between dominant firms and suppliers
- High degree of cooperation, linkages with external firms both locally and externally
- Moderate incidence of exchanges of personnel between customers and suppliers
- Low degree of cooperation among large competitor firms to share risk, stabilize market, share innovation
- Labour market internal to the district, less flexible
- Disproportionate share of blue collar workers
- Workers committed to large firms first, then to district, then to small firms
- High rates of labour in-migration, but less out-migration
- Evolution of unique local cultural identity, bonds
- Specialized sources of finance, technical expertise, business services dominated by large firms
- Little 'patient capital' within district outside of large firms
- Absence of trade associations that provide shared infrastructure – management, training, marketing, technical or financial help, i.e. mechanisms for risk sharing and stabilization
- Strong local government role in regulating and promoting core industries in local and provincial and national government
- High degree of public involvement in providing infrastructure
- Long-term prospects for growth dependent upon prospects for the industry and strategies of dominant firms

Satellite industrial platforms
- Business structure dominated by large, externally owned and headquartered firms
- Scale economies moderate to high
- Low rates of turnover of platform tenants
- Minimal intra-district trade among buyers and suppliers
- Key investment decisions made externally
- Absence of long-term commitments to suppliers locally
- High degree of cooperation, linkages with external firms, especially with parent company
- High incidence of exchanges of personnel between customers and suppliers externally but not locally
- Low degree of cooperation among competitor firms to share risk, stabilize market, share innovation
- Labour market external to the district, internal to vertically integrated firm
- Workers committed to firm rather than district
- High rates of labour in-migration and out-migration at managerial/professional/technical levels; little at blue and pink collar levels

- Little evolution of unique local cultural identity, bonds
- Main sources of finance, technical expertise, business services provided externally, through firm or external purchase
- No 'patient capital' within district
- No trade associations that provide shared infrastructure – management, training, marketing, technical or financial help, i.e. mechanisms for risk sharing and stabilization
- Strong local government role in providing infrastructure, tax breaks and other generic business inducements
- Growth jeopardized by intermediate-run portability of plants and activities elsewhere to similarly constructed platforms

State-anchored industrial districts

- Business structure dominated by one or several large, government institutions such as military bases, state or national capitals, large public universities, surrounded by suppliers and customers (including those regulated)
- Scale economies relatively high in public sector activities
- Low rates of turnover of local business
- Substantial intra-district trade among dominant institutions and suppliers, but not among others
- Key investment decisions made at various levels of government, some internal, some external
- Short-term contracts and commitments between dominant institutions and suppliers, customers
- High degree of cooperation, linkages with external firms for externally headquartered suppliers' organizations
- Moderate incidence of exchanges of personnel between customers and suppliers
- Low degree of cooperation among local private sector firms to share risk, stabilize market, share innovation
- Labour market internal if state capital, national if university or military facility or other federal offices for professional/technical and managerial workers
- Disproportionate share of clerical and professional workers
- Workers committed to large institutions first, then to district, then to small firms
- High rates of labour in-migration, but less out-migration unless government is withdrawing or closing down
- Evolution of unique local cultural identity, bonds
- No specialized sources of finance, technical expertise, business services
- No 'patient capital' within district
- Weak trade associations to share information about public sector client
- Weak local government role in regulating and promoting core activities
- High degree of public involvement in providing infrastructure
- Long-term prospects for growth dependent upon prospects for government facilities at core

---

Each spatial type is presented with a set of hypothesized traits, and the resilience and/or vulnerability of each to events in the changing global economy are noted. Districts which are sticky in one era may fail to cohere in the longer run – the glue may dry up, become brittle and lose its adhesive quality. Central to the differences among sticky places and their ability to persist are the presence (or absence) of distinctive and lopsided power

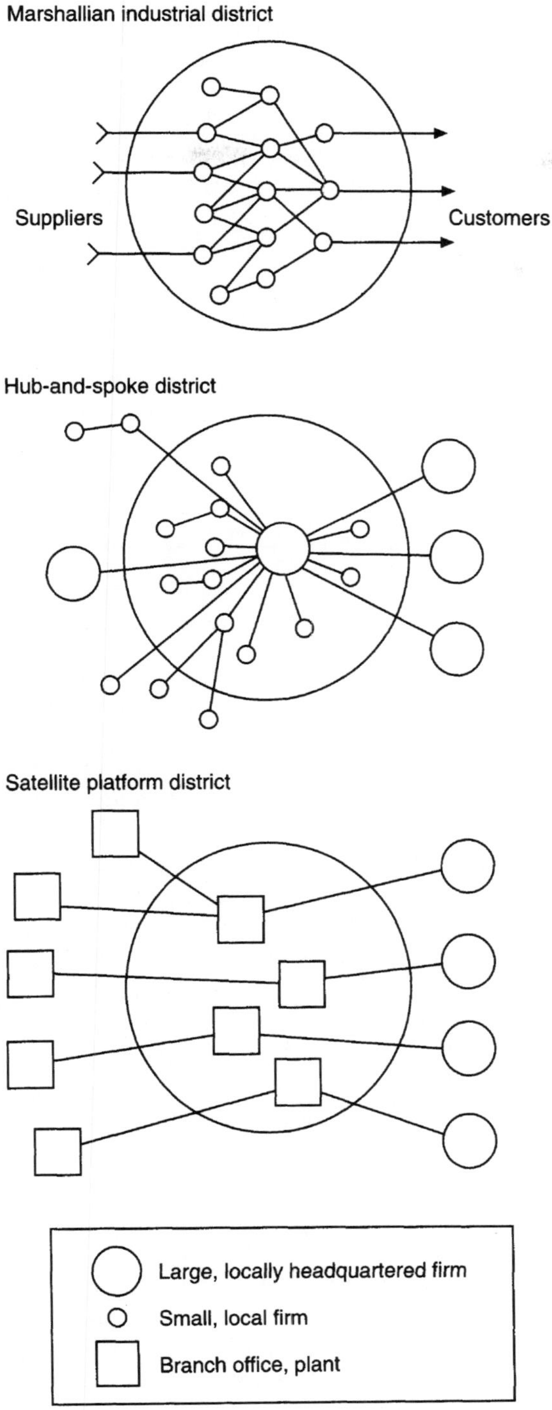

Figure 5.1 Firm size, connections and local versus non-local embeddedness

relationships, sometimes within the district and sometimes between district entities and those residing elsewhere. Examples of each type can only be mentioned in passing here, but are the subject of complementary papers (e.g. Golob *et al.* 1995; Gray *et al.* 1996; Markusen 1994; Markusen and Park 1993; Markusen and Sasaki 1994; Park and Markusen 1994).

The focus on rapidly growing industrial spaces helps us to develop an impressionistic sense of the relative contribution of each type to overall regional restructuring. In the United States, for instance, the fastest-growing industrial cities (as opposed to residentiary cities, where retirement communities account for the bulk of growth) include the fifteen listed in Table 5.2, all of which added manufacturing employment at rates of 50% or more over the period 1970 to 1990, compared with a zero rate of growth nationally. These may be contrasted with the performance of the four major older industrial centres of New York, Boston, Chicago and Los Angeles, at the bottom of the table. Very few of these fast-growing regions, I shall argue, can be characterized as NIDs, but many of them reproduce the conditions present in the other three models of 'sticky places' presented below.

Marshallian and Italianate industrial districts

An extensive and recent literature on industrial districts focuses on the Marshallian industrial district and its more cooperative, embedded Italianate progeny. Since the characteristics hypothesized for these districts are relatively well known, I summarize them briefly here, with particular emphasis on those which may be contrasted to the district types presented below.

In his original formulation of the industrial district, Marshall envisioned a region where the business structure comprises small, locally owned firms that make investment and production decisions locally. Scale economies are relatively low, forestalling the rise of large firms. Within the district, substantial trade is transacted between buyers and sellers, and often entails long-term contracts or commitments. Although Marshall did not explicitly say so, linkages and/or cooperation with firms outside the district are assumed to be minimal. The Marshallian industrial district is depicted in the top portion of Figure 5.1, with many small firms buying and selling from each other for eventual export from the region. The arrows show necessary purchases of raw materials and business services from outside the region on the left and sales to external markets on the right, in the form of purely exchange rather than cooperative relationships external to the region.

What makes the industrial district so special and vibrant, in Marshall's account, is the nature and quality of the local labour market, which is internal to the district and highly flexible. Individuals move from firm to firm, and owners as well as workers live in the same community where they benefit from the fact that 'the secrets of industry are in the air'. Workers are committed to the district rather than to the firm. Labour out-migration is minimal, while in-migration occurs as growth permits. The district is seen as

Table 5.2 Selected US metropolitan employment growth rates, 1970–90

	Employment, 1990 (in '000s)	*Employment, change (%), 1970–90*	*Manufacturing employment, 1990 (in '000s)*	*Manufacturing change (%), 1970–90*	*Service employment, 1990 (in '000s)*	*Service change (%), 1970–90*
Colorado Springs, CO	228	104	24	261	60	214
Austin, TX	471	178	50	249	131	253
Reno, NV	145	155	9	202	70	184
Tucson, AZ	316	123	28	199	101	219
Huntsville, AL	163	76	34	177	42	82
Orlando, FL	569	246	56	162	236	465
Albuquerque, NM	305	125	22	131	98	184
Melbourne/Titusville, FL	202	112	31	122	66	119
San Jose, CA	1,015	128	273	119	301	199
San Diego, CA	1,397	120	141	109	390	254
Anaheim/Santa Ana, CA	1,552	192	261	111	464	352
Raleigh/Durham, NC	513	123	66	94	145	175
Seattle, WA	1,339	114	227	73	362	206
Madison, WI	262	73	26	53	62	147
Elkhart/Goshen, IN	116	64	52	50	20	123
Los Angeles/Long Beach, CA	5,200	56	893	9	1,707	129
Boston/Lawrence/Salem, MA	1,672	30	340	–12	894	108
Chicago, IL	3,673	23	569	–33	1,128	101
New York, NY	4,765	2	428	–51	1,704	50
United States (total)	*110,321*	*56*	*19,742*	*0*	*37,573*	*126*

Source: US Department of Commerce, Bureau of Economic Analysis (1970, 1990). Estimates of suppressed data were computed by Andrew Isserman and Oleg Smirnov, Regional Research Institute, West Virginia University, and compiled by Ann Markusen and Mia Gray

a relatively stable community which enables the evolution of a local cultural identity and a shared industrial expertise.

The Marshallian district also encompasses a relatively specialized set of services which are tailored to the unique products/industries of the district. These services include technical expertise in certain product lines, machinery and marketing, and maintenance and repair services as well. They include local financial institutions offering so-called 'patient capital', willing to take longer-term risks because they have both inside information and trust in the entrepreneurs of local firms.

All of these features are subsumable under the notion of agglomeration, which suggests that the stickiness of a place resides not in the individual locational calculus of firms or workers, but in the external economies available to each firm from its spatial conjunction with other firms and suppliers of services. In Marshall's formulation, it was not necessary that any of these actors should be consciously cooperating with each other in order for the district to exist and operate as such. But in a more recent formulation, emerging from research on Italian industrial districts and extended to other venues in Europe and the United States, researchers have argued that concerted efforts to cooperate among district members and to build governance structures to improve district-wide competitiveness can improve prospects, i.e. increase the stickiness of the district.

Features characterizing Italianate districts are articulated in intensive case studies on the Italian case (Bellandi 1989; Bull *et al.* 1991; Goodman 1989; Piore and Sabel 1984; Sforzi 1989). These have been reworked and adapted to American cases – Orange County (Scott 1986; Scott and Paul 1990) and Silicon Valley (Saxenian 1994) – though not without debate (Florida and Kenney 1990; Malecki 1987; Saxenian 1991a). The unifying notion is that firms (often with the help of regional governments and trade associations) consciously 'network' to solve problems of cycles and overcapacity and to respond to new demands for flexibility (Amin and Thrift 1992). In the American version, rigidities in older industrial cities tend to encourage these agglomerations to root anew in relatively virgin locations (Markusen 1991; Scott 1988b; Storper and Walker 1989). Few cases have been identified outside Europe or the United States – candidates are subdistricts such as the southern sector of Tokyo and Kangwan, a south-side district in Seoul.

Unlike the passivity of Marshall's firms, Italianate districts exhibit frequent and intensive exchanges of personnel between customers and suppliers, and cooperation among competitor firms to share risk, stabilize markets and share innovation. Disproportionate shares of workers are engaged in design and innovative activities. Activist trade associations provide shared infrastructure – management, training, marketing, technical or financial help – as well as providing forums to hammer out collective strategy. Local and regional governments may be central in regulating and promoting core industries. Trust among district members is central to their ability to cooperate and act collectively (Harrison 1992; Saxenian 1994), although critics argue that the power of large corporations to shape Italian industrial districts has been understated (see the discussion in Harrison 1994: chapter 4).

In assessing growth, stability, equity and politics of Italianate industrial districts, the Italian variety must be distinguished from the Silicon Valley and Orange County cases, and each from their Marshallian predecessors. As for growth and stability, as long as agglomeration economies remain and are not replicated in other locales, both Marshallian and Italianate industrial districts retain good long-term prospects for growth and development. Although more standardized functions may be hived off and driven elsewhere by inflated regional costs, innovation (so the theory goes) will ensure the revitalization of these 'seedbeds of innovation'. But other hypotheses have been advanced. Agglomerative specialization and success in one industry, especially when associated with some degree of market power and/or dominance over region factor markets, can actually impede the development of other sectors whose presence might diversify the economy and counteract maturation or instability in the original sector. Pittsburgh in the late nineteenth and Detroit in the early decades of the twentieth century resembled Italianate districts and Silicon Valley, but the evolution of oligopoly and the crowding out of other sectors left both quite vulnerable to the inevitable maturation and decentralization of those industries (Chinitz 1960; Markusen 1985).

On the equity front, the high-tech Silicon Valleys and Orange Counties depart strikingly from the Italian industrial districts. The latter are often the creatures of resilient cultures, organized politically on the basis of long-standing communities, unions and the Italian communist party. Fundamental to their governance structures are strong leadership roles for unions and guarantees that most enterprises will be stabilized and nurtured, even during downturns. This has helped to stabilize incomes and assure relatively good income distributions within the districts. In the California cases, in contrast, district cooperation, where it exists, is purely between entrepreneurs and firms that operate in a non-union environment and where there is little pre-existing community to ameliorate vicious competition and failure in periods of instability. Income distribution tends to be highly dualized in such regions (Harrison 1994; Saxenian 1983). Furthermore, politics within such districts tends towards the conservative, laissez-faire end of the spectrum – Orange County is famous as the home of the John Birch society, and Silicon Valley as a hotbed of free trade and anti-union business activism.

Despite the often extravagant claims of some of its protagonists, the 'new industrial districts' approach has much to offer and has deservedly captured the imagination of scholars and local economic development activists alike. But many of the faster-growing regions of the world turn out not to be primarily characterized by these same features. Furthermore, other structural forms may be associated with superior welfare and political cultures. It is to these other types of sticky places that we now turn.

Hub-and-spoke industrial districts

Another quite different type of industrial district is represented by regions where a number of key firms and/or facilities act as anchors or hubs to the regional economy, with suppliers and related activities spread out around them like spokes of a wheel. Examples are Seattle and central New Jersey, USA; Toyota City, Japan; Ulsan and Pohang, South Korea; and São José dos Campos in Brazil. A simple version of this form is depicted in the middle frame of Figure 5.1, where a single large firm (e.g. Boeing in Seattle or Toyota in Toyota City) buys from both local and external suppliers, and sells chiefly to external customers who may be large (e.g. the airlines, the military in the case of Boeing) or masses of individual consumers (Toyota). Intensive case studies of hub-and-spoke districts include Seattle (Gray *et al.* 1996), central New Jersey (Fineberg *et al.* 1993), and São José dos Campos and Campinas, Brazil (Diniz and Razavi 1994).

The dynamism in hub-and-spoke economies is associated with the position of these anchor organizations in their national and international markets. Other local firms tend to have subordinate relationships to them. If over time the anchors evoke a critical mass of agglomerated skilled labour and business services around them, they may set off a more diversified developmental process where new firms form few connections to hub firms other than benefiting from the urbanization and agglomeration economies they have created.

Hub-and-spoke districts are thus dominated by one or several large, vertically integrated firms, in one or more sectors, surrounded by smaller and less powerful suppliers. Hub-and-spoke districts may exhibit either a strongly linked form, where smaller firms are quite dependent upon the large anchor firm or institution for either markets or supplies, or a weaker, more nucleated form, in which small firms enjoy the agglomerative externalities of larger organizations' presence without necessarily buying or selling to them. In some versions, the large player(s) may be oligopolists in a single industry, as with the big three auto corporations in Detroit or Toyota in Toyota City. Unrelated or loosely linked hubs in several industries may also co-exist in a region. In Seattle, for instance, the economy is organized around Weyerhauser as the dominant resource sector company, Boeing as the dominant industrial employer (commercial aircraft and military/spacecraft), Microsoft as the leading services firm, the Hutchinson Cancer Center as the progenitor of a series of biotechnology firms, and the Port of Seattle as the transportation hub. Core firms or institutions are embedded non-locally, with substantial links to suppliers, competitors and customers outside the district. Internal scale and scope economies are relatively high, and turnover of firms and personnel relatively low except in third-tier suppliers or in major downturns in hub industries. Key investment decisions are made locally but their consequences are spread out globally.

Hub-and-spoke districts may exhibit intra-district cooperation, but it will generally be on the terms of the hub firm. Substantial intra-district trade will take place among suppliers and hub firms, often embodied in long-term contracts and commitments. Cooperation may entail efforts to upgrade supplier quality, timeliness and inventory control, and it may extend outside district boundaries to suppliers further afield. Exchanges of personnel may take place, though not to the extent found in Italianate industrial districts. Markedly lacking is the cooperation among competitor firms to share risk, stabilize the market and share innovation. Strategic alliances on the part of the larger firms are more apt to be forged with partners outside the region.

The labour market in hub-and-spoke districts is internal to both large hub firms and to the district, though it is less flexible than in the Italianate model. Workers' loyalties are to core firms first, then to the district, and only after that to small firms. If jobs open up in hub firms, workers will often abandon smaller employers to get on to the hub firms' payroll. This factor makes it tougher for smaller firms in some segments of the industry to survive. Hub firms attract new labour into the conurbation, however, which helps to counterbalance the power imbalance in the labour market.

Hub-and-spoke districts do evolve unique local cultures related to hub activities. Detroit is known as Motor City, and sports teams of many cities have been named after dominant sectors – the Oilers, the Steelers, the Brewers, the Pistons, the Millers (the old Minneapolis team). They develop considerable expertise in the labour pool in specialized industrial capabilities, and they engender specialized business service sectors tailored to their needs. Although these latter are focused on the large hub firms, some can become less dependent by extending their markets to other competitor firms in far-flung locales. An extensive discussion of how a small firm experiences its position in a hub-and-spoke economy is included in Markusen (1994).

Districts of this sort lack some of the more celebrated governance structures of the Italianate industrial districts. They often lack 'patient capital', local venture capital specially tailored to start-ups in their industry. The largest returns to trade tend to be tied up as retained earnings in the major hub firms, who are happy to redeploy it wherever across the globe their strategic plans call for. The few trade associations that exist are relatively weak, often because top hub managers absent themselves from their deliberations and activities. Hub firms will concern themselves with state and local governmental activities that impinge upon their land use, tax and regulatory situations, and will try politically to ensure that area politicians represent the interests of their firm and industries at the national and international levels. They may also be actively involved in issues that affect their workforce and ability to do business – especially in improving area educational institutions and the provision of infrastructure.

In the long run, hub-and-spoke districts are quite dependent upon their major industries and firms within them for their stickiness. Growth and stability can be jeopardized by intermediate-run portability of plants and activities away from the region, or by the long-term decline of the industry, or by poor management of the principal firms. But stickiness also depends upon the degree to which mature sectors can release local resources into new, unrelated sectors. A sobering historical example of the vulnerability of hub-and-spoke districts is Detroit, where a turn-of-the-century Marshallian district (perhaps with some Italianate features) transformed itself into a hub-and-spoke district around the auto oligopoly by the 1930s. Here, to vastly oversimplify, Detroit's vitality was severely taxed by the oligopolistic rigidity of the locally headquartered auto industry combined with concerted investment on the part of the Japanese state and auto corporations in building a rival agglomeration around Toyota near Nagoya, Japan. Furthermore, tight oligopsonistic control over the Detroit area's resources prevented the diversification of its economy (Chinitz 1960). A counter example is Seattle, where several unique features of Boeing as the undisputed anchor to the regional economy (and the undisputed lead firm in the world aerospace industry) have contributed to (or at least not prevented) the region's diversification into other sectors – port-related activities, software, biotechnology – positioning it well to withstand retrenchment and global decentralization in the aircraft industry (Gray *et al.* 1996).

Hub-and-spoke industrial districts may be characterized by relatively good income distributions. If so, this is due to both structural and institutional causes. Market power, often present in hub-and-spoke cases, results in relatively high returns to capital, a necessary though not sufficient condition for the sharing of such returns with the workforce in the form of higher wages. The presence of large anchor firms, non-profit and public institutions may also reflect natural economies of scale which are associated with large capital outlays and therefore high levels of labour productivity, available for distribution in wages. Securing this labour share is most often dependent on the presence of unions or the threat of their emergence. More vigorous political competition between pro-business and pro-labour constituencies is apt to hold sway in such districts.

Satellite platforms

A third variant of rapidly growing industrial districts can be termed the satellite platform – a congregation of branch facilities of externally based multi-plant firms. Often these are assembled at a distance from major conurbations by national governments or entrepreneurial provincial governments as a way of stimulating regional development in outlying areas and simultaneously lowering the cost of business for competitively squeezed firms bristling under relatively high urban wages, rents and taxation. Tenants of satellite platforms may range from routine assembly functions to relatively sophisticated research, but they must be able to more or less 'stand alone', detachable spatially from either up or downstream operations within the same firm or from agglomerations of competitors and external suppliers or customers (Glasmeier 1988).

Satellite platforms can be found in almost all countries, regardless of development. An outstanding high-end example in the United States is the internationally much-admired Research Triangle Park, a collection of unrelated research centres of major multinational corporations (Luger and Goldstein 1990), while a comparable low-end US case is Elkhart, Indiana, where a number of auto-related branch plants have been attracted by relatively low-wage labour. In South Korea, Kumi constitutes a low-end textile and electronics platform, while Ansan operates as an odd collection of disparate industrial polluters grouped together (Park and Markusen 1994). In Japan, some of the better-performing technopoles, such as Oita and Kumamoto, fall into this category (Markusen and Sasaki 1994). In Brazil, a remarkable case is the state-sponsored expansion of Manaus as an import/export zone (Diniz and Borges Santos 1995).

In satellite platforms, business structure is dominated by large, externally situated firms that make key investment decisions. Scale economies within each facility are moderate to high, and rates of turnover of platform tenants are low. Minimal intra-district trade or even conversation takes place among platform tenants. Orders and commitments to local suppliers are conspicuously absent. Since platforms generally host heterogeneous firms in terms of product if not industry and are remotely controlled, they do not operate as cooperative ventures among resident plants to share risk, stabilize the market or engage in innovative partnerships. In this they differ from hub-and-spoke districts, where the large multilocational firm or institution is locally based. This type of sticky place is presented in the lower portion of Figure 5.1 – its most conspicuous feature is the absence of any connections or networks within the region and the predominance of links to the parent corporation and other branch plants elsewhere.

It is not as if branch operations, however, are not embedded in relationships external to the facility. They cooperate and communicate daily with the parent company. Personnel exchanges are common between branch operations and the headquarters firm, but not locally with other branch facilities. To buttress this non-place embeddedness, the labour market within which each facility operates, at least in the high-end version and for management and some technical talent in the low-end version, across district boundaries – it is internal to the vertically integrated firm, rather than to the district. This means that there will be high rates of labour migration in and out of the district at the managerial, professional and technical levels. Often skilled professionals who originated from the region will be disproportionately represented. Only blue and pink collar labour will be hired locally, which may, however, not be inconsequential.

Over time, districts built around platforms may begin to host growth of suppliers, oriented towards platform tenants, and they may enjoy some increase in local entrepreneurship because the platform enhances the pool of skilled personnel resident in the region. But in cases studied to date, the incidence of such activity is small, and the aggregate growth of the region is still very much tied to the number of tenants that can be attracted and to the ability to retain them (Howes 1993).

A number of features of the satellite platform constrain its development into a better-articulated regional economy. First of all, the main sources of finance, technical expertise and business services are external to the region, furnished through corporate headquarters. Satellite districts have little 'patient capital' to draw upon, and because substantive activities are diverse, they lack industry-specific trade associations that would provide shared infrastructure and help with management, training and marketing problems. These will only be partially compensated for by strong national or local government efforts and services offered by chambers of commerce and other associations of local fixed capital.

Satellite platforms' future growth is jeopardized by the intermediate-run portability of plants and activities elsewhere to similarly constructed platforms. Those concentrating on higher-end activities, where stability and amenities in the residential sphere are essential to drawing and keeping skilled personnel, will be less vulnerable in this regard, while purely low-cost districts will be more so, especially if fixed capital investment is low. Since individual plants and facilities are disparate and outward looking, satellite platforms do not engender the development of unique local cultural bonds or new identities, even though they may destroy pre-existing ones. Thus they may be less sticky, especially if less skilled, than other types of district. Hosting communities face the challenge of trying to parlay resources assembled by such facilities into other diversifying and home-grown sectors. They do remain sticky, however, to the extent that large capital investments are made in the process of occupying them.

The record on income distribution in satellite platforms is mixed. In all countries studied, the entry of such platforms into previously depressed regions does contribute to a higher overall per capita income (and perhaps a depression of those in regions of exit). Within the region, income distributional consequences depend on the nature of the industry and activity. Good blue collar jobs in a depressed agricultural region will improve the income distribution. In technical branch-plant platforms, the creation of a significant number of clerical and technician jobs may help to ameliorate the skewness introduced by operations that are top-heavy with managers and professionals. This seems to have occurred in the case of Research Triangle Park (Luger and Goldstein 1990). However, satellite platforms by their very nature artificially cordon off employment in some operations of a corporation from those in other regions, spreading income inequality out spatially. Somewhat better jobs for rural Japan or small-town Alabama placed on a satellite platform obscure the concentration of top-paid corporate jobs elsewhere and the deterioration in the income distribution in a Detroit or inner-city Tokyo, especially for blue collar workers.

The implications for the complexion of politics in satellite platform regions is also mixed. In some cases – Japan, for instance – the creation of such platforms under the technopolis strategy has coopted militant, often anti-business, prefectural movements for environmental cleanup and an improved quality of life, re-directing their energies and local resources into speculative economic development activities. In other cases, new satellite platforms have helped break the stranglehold of traditionally dominant 'good old boy' parties by introducing educated people and new immigrants into the region and contributing to more contested local politics.

State-anchored districts

A fourth form of sticky place is what we call the state-anchored industrial district, where a public or non-profit entity, be it a military base, a defence plant, a weapons lab, a university, a prison complex or a concentration of government offices, is a key anchor tenant in the district. Here, the local business structure is dominated by the presence of such facilities, whose locational calculus and economic relationships are determined in the political realm, rather than by private sector firms. This type of district is much more difficult to theorize about, because contingencies particular to the type of activity involved colour its operation and characteristics. It is apt to look much like the hub-and-spoke district in Figure 5.1, although a facility can operate with few connections to the regional economy, resembling the satellite platform case. Nevertheless, some commonalities can be noted.

Before doing so, however, we shall simply cite some of the examples of such districts. Many of the fastest-growing industrial districts in the United States and elsewhere owe their performance to the presence, new location or expansion of state facilities. Military bases, military academies and weapons labs, for instance, explain the phenomenal postwar growth of US cities like Santa Fe, Albuquerque, San Diego and Colorado Springs, while defence plants contributed dramatically to the growth of Los Angeles, Silicon Valley and Seattle (Markusen *et al.* 1991). State universities and/or state capitals explain the prominence of cities like Madison, Ann Arbor, Sacramento, Austin and Boulder among fastest-growing US cities. Denver owes much of its postwar growth to its hosting of the second largest concentration of federal government offices in the nation. In Japan and South Korea, the government research complexes at Tsukuba and Taejon, respectively, have fuelled growth in their environs. In Brazil, Campinas owes much to its top-ranked university, while São José dos Campos' growth is based on the government-owned, military-oriented aerospace complex (Diniz and Razavi 1994).

In general, scale economies are relatively high in such complexes. Because state-owned or state-dependent facilities are so large, supplier sectors do grow up around them, dependent upon the level of public expenditure. Short-term contracts and commitment do exist between state 'customers' and their suppliers, subject to political change. In the case of state capitals and universities, high degrees of cooperation may exist between the customer and suppliers, and activity will be relatively immune from the threat of exodus. This is less true for national facilities, especially in times of fiscal stringency or redundancy of function (e.g. the current closing of military bases in the

US). In nationally funded facilities, decisions are made external to the district and may be more indifferent to regional development impacts.

When government contracting is involved, especially in areas like defence, the arcane and elaborate nature of the contracting process may encourage the development of long-term supply relationships, based on a fairly strong degree of trust and cooperation. However, these ties need not be localized – they may span thousands of miles between Los Angeles or Silicon Valley and Washington, DC, for instance, or most of the length of a country like Korea as between Changwon and Seoul (Golob *et al.* 1995; Markusen and Park 1993).

Labour markets will be tailored to the particular state activity hosted. For state capitals, the labour market will tend to be relatively local or regional. Personnel may cycle between state customers and local suppliers. For universities and national facilities, labour markets will operate externally for the higher-skilled occupations. In the case of military bases, blue collar and unskilled positions will also be filled from a labour market national in scope. Workers' loyalties will be devoted to large state institutions and/or state-dependent facilities first, then to the district, then to firms.

Indigenous firms will play less of a role in these districts than in Marshallian or hub-and-spoke districts. Some may emerge out of specialized technology transfer (universities) or business service functions (lobbying). Firms will not tend to cooperate to stabilize markets or hedge against risk since they are not preoccupied with stabilizing demand in the same way that Marshallian districts with mature industries might. In general, trade associations will be relatively weak, and local government's role in regulating and promoting district activities will be minimal (think, for instance, of the District of Columbia's almost complete absence of power). Local fixed capital and government may adopt a sycophantic form of boosterism, designed to enhance the ability of an anchor facility to maintain or increase levels of external funding or protect it against closure.

In state-anchored industrial districts, long-term growth prospects depend on two factors – the prospects for the facility at the core of the region and the extent to which the facility encourages growth within the region by spawning local suppliers, spinning off new businesses, or supplying labour and other factors of production to the local economy. Often, the mammoth size of the facility – New Mexico's Los Alamos Laboratories, for instance, with an annual budget of $1.4 billion, mostly for personnel, or New London, Connecticut's Electric Boat submarine manufacturing facility, with its 20,000 workers – overwhelms any contribution, real or potential, that can be made through secondary effects. This means that local business and political energies tend to be focused on solidifying the facility's commitment and its level of funding. This must be pursued through politics at the relevant level and thus requires a relatively unique governance structure.

Politics in state-anchored industrial districts tends to be complex and tailored to the particularities of the form of government involvement. Military industrial districts range from the remarkably conservative (Colorado

Springs) to the remarkably liberal (New England). University towns and state capitals tend to be more liberal than cities of similar size, even within their own states, while towns hosting military bases and prisons tend to line up on the conservative end of the spectrum.

Sticky mixes

Although the presence of Marshallian industrial districts, even the Italianate version, can be confirmed in a number of American instances, the claims made for the paradigmatic ascendancy of this form of new industrial space (Scott's rubric) do not square with the experience of most rapidly growing agglomerations in industrialized and industrializing countries. In the United States, for instance, most rapidly growing industrial regions do not exhibit the characteristics of the Third Italy. Indeed, the lessons of the Italian industrial district experience are being adopted most fruitfully in the industrial Midwest as a way of stemming deindustrialization and retaining jobs in small and medium-sized firms, not in explaining new industrial spaces. Even Silicon Valley, as we show elsewhere, is more a mix of industrial district types than a pure case of Italianate industrial district (Golob *et al.* 1995). In Japan, South Korea and Brazil, it is difficult to find a single instance of a flexibly specialized industrial district outside of subareas of the major metropole. Most rapidly growing metropolitan areas owe their performance to hub firms or industries, satellite platforms and/or state anchors, or some combination thereof.

The United States can be looked at more closely in this regard. The fast-growing industrial cities in Table 5.2 can be allocated to one or more of our industrial district types. Colorado Springs, Huntsville, Melbourne/Titusville and San Diego, all military or space-dependent cities, belong in the fourth, government-facility-anchored growth areas. Madison, Austin and Albuquerque also belong in this category, the first two with both the state university and state capital, the latter with the state capital, university and various military-related facilities, including nearby Los Alamos and Sandia laboratories. Reno and Orlando's growth is primarily entertainment related, although in recent years Reno has benefited from warehousing and related operations fleeing California's tax structure. Seattle, Los Angeles and the latter's Anaheim/Santa Ana neighbour are hub-and-spoke districts organized around large defence and commercial corporations, with universities playing larger or smaller roles. Raleigh/Durham is a prototypical case of a successful high-tech satellite platform, while Elkhart/Goshen has flourished from low-wage, non-union capacity additions in aging industries.

The models of sticky places presented above are suggestive rather than definitive products of an inductive research method. Further application of these to an even broader set of regional economies will be necessary to determine how well each is constructed and how common its incidence in real space. Comprehensive comparative work across a larger applied set could tell us much about district forms and how they vary by type of industry and degree of maturity, national and regional rules and cultures, and firm and local economic development strategy.

Many localities, especially larger metropolitan areas, exhibit elements of all four models. Silicon Valley, for instance, hosts an industrial district in electronics (Saxenian 1994) but also revolves around several important hubs (Lockheed Space and Missiles, Hewlett Packard, Stanford University) as well as hosting large 'platform'-type branch plants of US, Japanese, Korean and European companies (e.g. IBM, Oki, NTK Ceramics, Hyundai, Samsung). Furthermore, it is now the fourth largest recipient of military spending contracts in the nation, shaping the defence electronics and communications sector in the Valley (Golob *et al.* 1995; Markusen *et al.* 1991; Saxenian 1985).

An intriguing question is whether regions can maintain their stickiness by transforming themselves from one type of district to another. Historically, as we have pointed out, Detroit made the transition from a Marshallian district to a hub-and-spoke district. Localities which host satellite platforms may be able to encourage backward and forward linkages that transform them into more Marshallian or hub-and-spoke-type districts – scholars debate whether this is occurring around large Japanese auto transplants in the United States. A state-centred district might do the same. A hub-and-spoke district which loses its anchor tenant may be able to create a Marshallian district in its wake, as some are trying to do in the Los Angeles aerospace industry. Recruitment or incubation of a new hub could transform a Marshallian or state-centred district into a hub-and-spoke variant, which is what Colorado Springs has been doing with new organizational headquarters like the US Olympics and the right-wing Christian Focus on the Family. More work could be done on the conditions which impede or facilitate these mutations.

This research was methodologically confined to places doing better than average, simply because this ensured they met the criterion of superior growth performance. However, many localities with stable or slowly declining growth patterns are struggling to be sticky places, and many are succeeding in stanching their losses by remaking their industrial structures. New England, for instance, began as early as the 1950s to transform itself into a diversified military industrial complex, escaping the deeper displacement that occurred post-1970 in the industrial Midwest (Markusen *et al.* 1991). Although New England has not as a region posted above-average long-term growth rates, even during the Reagan military buildup, it deserves study as a sticky place. Midwestern cities like Chicago, Milwaukee and Cleveland, with little comparative advantage in military industrial sectors, are trying to make themselves more sticky by anchoring and upgrading existing expertise in industries like metals, machining and automobiles.

Our study was conducted at the metropolitan scale, equivalent more or less to a regional labour shed. However, industrial district features can characterize smaller agglomerations within metropolitan areas. Extension of these models to the subregional scale might require relaxing one or more assumptions and altering some hypotheses.

Research and policy implications

This exercise in distinguishing among types of sticky places illustrates the diversity in spatial form, industrial complexion and maturity, institutional configurations and welfare outcomes found in contemporary regional economies. It cautions that the singular enthusiasm for flexibly specialized industrial districts, especially the high-tech American variant, is ill founded on both growth/stability and equity grounds. In large part, the problem here lies in the limits of the research strategy used in the NIDs literature – the intensive study of particular localities extracted from their embeddedness in a larger global economy. It is useful to study why certain places appear to be different and/or more successful as a means of developing hypotheses regarding features that may contribute to such success. Once identified, these then need to be tested against a larger sample, one more representative of the universe of localities.

Furthermore, the study of industrial districts and networks within them has generally been confined to smaller firms in particular industries – their links to larger firms and their links to other firms and institutions outside the region have been ignored. As a result, conclusions have been drawn about the endogenity of growth in such districts that, when viewed on a larger, more comprehensive canvas, are not warranted. Nor is the zero-sum nature of much of this growth acknowledged – that certain places grow at the expense of other places, that high-wage employment in some regions is linked to low-wage employment in others, and that only a few places can possibly aspire to becoming Silicon Valleys of the future.

In reality, sticky places are complex products of multiple forces – corporate strategies, industrial structures, profit cycles, state priorities, local and national politics. Their success cannot be studied by focusing only on local institutions and behaviours, because their companies (through corporate relationships, trade associations, trade, government contracts), workers (via migration and international unions) and other institutions (universities, government installations) are embedded in external relationships – both cooperative and competitive – that condition their commitment to the locality and their success there.

These reflections on research approach are applicable to economic development policy at both regional and national levels as well. At the former level, economic developers would be well advised to assess their existing district structures accurately and design a strategy around them, rather than committing to a fashionable strategy of small firm networking within the region. Improving cooperative relationships and building networks that reach outside the region may prove more productive for some localities than concentrating on indigenous firms. Furthermore, our work on hub-and-spoke and satellite platform structures suggests that large firms can be significant contributors to regional development, albeit posing problems of dominance and vulnerability, and that recruitment of an external firm or plant may be a good strategy for a region at a particular developmental moment. Regions might also be well advised to target national level policies shaping the competitive status of their industries and allocating public infrastructure and procurement contracts.

At the national level, a strategy to ameliorate regional competition and differential growth rates would:

- attempt to determine how many districts of each type the national economy might be expected to sustain;
- develop a strategy for stabilizing existing districts and channelling new ones to deficit areas;
- ban the use of public funds to subsidize competition among regions;
- monitor and if necessary alter national policies with substantial regional implications – devolution of powers and responsibility to subnational levels, new trade regimes (e.g. NAFTA, GATT), macroeconomic policy initiatives (e.g. deficit reduction and fiscal austerity versus stimulus), financial market structures, Third World development, international labour and human rights, international environmental standards, immigration restrictions, social safety nets, and infrastructure provisions.

In the United States at present, only the third of these has any near-term possibility of being undertaken and then only as a result of considerable bipartisan clamour in Congress.

The prominence of hub-and-spoke and satellite platforms among US sticky places suggests that economic development strategies built on cross-regional alliances might be as important to localities as purely local networking approaches. Cross-regional networks might be forged to shore up progressive institutions under attack (labour, environmental and community development gains) and create better ones at national and international levels to curb the worst products of capitalist development – poverty, insecurity, income inequality, environmental degradation. While builders of NIDs struggle to create governance structures at the local level, multinational finance and industrial leaders are crafting a World Trade Organization which would be highly undemocratic and pre-empt many of the existing rights and safeguards that workers and communities have fought for and won. More sophisticated and pluralistic profiles of industrial districts and how they operate, both internally and externally, must be joined with more intensive study of multinational corporations and state institutions if a more powerful geographical contribution to progressive strategy is to emerge.

Acknowledgements

This chapter appeared originally as 'Sticky places in slippery space: a typology of industrial districts', *Economic Geography* (1996, 72: 293–313).

Bibliography

Amin, A. and Robins, K. (1990) 'The re-emergence of regional economies? the mythical geography of flexible accumulation', *Environment and Planning D: Society and Space* 8: 7–34.

Amin, A. and Thrift, N. (1992) 'Neo-Marshallian nodes in global networks', *International Journal of Urban and Regional Research* 16(4): 571–87.

Bellandi, M. (1989) 'The industrial district in Marshall', in E. Goodman and J. Bamford (eds) *Small Firms and Industrial Districts in Italy*, London: Routledge: 136–52.

Best, M. (1990) *The New Competition: Institutions of Industrial Restructuring*, Cambridge, MA: Harvard University Press.

Bull, A., Pitt, M. and Szarka, J. (1991) 'Small firms and industrial districts: structural explanations of small firm viability in three countries', *Entrepreneurship & Regional Development* 3: 83–99.

Chinitz, B. (1960) 'Contrasts in agglomeration: New York and Pittsburgh', *American Economic Association, Papers and Proceedings* 40: 279–89.

Christopherson, S. (1993) 'Market rules and territorial outcomes: the case of the United States', *International Journal of Urban and Regional Research* 17(2): 274–88.

—— (1994) 'Rules as resources in investment and location decisions', paper presented at the Centenary Conference for Harold Innis, University of Toronto, September.

Christopherson, S. and Storper, M. (1986) 'The city as studio, the world as back lot: the impact of vertical disintegration on the location of the motion picture industry', *Environment and Planning D: Society and Space* 4: 305–20.

Dicken, P. (1992) *Global Shift: The Internationalization of Economic Activity*, 2nd edn, New York: Guilford Press.

Diniz, C.C. and Borges Santos, F. (1995) 'Manaus: a satellite platform in the Amazon Region', Working Paper, CEDEPLAR, University of Minas Gerais, Brazil, May.

Diniz, C.C. and M. Razavi (1994) 'Emergence of New Industrial Districts in Brazil: São José dos Campos and Campinas Cases', Working Paper, CEDEPLAR, University of Minas Gerais, Brazil, November.

Ettlinger, N. (1992) 'Modes of corporate organization and the geography of development', *Papers in Regional Science* 71: 107–26.

Feldman, M. (1993) 'Agglomeration and industrial restructuring', CPAD Working Paper 93-02, Graduate Program in Community Planning and Area Development, University of Rhode Island, June.

Fineberg, D., Wilson Gilmore, R., Krantz, J., Lianes, M., Miller, R., Mann, U.and Schmitt, B. (1993) 'The biopharmaceutical industry in New Jersey: prescriptions for regional economic development', Report to the Princeton/Rutgers Research Corridor, Department of Urban Planning and Policy Development, Rutgers University.

Florida, R. and Kenney, M. (1990) 'Silicon Valley and Route 128 won't save Us', *California Management Review* 33: 68–88.

Gereffi, G. and Korzeniewicz, M. (eds) (1994) *Commodity Chains and Global Capitalism*, Westport, CT: Praeger.

Gertler, M. (1988) 'The limits to flexibility: comments on the post-Fordist vision of production and its geography', *Transactions of the Institute of British Geographers* 13: 419–32.

Glasmeier, A. (1988) 'Factors governing the development of high tech industry agglomerations: a tale of three cities', *Regional Studies* 22: 287–301.

Golob, E., Gray, M., Markusen, A. and Park, S.O. (1995) 'Valley of the heart's delight: Silicon Valley reconsidered', Working Paper, Project on Regional and Industrial Economics, Rutgers University, presented at the Regional Science Association Annual Meeting, Niagara Falls, Canada, November.

Goodman, E. (1989) 'Introduction: the political economy of the small firm in Italy', in E. Goodman and J. Bamford (eds) *Small Firms and Industrial Districts in Italy*, London: Routledge: 1–3.

Goodman, E. and Bamford, J. (eds) (1989) *Small Firms and Industrial Districts in Italy*, London: Routledge.

Granovetter, M. (1985) 'Economic action and social structure: the problem of embeddedness', *American Journal of Sociology* 91: 481–510.

Gray, M., Golob, E. and Markusen, A. (1996) 'Big firms, long arms: a portrait of a "hub and spoke" industrial district in the Seattle region', *Regional Studies* 30(7): 651–66.

Harrison, B. (1992) 'Industrial districts: old wine in new bottles?', *Regional Studies* 26(5): 469–83.

—— (1994) *Lean and Mean: The Changing Landscape of Corporate Power in the Age of Flexibility*, New York: Basic Books.

Harvey, D. (1982) *The Limits to Capital*, Oxford: Basil Blackwell.

Healey, M. and Rawlinson, M. (1993) 'Interviewing business owners and managers: a review of methods and techniques', *Geoforum* 24: 339–55.

Howes, C. (1993) 'Constructing comparative disadvantage: lessons from the U.S. auto industry', in H. Noponen, J. Graham and A. Markusen (eds) *Trading Industries, Trading Regions*, New York: Guilford Press: 45–91.

Howes, C. and Markusen, A. (1993) 'Trade, industry and economic development', in H. Noponen, J. Graham and A. Markusen (eds) *Trading Industries, Trading Regions*, New York: Guilford Press: 1–44.

Krumme, G. (1969) 'Toward a geography of enterprise', *Economic Geography* 45: 30–40.

Linge, G.J.R. (1991) 'Just-in-time: more or less flexible?', *Economic Geography* 67: 316–32.

Linge, G.J.R. and Rich, D.C. (1991) 'The state and industrial change', in G.J.R. Linge and D.C. Rich (eds) *The State and the Spatial Management of Industrial Change*, London: Routledge: 1–21.

Lovering, J. (1990) 'Fordism's unknown successor: a comment on Scott's theory of flexible accumulation and the re-emergence of regional economies', *International Journal of Urban and Regional Research* 14: 159–74.

—— (1991) 'Theorising Post-Fordism: why contingency matters (a further response to Scott)', *International Journal of Urban and Regional Research* 15(2): 298–301.

Luger, M. and Goldstein, H. (1990) *Technology in the Garden*, Chapel Hill, NC: University of North Carolina.

Luria, D. (1990) 'Automation, markets and scale: can "flexible niching" modernize U.S. manufacturing?', *International Review of Applied Economics* 4: 127–65.

McNee, R. (1960) 'Toward a more humanistic economic geography: the geography of enterprise', *Tijdschrift voor Economische en Social Geografie* 51: 201–5.

Malecki, E.J. (1987) 'Comments on Scott's high tech industry and territorial development: the rise of the Orange County complex, 1955–1984', *Urban Geography* 8: 77–81.

Markusen, A. (1985) *Profit Cycles, Oligopoly and Regional Development*, Cambridge, MA: MIT Press.

—— (1991) 'The military industrial divide: Cold War transformation of the economy and the rise of new industrial complexes', *Environment and Planning D: Society and Space* 9: 391–416.

—— (1994) 'Studying Regions by Studying Firms', *The Professional Geographer* 46: 477–90.

—— (1995) 'The Interaction of Regional and Industrial Policies: Evidence from Four Countries', in *Proceedings, World Bank's Conference on Development Economics, 1994*, Washington, DC: World Bank.

Markusen, A., Hall, P., Campbell, S. and Deitrick, S. (1991) *The Rise of the Gunbelt*, New York: Oxford University Press.

Markusen, A. and Park, S.O. (1993) 'The state as industrial locator and district builder: the case of Changwon, South Korea', *Economic Geography* 69: 57–181.

Markusen, A. and Sasaki, M. (1994) 'Satellite new industrial enclaves: a comparative study of United States and Japanese cases', Working Paper, Project on Regional and Industrial Economics, Rutgers University, January.

Massey, D. (1984) *Spatial Divisions of Labor: Social Structures and the Geography of Production*, New York: Methuen.

Massey, D. and Meegan, R. (1982) *The Anatomy of Job Loss: The How, Why and Where of Employment Decline*, London: Methuen.

Park, S.O. and Markusen, A. (1994) 'Generalizing new industrial districts: a theoretical agenda and an application from a non-Western economy', *Environment and Planning A* 27: 81–104.

Piore, M. and Sabel, C. (1984) *The Second Industrial Divide: Possibilities for Prosperity*, New York: Basic Books.

Pollert, A. (1988) 'Dismantling flexibility', *Capital and Class* 34: 42–75.

Sabel, C. (1989) 'Flexible specialization and the re-emergence of regional economies', in P. Hirst and J. Zeitlin (eds) *Reversing Industries Decline*, New York: St Martin's Press: 17–70.

Saxenian, A. (1983) 'The urban contradictions of Silicon Valley', *International Journal of Urban and Regional Research* 17(2): 236–57.

—— (1985) 'The genesis of Silicon Valley', in P. Hall and A. Markusen (eds) *Silicon Landscapes*, Boston, MA: Allen & Unwin: 20–34.

—— (1990) 'Regional networks and the resurgence of Silicon Valley', *California Management Review* 32: 89–112.

—— (1991a) 'Silicon Valley and Route 128 won't save us: response to Richard Florida and Martin Kenney', *California Management Review* 33: 136–42.

—— (1991b) 'The origins and dynamics of production networks in Silicon Valley', *Research Policy* 20: 423–37.

—— (1994) *Regional Networks: Industrial Adaptation in Silicon Valley and Route 128*, Cambridge, MA: Harvard University Press.

Sayer, A. (1989) 'Post-Fordism in question', *International Journal of Urban and Regional Research* 13: 666–95.

Schoenberger, E. (1985) 'Foreign manufacturing investment in the United States: competitive strategies and international location', *Economic Geography* 61: 241–59.

—— (1988) 'From Fordism to flexible accumulation: technology, competitive strategies, and international location', *Environment and Planning D: Society and Space* 6: 245–62.

—— (1991) 'The corporate interview as a research method in economic geography', *The Professional Geographer* 44: 180–9.

Scott, A. (1986) 'High tech industry and territorial development: the rise of the Orange County complex, 1955–1984', *Urban Geography* 7: 3–45.

—— (1988a) 'Flexible production systems and regional development: the rise of new industrial space in North America and Western Europe', *International Journal of Urban and Regional Research* 12(2): 171–86.

—— (1988b) *New Industrial Space*, London: Pion.

Scott, A. and Paul, A. (1990) 'collective order and economic coordination in industrial agglomerations: the technopoles of southern California', *Environment and Planning C: Government and Policy* 8: 179–93.

Sforzi, F. (1989) 'The geography of industrial district in Italy', in E. Goodman and J. Bamford (eds) *Small Firms and Industrial Districts in Italy*, London: Routledge: 153–73.

Storper, M. (1989) 'The transition to flexible specialization in industry: external economies, the division of labor and the crossing of industrial divides', *Cambridge Journal of Economics* 13: 273–305.

Storper, M. and Harrison, B. (1991) 'Flexibility, hierarchy and regional development: the changing structure of industrial production systems and their forms of governance in the 1980s', *Research Policy* 20: 407–22.

Storper, M. and Walker, R. (1989) *The Capitalist Imperative: Territory, Technology and Industrial Growth*, New York: Basil Blackwell.

Yin, R. (1984) *Case Study Research: Design and Methods*, Applied Social Research Methods Series 5, Beverly Hills, CA: Sage.

Part II
Regulation

6 Harnessing the region

Changing perspectives on innovation policy in Ontario

David Wolfe

Introduction

The current era is marked by a profound degree of uncertainty in prevailing economic and political relations. At the root of this uncertainty are three interrelated processes: the emergence of a new information technology paradigm that is dramatically altering the economic calculus of production and distribution; the phenomenon of globalization which is increasing the linkages and interdependence between the economies of Europe, North America and East Asia; and the gradual decline of Fordist methods of standardized mass production and distribution with profound implications for the occupational structures and patterns of employment throughout these economies. The resulting dislocation raises fundamental questions about the future roles and relationships of different levels of governance – at the global, national and regional levels of the economy and society.

A number of developments associated with the trend towards globalization reinforce the growing salience of supra-national institutions: the internationalization of production and of financial markets; the integrative capacity of information technologies that overcome the previous economic barriers in transportation and communications; the increased power of international regimes and organizations in the management of economic affairs; and the increasing scope of power and authority delegated upward to supra-national bodies. Collectively, these trends affect the context within which national levels of government exercise the sovereignty with which they are endowed.

Conversely, these developments are also focusing attention on the changing role of regions. A number of factors contribute to the increased salience of regions in the emerging global economy. Complex systems of technology, production processes and industrial organization, and their supporting infrastructures of social and political institutions, exhibit distinctive spatial characteristics. Production relations tend to aggregate over time among networks of firms following the pattern of input–output relations, or traded interdependencies, that form the basis of information exchange in the local economy. The value of face-to-face interaction, particularly in the context of an abundant technical and professional labour force and a supportive regional institutional infrastructure, is inestimable. Periods of transition from one set of technologies to another, such as the present, coincide with a reorganization of the spatial distribution of production. The ensuing period of adjustment highlights the changing relationship between national and subnational, or regional, levels of governance. As Charles Sabel has argued, at root, 'the relationship between the economy and its territory is changing' (Sabel 1989).

These broad developments at the global level are reflected in, and intensify changes in, the Canadian political economy. A consistent theme in Canadian history has been the tension between the forces of centralization, making for a strong federal government, and those of regionalism, reinforcing the role of the provinces. The overwhelming tendency has been to attribute the rise of regionalism and the loss of effective national leadership to the growing integration of Canada into a continental and global economy. Inevitably, this trend is viewed as a sign of the weakening of the nation. However, the impact of new transportation and communications technologies and the rediscovery of the region as a dynamic source of growth raises critical questions for this interpretation of the Canadian political economy. What does the emergence of these new technologies imply for the role of the regions in Canadian economic development? Is it necessary to re-evaluate the appropriate balance between the national and regional levels of government in framing economic development policies for Canada?

A number of writers in the literature on evolutionary economics and technological change attach special importance to the role of institutional supports for technological innovation and diffusion. The work of Lundvall, Nelson and Freeman focuses on how effectively the institutions supporting innovation cohere into national systems of innovation. A similar body of literature in economic geography and regional science specifies the valuable role that institutional infrastructures at the regional and local level have played in supporting the economic dynamism of some of these localities. This paper draws upon these theoretical perspectives to suggest a potential resolution of the tension between the role of the nation and the region in Canadian industrial policy. It deploys these insights in an examination of the recent experience in the province of Ontario to suggest that policies to promote dynamic competitiveness and economic growth at the regional level can serve as a valuable complement to those pursued at the national level.

Paradigm shifts and national systems of innovation

Recent work in the neo-Schumpeterian tradition emphasizes the consequences of a shift in techno-economic paradigm. Following Schumpeter, it stresses the dynamic role played by major technological innovations in generating economic and social change in a capitalist system. Differentiation is made between lesser magnitudes, or incremental orders, of innovation and greater magnitudes. The current magnitude of change is described as a new technological revolution or the emergence of a new techno-economic paradigm. The concept of a techno-economic paradigm applies to changes in the underlying technology system which are so far-reaching in their effects that they exert a transformative influence on every aspect of behaviour throughout the industrial economy. Technological changes of this magnitude alter not only the competitive structure of specific branches or sectors of the economy, but the entire input cost structure and conditions of production and distribution throughout the economy. The emergence of a new techno-economic paradigm is distinguished from less pervasive forms of technological innovation by the specific set of characteristics associated with its most important input or key factor: a relatively low and constantly falling cost curve, plentiful supply, and ease of application across many sectors of the economy. The new key factor does not diffuse throughout a modern economy as an isolated input, but rather at the core of a rapidly growing system of technical, social and managerial innovations (Freeman and Perez 1988: 58–61).

The approach outlined above has sometimes been accused of technological determinism; in reality, this approach emphasizes the mutual interdependence between the underlying technical and economic changes associated with the core technology and the set of social and political changes required to support its broad diffusion and application. The successful outcome of such a shift is always contingent, not necessary; it depends on a complex process of change in forms of social organization and the resolution of political conflict.[1]

At the heart of the new techno-economic paradigm is the convergence of an integrated set of computer, communications and video technologies that are based on semiconductors and share the capacity to process and transmit data in digital form. The current diffusion of these technologies throughout the industrial economies is exerting effects as vast and sweeping as those that accompanied the second industrial revolution at the turn of the century (Organisation for Economic Co-operation and Development 1988: 35). A recent report by the US Department of Commerce indicates that the information technology sector (computers and communications) of the economy grew from 4.9% in 1985 to 8.2% in 1998. When allowance is made for the fact that prices in this sector have been falling, while those in most others have been rising, the rate of growth is even greater. Even more dramatic has been the rise in the proportion of business spending on equipment accounted for by IT. In the 1960s it accounted for 3% of total spending; in 1996, IT's share rose to 45% (Margherio *et al.* 1998: 4–6).

While the microelectronics revolution is exponentially increasing the capacity to handle information, knowledge-based inputs are simultaneously becoming an increasingly salient component of every aspect of production. Some analysts have argued this development signifies the shift to a new form of 'post-industrial' (Bell 1973) or 'post-capitalist' (Drucker 1993) society. In reality, the new paradigm mobilizes knowledge, collective or social intelligence, and innovative capacity in a dynamic way within the context of a capitalist mode of production. If knowledge is understood to include not just R&D, but also design, engineering, advertising, marketing and management, then it is clear that knowledge-based inputs are becoming the defining feature of both manufacturing and service industries in the contemporary economy. These developments lead to the characterization of the emerging period more appropriately as one of 'knowledge-intensive' capitalism (Mytelka 1987; Florida 1995).

The increasing role of knowledge and innovation in the new economy emphasizes the importance of the innovative capacity of national economies. Periods of rapid technological change are characterized by extreme economic uncertainty as the frontier of technological possibilities changes dramatically. Past technological trajectories are no longer adequate guideposts in the emerging economic and technological environment. These periods place a high premium on the ability to acquire, absorb and diffuse relevant scientific and technological information throughout the educational, economic or political institutions of a society. They also accentuate the ability of national institutions to search for and apply relevant pieces of knowledge. Innovation and technical progress are sustained by a complex set of relationships among the institutions which produce, distribute and apply various kinds of knowledge. The innovative performance of individual countries is influenced by the way elements of this institutional system interact with each other in the creation and application of knowledge.

The central role of institutional structures in national responses to a new techno-economic paradigm has led to the recent interest in the concept of national systems of innovation. The systems of innovation approach emphasizes the role of various institutional structures and social forces in influencing the innovation process. The concept was first applied by Freeman (1987) in his study of technological change in the Japanese economy and has subsequently been developed and expanded in the work of Lundvall (1992) and Nelson (1993).[2] Freeman initially defined national systems of innovation as 'the network of institutions in the public and private sectors whose interactions initiate, import, modify and diffuse new technologies' (Freeman 1987: 1). Freeman emphasizes the role that social and political institutions play in supporting the adoption and dissemination of scientific and technical knowledge. In his study of the Japanese system of innovation, he analyses the contribution of four components: government policy; corporate R&D; the education and training system; and the general structure of industry.

Lundvall provides a somewhat more inclusive definition of the concept. One of the crucial differences between his approach and that of Freeman is the importance he attaches to the patterns of interaction between firms as part of a collective learning process in the acquisition and use of new technical knowledge. This flows from his belief that innovation is increasingly tied to a process of interactive learning and collective entrepreneurship, especially in terms of the relationships between producers and users of new technology. For him 'a system of innovation is constituted by elements and relationships which interact in the production, diffusion and use of new, and economically useful, knowledge and ... a national system encompasses elements and relationships, either located within or rooted inside the borders of the nation state' (Lundvall 1992: 2). The main elements of the system include: the internal organization of firms; the network of inter-firm relationships; the role of the public sector; the institutional set-up of the financial sector; and the degree of R&D intensity and the nature of R&D organization.[3]

Stan Metcalfe provides a somewhat more synthetic and simple definition of the national system of innovation. According to him, '[a] national system of innovation is that set of distinct institutions which jointly and individually contribute to the development and diffusion of new technologies and which provides the framework within which governments form and implement policies to influence the innovation process. As such it is a system of interconnected institutions to create, store and transfer the knowledge, skills and artifacts which define new technologies' (Metcalfe 1997: 285).[4]

Although most innovative activity in national economies occurs within the boundaries of the private firm, the role of the public sector in stimulating and sustaining innovative behaviour is critical. In most of the industrial countries, the government-supported share of funding on R&D ranges from a low of 20% to in excess of 50%. Moreover, the public sector maintains a vast array of infrastructural supports critical for the innovation process in the form of the post-secondary educational system, public R&D facilities and a wide range of institutions that support the process of technology transfer. The concept of a national system of innovation thus draws attention to the effectiveness of public policies in fostering the kinds of private sector activity necessary to develop and maintain a sustained innovative capacity (Niosi *et al.* 1993: 212).

The dynamic role of the region

While most of the work in the neo-Schumpeterian tradition on systems of innovation has focused on the national level, an alternative stream of work has drawn attention to the role of the regional or subnational units of government in supporting and sustaining the innovation process. Some observers suggest that the emerging paradigm is also shifting the locus of activity between national and subnational, or regional, levels of government. Indeed, recent analyses have begun to adopt the concept of national systems of innovation for use at the subnational level as well.

The emerging knowledge-intensive industries in the new paradigm exhibit a marked tendency to cluster around regional growth poles – not only are the firms in these industries closely linked to each other, but they also tend to locate close by their clients. Further, the service industries that provide inputs to them also tend to be located close by. Innovative capabilities are sustained through regional communities that share a certain base of knowledge and the increments to that knowledge base. Technological knowledge, in the collective and cumulative sense described above, is often highly local in nature, in contrast to scientific knowledge that is grounded in a broad international community of scholars and researchers. The cumulative technical knowledge necessary to transform new scientific possibilities into innovative products or processes grows out of the myriad of relationships built up among research laboratories, networks of suppliers and a collection of innovative firms (Malecki 1990: 110–12).

Geographer Michael Storper uses the term 'territorialization' to describe the range of economic activity that depends on resources which are territorially specific. The types of resources involved can include specific assets that are only available in a certain place, or more critically, assets whose real value emerges out of the context of particular interorganizational or firm–market relations that depend upon geographic proximity. Relations based upon geographic proximity constitute valuable assets when they generate positive spillover effects in an economic system. The more grounded the economic activities of a region are to the specific assets of that region, the more fully territorialized are those activities (Storper 1997: 170). Michael Porter notes that local concentrations constitute an important source of competitive advantage in the emerging global economy:

> In a world of global competition, then, the sources of competitive advantage are becoming increasingly localized. ... The process of creating true competitive advantage is localized and benefits greatly from the proximity of lead customers, suppliers, educational institutions and rivals.
> (Porter 1991: 41)

Economic practices are rooted in a broad array of social and political institutions, both private and public, that provide the necessary support for their effective operation. A critical variable in the ability of different regions to maintain the conditions that support a dynamic technological trajectory is the capacity for self-organization on the part of their public and private institutions. This capacity for self-organization has recently been linked to the existence of the stock of social capital in the region. Social capital refers to various features of the social organization of a region, such as the presence of shared norms and trust that facilitate coordination and cooperation among individuals, firms and sectors for their mutual advantage. It secures the conditions that enhance the benefits derived from more tangible investments in physical and human capital. Without its supportive functioning, high levels of these more tangible forms of investment may fail to produce the benefits that should potentially result from them (Cooke 1998).

More and more cases can be found of emerging cooperative relationships between networks of producers – between large assemblers and smaller suppliers in the auto industry, between networks of small producers, such as exists in the Emilia-Romagna industrial district of Italy, and even among large producers in the computer and telecommunications industries that make up the core of the new information technologies. The growing costs of R&D, as well as the increasing complexity and knowledge intensity of new scientific research and product development, make the challenge more forbidding for individual firms – hence the growing importance of regional agglomerations of innovative firms in the collective advance of technical knowledge. The key elements of a networked regional economy include a dense network of public and private industrial support institutions, high-grade labour market intelligence and related vocational training mechanisms, rapid diffusion of technology transfer, a high degree of inter-firm networking, and receptive firms well disposed towards innovation. The very density of these networks and institutional supports is often interpreted as a sign of the vibrancy of a regional economy (Cooke and Morgan 1993: 562).

Geographic proximity is equally important for manufacturers in the more traditional industries associated with the old paradigm and the suppliers of their production equipment. As production equipment incorporates more of the sophisticated microelectronics associated with information technology, the ease of interaction between producers and end-users may be a critical variable in explaining the relative success with which firms in mature industrial districts manage the transition to the new economy (Gertler 1993: 670–1).

The consequences of regional agglomeration for firms in both the emerging information-intensive and the mature restructuring sectors draw attention to the role played by subnational or regional levels of governance. Regional economies consist of more than just individual behaviours of firms, or even networks of firms, and their employees. They are constituted by the cultural traditions and institutional structures that facilitate and regulate economic behaviour and social activity. Indeed, one of the most striking assertions advanced recently is that dynamic region states are supplanting the historical role played by nation states. According to Kenichi Ohmae, the nation state has become progressively more dysfunctional as a unit for coordinating economic activity in a globalized economy: 'On the global economic map the lines that now matter are those defining what may be called "region states" '. For Ohmae, 'region states' circumscribe natural economic zones that tend to have strong linkages with the emerging global economy. They must be small enough for their members to develop shared economic interests, but of adequate size to maintain the communications and transportation infrastructure and supporting professional services needed to support the regional concentration of firms capable of participating actively in the global economy (1993: 78–80; 1995).[5]

Ohmae exaggerates the extent to which the dynamic new region states are supplanting the nation state. This arises partly from his tendency to conflate two distinct categories – small, but sovereign, city states, such as Singapore, and dynamic subnational governments that form part of larger, sovereign states. While his argument has some validity in the former case, he underestimates the extent to which dynamic regional governments operate within the broad cultural and political context defined by national governments in the latter. This ambiguity over what constitutes a 'region state' raises the question of how to define a region. Recent work draws an important distinction between two types of regions: 'cultural' and 'administrative'. Cultural regions share certain features in common with 'the classical definition of nation as a people sharing a common culture, language and territory but which either have not become states (e.g. the Basque Country) or forfeited that status (e.g. Scotland)', while the latter category includes subnational areas of jurisdiction within larger federal systems, such as the German Länder or US states, or newer forms of regional government within traditionally centralized democracies, such as France or Italy. All such regions are defined as 'territories smaller than their state possessing significant supralocal governance capacity and cohesiveness differentiating them from their state and other regions' (Cooke *et al.* 1997: 479–80).

Within this context of regional studies, increasing attention has been devoted to the question of regional innovation systems (RSIs). While definitions may vary, central to the idea of the RSI is the notion of how the institutional and cultural environment of a region either supports or retards the innovation process. This may be defined as 'the set of economic, political and institutional relationships occurring in a given geographical area which generates a collective learning process leading to the rapid diffusion of knowledge and best practice' (Nauwelaers and Reid 1995: 13; Cooke 1998).

Given the expanding role of regions as a locus of activity and competitive advantage, it is not surprising that a large number of regional governments have begun to replicate the range of policy instruments to promote regional innovation found in the more successful regional economies. Innovation strategies to promote regional innovation target government support through a number of specific policy instruments: the provision of technology infrastructure support; the creation of sector-wide consortia for the collective provision of basic services, such as accounting, design, payroll preparation and marketing information; the promotion of joint ventures, strategic alliances and a strategic role for trade associations to foster the creation of inter-firm synergies; the creation and upgrading of labour force skills through apprenticeship programmes, vocational training schemes and the establishment of specialized training institutes; and finally, the creation of specialized, regionally or sectorally based development agencies (Murray 1991: 70–2; Scott and Storper 1992: 225–6) [6] These approaches represent a new innovative form of regional policy-making, characteristic of what has been termed the *intelligent region*, which is *institutionally reflexive* in its nature. The governments of these intelligent regions are fundamentally learning organizations, constantly concerned with enhancing their capability to evaluate and refine their policies for promoting regional innovation patterns (Florida 1995; Cooke 1997).

The roots of industrial policy in Ontario

Industrial policy in Ontario has historically been characterized more by a state of benign neglect than one of conscious direction, although there have been periods of notable exception. Traditionally, as the industrial heartland of the staples-producing hinterland, Ontario benefited disproportionately from the national policies of import substitution industrialization associated with the National Policy tariffs, patent legislation and the exploitation of Canada's preferred status within the British Empire. The result was a strong manufacturing sector, based excessively on the presence of branch plants of foreign multinationals with production geared to the domestic economy. In the expansionary atmosphere of the 'golden age' after World War II, provincial governments in Ontario were content to rely upon federal macroeconomic management of the economy and Canada's improved trade relations to create the appropriate context for provincial economic development. To the extent that they pursued any consistent set of economic development policies, they focused on the supply side, rather than the demand side. Provincial governments in Ontario viewed their primary role as the provision of infrastructure investment in highways, electric power generating capacity, support for municipalities in building water and sewage systems, and, in the decade of the 1960s, a dramatic expansion of the post-secondary educational system. In policy areas of critical import for the provincial economy, such as the imbalance in automotive trade between Canada and the United States, the provincial role was constrained by its relative exclusion from jurisdiction over trade issues. The Automotive Products agreement negotiated by the federal government with the US in 1965 was the most significant piece of industrial policy for the province in this period. Overall, the Conservative governments which ruled from 1943 to 1985 were preoccupied with maintaining a 'favourable investment climate' for private business in the province by controlling spending and managing the provincial debt (Rea 1985: 22–3, 204–5).

This complacency began to fade in the late 1970s as the industrial heartland experienced the economic slowdown and restructuring that affected other industrial economies in the wake of the oil price shock and mid-1970s recession. In the late 1970s and early 1980s, the provincial government also came under pressure to provide financial assistance to firms facing the prospect of industrial restructuring, especially in the automotive industry. The North American industry experienced a massive process of restructuring in the late 1970s, involving substantial capital outlays. Faced with intense competition from Japanese manufacturers and the possibility of global relocation, North American manufacturers looked to the federal and provincial governments to provide financial assistance.[7] Faced with these growing pressures, successive governments in Ontario have become convinced of the need to adopt a more coherent framework for industrial and technology policies. Taken as a whole, they provide a fascinating study in contrasts – given the different partisan composition of the four governments that have held office since 1980. They also provide some interesting lessons in the difficulty of moving older industrial economies towards the category of the learning region discussed above.

The first period of response occurred under the Conservative government from 1980 to 1985. It began with the formation of the Board of Industrial Leadership and Development (BILD) in January 1981. The Board, a cabinet committee, was charged with responsibility for coordinating all government spending on industrial, resource, transportation and regional development, budgeted at $2 billion in 1980–1. In addition, it was assigned a new series of economic initiatives which were to amount to $750 million over the next five years. The larger portion of this figure amounted to a repackaging of existing funds. However, by the 1983 budget, the government had raised the planned allocation to $1.1 billion, of which $503 million was designated for science and technology projects. The new portion of these funds represented a notable shift in the focus of provincial industrial and technology policy – towards a downstream emphasis on encouraging the process of technology transfer through the commercialization of research results, as well as the adoption of new process technologies by existing industries.

Principal among the new policy initiatives were the creation of the Innovation Development for Employment Advancement (IDEA) Corporation and the establishment of five new technology transfer centres. Funds were advanced to the IDEA Corporation to use as seed capital in setting up five technology funds that would invest in industries based on microelectronics, biological and medical sciences, information processing and transmission, chemical and processing technologies and manufacturing automation. In addition, the Board committed $100 million over five years to fund five industry-oriented technology centres: Automotive Parts Technology; Resource Machinery; Farm Equipment and Food Processing; Advanced Manufacturing (two separate CAD/CAM and Robotics centres); and Microelectronics. The mission of the centres was to enhance the competitiveness of Ontario industry and support the diffusion of new technology by the following: aiding in the development of high-technology production through advice, funding and prototype development; providing training programmes in advanced technologies to industry; providing information, seminars and technology awareness activities; and demonstrating technology hardware and software applications. In part, the establishment of the centres responded to the concerns raised in the report of a provincial task force on microelectronics about the slow pace of adoption of new process technologies (Jenkin 1983: 73; Miller 1983: 18–19; Grossman 1984).

In the eyes of many, this initiative represented a cynical attempt to make a tired government appear forward-looking and innovative. However, others saw in it the first halting step towards shaking off the complacency of Ontario's industrial policy and confronting the reality of the structural changes reshaping the provincial economy. The various measures that made up the overall initiative had a limited effect. The IDEA Corporation was widely judged to be a failure. The technology centres achieved a more mixed degree of success. Some, such as the Automotive Parts Centre in St Catherines, were credited with helping Ontario's parts manufacturers to successfully adopt the new technology of statistical process control in the early 1980s and position themselves to participate in the tremendous boom that occurred in the latter part of the decade. However, a condition of their creation was that they achieve 50% self-sufficiency by the fourth year of their existence. An evaluation conducted for the new Liberal government in 1986 concluded that they were achieving a high benefit/cost ratio and were playing a 'critical role' in promoting economic development. Nonetheless, the government instructed the centres to submit new business plans with provision for higher levels of cost recovery, streamlined operations and reduced expenditures. In the end the government sold or privatized most of the centres and by 1990 all but one had ceased operation.

The minority Liberal government that assumed office in 1985 on the basis of a formal accord with the social democratic New Democratic Party represented a significant break with the previous forty years of conservative rule. The Liberals were determined to put their own stamp on the conduct of the province's affairs, especially in the area of economic policy. This included a vocal and persistent opposition to the federal government's neo-conservative agenda, symbolized by the Free Trade Agreement with the US. One of the first steps taken by the Liberal Premier in April 1986 was to announce the formation of the Premier's Council, a multipartite body that included cabinet ministers, some of the most influential business people in the province, and a small representation of labour leaders and people from educational institutions. It was charged with responsibility for analysing the competitive strengths of the provincial economy, determining its weaknesses, and proposing new policy directions for Ontario. The more activist role for the provincial government assigned to the Council was symptomatic of the growing divergence between Ontario's perception of its need for a regionally based development strategy and the federal government's reliance on a trade-led adjustment strategy (Cameron 1994: 114–17).

Two years later, the Council produced a path-breaking study entitled *Competing in the New Global Economy*. The Premier's Council Report released in April 1988 presented the most coherent vision of an industrial and technology strategy espoused by either of the two mainstream parties in this country. The study, and the policy solutions it advocated, were noteworthy for the dramatic break they constituted with the prevailing neo-conservative orthodoxy in North America. Rather than viewing international competition as a threat to workers' wages, the Premier's Council depicted effective international competition as the key to a high-wage economic strategy and higher standards of living.

> In the future our prosperity will depend increasingly upon our ability to sustain a sufficiently large base of companies competing in world markets,

> not on the basis of lower labour or raw materials costs, but rather through technological innovation, skilled labour, adept marketing, and high productivity. ... When nations cannot maintain productivity growth in their internationally traded goods and services at rates equal to their competitors, they have only one alternative to remain viable in international markets: they must reduce their wages. The usual method for this is a currency devaluation. ... A long-term devaluation strategy, however, is nothing more than a program of achieving international competitiveness through steady reductions in living standards.
>
> (Premier's Council 1988: 35–7)

The Premier's Council counterpoised to this a strategy of achieving higher value-added per employee by realizing higher productivity in the existing mix of goods and services, or by shifting the industrial structure of the province towards goods and services that are inherently higher value-added per employee activity. They termed the process of shifting production towards higher value-added per employee activities 'industrial restructuring'. The Council argued that this strategy could best be pursued by focusing its economic policies on traded businesses – those exposed to world trade and competition. Gains realized through improvements in traded goods and services would generate increased prosperity throughout the provincial economy. Hence, 'the traded sectors must be viewed as the fundamental drivers of our future wealth and prosperity' (1988: 41). The key to accomplishing this goal was to increase the number of indigenous world-scale companies capable of competing effectively in global markets. The Council viewed indigenous firms as more likely to provide higher value-added jobs, generate indirect employment, and create spin-off companies in the province. The Council defined Ontario's challenge as needing to accelerate the growth of indigenous threshold firms in the traded sectors with the potential to reach world-scale levels of activity, while expanding the strengths of the existing non-indigenous base of companies (1988: 75).

Not content to wait for the full results of the Council's deliberations, however, the Liberal government simultaneously announced the creation of a ten-year $1 billion Technology Fund in 1986 to be partly under the direction of the Premier's Council. The speedy implementation of a wide range of programmes under the aegis of the Technology Fund significantly enhanced the government's role in the regional innovation system. An existing programme, the University Research Incentive Fund, was revamped and brought under the umbrella of the Technology Fund. The purpose of this programme was to encourage universities to collaborate with the private sector in joint research initiatives by providing matching funding for private sector investments in short-term university contract research. In June 1987 the Council chose seven provincial Centres of Excellence to carry out long-term basic research in Ontario universities. Each of the seven designated centres involves collaborative research between faculties at more than one university and industry partners. Funded at an initial level of $204 million over five years, the centres were as follows: Advanced Laser and Lightwave Research; Space and Terrestrial Science; Integrated Manufacturing; Groundwater Research; Information Technology; Materials Research; and Telecommunications Research.

The third major component announced by the government was the Industry Research Program. The programme was designed to stimulate leading-edge industrial R&D in areas of strategic importance with a demonstrated potential for export or import replacement. The projects were to be based on sound scientific principles and display a degree of risk, as well as economic and social benefits. Successful applicants were required to fund a portion of the project as well. At its peak in the early 1990s, the Industry Research Program was providing funding for 24 separate projects with a total annual expenditure of $23 million. The Technology Fund also supported a number of smaller programmes, including the Technology Personnel Program, designed to assist smaller manufacturing firms in hiring new engineering and technical staff (Premier's Council on Economic Renewal 1993: 98–113).

The Technology Fund enjoyed a better record of achievement than most of the rest of the Premier's Council's recommendations. The other major recommendation implemented in the budget of April 1988 introduced a new R&D Super Allowance that provided a tax incentive for incremental R&D expenditures above a company's three-year rolling average of R&D performed in Ontario. The tax incentive provided an additional benefit for firms undertaking R&D in Ontario to existing federal and provincial incentives. Other recommendations of the Council called for the creation of a Strategic Procurement Committee to be composed of independent business, academic and labour leaders; a Growth Ventures programme to provide $100 million over five years in loan guarantees to venture capital companies investing in eligible small and medium-sized companies; and a risk sharing fund to assist Ontario-based firms on the threshold of becoming multinationals were either announced and then dropped or never made their way successfully through the Cabinet process. In the end, the coherent policy framework outlined by the Premier's Council was only partially implemented before the government's defeat in the election of 1990.

The varying degree of success enjoyed by the Council's proposals resulted partly from the lack of consensus over its approach within the Ontario public service and the limited support it enjoyed in the two key ministries, Industry, Trade and Technology and the Treasury. For its part, the Treasury resisted many of the Council's key recommendations partly because of their expense, and partly due to its preference for tax incentives as a policy instrument. The one initiative that it supported, the R&D Super Allowance, was implemented at the expense of the Technology Fund's ability to carry out the rest of its mandate. In addition, it was never clear that the Council enjoyed the full support of the business community. The business members of the Council were appointed as individuals or heads of their respective companies, but did not speak for their industries or constituencies as a whole. It is questionable how successful the Council was in mobilizing a consensus around its vision among the members of the broader business community. Although three of the leading trade unionists in the province also signed the report, they generally viewed it as the business agenda and held their fire until a promised second report in which they would get to deal with the questions of education, training and labour force adjustment. In the end, the Premier's Council Report represented a vanguard of thinking among selected government, business and labour leaders in the province and suffered from the inability to mobilize a broad 'development coalition' around its vision of the province's future path for economic development.

Towards institutional reflexivity?

The election of the New Democratic Party government in Ontario in September 1990 was regarded as one of the great political upsets in the province's history. Few observers, even those closest to the party's campaign, seriously believed it would win until a few short days before the election. The New Democratic Party took office just as the worst recession since the 1930s hit the province. While some had foreseen that the Free Trade Agreement with the US would force a major adjustment upon the provincial economy, few anticipated that it would occur in the context of high real interest rates, an overvalued Canadian dollar, and a severe cyclical recession. The recovery, which began in 1991, was hesitant at best and the overall level of employment did not surpass the 1989 peak until July 1994.[8]

The New Democratic Party, both federally and provincially, had long advocated the adoption of an industrial strategy, but was somewhat vague on specifics. Policy resolutions adopted at party conventions regularly called for the nationalization of leading corporations, but there was little active consideration of this option by the ministers of the new government. Those political advisors and senior bureaucrats responsible for formulating economic policy were determined to build on the foundations of a more active industrial and technology policy begun by their predecessors, but to avoid some of the problems encountered in the past.[9] The literature on the potential value of regional networking and cooperation in enhancing competitiveness provided a useful starting point to build that alternative (Best 1990; Murray 1991). Some of these ideas had been explored through the economic policy review coordinated between 1988 and 1990 by the then Treasury critic for the party, Floyd Laughren. The ideas developed in this review formed the backdrop for the evolution of the NDP's industrial and technology policies (Walkom 1994: 92–6; Ernst 1995).

Three strategic concerns underlay the development of the government's industrial and technology policy. The first concern was to prevent a philosophical gap between the broader macroeconomic focus of the Ministry of Finance and the narrower emphasis on technology and innovation that framed the industrial and technology policy. The second concern was to overcome the internal divisions within the bureaucracy that had characterized the previous government's efforts. The third concern was to devolve responsibility for economic development on to the broadest range of actors, both within and without the government, in keeping with some of the precepts of associative democracy discussed above.

A final challenge for the NDP to cope with was the business hostility that quickly developed towards its broader equity and industrial relations agenda. While never comfortable with the thought of a social democratic government in Ontario, organized business interests were cautious in their approach for the first nine months. However, the introduction of a number of major initiatives in early 1991 quickly galvanized the business community into opposition. By the time the government's industrial policy framework was introduced formally in mid-1992, there was substantial business hostility to overcome before it could gain their participation. On the other side of the spectrum, there was little direct aid from the government's traditional supporters in the labour movement and elsewhere to offset this opposition (Walkom 1994: 98–105; Rachlis and Wolfe 1997).

The initial attempt to articulate an alternative economic vision was presented in the first budget of April 1991. Although the budget itself was widely condemned for its naive Keynesianism, a background paper outlined a more comprehensive approach to economic policy. The budget paper, *Ontario in the 1990s*, established sustainable prosperity based on equitable structural change as its goal. The paper recognized that competitiveness was important to attaining this objective, but argued that it could best be realized through the creation of high-value-added, high-wage jobs and of strategic partnerships. The most important adjustment challenge in the 1990s was to increase the overall productivity of Ontario's economy. The key to meeting this challenge did not lie in minimizing cost levels for the existing mix of product and processes, but rather in fostering productive systems that promote continuous improvement in products and processes across the networks of firms and sectors in the provincial economy. The budget paper argued that a high-wage, high-value-added strategy must be based on a defence, and extension, of social equity to generate the required degree of social cohesion. The key to long-term competitiveness lay in a recognition of the increased importance of knowledge-based inputs, or technology, in every aspect of the production process. The challenge for public policy was to promote an organizational culture supportive of technology and innovation in the workplace and society at large (Laughren 1991).[10]

Some of the themes introduced in this budget paper were reinforced and expanded in the succeeding budget of 1992. The supplementary budget paper, *Investing in Tomorrow's Jobs*, argued that:

> Investment in plant, technology, training, infrastructure and flexible organizations is critical for renewed productivity growth in Ontario. This

> requires a joint effort among business, labour and government. Government programs and private activities must be redirected to promote the kinds of change that lead to a new, more flexible and knowledge-intensive economy.
>
> (Laughren 1992: 19)

The paper outlined the series of economic policies being implemented to achieve these goals, including: enhanced measures for labour market training and adjustment; the creation of an Ontario Training and Adjustment Board (recommended in the second Premier's Council Report); improvements in the area of social infrastructure, especially child care facilities and affordable housing; a strategic programme of investment in upgrading the province's physical infrastructure; a regional development strategy to ensure that communities were involved in the process; and measures to finance investments in more innovative and knowledge-based types of production, including support for worker ownership and the creation of an Ontario Lead Investment Fund.

The other key theme articulated in both the 1991 and 1992 budget papers was that of partnership. In Budget Paper E, the government had indicated that the realization of its economic strategy must be based on a broad social partnership. It required strategic public and private initiatives in a climate that allowed the respective partners to develop a sense of collective responsibility. A concerted and cooperative approach was deemed essential to achieve the government's goals with respect to economic development and sustainable prosperity (Laughren 1991: 101). This emphasis on partnerships and cooperative action indicated that the government was contemplating serious changes both in the way it influenced private sector behaviour and in the policy instruments used to achieve these goals. The government was also attempting to forge a new analytical and policy framework for the delivering of economic development policy – one which diverged from the traditional command and control form of policy implementation and from the use of traditional policy instruments, such as tax incentives and direct subsidies, to accomplish its goals.

At the centre of the new strategy was the Industrial Policy Framework. The Industrial Policy Framework built on the analysis of the Premier's Council Report, but supplemented it with insights drawn from the experience of some US states and the more innovative subnational jurisdictions in Europe. The overall goal was to promote the transition of Ontario's economy towards those sectors and firms with the capacity to generate higher wage, higher value-added and environmentally sustainable jobs. The framework focused on ways of developing higher value-added activities throughout the economy to increase competitiveness and create more, and better, jobs. It consisted of three main elements:

1 changing the way the government invests, including measures to enhance

the quality of physical and technological infrastructure through institutions, such as the seven provincial Centres of Excellence (funding for the centres was renewed in July 1992 for an additional five years);
2 changing the way the government works with companies, specifically through the negotiation of strategies developed in cooperation with the firms and unions in specific sectors to improve their competitiveness. This goal was also to be achieved through focusing the government's support on strategic groups of firms, such as those committed to continuous innovation and to improving their technological capabilities;
3 changing how the government responds to economic change, through measures to support investment in green industries and enhanced support for organizational change in Ontario firms (Ontario, Ministry of Industry, Trade and Technology 1992).

The most significant change envisioned in the framework was the increased emphasis placed on working with sectors. One source of inspiration for this approach came from the analytical work of people like Michael Best and Robin Murray referred to above. Another was the emphasis placed by Michael Porter on the role of industrial clusters in shaping competitive advantage (Porter 1990). Not by coincidence, the province of Quebec also developed a cluster-based development strategy at this time (Gagné and Lefèvre 1993). This approach was predicated on the assumption that the institutional infrastructure of the sector can constitute an important source of competitive advantage. The relevant infrastructure can include a variety of inter-firm practices and extra-firm agencies, such as trade associations, apprenticeship programmes, labour education facilities, joint marketing arrangements and regulatory commissions, each of which facilitates inter-firm cooperation. These sector-based institutions can play a critical role in improving the collective competitiveness of firms relative to those in sectors elsewhere. Following Best's argument, the Sector Partnership Fund assumed that within individual sectors, competition and cooperation can be complementary activities.

The Sector Partnership Fund announced in the budget of April 1992 was a three-year (later extended to six years) initiative, budgeted at $150 million, and designed to implement the sectoral component of the Industrial Policy Framework. The Sector Partnership Fund provided assistance to approved cooperative sector projects that led to higher value-added activities. The Sector Partnership Fund was based on the four principles of flexibility, cooperation, leverage and accessibility. It recognized that each sector faces unique competitive challenges and it was designed to respond to those unique circumstances. Individual industrial sectors are characterized by distinctive sectoral properties, shaped by the specific nature of the technology they use and the constraining effects of their products and product markets (Hollingsworth and Streeck 1994: 271).

Out of these efforts, strategic plans and concrete initiatives were to be developed for potential funding from the Sector Partnership Fund. Sector Partnership Fund support was intended to lever project funding from industry, labour and other levels of government. The process was based, in part, on the assumption that eligible projects constituted a form of quasi-public goods, whose utility to industry partners was strong enough to attract some private investment, but insufficient to be self-financing. It was also seen as a way of subjecting the sectoral initiatives to a form of market test to determine if the private sector was willing to support them itself. Finally, all sectors were deemed potentially eligible for Sector Partnership Funds.

While the hallmark of the Sector Partnership Fund was to choose winning activities, not winning sectors, the government designated a number of areas as priority sectors for policy development. One of these was green or environmental industries. Green industry involves products and processes that contribute to energy efficiency, water conservation, pollution prevention and the three R's. The thrust of the strategy was to foster the development of green products by Ontario industries, as well as to create a global demand for these products. The goal was to support Ontario firms in manufacturing the green products and intermediate goods that would be stimulated by a leadership approach on environmental standards and energy efficiency. Early measures adopted to support this strategy focused on using energy efficiency and environmental retrofit programmes as a way of leveraging demand for green products within the province.

By any criteria of measurement, the initial stage of sector consultation and strategy formation must be viewed as a success. Both the number of sectors involved and the extent of participation by key sector players in the consultative process exceeded the expectations of government officials by a wide margin. Between the summer of 1992 and the provincial election in June 1995, the Ministry of Economic Development and Trade, along with a number of other ministries assigned lead responsibility for their respective sectors, worked with a wide range of industry associations and trade unions to develop comparable strategies for their sectors. In addition to the sector mentioned above, consultative efforts produced approved strategies in 14 others: Telecommunications, Food Processing, Computing, Tourism, Cultural Industries, Aerospace, Auto Parts, Mines and Minerals, Construction, Health Industries, Forestry, Plastics, Residential Furniture and Chemicals. By the spring of 1995, work plans were approved and strategies under development in a range of additional sectors, including: Biotechnology, Consulting Engineering, Design, Machinery, Tool, Die and Mould, Retail, and the Electrical and Electronics industry. The last of these strategies was released formally in May 1996.

In each case, the consultative efforts were broad and inclusive, drawing in as many as 150 individuals in the sector to prepare detailed analyses of sectoral strengths and weaknesses and propose a course of action. In total, the approach involved 28 different sectors and over 2,000 individual participants. In the process, the sector partners included 22 different unions, 93 industry associations and 28 universities and colleges (Ontario, Ministry of Economic Development and Trade 1995). This was a major accomplishment for the process, given the continuing opposition by industry to some of the government's key equity initiatives, such as labour relations reform, the introduction of employment equity regulations and minimum wage increases. Most participants acknowledged that the process itself was one of its most valuable products; new relationships were developed among business competitors, a greater sense of trust was generated among all the partners, and the effective identification of common sectoral interests occurred.

One example of the early success of the approach was the report of the Advisory Committee on a Telecommunications Strategy for Ontario presented to the Minister of Culture and Communications, in August 1992. The report set out an ambitious vision for the telecommunications industry of the province. The government responded to its recommendations by establishing an Ontario Network Infrastructure Program (ONIP) in February 1993 to accelerate the development of telecommunications-based information networks in the province. It also announced the establishment of four priority areas for funding under the Sector Partnership Fund: developing new telecom applications; forming innovative business enterprises; establishing specialized sectoral infrastructure; and enhancing market development and promotion. A number of initial projects were funded subsequently under this programme, including OCRInet, a wide area network linking a number of post-secondary research institutions and private research centres in the Ottawa/Carleton region, and several local community-based information networks.

The high number of sectors that participated in the strategy development process and their relative success in achieving consensus on their strategic plans would suggest that demands on the Sector Partnership Fund should have been high. Indeed there was no lack of recommendations for concrete initiatives in virtually all of the plans. These initiatives tended to be grouped into four categories: access to capital, technology and R&D, education and training, and export trade development. Despite this fact, the Sector Partnership Fund underspent its allocation in every year that it existed and at the time of its termination in July 1995, little more than half of the $150 million allocation had been committed. A number of factors accounted for this outcome. One that created a substantial barrier was the expectation of industry funding for the initiatives. The imposition of the 'quasi-market test' on Sector Partnership Fund initiatives clearly imposed a hurdle that many private sector participants had difficulty surmounting.

Many of the concrete initiatives that eventually emerged were oriented towards the creation of sector-based technology centres. Examples included: the Guelph Food Technology Centre, designed to increase effective technology and information transfer, as well as to provide accessible pilot plant facilities for the food industry; an Ontario Centre for Environmental Technology Advancement to provide technical support services, financial advice and business counselling to help young firms commercialize environmental technologies; and Connect-IT, a computing sector resource facility to assist the many small and medium-sized firms in Ontario's industry in developing sector-specific competency in management, standards, marketing expertise and export readiness. In the computing sector funding was also provided to support the Electronic Commerce Institute to promote the adoption and use of electronic data interchange in Canadian industry. Other areas that received some funding included export market development through Interhealth Canada, a private, not-for-profit corporation designed to pursue and gain international contracts for Canadian firms in key markets around the world; and the plan to establish representatives for the auto parts sector in Japan and Europe to help increase sales to Japanese and European assemblers in their North American and foreign operations.

In addition to its sectorally related activities, the government took a number of other measures to assist smaller, innovative, high-growth companies. One such measure was the creation of the Ontario Innovation and Productivity Service. Modelled after aspects of several other institutions, including the Michigan Modernization Service, the Australian National Industrial Extension and elements of Ontario's own Manufacturing Recovery Program, the Innovation and Productivity Service was designed to help innovative growth firms overcome barriers to their further expansion. The Innovation and Productivity Service worked with a selected group of target firms to help them identify challenges and opportunities for growth and develop a strategic business plan. It provided funding for strategic projects and facilitated enhanced access to other provincial and federal government programmes. The programme worked effectively with a cadre of good small to medium-sized enterprises in helping to improve their competitive fundamentals.

The creation of multiple sector-based institutions in the areas of industrial policy, labour market policy and financing mechanisms began to raise some fundamental questions with respect to the coordination of industrial and technology policy in Ontario. Among the key issues which emerged was that of sectoral linkages – namely how can the government more effectively coordinate the various sectoral initiatives, both across sectoral lines where potential synergies exist and between policy areas where overlapping jurisdictions may create problems. A report issued on the economic impact of the Centres of Excellence drew attention to the importance of viewing these multiple initiatives as parts of a complex and integrated provincial or regional system of innovation. The report drew attention to the need to assess the overall degree of integration among the other elements of the system and target areas in need of more effective communication (The Impact Group *et al.* 1994).While this analysis focused on the role of the Centres of Excellence, there was clearly a strong case to be made for using a similar framework to assess the degree of integration among the other elements of the system and target areas in need of more effective coordination.

Rolling back the tide

The considerable progress made in this direction during the Liberal and NDP interregnum came to an abrupt end with the election of a new Conservative government in 1995. The Tory platform, labelled the Common Sense Revolution, called for an abrupt shift in the direction of government spending, in general, and its economic development policies, in particular. The CSR evinced a preference for the use of broad framework policies, such as a reduction in the tax and regulatory burden to stimulate growth, in contrast to the more targeted spending policies favoured by the Premier's Council and the NDP government. Within the first six months of assuming office, nearly all of the initiatives put in place by the two previous governments were cancelled or wound down. Virtually all that remained were the Centres of Excellence, and their survival was not assured until December 1996 when the Minister of Economic Development announced their renewal for the next five years with an annual budget of $32.5 million and a consolidation of the seven centres down to four. The Minister indicated that the renewed centres would be tied more closely to the private sector for the purpose of promoting economic growth and job creation. Their primary purpose was to encourage collaboration between universities and the private sector through partnerships that give industry better access to university research expertise.

For the first two years of its mandate the issue of industrial and technology policies took a back seat, as the Conservative government struggled with a broader agenda of reducing expenditure and personal income taxes, reforming the welfare system and engineering a massive redistribution of responsibility between the provincial and local governments. It was not until the 1997 budget that some of the elements of the province's industrial and technology policy re-emerged on the agenda. The budget contained a major new spending programme and several additional tax incentives. In addition, it included a long budget paper on the benefits of investing in innovation and R&D for the Ontario economy and a rationale for the new spending programme and tax incentives being introduced with the budget. Both the budget speech and the accompanying budget paper were filled with references to the need for increased partnership between the private sector and other elements of the innovation system, especially the university-based research institutions.

Of the numerous changes introduced, the $500 million R&D Challenge Fund was the most significant. Its primary rationale is to promote business–university partnerships and research excellence. The stated objectives of the fund are to support job creation and economic growth; to promote world class research of interest to the private sector; and to encourage more collaboration between the private sector and research institutions. According to the government, the main priority of the fund is to attract and keep world class researchers in Ontario. It has the flexibility to provide support for leading-edge research that benefits today's growing industries and helps create the industries of the future; state-of-the-art equipment and facilities;

and incentives for gifted researchers to work in Ontario, including endowed chairs. The funding will be awarded on a competitive basis, according to the proposal's contribution to research excellence and economic growth. One criterion of its economic benefit is the ability to attract private sector support. However, the fund will also be used to allow provincial research centres to match funds from other federal and international grant-giving councils. Of the various tax incentives introduced in the budget, the most significant is the Ontario Business-Research Institute Tax Credit – a 20% refundable R&D tax credit for corporate-sponsored R&D performed in Ontario by eligible universities or other approved post-secondary educational institutes or research associations (Eves 1997: 177–83).

The gradual, but significant, shift in the government's policy focus continued with the 1998 budget. The government announced several more policy initiatives with a strong emphasis on educating and training the labour force needed for the emerging knowledge-based economy. Another background document released with the budget provided the overarching rationale for these measures. The budget paper identified strategic skills as the critical nexus between the emergence and rapid spread of new technologies and the resulting opportunities for growth in the local economy. The adoption and use of new technologies creates a demand for new kinds of skills needed to use the technologies in a diverse range of sectors, from automotive parts, to banking and software design. From the perspective of the local or regional economy, a ready supply of skills are *essential to exploiting the opportunities for economic growth* in any sector. In addition, they support additional spin-off jobs in related occupations. Conversely, a shortage of these strategic skills can block the expansion of jobs in the regional economy. A number of recent surveys documented the shortage of required skills as a major obstacle to growth in the dynamic sectors of the provincial economy. The government actions were designed to remedy this situation (Eves 1998: 148–50).

The budget announced two new measures designed to deal with the critical skill shortages. The first was the creation of a new $150 million Access to Opportunities Fund to create an additional 17,000 places at Ontario universities in the high demand computer science and engineering programmes over the next three years. The government indicated that it would apply a 'market test' to this programme by asking industry to match the start-up costs, although it is not exactly clear what is included in this dimension. In addition, the government provided $10 million to support four innovative training programmes at cooperative research institutes and community colleges in the areas of automotive parts design and manufacturing technology, new media skills, telecommunications and metal machining and engineering. It set aside a further $20 million to support other effective partnerships to develop strategic skills (Eves 1998: 145–6).

While the various measures do not offset the full weight of the programmes and incentives eliminated in the first two years of the government's mandate, they indicate a substantial shift in the approach that it is taking to the issue of innovation and economic development. The current government has been consistent in its view that there is no rationale for directly subsidizing private industry to achieve these goals. However, in response to pressures from industry and the education sector, it seems to recognize that the public sector plays a critical role in supporting the innovation process through the provision of infrastructure – especially in the two critical areas of basic research and education and training of the highly skilled labour force demanded by the knowledge-based industries. While its current policies are a far cry from the type of reflexive regional states described above, there is little doubt that the two recent budget papers have begun to echo some of the themes expressed in the previous Premier's Council reports – especially the one on skills (Premier's Council 1990) – and the Industrial Policy Framework (Ontario, Ministry of Industry, Trade and Technology 1992).

Recent interpretations of the political *wende* in Ontario have used some of the concepts described above to argue that the current government is the first to appreciate the potential for Ontario to operate as a true 'region state' in an integrated North American economy. According to Thomas Courchene, Ontario has both the economic capacity and the political–administrative infrastructure to emerge as the first true 'region state' in North America. It is being driven ever faster in this direction by the 'pull' of continental integration and the 'push' of federal devolution. The current conservative policies of fiscal retrenchment and administrative streamlining are engineering the improvements in public sector productivity that Ontario requires to compete effectively for investment and growth in North America (Courchene and Telmer 1998).

Ontario has undoubtedly been moving down the path towards 'a learning region' over the past decade and a half. Unfortunately, the actions of the current government are not contributing to this direction as clearly as Courchene maintains. There are a number of problems with his interpretation. The fiscal policies of the first two years, and the more recent discovery of innovation policies, are contradictory, not complementary. The deep cuts introduced to the education, social and municipal sector have both undermined the capacity to deliver quality services and weakened the conditions of trust and social capital that most analysts associate with dynamic regional economies. In this sense, they are weakening, rather than strengthening, the untraded interdependencies in the regional economy. While the policy shift and fiscal relaxation in the last two budgets have begun to reverse the trend, they have not undone it. Furthermore, Courchene seriously underestimates the extent to which national cultural and institutional patterns still matter; a dynamic regional economy must operate within the context of existing national structures (Gertler 1997; Pauly and Reich 1997). This is true for the vast majority of region states.

Conclusion

The measures adopted in Ontario between 1985 and 1995 did not qualify it for inclusion in the select group of regional states advancing the frontier of innovative industrial and technology policy. Yet the series of initiatives undertaken in this period described a gradual evolution towards a more reflexive and comprehensive approach to managing the process of technological change. They were comparable to developments underway in numerous other subnational jurisdictions that assumed a more active stance in responding to the challenge of a shift to a new techno-economic paradigm. The reality confronted by the provincial governments in this decade is that of regional economies linked into an ever more tightly integrated North American economy. In a situation where the federal government was preoccupied with systematically dismantling the institutions and policies capable of managing the transition to a new economic paradigm, who else could fill the leadership void, but the provinces.

The policy innovations described above suggest that Ontario had begun the process of adapting its industrial and technology policies in response to the deep structural changes under way in the economy. While these initiatives fell short of the full requirements of *institutional reflexivity*, they pointed in a new direction. The termination of many of these initiatives as a result of the election in 1995 signified that Ontario was reverting to the more market-led to structural adjustment that characterized its policies during most of the postwar period. However, the new initiatives of the last two budgets and the striking similarity to some of the analysis employed by its predecessors suggest that the current government may slowly be recognizing that competitive and innovative regional economies are not built on cost reductions alone. The tentative process of adapting its public and private institutions to respond to the challenges of new technologies and continental integration has followed a tortuous path. It is too early yet to tell which tendency will prevail and whether Ontario will continue along the path towards a more reflexive, learning economy embarked upon in the previous decade.

Acknowledgements

Research support for this paper was provided, in part, by SSHRCC Research Grant No. 809-95-0009. The paper benefited from the helpful comments of Helen Burstyn, Jeff Finkelstein, Bob Marshall, Ammon Salter and the editors of this volume. The author is responsible for any remaining errors or omissions.

Notes

1 The work of Freeman and Perez has been contrasted recently with two alternative approaches that have been used to explain the end of the era of standardized mass production – the flexible specialization approach expounded in the work

of Piore and Sabel and the regulation school associated with the work of Aglietta, Boyer and others. Two recent attempts to compare and contrast the three approaches are found in Elam (1990) and Nielsen (1991). These three approaches differ in a number of important respects, not least the level of analysis which they emphasize. Most discussions of these contending approaches stress the differences between them, but in some respects it may be more useful to draw upon various elements of each of them. For instance, Freeman and Perez and the regulation school authors tend to emphasize the significance of the national level, while the flexible specialization approach underlines that of the regional level. The discussion that follows draws from the insights of both perspectives.

2 For a helpful overview of the differing approaches see McKelvey (1991).

3 A third approach to the concept can be found in the work of Richard Nelson who tends to see national systems of innovation in more institutional terms, looking at the role of government policy at the national level, formal regulation and informal coordination, levels of R&D funding and the supporting role played by the educational infrastructure (Nelson 1993).

4 The above references provide a small sampling of the different approaches to the national system of innovation. For a more comprehensive overview, and a useful distillation of the key features they share in common, see Edquist (1997).

5 I have examined these and related aspects of region states in greater detail in Wolfe (1997).

6 For a preliminary overview of a range of the relevant policies see Wolfe (1994).

7 For a good overview of the experience of restructuring in the Canadian auto industry see Holmes (1987).

8 A broader overview of the state of Ontario's economy and the structure of its regional innovation system in the early 1990s is provided in Wolfe and Gertler (1997).

9 The author was an active participant in many of the policy debates and some of the policy documents discussed below. As such, what follows is anything but an objective analysis.

10 For a fuller discussion of these themes see Ernst (1995).

Bibliography

Bell, D. (1973) *The Coming of Post-Industrial Society: A Venture in Social Forecasting*, New York: Basic Books.

Best, M.H. (1990) *The New Competition: Institutions of Industrial Restructuring*, Cambridge: Polity Press.

Cameron, D.R. (1994) 'Post-modern Ontario and the Laurentian thesis', in D.M. Brown and J. Hiebert (eds) *Canada: The State of the Federation 1994*, Kingston: Institute of Intergovernmental Relations, Queen's University.

Cooke, P. (1997) 'Institutional reflexivity and the rise of the region state', in G. Benko and U. Strohmayer (eds) *Space and Social Theory: Interpreting Modernity and Post-Modernity*, Oxford: Blackwell.

—— (1998) 'Introduction: origins of the concept', in H. Braczyk, P. Cooke and M. Heidenreich (eds) *Regional Innovation Systems: The Role of Governances in a Globalized World*, London: UCL Press.

Cooke, P. and Morgan, K. (1993) 'The network paradigm: new departures in corporate and regional development', *Environment and Planning D: Society and Space* 11: 543–64.

Cooke, P., Uranga, M.G. and Etxebarria, G. (1997) 'Regional innovation systems: institutional and organizational dimensions', *Research Policy* 26: 475–91.

Courchene, T.J. with Telmer, C.J. (1998) *From Heartland to North American Region State: The Social, Fiscal and Federal Evolution of Ontario*, Monograph Series on Public Policy, Centre for Public Management, Toronto: Faculty of Management, University of Toronto.

Drucker, P.F. (1993) *Post-Capitalist Society*, New York: HarperBusiness.

Edquist, C. (1997) 'Introduction: systems of innovation approaches – their emergence and characteristics', in C. Edquist (ed.) *Systems of Innovation: Technologies, Institutions and Organizations*, London: Pinter.

Elam, M.J. (1990) 'Puzzling out the post-Fordist debate: technology, markets and institutions', *Economic and Industrial Democracy* 11: 9–37.

Ernst, A. (1995) 'Towards a progressive competitiveness?: economic policy and the Ontario New Democrats, 1988–1995', paper presented to the Annual Meeting of the Canadian Political Science Association, Université du Québec à Montreal, Montreal, 5 June.

Eves, E. (1997) 'The R&D opportunity: cutting taxes and creating jobs', Budget Paper E, in *1997 Ontario Budget*, Toronto: Queen's Printer for Ontario, 6 May.

—— (1998) 'Strategic skills: investing in jobs for the future today', Budget Paper E, in *1998 Ontario Budget*, Toronto: Queen's Printer for Ontario, 5 May.

Florida, R. (1995) 'Toward the learning region', *Futures* 27(5) May/June: 527–36.

Freeman, C. (1987) *Technology Policy and Economic Performance: Lessons from Japan*, London and New York: Pinter.

Freeman, C. and Perez, C. (1988) 'Structural crises of adjustment, business cycles and investment behaviour', in G. Dosi, C. Freeman, R. Nelson, G. Silverberg and L. Soete (eds) *Technical Change and Economic Theory*, London and New York: Pinter.

Gagné, P. and Lefèvre, M. (1993) *L'Atlas Industriel Du Québec, Avec le concours de Gérald Tremblay*, Montréal: Publi Relais.

Gertler, M.S. (1993) 'Implementing advanced manufacturing technologies in mature industrial regions: towards a social model of technology production', *Regional Studies* 27(7): 665–80.

—— (1997) 'Barriers to technology transfer: culture and the limits to regional systems of innovation', Working Papers in Geography 97-3, Oxford: School of Geography, University of Oxford.

Grossman, H.L. (1984) *Economic Transformation: Technological Innovation and Diffusion in Ontario*, Toronto: Queen's Printer for Ontario.

Hollingsworth, J.R. and Streeck, W. (1994) 'Countries and sectors: concluding remarks on performance, convergence and competitiveness', in J.R. Hollingsworth, P.C. Schmitter and W. Streeck (eds) *Governing Capitalist Economies: Performance and Control of Economic Sectors*, New York and Oxford: Oxford University Press.

Holmes, J. (1987) 'The crisis of Fordism and the restructuring of the Canadian auto industry', in J. Holmes and C. Leys (eds) *Frontyard Backyard: The Americas in the Global Crisis*, Toronto: Between the Lines.

The Impact Group, Hickling, KlasTek Ltd and IFIAS (1994) *Innovation and Wealth Creation: Performance Measures for the Ontario Centres of Excellence*. Toronto.

Jenkin, M. (1983) *The Challenge of Diversity: Industrial Policy in the Canadian Federation*, Science Council of Canada Background Study 50, Ottawa: Supply and Services Canada.

Laughren, F. (1991) 'Ontario in the 1990s: promoting equitable structural change', Budget Paper E, in *1991 Ontario Budget*, Toronto: Queen's Printer for Ontario, 29 April.

—— (1992) 'Investing in tomorrow's jobs: effective investment and economic renewal', Supplementary Paper, in *1992 Ontario Budget*, Toronto: Queen's Printer for Ontario, 30 April.

Lundvall, B.-Å. (1992) 'Introduction', in B.-Å. Lundvall (ed.) *National Systems of Innovation: Towards a Theory of Innovation and Interactive Learning*, London: Pinter.

McKelvey, M. (1991) 'How do national systems of innovation differ? A critical analysis of Porter, Freeman, Lundvall and Nelson', in G.M. Hodgson and E. Screpanti (eds) *Rethinking Economics: Markets, Technology and Economic Evolution*, Hants, England: Edward Elgar.

Malecki, E.J. (1990) 'Technological innovation and paths to regional economic growth', in J. Schmandt and R. Wilson (eds) *Growth Policy in the Age of High Technology: The Role of Regions and States*, Boston: Unwin Hyman.

Margherio, L., Henry, D., Cooke, S. and Montes, S. (1998) *The Emerging Digital Economy*, Washington, DC: Secretariat on Electronic Commerce, US Department of Commerce, http://World Wide Web.ecommerce.gov/emerging.htm.

Metcalfe, J. (1997) 'Technology systems and technology policy in an evolutionary framework', in D. Archibugi and J. Michie (eds) *Technology, Globalisation and Economic Performance*, Cambridge: Cambridge University Press.

Miller, F.S. (1983) *R&D and Economic Development in Ontario: A Discussion Paper*, 1983 Ontario Budget Paper, Toronto: Queen's Printer for Ontario.

Murray, R. (1991) *Local Space: Europe and the New Regionalism*, Manchester and Stevenage, Herts: Centre for Local Economic Strategies and South East Economic Development Strategy.

Mytelka, L.K. (1987) 'Knowledge-intensive production and the changing internationalization strategies of multinational firms', in J.A. Caporaso (ed.) *A Changing International Division of Labour*, Boulder, CO: Lynne Reiner.

Nauwelaers, C. and Reid, A. (1995) *Innovative Regions? A Comparative Review of Methods of Evaluating Regional Innovation Potential*, European Innovation Monitoring System (EIMS) Publication No. 21, Luxembourg: European Commission, Directorate General XIII.

Nelson, R.R. (ed.) (1993) *National Innovation Systems: A Comparative Analysis*, New York and Oxford: Oxford University Press.

Nielsen, K. (1991) 'Towards a flexible future – theories and politics', in K. Nielsen *et al.* (eds) *The Politics of Flexibility*, London: Pinter.

Niosi, J., Saviotti, P., Bellon, B. and Crow, M. (1993) 'National systems of innovation: in search of a workable concept', *Technology in Society* 15: 207–27.

Ohmae, K. (1993) 'The rise of the region state', *Foreign Affairs* 72: 78–87.

—— (1995) *The End of the Nation State: The Rise of Regional Economies*, New York: The Free Press.

Ontario, Ministry of Economic Development and Trade (1995) *Ontario Sector Snapshots* (A progress report on the sector development approach), Toronto: Queen's Printer for Ontario.

Ontario, Ministry of Industry, Trade and Technology (1992) *An Industrial Policy Framework for Ontario*, Toronto: Queen's Printer for Ontario.

Organisation for Economic Co-operation and Development (1988) *New Technologies in the 1990s: A Socio-economic Strategy* (Report of a group of experts on the social aspects of new technologies), Paris: OECD.

Pauly, L.W. and Reich, S. (1997) 'National structures and multinational corporate behaviour: enduring differences in the age of globalization', *International Organization* 51(1) Winter: 1–30.

Porter, M.E. (1990) 'The competitive advantage of nations', *Harvard Business Review* March–April: 73–92.

—— (1991) *The Competitive Advantage of Massachusetts*, Boston: Monitor Company, Inc. and Harvard Business School.

Premier's Council (1988) *Competing in the New Global Economy*, Vol. 1, Toronto: Queen's Printer for Ontario.

—— (1990) *People and Skills in the New Global Economy*, Toronto: Queen's Printer for Ontario.

Premier's Council on Economic Renewal (1993) *Ontario 2002: A Report of the Task Force to Review the Ontario Technology Fund in the Context of an Innovation-Based Society*, Toronto: Queen's Printer for Ontario.

Rachlis, C. and Wolfe, D. (1997) 'An insider's view of the NDP government of Ontario: the politics of permanent opposition meets the economics of permanent recession', in G. White (ed.) *The Government and Politics of Ontario*, 5th edn, Toronto: University of Toronto Press.

Rea, K. (1985) *The Prosperous Years: The Economic History of Ontario, 1939–1975*, The Ontario Historical Studies Series, Toronto: University of Toronto Press.

Sabel, C.F. (1989) 'Flexible specialisation and the re-emergence of regional economies', in P. Hirst and J. Zeitlin (eds) *Reversing Industrial Decline*, Oxford: Berg.

Scott, A.J. and Storper, M. (1992) 'Industrialization and regional development', in M. Storper and A.J. Scott (eds) *Pathways to Industrialization and Regional Development*, London and New York: Routledge.

Storper, M. (1997) *The Regional World: Territorial Development in a Global Economy*, New York: The Guilford Press.

Walkom, T. (1994) *Rae Days: The Rise and Follies of the NDP*, Toronto: Key Porter Books.

Wolfe, D.A. (1994) 'The wealth of regions: rethinking industrial policy', Program in Law and the Determinants of Social Ordering, Working Paper No. 10, Toronto, Ontario: Canadian Institute for Advanced Research, May.

—— (1997) 'The emergence of the region state', in T.J. Courchene (ed.) *The Nation State in a Global/Information Era: Policy Challenges*, The Bell Canada papers on economic and public policy 5, Kingston: John Deutsch Institute for the Study of Economic Policy, Queen's University.

Wolfe, D.A. and Gertler, M.S. (1997) 'The regional innovation system in Ontario', in H. Braczyk, P. Cooke and M. Heidenreich (eds) *Regional Innovation Systems: Designing for the Future*, London: UCL Press.

7 Rules as resources

How market governance regimes influence firm networks

Susan Christopherson

Introduction

Two truisms lie at the heart of economic geography. The first is that investment decisions are location decisions. The second is that investment (and location) decisions produce differences in economic development potential across space. While these truisms remain central to locational analysis, the intellectual terrain within which they are interpreted has shifted dramatically. From relatively straightforward models of industrial location based on factor prices, the theoretical base of industrial location has developed to include an increasingly sophisticated political–economic dimension. This reconceptualization of the terrain of industrial location is an aspect of a broader re-thinking of markets, how they operate, and how they are governed. As Thrift and Olds (1996: 315) describe, the 'realization of the social nature of markets has changed the idea of the market as a neutral arena in which pure exchange takes place to an arena in which there are complex moral and institutional orders regulating not only the conduct of exchange but also what is defined as exchange in the first place.'

The way in which we see industrial districts and networks has been particularly influenced by ideas about market mediation and governance. There is now a substantial literature in planning, geography, sociology, and political science illustrating how trust, and various forms of social connection, create the conditions for market transactions. While these stories are very convincing, the diversity of forms of inter-firm connection raises another set of questions (Dicken 1998; Gereffi 1994, 1996; Harrison 1997; Markusen 1996). What factors shape firm decisions to connect in some ways and not in others? How do we link network form to socio-economic function?

Although there is plenty of talk about 'embeddedness' in accounts of firm networks, we have only the barest outline of a theory about how particular market governance and coordination structures arise and how they influence firm decisions about where and in what ways to interact with their suppliers and customers. What we have, at present, is 'a spectrum of different forms of coordination which consist of networks of inter-relationships within and between firms structured by different degrees of power and influence' (Dicken

1998: 8). One promising avenue for theoretical development, however, begins with the insight that at the heart of coordination is power; and that power is established and maintained through social, political, and legal institutions. If we take the concept of embeddedness as implying that firms operate within a set of institutions and associated rules and norms that create incentives for some behavior and disincentives for others, we may be able to trace the reasons for different coordination mechanisms.

In what follows I look at political–legal frameworks that govern markets and their potential influences on inter-firm coordination. I then briefly lay out how these different incentive systems constitute a set of resources for firms in the international trade and production arenas. This is an exploratory exercise and intended to develop a more institutionally informed understanding of firm networks and their geographic consequences. It is not intended to be definitive but rather to raise a series of issues about the relationship of function, form, and spatial outcome.

National systems governing investment and financial markets

One place to see how governance systems influence firm behavior in networks is via the market rules governing the 'home base' or domestic economy of the core firm or firms in a network. There are both empirical and theoretical reasons for examining the role of national market rules in influencing network form and practice. Despite the globalization of markets, the majority of production remains situated within national borders. Foreign direct investment as a percentage of the world's total output is only marginally higher than it was in 1913.[1] There is also evidence of persistent differences in the technological styles of national production and innovation systems (Gertler 1995) and in national labor practices (Christopherson 1998; Darbishire and Katz 1998; Fukao 1995; Shaikh 1996). These factors, as well as the documented tendency of transnational firms to retain their headquarters and research and development activities in their country of origin, all point to 'national identity' as a continuing influence on firm decision-making, including multinational firms (Dicken 1998; Doremus *et al.* 1998).

Although a multinational firm may wish to take advantage of factor or market conditions in different national economies (whether low wages or high skills) its market authority and the coherence of its business strategy are fixed within the rules of its home base. So, for example, while a firm may operate in or have strategic alliances with firms in other countries, its management's fiduciary responsibilities are defined by the rules governing firms in its country of origin. A firm will find it incongruous to, at the same time, exercise strategies which entail providing high short-term returns to shareholders and those which entail making long-term investments in research and development and worker skills.[2] As Ruigrok and van Tulder (1995) describe, governance systems define what constitutes success for a capitalist enterprise. A firm's ultimate preference, therefore, will be to sustain the logic of its production organization, even outside the national context.

In an important sense, then, the rules that govern domestic markets constitute both a set of constraints and a set of resources that affect the evolution of firm networks as forms of coordination and as market and production strategies. Although it is flirting with reductionism to do so, we can distinguish two 'ideal type' governance structures for the purposes of illustrating how these corporate and financial market rules influence coordination decisions.

One type of market governance system, manifested particularly in Germany and Japan, has a *centripetal* character. The matrix of public and private regulation governing financial markets, firm asset ownership and control, and labor market conduct provides continuous collective regulation of firm behavior. A 'thick' regulatory system, it tends to produce relatively less differentiated investment strategies among firms within sectors because innovation on the part of an individual firm would imply pulling away from rigorously applied collective standards. In addition, it increases 'sunk costs', that portion of fixed costs that would remain even if output was zero. Sunk costs include such investments as those in initial infrastructure, labor force training, and pension benefits owed to workers (Clark 1992; Clark and Wrigley 1997). Sunk costs decrease capital mobility but they may also be necessary to enable firms to shift from a low-value-added to a high-value-added market or to dominate a market against firms unwilling to take on such costs (Clark 1992).

A second type, as manifested in the US and the UK, could be described as a *centrifugal* governance system. At the heart of the Anglo-American market governance system are very different assumptions about the roles and rights of actors in the economy and therefore about property rights and about the rights of stakeholders in the firm (Fukao 1995). Regulation tends to encourage individual firm adjustment and innovation within a 'thin' context of legal minimum requirements. The regulatory framework works against firm investment in sunk costs and in favor of capital mobility and cost reduction as methods of achieving efficiency.

Reciprocity is rooted in specific contracts rather than based on norms governing relationships, with important implications for relations of trust and obligation. To the extent that the Anglo-American system is self-regulating, it is dependent on individually internalized standards inculcated through professional training and class associations rather than on the operation of collective market institutions.[3]

While governance systems can be conceived of as bargaining environments for firms (Ruigrok and van Tulder 1995), the approach used here emphasizes the role of the firm as a 'vehicle' for investment rather than as an independent actor in a bargaining framework. To make the differences among investment regimes more concrete, I will examine market rules in some detail, delineating how they solve some important problems for capitalist market economies in quite different ways.

Alternative solutions to market governance

One way to think about market rules is in terms of how they solve problems central to the operation of capitalist market economies. A realist (and realistic) analysis of capitalist market economies recognizes that market regulation inherently reflects power relations and that power is vested unequally. Attempts to create or reproduce power are at the source of rules governing markets. These rules create substantive roles for actors and regulate the investment process within and across firms. They incorporate norms and beliefs about the roles of actors and regulatory institutions (Heilbroner 1996). They prescribe what types of information are necessary to make markets work effectively. They determine the information available to various actors. So, for example, what is described as an 'agency' problem in models of asymmetric information is inherently a problem of how and where power can be exercised. Information cannot be separated from control and control implies power (Jacobs 1993). If we understand firm networks as solutions to asymmetric information problems, we can posit that they are governed differently because the power and control conditions that underlie imperfect information differ from one society to another.

Major 'problems' in market economies include: (1) capital allocation and its attendant risks for the investor; (2) the extent and nature of competition among actors; (3) the investor–manager or principal–agent relationship; and (4) the capital–labor relationship.

These problems are universal to the replacement of reciprocity-based socio-economies with the impersonal transactions of the market. Obviously, though, this transformation is incomplete and market systems exist along a continuum between 'pure market' in which price is the only consideration and reciprocity-based exchange where price is meaningless. The differences among capitalist market economies are the subject of a now 'classic' literature on how political actors shape market regulation and industrial policy, affecting the ability of the nation state to achieve economic performance goals. More recent works have dealt specifically with the question of political contingency and the effect of different types of institutional structures on economic outcomes (Berk 1994; Skowronek 1982).

The politically contingent nature of the rules governing markets is demonstrated in varying definitions of the boundaries of private property rights (Dolzer 1992). The balance between the individual's right to use or dispose of property and the public/social needs inconsonant with those rights can be worked out in very different ways. The German Basic Law, for example, explicitly expresses an interpretation of ownership that strikes a balance between individual rights and public needs. According to Article 14: '1) Private property and the right of inheritance shall be protected. Substance and limitations are determined by the laws. 2) Property entails obligations. Its use shall also serve the public good.'[4]

This definition of the limits of property rights has important implications for the prerogatives of firms. Property ownership and control are separated in the German system. One can own property and yet face significant constraints on using or disposing of that property. In the US, by contrast, property ownership and control are conjoined, vesting all interests in the property owner.

A specific example of how politics can produce different institutional outcomes over time and space is evident in the changing interpretation of the origins of the firm in the US, from the concessional firm of the mid-nineteenth century, a creation of the state and public interest with strong public obligations, to the legally enforceable conception of the firm as it exists today, a nexus of contracts with no public obligation (Weber 1995).

The insights of political–institutional analysts have been neglected, however, in the wake of expanding international financial markets and the conceptualization of the global market economy as operating 'beyond rules' and the influence of nation states and according to pure market principles. Recent work on the development of international regulatory frameworks, though, presents a different picture of the globalization process, one in which interests based in national regulatory systems are constructing and contesting international regulatory spaces (Hancher and Moran 1989; Roberts 1994). This work suggests that politics, though originating within the governance structure of the nation state, does not end at its borders.[5]

Although national differences in market governance and industrial policy are frequently vaguely attributed to values and ideology, it is through institutions that culture is realized and reproduced. The rules governing investment are embedded in broader national systems of governance which, although they may be inconsistent on some accounts, are internally coherent when compared with other systems (Doremus *et al.* 1998). So, the next step is to examine how some problems common to capitalist economies are resolved via distinctive governance institutions.

The investor and capital allocation

One characteristic that distinguishes the different market regimes of Japan, Germany, and the US is ownership structure. The US and Anglo-American regimes, in general, have more fragmented, less stable ownership structures than those of Japan and Germany. The most recent data available (from the early 1990s) indicate that in the US 90% of the voting shares of publicly held corporations are held by individual households, pension funds, and mutual funds. Banks hold only 1% of the publicly listed shares. In Japan, banks hold approximately 25% of publicly listed shares and individuals, pension funds, and mutual funds, about 30%. In Germany, the differences are even more dramatic with only 15% of publicly listed shares being held by individuals, pension funds, and mutual funds and 10% by banks. Non-financial firm holdings are negligible in the US but 25% in Japan and 40% in Germany.[6]

Another strong indication of differences in capital allocation institutions is the considerable variation in the role of stock markets. The number of listed companies and their capitalization relative to the size of the economy differs considerably among the three economies. Although Japan has the highest percentage of capitalization, it also has a very stable ownership structure dominated by banks and non-financial firms, which function as interlocking networks (cross-shareholding) of ownership and control.[7]

These differences in the character of financial markets and in the risk assumed by investors have implications for the cost of capital which is roughly twice as high in the US as it is in Germany and Japan, and for expectations of the investment process (Jacobs 1991). They also have implications for the degree of investor pressure on firms, which is significantly higher in the US where more firms are publicly traded (Capelli *et al.* 1997). The dominant role of banks in corporate finance in both Japan and Germany creates a capital market in which long-standing relationships between corporations and banks regulate risk, and in which holdings are bigger than in the US and more stable (Charkham 1994). In Japan, this regulation is expressed in cross-shareholding as an aspect of a trading relationship among customers and suppliers (Fukao 1995).[8] Cross-shareholding creates a strong institutional basis for collective regulation among these inter-related firms.

A compelling explanation for differences in investment markets is that market governance systems allocate information and risk in different ways. In Germany and Japan, risk is absorbed by intermediary institutions while in the US it rests with the investor as an individual. As a result, individual investment risks are appreciably higher in the US because investors have relatively little control over the day-to-day operations of companies (Kester 1991). Market institutions in the US deal with risk through the relative cost of capital and through credit rationing (Stiglitz and Weiss 1981). In Japan and Germany, investment risk is reduced by institutions which allow close investment oversight and by integration of the finance and production sectors through bank ownership of industrial enterprises and cross-shareholdings. These long-term risk reducing institutions affect the cost of capital, the investments to which it is allocated, and the time frame within which a return is anticipated.

In the US higher risk is associated (via property rights law, for example) with potentially higher gain. Thus, the balance tips in favor of short-term, 'venture' investments. This high-risk, high-gain regime is supported by easy exit policies and procedures (bankruptcy law) and by impersonal contract law which encompasses relationships ranging from employment to marriage.[9]

The investor–manager or principal–agent problem

The principal–agent problem is closely related to the capital allocation problem. In centrifugal market governance systems such as the US, it is difficult for the investor to monitor a company's performance because of fragmented ownership and the 'arm's-length' relationship between investor and investment manager. Differences in handling this problem are exemplified by the hundreds of hostile takeovers affecting US firms in the 1980s (with their attendant acquisition costs) and the total absence of such takeovers in the German system.

In the US a conception of the investment process as one dominated by large numbers of small investors combined with trust-breaking regulation in the 1930s to produce a financial market in which investment is driven by transactions. Investment decisions are made with no specific information about the firm (as in Index funds) or on the basis of limited and formal public information that is accessible to all investors. By contrast, in centripetal systems, financial market rules may enable concentrated ownership. In these systems corporate or institutional owners exert considerable influence over the management of the firm, using 'inside' information which is not publicly available (Fukao 1995).

The explicitly codified objective of the vast majority of US firms is to 'maximize shareholder value, measured by current stock price' (Porter 1992: 53). The strength of this 'rule' is such that managers who favor (by internal investment) long-term shareholder value over short-term stock price risk law suits for fiduciary mismanagement. One manifestation of this priority is that US non-defense research and development spending by private firms in the 1980s was ranked twentieth out of 23 industrial countries (Thurow 1993: 157).

The contemporary orientation to high short-term returns for shareholders is reinforced by what have become standard practices in centrifugal system firms. For example, managers are rewarded for performance with stock options, giving them further incentives to keep short-term returns at a high level. And managers are chosen for their financial acumen rather than their technical expertise in the industry. Again, by contrast, short-term returns on investment do not dominate internal investment decisions in centripetal systems to the extent that they do in the US. For example, a study of shareholder concerns in large US and Japanese firms in the late 1980s showed that 80% of US shareholders want share prices to increase rapidly. Eighty percent of Japanese investors find either growth or stability more important (Fukao 1995: 42). While there may be some recent changes in attitude, investment decisions have been driven historically by goals which are oriented more frequently toward corporate position in the long term. These goals may be met in a variety of ways, including technical superiority and increasing market share, but require investment in inter-related assets, such as research and development, capital equipment, and job training. Some of these investments can be valued easily while others, such as job training or positioning in an international market, cannot.

The extent of competition and the distribution of risk

The degree of competition and the distribution of risk among firms is a key dynamic defining industrial systems (Cawson *et al.* 1990). Although frequently subsumed under descriptions of trust, there are a wide range of options for structuring inter-firm relationships: (1) cooperation; (2) competition; (3) compliance; (4) coalition; (5) direct control; and (6) structural control (Ruigrok and van Tulder 1995).

In centripetal systems, market governance is carried out by strong intra-sectoral institutions and organizations, such as employer associations and credentialing bodies, in cooperation with the government. And the prerogatives of concentrated ownership and private sector governance occur in conjunction with broader fiduciary responsibilities and more exacting collective norms than is the case in centrifugal systems.

Long-term relationships among firms, buttressed by equity ownership, allow core firms in centripetal political economies to produce at lower levels of vertical integration and yet to rely on fewer input providers than firms in centrifugal systems. Long-term, stable contracts also allow input providers to invest in certain types of specialized assets, thus increasing their productivity and the quality of their inputs (Kester 1991).[10] Over the long term, these investments, whether in technology or skills, result in a virtuous circle of learning that increases the productivity of both the supplier and the buyer.

At all levels of production, there are 'clubs' that increase information flow across suppliers and buyers, and between them. These governance system characteristics are particularly valuable in sectors, such as automobiles, where quality control and continuous improvement are pre-eminent objectives.

Although they have many of these 'cohesive' features in common, the Japanese and German governance systems represent distinctive variants with respect to inter-firm relations. The German variant is the result of continuous bargaining among a coalition of partners in the production process with much of the bargaining taking place at the societal rather than at the firm level. The Japanese variant, sometimes described as 'distributed cooperation', is characterized by strong structural control by core firms over the entire industrial complex.

The difference between this type of control and that exercised by firms in the less cohesive centrifugal systems is captured by the insight that in centrifugal systems, a contract will mark the end of a bargaining process while under centripetal systems, signing a contract will mark the beginning of extensive bargaining (Ruigrok and van Tulder 1995: 114).

The inter-firm relationships typical of centrifugal regimes are most visible in sectors where a short-term 'product' is the ultimate goal – the advertising campaign, the financial 'deal', the television program, the technological innovation. In these situations, governance rules that encourage individual investment in specialized skills and realization of those assets through high fees may be more effective in producing a quality 'product' (Christopherson 1998).

The capital–labor problem

Another key set of institutions that affect investment across and within firms are those that govern firm conduct with respect to the labor market (Christopherson 1998). In a highly simplified form, different labor practices among regimes can be explained in terms of the relative positions of various stakeholders in the firm. Fukao (1995) describes these relationships as follows:

> *Relationship A: Japan and Germany*
> Creditors > a large number of core employees > top executives > shareholders (strictly defined earned profit) > other employees;
>
> *Relationship B: United States*
> Top executives > creditors > a very small number of core employees > shareholders (liberally defined earned profit plus a part of paid-in capital) > a large number of other employees.

These unequal relationships are fixed by law (particularly bankruptcy law) but also by implicit contracts supported by court rulings as well as custom.

In centripetal regimes, both direct state regulations (originating in labor bargaining power), such as those governing lay-offs or redundancies, and collective bargaining agreements between unions and employer associations restrict the options available to firms in relation to labor use and redeployment. These restrictions essentially force employers to move to strategies to improve workforce productivity through training or capital investment. Alternative strategies to reduce costs, such as longer opening hours or branch closure and worker lay-off, are costly and difficult to implement.

In German firms with more than 2,000 employees, for example, representatives of employees and trade unions hold 50% of the seats on supervisory boards of stock corporations. And, within firms, 'works councils' have rights regarding changes in employment or dismissal. These legislatively guaranteed rights, along with other rights granted to management, dilute the control of firm owners to dispose of firm assets once they are acquired.

Although potential owners can acquire German firms with some ease, their ability to control the assets they acquire is severely limited. As has already been indicated, property ownership in the German system is not concomitant with control. Control is shared among the stakeholders.

In centrifugal systems, most notably the US, the doctrine of the individual employment contract combines with property law to provide a legal basis for limiting the options for collective action by labor and, therefore, for coordination between labor and management.

Within centripetal systems, peak bargaining at the national level also mutes intra-national interjurisdictional competition in wages and working conditions and leverages the power of unions in the most productive and competitive sectors to raise wages in less competitive sectors, such as non-traded services. As a consequence, employers are less able to use the threat of capital mobility as a bargaining tool. Without the leverage for labor produced by peak bargaining, the threat of capital mobility is used to force jurisdictions to provide a 'competitive' business environment (Molotch 1998).

Market rules and firm strategies

Again, by way of illustration, we can sketch two ways in which politically constituted market rules affect firm strategies and the coordination of firm networks. First, just as they shape relationships among stakeholders within firms, investment rules and property rights construct incentives for core firms to relate to their suppliers in quite distinct ways. Second, by defining the boundaries of inter-firm competition and cooperation, they create a political–economic basis for different types of state intervention in the market.

Risk redistributing versus risk sharing international networks

A comparative look at multinational networks suggests some ways in which national market rules affect both the objectives and form of firm network governance structures. Although not strictly analogous with the investment-oriented framework presented in this analysis, Ruigrok and van Tulder (1995) have identified types of networks emerging out of bargaining systems. Via their typology, we can see some key differences among networks in the configuration of activities in a core firm's value chain in space, and the ways in which the activities in the value chain are coordinated. Major differentiating variables include: (1) the spatial division of labor; (2) the extent of decentralized decision-making; (3) the propensity and duration of strategic alliances among core firms; and (4) expansion/growth strategies (see Table 7.1).

The types of firm networks that arise when core firms originate in centripetal systems, such as Japan and Germany, emerge out of both the constraints and the possibilities presented by longer investment time horizons, as well as more patient investment capital and investor expectations. Firms with longer time horizons, for example, opt for strategies and firm networks that allow for the achievement of scale economies and long-term market coverage rather than 'first mover' advantages.

The differences among the two centripetal regimes are instructive, however. Japanese core firms are more likely to pursue a strategy of 'glocalization', that is developing greenfield sites in a target national market and becoming a local producer, using local suppliers. At the same time, Japanese firms typically do not shift major decision-making authority (for

Table 7.1 Network characteristics by market governance regime types

	Spatial division of labor	*Locus of decision-making*	*Core strategic alliances*	*Expansion strategies*
Centripetal regime I, e.g. Germany	Multi-domestic; regional–European division of labor	Coalition	Horizontal, long-term alliances	Mergers, e.g. to share multi-domestic marketing
Centripetal regime II, e.g. Japan	'Glocalization'	Concentrated in core firm	Relatively rare	Greenfield
Centrifugal regime, e.g. US	International	Decentralized based on contracts	Instrumental, short term	Mergers, acquisitions (including hostile takeovers)

finance, or technological innovation) to the local network. In this case, the core firm and its network of suppliers in Japan is akin to a 'mothership' in space with replicated networks in other national locations. Strategic alliances are few and capitalization remains largely a domestic responsibility. Japanese auto manufacture and consumer electronics represent the use of these strategies (Fruin 1992; Fukao 1995).

The German, and more broadly European, pattern of development, while also reflecting longer investment time horizons and patient capital, has distinctive features rooted in the history of interaction among European economies. Firms may organize production around a regional division of labor while at the same time pursuing long-term strategic alliances and horizontal mergers as a method of expansion. A multi-domestic strategy, sharing production innovation and marketing costs, leads to coalition-style decision-making.

The characteristics of this type of multi-domestic network organization are exemplified by the way German government and industry found to deal with a perceived lag in semiconductor development. The Bundesministerium für Forschung und Technologie collaborated with Siemens, the major German firm with a stake in semiconductor production, in a 'Megaprojekt' to produce one-megabyte memory chips by 1988. The project also included the Bundesministerium's counterpart in the Netherlands and the Dutch firm, Philips. According to Ziegler (1994):

> ... this arrangement allowed the firms to spread the risk of costly research and development and gave both governments the assurance that the firms would be closely monitored by one another. As the BMFT helped Siemens and Philips to finance this costly project, it also initiated a series of

> programs to promote the diffusion of microelectronics to small and medium sized firms and also bolstered the industry infrastructure by subsidizing several new institutes for applied semiconductor research.

This bi-national project later resulted in the Joint European Silicon Structures Initiatives (JESSI).

The high proportions of inter-European investment reflect a horizontal internationalization strategy and the propensity of firms in relatively comparable diversified economies to internationalize to achieve long-term market positioning and scale economies. While European countries account for some 43% of world imports, if one combines the twelve European Community nations with the EFTA to eliminate intra-European trade, Europe's share of world imports drops to 12% (Dicken 1998).

There is also evidence that German firms locating production outside their home economies use the advantages created in their 'home base' supplier networks to leverage development in new arenas. For example, German auto parts producers have been building new capacity in the US in conjunction with their long-term contracts with Daimler-Benz. According to Kester (1991), 'the strength of German supplier relations with Daimler-Benz has been critical to the initiation of these investments.' In this case, the strength of home base network relations has enabled international capital mobility and new investment. It is notable that German investment in the US auto parts industry has not sought out locations with the lowest cost labor but those in which it can maintain the high quality necessary to meet the specifications of its buyer firm. In this way, German firms may be concentrating in and near Spartanburg, South Carolina (now dubbed 'the autobahn') because concentration allows them to reproduce the labor market conditions which produce high-quality production in Germany. They are pursuing a modified 'glocalization' strategy, one which entails maintaining close ties to their domestic suppliers.

Horizontal firm networks, such as those common in European centripetal economies, are frequently characterized by equity sharing agreements among firms. Partners participate jointly in critical decisions and frequently have long-term relationships with their suppliers, domestic and foreign. The Airbus Project is another example of the horizontal investment strategy. It takes advantage of strong state–firm relationships, shares risks, and has the strategic objective of securing the European market for a European product.

In centrifugal economies, network organization reflects a deep division of labor between core firms and suppliers. In this vertical international firm network structure, participant firms are arranged in a hierarchy, with the core firm assuming dominant control over critical production decisions, marketing, and distribution methods, and technology transfer. This requires massive coordination capacity. The core firm identifies and allocates property rights via cost-based, short-term contracts, and attempts to redistribute risk downward through the commodity chain (Gereffi 1994, 1996; Golich 1992).

By contrast with the strategy of locating a fully formed network in another market (glocalization), international sourcing is the preferred form of organization. A sizable portion of this outsourced production is re-imported into the home base.

The core firm may not even perceive itself as a product producer but as a merchandiser or platform, the driver of a buyer-driven commodity chain. Such is the case with Nike athletic footwear (Korzeniewicz 1994). According to Gereffi (1994: 99, cited in Dicken 1998):

> The main job of the core company in buyer-driven commodity chains is to manage production and trade networks and make sure all the pieces of the business come together as an integrated whole. Profits in buyer-driven chains derive not from scale economies and technological advances as in producer-driven chains, but rather from unique combinations of high value research, design, sales, marketing and financial services that allow the buyers and branded merchandisers to act as strategic brokers in linking overseas factories and traders with evolving product niches in their main consumer market.

This merchant model of production organization is consonant with the short-term investment orientation of the centrifugal regime. It implies less cohesive relationships among participants in the production network and a higher level of volatility in the system as a whole. The differences between the cohesive networks of the centripetal regime and the opportunistic, strategic networks of the centrifugal regime are also reflected in their domestic policy networks and relationship to the state.

Coordination versus firm-specific policies: the significance of a sectoral voice

Both centripetal and centrifugal investment regimes influence state policy and use the state apparatus in an instrumental way to construct favorable international environments for trade and production. Policy outcomes are not a simple matter of influence. They are affected by the policy-making mechanisms in the state as well as the character of the domestic policy network – the organizational and ideological links between state and society (Katzenstein 1984).

Centripetal regimes facilitate intra-sectoral coordination and create a strong political foundation for sectorally based industrial policy. By contrast, those regimes whose market rules place both rights and risks in the individual firm promote intra-sectoral competition and discourage cooperation, favoring a 'winner-takes-all' approach to state support. In these regimes it is difficult to develop a political consensus for a sectorally based industrial policy that involves investment in services or infrastructure which benefits industries rather than individual firms. If firms cannot see a direct, short-term effect on their profits, they are unlikely to cohere around an industrial policy. In lieu of such coherence, subsidies of various sorts directed at individual firms become the only acceptable policy initiative.[11]

A significant aspect of coordinated regimes is their ability to construct a sectoral 'voice' with respect to state policy. Reich (1989) describes, for example, how VW orchestrated a process of coordination and cooperation within the automotive sector in order to shape government policy in its favor. In another instance, regional coalitions of firms and unions have been able to force state investment in industrial areas whose infrastructure needs rebuilding in order to be competitive. Such was the case with the German port city of Bremen. Although these policies and others, including those of the German government to protect domestic producers from foreign purchase, can be characterized as emanating from state interests, they also reflect the power of a strong coherent sectoral voice. The sectoral orientation of state industrial policy inherently favors domestic firms over foreign investors.

The sectoral voice assumes even more significance given the insecure positions of public policy-makers and the tendency for their decisions to be influenced by the ideology delimiting acceptable state–economy relationships (Ikenberry 1986). In the centrifugal regimes, firms organize trade associations to influence public policy but rarely are able to participate in the implementation of policies (such as job training programs) as a sectoral unit. The absence of coherent sectoral voices leaves an opening for *ad hoc* industrial policy, such as that represented by the relationship between national security and defense industries.

Industrial policy in centrifugal regimes focuses attention on the individual firm (e.g. Chrysler, Boeing) rather than on the sector and increases individual firm bargaining power. Within the US this has produced an industrial policy oriented around individual firms and firm-specific subsidies.[12] One of the consequences of this orientation is a perception on the part of firms that the only acceptable form of state intervention in the economy is firm specific. Firms see state subsidies as something akin to what Susan Strange (1986) describes as 'casino capitalism' ('You can't win if you don't play.')

Industrial policy in the US reflects, in microcosm, the state–state, state–firm, firm–firm bargaining structure put forward by Stopford and Strange (1991). Firm bargaining takes place against a background of interjurisdictional competition to provide the most 'efficient' conditions for firms (Molotch 1998). Firms bargain for tax abatements, infrastructural provision, and exemption from onerous environmental regulation.

One of the most important bargaining arenas is over wage concessions. To some observers, this local bargaining would appear unnecessary – the US has experienced serious wage decreases for 80% of the workforce since the 1970s (Mishel and Bernstein 1995) and regional wage differentials have eroded. Bargaining by firms to maintain or further decrease local wage costs is effective, however, because threats to relocate intra-regionally have become more persuasive. These threats are credible, not because of market-determined factor input costs, but because of subsidy packages offered by adjacent localities with equally low wage costs.

Ironically, concessions to individual firms made by labor and the state reduce the firm's sunk costs in any one location and enable an even stronger bargaining position in the next round.[13] One of the most significant aspects of this bargaining regime is the scale at which bargaining occurs. Locality level bargaining is the norm and maximizes the power of the firm vis-à-vis the state. The locality, in effect, acts as a lobbying agent for the firm. Firms may threaten to move or make initial investments within a regionally defined consumer or labor market, based on the conditions offered by various localities within the region. This allows them maximum bargaining power within the region which meets their primary locational requirements.

The subsidies demanded by US firms ultimately rebound to the detriment of the regional and local economy. Infrastructural investments for individual firms, such as those for access roads or fiber optic cables, serve the needs of the individual firm but do not constitute the type of infrastructural investment that will support broader industrial development. In the worst case scenario, such as that represented by the Saturn plant in Tennessee, tax concessions to the plant were of such magnitude that no resources were available for investment in the basic infrastructure needed to support the supplier firms that were expected to move to the site to serve the plant. The plant thus remains the dominant employer in the region (with low sunk costs) and its bargaining position vis-à-vis the state is further enhanced.

The sectoral voice and trade policy

The nature of state–industrial sector relations also inevitably influences the extent to which an economy is open or closed to trade. In centripetal systems, the presence of a strong sectoral voice provides a coherent political base for protectionist measures. For example, while Germany maintains a policy of open access to foreign investment, state policies also discriminate in favor of domestic firms (Reich 1989). This stance is exemplified by government intervention to prevent takeovers and buy-outs of firms considered 'national assets'.

Centrifugal regime, particularly Anglo-American, treatment of foreign direct investment differs considerably, in part, because of the lack of coherent political support for protectionist measures. The 'free trade' stance is strongly supported by international sourcing retailers in order to keep prices down and is buttressed by an ideology of comparative advantage which is solely commodity price based. US and British governments encourage foreign investment (in association with a free trade position) on the assumption that such investment will equalize national comparative advantage. However, if comparative advantage or, more accurately, competitive advantage is not simply cost-based and equalized by locating production in an environment with the same production costs, but is based on other factors, such as home country market institutions, then foreign firms maintain a competitive advantage whatever their location.

In addition, as Reich (1989) points out, if the state affords foreign firms the same treatment as domestic firms, it will incur significant long-term tangible costs because foreign producers face more realistic choices between exit and loyalty than do domestic producers.

Less obvious are the ways in which market rules inhibit foreign investment or competition in domestic markets via high 'sunk costs' and supplier–retailer relationships. Sunk costs are those investments in plant facilities, job training, pension benefits, or community goodwill which are never available for potential investment returns. In economies where sunk costs are high (as they frequently are in centripetal systems such as Japan and Germany), firms cooperating within the constraints of centrifugal systems and under pressure to produce short-term returns will be discouraged from investing. More likely to invest will be firms interested in long-term integration in the foreign economy, whatever their domestic origins.[14] So, outward investment by German transnational corporations increased dramatically over the 1980s (Dicken 1998), while inward investment declined during the same period (Julius 1991).

Firms expecting 'equal treatment' in centripetal systems must buy into high sunk costs. The 'equal treatment' disadvantage for firms operating under centrifugal market rules is exacerbated if the conventional industrial policy is one of individual firm subsidy. This has the effect of eliminating the sunk costs that would tie a foreign investor to a new production location.

On the consumption side, both high sunk costs and supplier–retailer relationships effectively discourage foreign firms from entering consumer markets. Like manufacturers, retailers in centripetal systems must join trade associations, buy community goodwill, and commit themselves to job training programs and apprenticeships in order to locate in a community. As a consequence they tend to be concerned with market share rather than quick profits. All of these practices, plus high labor costs and government regulations which favor the interests of existing businesses over those of potential newcomers, make the entry of short-term-oriented foreign competitors very costly and difficult, thereby protecting domestic markets for domestic producers (or those willing to play by local rules).

Once again, it is important to remember that in centripetal economies the rules governing enterprises are most frequently private, administered by trade associations and unions. So, for example, in Germany, it is the industry-run Central Institute for Combating Unfair Competition that enforces rules against illegal 'sales' (allowed only twice a year in Germany) and other violations of norms of competitive practice (Davis *et al.* 1995). Attempts to 'de-regulate' centripetal systems fall on deaf ears because the government plays an ancillary rather than a central role in market regulation. This private regulatory structure provides an effective fortress against foreign competition via trade or investment and moves together to maintain its collective competitive advantage. So, again in Germany, the retail banking sector provides services that in the US and UK are provided through a specialized fragmented financial service sector. The fact that there is one branch bank for every 1,400 Germans makes it difficult for foreign financial service firms to identify or reach customers for niche financial products.

The capacities and constraints constituted by market regulation systems support and expand recent work in geography on corporate decision-making (Schoenberger 1997) and the consequences of regulatory frameworks and their spatial characteristics (Christopherson 1993, 1998; Clark 1992; Marsden and Wrigley 1995: 33–47). If we accept their influence as institutions that can construct interests and thus political–economic space, they also lend themselves to a critique of some of the assumptions used to explain 'globalization' and the critical processes constructing the new world economy.

Conclusion: new parameters for interpreting networks

One consequence of accepting the continuing influence of politically constituted market regulation on the character of the world economy is a richer set of parameters within which to interpret firm investments and their locational outcomes, including network behavior.

At one level, this complexity arises from bringing a different set of theoretical materials to bear in explaining inter-firm relationships. Although we have theories that attempt to explain how firm networks interact to reduce costs and increase production flexibility, these theories focus almost exclusively on production cost variables (neglecting other sources of competitive advantage) or on governance at the local scale. The reasons for this may be found in intellectual history, and in the paradigms we have used to explain investment and location processes under contemporary global economic conditions. The first paradigm, that of the decline of the efficacy of the nation state, depends on the classical literature on political economy, which fixes the interests of political actors and the rules they institute within the territorial boundaries of the nation state. The paradigm we most frequently use retains that separation and treats the international economy as 'pure' market and the subnational region as a space of residual political–economic action. If, instead, we view political–economic actors as in the business of constructing 'regulatory spaces', the processes constructing the global economy become, at once, more transparent and more political (Roberts 1994).

In addition, an almost incidental initial focus on regional political economy in a country, Italy, with a singularly weak national market governance system, drove comparative studies, which then assumed that regional economies should be treated as relatively autonomous. From a perspective which starts first from the way in which political–economic actors construct regulatory space, the degree and kind of spatial differentiation in a nation state is the product of its market governance system and not a residual effect of globalization (Christopherson 1993).

A focus on market rules is, at base, a way to develop a framework within which to reassert the role of politics in the creation of regulated spaces, from that of the firm to that of the global economy.

Notes

1 The mid-1990s figure compares with 44% in 1960 (Uchitelle 1998).

2 Through a strategic alliance or supplier contract, a core firm can take advantage of the capacities produced by market governance systems distinctly different from its own but only insofar as they are consonant with its essential market strategy.

3 For an effective description of the workings of individual networks in the US context, see Saxenian (1994).

4 Both Germany and the US have a concept of 'the public interest' that enters into determinations of the limits of private property rights. In Germany, however, the public interest is much more specifically defined than in the US. In environmental or land use law, for example, the decisions of German courts reflect a 'rule and exceptions' scheme.

5 One manifestation of the international 'contest over rules' to govern international markets is in the area of intellectual property rights. Under the provisions of the Berne Convention, which governs property rights in most countries, the producers of intellectual property, whether artists or directors or authors, retain rights in the property apart from ownership rights to hold or distribute it. The US has never agreed to these provisions of the Berne Convention because they violate US property rights law which vests sole control of all property, including the right to alter it or destroy it, in the owner. Thus, politically contingent rules emerging out of nationally constituted political interests compose paradigms for the creation of international regulatory spaces. By extension, to understand the precepts underlying emerging international regulatory regimes, we need to understand their origins in national market regulation.

6 Data are from Deutsche Bundesbank, Tokyo Stock Exchange, Proshare, and the US Federal Reserve Board cited in Kester (1991).

7 Ninety-nine percent of all Japanese firms are unquoted and look to the banking system as the only source of external capital (Charkham 1994).

8 Some estimates place cross-shareholdings in Japan at just under half of all shareholdings (*Economist*, 1997).

9 By contrast, in many European countries bankruptcy is considered an irredeemable failure, and in Japan litigation is considered 'shameful'. Institutional capacities reflect these perceptions.

10 The risks associated with these investments are increased to the extent that they are location specific. So, systems which lower risks via long-term business relationships deal with location-specific risks via the private sector while in the US these risks can be relegated to the public sector via firm-specific subsidies.

11 Countries, most notably the US, in which the political risks of a sectoral industrial policy outweigh the benefits because of the absence of clear sectoral 'voices' will tend to oppose such policies in other regimes labeling them as unfair subsidies. This stance is justified on the grounds that in a 'winner-takes-all' situation and under conditions of equal treatment, every firm may compete for a subsidy while sectoral industrial policies have tended to promote the interests of domestic producers.

12 Individual firm-specific subsidies are also linked to a form of electoral politics dependent on individual contributions.

13 The one sector in which capital mobility has aroused public attention in the US is that of professional sports. A recent satire of the increasing tendency to sell sports teams to the highest bidder describes a departure scenario: '1) initiate secret meetings with cities that want a team; 2) choose your new city and then leak stories about how much money you are losing in your current home; 3) sign your lease with the city that's just enacted a new lottery, passed new taxes on alcohol, bowling and tap shoes and closed down two high schools to give you that $300 million stadium and $50 million signing bonus.' The story ends with 'Scenario II: move – then move some more' (Sandomir 1995).

14 A preliminary analysis of the approximately 300 US firms in Germany indicates three major reasons for location in Germany: (1) a German connection and familiarity if not a positive preference for German market regulation; (2) association with defense activities located in Germany; and (3) access to industrial markets.

Bibliography

Berk, G. (1994) *Alternative Tracks, The Constitution of American Industrial Order, 1865–1917*, Baltimore, MD: Johns Hopkins University Press.

Cawson, A., Morgan, K., Webber, D., Holmes, P. and Stevens, A. (1990) *Hostile Brothers: Competition and Closure in the European Electronics Industry*, Oxford: Clarendon Press.

Charkham, J. (1994) *Keeping Good Company, A Study of Corporate Governance in Five Countries*, Oxford: Clarendon Press.

Christopherson, S. (1993) 'Market rules and territorial outcomes: the case of the United States', *International Journal of Urban and Regional Research* 17: 274–88.

—— (1998) *Why do National Labor Market Practices Continue to Diverge in a Global Economy? An institutional perspective on the persistence of difference*, Washington, DC: US Department of Labor, International Labor Affairs Bureau.

Clark, G.L. (1992) 'Real regulation: the administrative state', *Environment and Planning A* 24: 615–27.

Clark, G. and Wrigley, N. (1997) 'Exit, the firm and sunk costs: reconceptualizing the corporate geography of disinvestment and plant closure', *Progress in Human Geography* 21(3): 338–58.

Darbishire, O. and Katz, H. (1996) Converging divergences: worldwide changes in employment relations, manuscript, Ithaca, NY: NYSSILR, Cornell University.

Davis, B., Gumbel, P. and Hamilton, D. (1995) 'To all U.S. managers upset by regulations: try Germany and Japan', *Wall Street Journal*, 14 December: 1, 3.

Dicken, P. (1998) *Global Shift: Transforming the World Economy*, 3rd edn, New York: Guilford Press.

Dolzer, R. (1992) *Property and Environment: The Social Obligation of Ownership*, IUCN Environmental Policy and Law Paper No. 12, Morges, Switzerland: International Union for Conservation of Nature and Natural Resources.

Doremus, P., Keller, W., Pauly, L. and Reich, S. (1998) *The Myth of the Global Corporation*, Princeton, NJ: Princeton University Press.

Fruin, M. (1992) *The Japanese Enterprise System*, Oxford: Clarendon Press.

Fukao, M. (1995) *Financial Integration, Corporate Governance and the Performance of Multinational Companies*, Washington, DC: The Brookings Institution.

Gereffi, G. (1994) 'The organization of buyer-driven global commodity chains: how U.S. retailers shape overseas production networks', in G. Gereffi and M. Korzeniewicz (eds) *Commodity Chains and Global Capitalism*, Westport, CT: Praeger: Chapter 5.

—— (1996) 'Global commodity chains; new forms of coordination and control among nations and firms in international industries', *Competition & Change* 1: 427–39.

Gertler, M. (1995) ' "Being there": proximity, organizations and culture in the development and adoption of advanced manufacturing technologies', *Economic Geography* 71: 1–26.

Golich, V. (1992) 'From competition to collaboration: the challenge of commercial-class aircraft manufacturing', *International Organization* 46(4): 899–934.

Hancher, L. and Moran, M. (1989) 'Organising regulatory space', in L. Hancher and M. Moran (eds) *Capitalism, Culture and Regulation*, Oxford: Clarendon Press.

Harrison, B. (1997) *Lean and Mean, The Changing Landscape of Corporate Power in the Age of Flexibility*, New York: Guilford Press.

Heilbroner, R. (1996) 'Reflections on a sad state of affairs', in J. Eatwell (ed.) *Global Unemployment, Loss of Jobs in the '90s*, London: M.E. Sharpe.

Ikenberry, G.J. (1986) 'Conclusion: An institutional approach to American foreign policy', in G.J. Ikenberry, D. Lake and M. Mastanduno (eds) *The State and American Foreign Economic Policy*, Ithaca, NY: Cornell University Press.

Jacobs, M.T. (1991) *Short-term America: The Causes and Cures of our Business Myopia*, Boston, MA: Harvard Business School Press.

—— (1993) 'National financial systems and the sensitivity of aggregate investment to the cost of capital', paper presented to the Allied Social Science Association, 3 January 1994, Boston.

Julius, D. (1991) *Global Companies & Public Policy*, New York: Council on Foreign Relations Press.

Katzenstein, P. (1984) *Small States in World Markets*, Ithaca, NY: Cornell University Press.

Kester, W.C. (1991) *Governance, Contracting and Investment Time Horizons*, Washington, DC: Council on Competitiveness.

Korzeniewicz, M. (1994) 'Commodity chains and marketing strategies: Nike and the global athletic footwear industry', in G. Gereffi and M. Korzeniewicz (eds) *Commodity Chains and Global Capitalism*, Westport, CT: Praeger.

Markusen, A. (1996) 'Sticky places in slippery space: a typology of industrial districts', *Economic Geography* 72: 293–313.

Marsden, T.K. and Wrigley, N. (1995) 'Retailing, the food systems, and the regulatory state', in N. Wrigley and M. Lowe (eds) *Retailing, Consumption and Capital: Towards the New Retail Geography*, London: Longman, pp. 33–47.

Mishel, L. and Bernstein, J. (1995) *The State of Working America*, Washington, DC: Economic Policy Institute.

Molotch, H. (1998) 'Urban America crushed in the growth machine', in C.Y.H. Lo and M. Schwartz (eds) *Social Policy and the Conservative Agenda*, Oxford: Blackwell.

Porter, M. (1992) *Capital Choices: Changing the Way America Invests in Industry*, Washington, DC: Council on Competitiveness.

Reich, S. (1989) 'Roads to follow: regulating direct foreign investment', *International Organization* 43: 543–84.

Roberts, S. (1994) Competition, risk and regulation in international finance: changing relations of states and capital, unpublished manuscript, Lexington, KY: Department of Geography, University of Kentucky.

Ruigrok, W. and van Tulder, R. (1995) *The Logic of International Restructuring*, New York: Routledge.

Sandomir, R. (1995) 'Moving teams for fun and profit', *New York Times*, 26 November: Section E:6.

Saxenian, A. (1994) *Silicon Landscapes*, Cambridge, MA: Harvard University Press.

Schoenberger, E. (1997) *The Cultural Crisis of the Firm*, Oxford: Blackwell.

Shaikh, A. (1996) 'Free trade, unemployment, and economic policy', in J. Eatwell (ed.) *Global Unemployment, Loss of Jobs in the '90s*, London: M.E. Sharpe.

Skowronek, S. (1982) *Building a New American State: The Expansion of National Administrative Capacities, 1877–1920*, Cambridge: Cambridge University Press.

Stiglitz, J. and Weiss, A. (1981) 'Credit rationing in markets with imperfect information', *American Economic Review* 71: 3.

Stopford, J.M. and Strange, S. (1991) *Rival States, Rival Firms: Competition for World Market Shares*, Cambridge: Cambridge University Press.

Strange, S. (1986) *Casino Capitalism*, Oxford: Blackwell.

Thrift, N. and Olds, K. (1996) 'Refiguring the economic in economic geography', *Progress in Human Geography* 20(3): 311–37.

Thurow, L. (1993) *Head to Head*, New York: William Morrow.

Weber, R. (1995) 'The state as corporate stakeholder: governing the decline of the military-industrial complex', PhD dissertation, Cornell University, Ithaca, NY.

Uchitelle, L. (1998) 'Global tug; national tether', *New York Times*, 30 April: D1, 6.

Ziegler, N. (1994) 'Recent changes in Germany's public strategies for technology promotion', paper presented at a conference on the Political Economy of the New Germany, Cornell University, Ithaca, NY.

8 Continentalism in an era of globalization

A perspective from Canada's resource periphery

Roger Hayter and John Holmes

Introduction

In this chapter, we examine the idea of (North American) continentalism from a Canadian perspective that is centred on resource or 'staple' industries and regions. In theory and practice, it is widely accepted that continentalism is a quintessential example of a global trend towards regionalism in international trade and investment, formally underpinned by the Free Trade Agreement (FTA) between Canada and the US in 1989 and subsequently extended to include Mexico in the North American Free Trade Agreement (NAFTA) of 1992 (Gibb and Michalak 1994; McConnell and MacPherson 1994). What is at issue is whether or not the FTA and NAFTA (and other cases of international regionalism) are stepping stones towards, or steps backwards from the multilateralism advocated by the General Agreement on Tariffs and Trade (GATT) since 1947 (Gibb 1994; Michalak 1994). Even within North America, an unequivocal march to free trade practice is not apparent (Gertler and Schoenberger 1992; Hayter 1992). Indeed, for Canada, specifically its resource industries and regions, the regulatory framework of continentalism has changed substantially over the last twenty years and for established Canadian-based resource industries, such as the forest industries, continentalism typically implies more restrictive conditions and opportunities than was previously the case. A key to understanding this apparently paradoxical development, as Glasmeier *et al.* (1993) emphasize, is to recognize that trade relations and agreements, implicit and formal, are motivated by principles of self interest and political economy that do not entirely conflate with the assumption of enlightened mutual interest that underlies notions of 'free trade'.

For the purposes of this chapter, the idea of a regulatory framework refers to broadly accepted 'norms' of behaviour that shape international relations, whether buttressed by formal policy or not. As an illustration of this conception, continentalism has been a powerful ideology underpinning trade, investment and indeed labour relations between Canada and the US for a long period of time, certainly for most of the twentieth century. Indeed, continentalism may be seen as an adjunct of, even the basis for, Pax

Americana. In effect, until the FTA and NAFTA, continentalism existed as an implicit policy or, to use Storper's (1997) term that is normally applied at local scales, as a broadly based 'convention' underlying the behaviour of business, governments and unions. The significance and nature of continentalism is not in dispute. Thus the US and Canada have long forged the most significant bilateral trading relationship in the world and one which has largely cast Canada's global visible trading role as that of resource supplier to the US metropole in return for manufactured goods delivered as imports or via branch plants. In Canada, however, continentalism has been, and remains, contentious. On the one hand, the economic benefits of continentalism are equated with free trade and Canada's role as resource supplier is 'seen as a natural development' reflecting the benign allocations of comparative advantage (Mackintosh 1967). Canadian critics, on the other hand, see continentalism as institutionalizing over-dependency on staple exports (raw materials and primary manufactures), as a reflection of Canadian economic and political subservience, and the manner in which the US has cast a shadow over the northern half of the continent (Watkins 1989: 28; see also Clement 1989; Innis 1967; Rotstein 1977; Watkins 1963). From this perspective, continentalism represents Canadian acquiescence to US hegemony in a way that has limited Canadian policy options. Hence the approbation: 'Canada is rich in resources, poor in policy' (Kierans 1987: xiv).

On the face of it, the FTA and NAFTA provide a stamp of approval for the idea of North America as a trading bloc, a triumph for the voices of continentalism. Yet, by the 1980s continentalism was a mature policy that to a significant degree had been implemented in the arena of trade and investment relations. Even Canada's free trade economists and advocates argue that by the 1980s Canada had already reaped the benefits of free trade with the US and that Canada should not expect to gain too much from NAFTA, at least in the foreseeable future (Cox and Harris 1992; Watson 1987). Indeed, we suggest that from a Canadian perspective, the rhetoric and reality of continentalism are following different trajectories. Thus, despite FTA and NAFTA, many of Canada's staple sectors and communities are facing renewed US protectionism. In the case of lumber, such protectionism was grandfathered in the agreements themselves (Hayter 1992). Moreover, the trade dispute mechanisms negotiated as part of the trade agreements have politicized issues in a way that is not to Canada's advantage, added new layers of bureaucracy that counters the idea of free markets and have in any case not removed US discretionary powers over trade matters. In practice, the survival of many Canadian staple producers depends upon shifting away from the strictures of continentalism. For these producers, the creation of the North American trading bloc is not providing a defence, and certainly not a 'fortress', against broader forces of globalization. Moreover, if continentalism has traditionally meant Canadian specialization and commodity standardization for US markets, globalization is demanding greater flexibility, diversity and differentiation among Canadian staple producers and communities. In the present period of globalization, continentalism is providing less of a security blanket to Canadian staple exporters than has been the case in previous decades.

In this chapter, with specific reference to the Canadian paper industry and to the experience of the Powell River paper mill in British Columbia, we explore the evolution and contemporary transformation of continentalism as a regulatory framework, especially with respect to trade and investment. In a widely held view, Canada's staple industries and regions are the result of market forces. Yet these market forces are themselves subservient to the regulatory framework of continentalism. Thus the restructuring of Canada's staple industries, specifically the paper industry, is not only the result of market-driven changes in prices, but also a consequence of more fundamental shifts in regulatory effects. Recently a number of studies have examined the restructuring of paper mills across Canada, including Powell River, as exemplars of the shift from Fordism to post-Fordist industrial structures (Hayter 1996; Hayter and Holmes 1993, 1994; Holmes 1997; Mackenzie and Norcliffe 1997; Norcliffe and Bates 1997; Preston *et al.* 1997; Rose and Villemaire 1997). These studies, however, do not link processes of restructuring with the theme of continentalism. Yet, a few caveats aside, continentalism has been the guiding principle shaping the location, structure and performance of the wood-based Canadian paper industry virtually from its origins. To be comprehensively understood, the restructuring of paper mills, such as Powell River, across Canada has to be placed in the context of the legacy and changing imperatives of continentalism.

In broader conceptual terms, as Michalak (1994) observes, the restructuring literature in general has not explicitly incorporated literature dealing with international regionalism, especially the creation of trading blocs. This omission is especially surprising since multilateralism was such an important feature of the international environment of Fordism and the subsequent upheaval of Fordist production structures has been paralleled by complications and caveats to multilateralism. Indeed, Michalak (1994) intimates that the restructuring of Fordist industrial structures towards more flexible arrangements implicates, in one way or another, the shift towards international regionalism. This study seeks to contribute towards bridging this research gap.

As a final introductory comment, we acknowledge a debt to Harold Innis (1930, 1950, 1956, 1967) and the Innisian tradition he spawned (Barnes 1987, 1993a, 1993b; Britton and Gilmour 1978; Clement and Williams 1989; Hayter and Barnes 1990; Kroker 1985; Melody *et al.* 1981; Neill 1972; Rotstein 1977; Watkins 1981). Without offering a further review, we simply note that an important dimension of the Innisian tradition constitutes a set of criticisms about the manner in which the staple sector in Canada has been exploited to serve primarily the interests of foreign, metropolitan powers. Indeed, Innis was the most consistent, and necessarily effective, of opponents against the quick absorption of Canadian society into the continentalist strategy of the

American empire (Kroker 1985: 97). This criticism, by the way, implies not only a concern for Canadian dependency on the American metropole (and previously on the British metropole) but also disillusionment with the complicity of Canadian policies, a disillusionment reflected in Innis's accusation of Canadian 'political lethargy', and 'an infinite capacity for self-congratulation' (Innis 1956: 398–9). Similar comments have been made regarding Canadian proponents of the FTA. Thus Atkinson and Coleman (1989: 51) suggest that the Canadian government's enthusiasm for the FTA was because it constituted 'the least demanding industrial policy option'. Certainly, no new ideas were needed as Canadian economists had been urging just such a policy for decades; in Canada economic liberalism provides a deeply rooted philosophy which is sceptical about government interference in economic matters, including trade; while tariffs between the US and Canada had been declining for decades and on many Canadian staples were already non-existent. In fact, the FTA and NAFTA may well have stimulated some unintended effects, especially in relation to the resource sector.

Continentalism and the regulation of Canada's staple industries

A shared continent and much common cultural heritage inevitably facilitated a close integration of the US and Canadian economies. In an oft quoted phrase, Mackintosh (1967: 15) argued that 'Canada is a nation created in defiance of geography', by which he meant that the 'natural' – in the sense of economically rational – flow of commerce and trade is north–south. Notwithstanding such 'natural' links, prior to the twentieth century Canadian staples, notably fur, fish, square lumber and wheat, were developed as an alternative to, and sometimes in competition with, American sources, primarily to serve British markets and imperial interests. For these staples, the 'natural flow' of trade was east–west across Canada (and the Atlantic) and for Innis (1930) it was the fur trade that defined the realm of Canada. But the extraordinarily rapid industrialization of the US economy inevitably re-cast trade along north–south lines so that the Canadian staples developed in the twentieth century, notably pulp, paper, lumber, various metallic minerals and petroleum, have typically complemented US growth (Norcliffe 1996). Indeed, in the manner prescribed by continentalism, these staples have developed principally, sometimes almost exclusively, to serve US economic and strategic interests.

Principles of continentalism

Continentalism does not solely imply the 'close integration' of the Canadian and US economies. Rather, the implementation of continentalism has involved specific policy attitudes and choices. In particular, continentalism has implied a distinct model of international relations, a distinct set of economic beliefs and a specific spatial division of labour between the two countries. Baldly stated, the three principles of continentalism comprise: the political hegemony of the US; an economic commitment to free trade and the free flow of investment; and a continental spatial division of labour that emphasizes Canada's role of staple supplier to US markets and the US as supplier of industrial goods. Moreover, within staple industries, continentalism implies a similar spatial division of labour in which Canada's emphasis is on bulk commodities with value-added activities occurring in the US. Within Canada itself, continentalism is further equated with antagonism towards political support for economic sovereignty.

Defined in these terms, although never expressed in a formal treaty, the roots of continentalism can be traced to the latter part of the nineteenth century and to the American formulation of 'manifest destiny', a concept supported by American unions as well by business and government. Within Canada, where the idea of continentalism has always been more controversial, since before Confederation debates about economic development have invariably engaged 'continentalists' or 'free traders', whose priority is the creation of linkages with the US, and the 'nationalists', whose priority is the creation of linkages within Canada. Occasionally, this argument surfaced as free trade or reciprocity debates, which dominated federal elections including John A. Macdonald's election victory, which led to the National Policy of 1879, and the 1911 election, which was again won by the conservatives on the basis of a nationalist, anti-free trade stance. As it turned out, the National Policy and the 1911 election were illusory victories for the forces of nationalism. Thus the National Policy, by combining high tariffs and an open door policy to foreign investment, greatly stimulated the establishment of American branch plants to serve the Canadian market, and thereby strong north–south linkages in terms of lines of control and affiliated linkages. Indeed, the absorption of the Canadian economy within that of the US was fully supported by Canadian federal and provincial policies, which emphasized exploiting staples for export, principally by subsidizing infrastructure, establishing low resource-rent regimes and encouraging entry by foreign, especially American, capital. With a few exceptions restricted to primary processing only, since Confederation Canadian policies have not sought to add value to staples or to promote backward linkages in the form of machinery and equipment which has often enjoyed low-duty or duty-free status entering Canada. Moreover, beginning after 1911 the US introduced tariff policies that favoured the import of Canadian resources and in some cases primary manufactures but discriminated substantially against secondary manufactures. At the same time, the formation of unions in Canada was strongly affected by US organizations.

As Marshall *et al.*'s (1936) study documents, a continentalist economy existed by the 1930s. While the 1930s Depression and the Second World War provided an opportunity for Canada to re-think its philosophy, government, business and even union strategies and structures on both sides of the border combined to reinforce continentalism, which reached its zenith in the 1950s and 1960s. For its part, the Canadian federal government, which had apparently been quietly lobbying for continentalism since at least the 1940s (Clark-Jones 1987), maintained its liberal philosophy towards direct foreign investment while provincial governments' zeal for resource mega projects and to establish themselves as 'stable and secure' resource suppliers to the US remained unabated (Haglund 1989; Weaver and Gunton 1982). On the US side, the most obvious confirmation of continentalism was the Paley Report of 1952, which stressed the threat of communism to global security and the need for the US to import low-cost and 'strategic' raw materials to meet its political and economic obligations. Canada was regarded as a particularly desirable source of resources, including newsprint, then considered a 'strategic' commodity. The US also introduced or retained zero or low tariffs on resource imports while maintaining protection for its secondary manufacturing sector. Moreover, as Watkins (1989: 30) reminds us, during the 1950s and 1960s the US was willing to grant special concessions or exemptions to Canada from otherwise punitive US policies. In the 1960s, for example, Canada was made exempt from balance of payments directives affecting American branch plants in foreign countries while the Auto Pact increased the efficiency of the auto industry and gave Canada access to American markets, albeit at the same time entrenching Canadian complete managerial and technological dependency on US firms.

For Canada, continentalism has bequeathed some highly unusual characteristics to the economy. First, Canada has traditionally relied on trade to a greater degree than most other advanced countries, whether they are larger or smaller. In the mid-1980s, for example, the value of exports accounted for almost 27% of Canada's GNP but less than 7% of US GNP and only 15% of Australian GNP (Clement 1989: 43). Second, caveats to the Auto Pact aside, Canada has remained unusually dependent on exports of large volumes of standardized staples produced in large operations located in specialized communities within Canada's periphery. Third, Canada's trade remains usually, indeed remarkably, specialized on one partner, the US. For decades, over three-quarters of Canada's imports and exports have been with the US; countries such as Australia and Mexico have a far more geographically diversified trade structure. Fourth, the Canadian economy has experienced a remarkably high level of foreign, primarily American, ownership, especially in the staple and secondary sectors, for a long period of time (Britton and Gilmour 1978). As Rotstein (1977) notes, during this century Canada has been at the leading edge of the explosion of multinational investment. Fifth, in comparison with other industrialized countries, larger and smaller, Canada's per capita R&D investments in the private sector are low throughout the industrial sector, including the staple industries. Sixth, since the end of the nineteenth century American unions have expanded into Canada, which 'is unique in that it is the only country in the world with unions whose headquarters are located in a foreign country, unions which at the same time are subject to the laws and labour legislation enacted in the country where the headquarters are situated' (Scott 1978: 7). That is, 'international unions' in Canada are themselves branch organizations, which in 1921 accounted for almost 73% of union membership and for an even higher percentage in the early 1960s when union membership in Canada was much greater. Elsewhere, of course, international unionism has the very different connotation of cooperation between independent, national organizations.

Critics of continentalism from a Canadian perspective

These structural features of Canada's industrial economy, and related trading patterns, are interpreted differently by continentalists and nationalists. For continentalists, these features elicit a 'so what?' response; for the continentalists what is important are the efficiencies and growth generated by free trade and the free flow of foreign investment. In their view, access to the huge American market and to American direct foreign investment that provides critical inputs of know-how, capital and access to affiliated (and stable) markets, facilitates growth in the Canadian economy and helps sustain high standards of living. For the continentalists, the landscape of continentalism is essentially the realistic expression of comparative advantage. In effect, the continentalists argue that, at least for Canada, ownership does not matter in terms of economic behaviour. This position is supported by studies which claim that they cannot find any differences in the secondary manufacturing sector between the behaviour of foreign-owned branch plants and of indigenous firms (Safarian 1966) and by rather more vague suggestions that resource producers in the US are more or less in the same position as resource producers in Canada.

For nationalists, the Canadian economic landscape is a 'truncated' one. In this view, the Canadian industrial economy is too narrowly specialized on commodities and low-value industries as the landscape of continentalism has left Canada with fewer head-office activities, less R&D capability, fewer value-added activities, more limited trading contacts and fewer exports of manufactured goods than can be reasonably expected for an economy of Canada's size and complexity (Britton and Gilmour 1978; Hayter 1982; Rosenbluth 1981; Watkins 1989). This view is supported by studies which have detected significant differences in Canada's secondary manufacturing sector and the tendency for branch plants to reduce local multiplier effects and R&D capability by transferring demands back to donor economies (Britton 1976) while resource-based industries that rely on commodity exports, imported technology and decisions made by foreign-based corporations have structures and face problems which are different from resource producers accessing domestic markets and which are locally controlled and supported by indigenous technological capability. These studies further suggest that care needs to be exercised in conducting comparisons to determine whether or not truncation exists while also noting that observed differences in behaviour may or may not be critical (Hayter 1982). Rosenbluth asks, for example: 'Suppose the right to vote in Canadian elections were confined to the inhabitants of ... Cleveland, Ohio. Would that be alright? Would it be necessary to show that the resulting Canadian government was worse than the one elected by the residents of Canada? It might well be impossible to demonstrate this.' (Rosenbluth 1981: 345). To some extent, the nationalist argument is a plea, not for autarky, but for greater independence and control in economic matters and a recognition of the primacy of political economy rather than simply economics.

Within the crucial staple sector, Innis (1950) saw continentalism as creating within Canada an 'unbalanced' landscape featuring intense cycles of boom and bust according to the demands of the US metropole, a vulnerability often reinforced by changes in supply conditions, technology and the policies of multinational corporations. As Innis noted in an oft quoted sentence: 'Each staple in its turn left its stamp, and the shift to new staples invariably produced periods of crisis in which adjustments in the old structure were painfully made and a new pattern created in relation to a new staple' (Innis 1950: 5–6). Unfortunately, in the view of Innisians, continentalism has left the Canadian economy, including the staple sector, in a weak bargaining position. In this view, high levels of foreign ownership and a lack of decision-making autonomy and R&D capability within Canada's private sector, an unusual reliance on the resource sector whose terms of trade and job potential inevitably deteriorate over the long term and the assumed priority of US security and military interests have collectively conspired to cast Canadian policy to the US coat-tail (McGee 1990). In this latter regard, the extent of Canadian acquiescence should not be underestimated. Indeed, during the free trade debate of the 1980s Canadian continentalists desired an agreement which, at least with respect to foreign investment and energy, 'would place any future nationalist initiative ... permanently beyond the legislative capability of the Canadian state' (Williams 1983: 137).

After Fordism: the modification of continentalism

Since the early 1970s, the transformation of the global economy has gathered momentum, driven by dynamic markets, increasing competition and technological change. While new industrial spaces have been created, established Fordist production systems have been undermined, and the industrial hegemony of the US has at least been questioned. Industrial restructuring within North America, and beyond, has also provided context for the emergence of cracks in continentalism as it had been practised under Fordism, and even for changes in the nature of continentalism as a regulatory framework. From this perspective, the FTA and NAFTA cannot be simply regarded as rubber-stamping an existing regime of continentalism; rather they herald a different, in some ways more complex, form of regulating the trade and investment relationships between the two countries.

Cracks in continentalism, as practised in the high noon of Fordism, are reflected in several ways relating to trade, labour and investment. The most obvious expression of continental tension is that US protectionist sentiment continues to be directed against Canadian staple exporters and the FTA/NAFTA seems to be having little effect in dampening US enthusiasm in this regard. Thus, by 1994, 59 trade conflicts, or about one a month, have gone to the dispute settlement mechanism set up by the FTA, including softwood lumber, which by 1998 had been in dispute for sixteen years although for the previous forty years it had been exported duty free to the US (Hayter 1992). With respect to investment, as staple trade links have become more vulnerable US corporations in the 1980s have occasionally sold off their Canadian operations. According to Marchak (1983), for example, an important dimension of restructuring in the British Columbian forest industry of the early 1980s was the withdrawal of long-established American multinationals as they sought to place priority on modernization and expansion within the US. Such examples exist across Canada (see Hayter 1985, 1993). One implication of such divestments is to reduce anti-protectionist lobbies within the US, which in effect means a reduction in Canadian bargaining power.

With respect to labour, with gathering momentum (from the early 1960s onwards) one Canadian local union after another has democratically voted to break away from their branch-plant status as part of American 'international' unions. Thus the proportion of Canadian union members who were part of American unions dropped from 75% in 1961 to just over half in 1973 to 31% in 1992 as an increasing number of unions have been Canadianized (Kumar 1993: 2; Laxer 1976). This trend reflects various motives including the fact that unionism in the two countries evolved along different trajectories. Thus while the philosophy of 'business unionism' gained ascendancy in the US, in Canada unions have typically pursued a broader social and political agenda. Moreover, while American unions have often argued the need for international unions to respond effectively to international capital, Canadian locals since the turn of the century have complained about the financial drain of membership dues to US-based head offices and a continuing failure to support Canadian priorities. Indeed, historically American unions were a strong voice supporting continentalism and the implied restrictions on Canadian job opportunities while in recent times American unions have often supported protectionist measures regardless of Canadian concerns (Laxer 1976; Scott 1978). It should also be emphasized that the creation of independent Canadian unions is not merely symbolic; rather, since their formation, whether in the lumber, paper or automobile industries, the policies and contracts of Canadian unions have increasingly diverged from their American counterparts. Labour relations in the automobile industry following the formation of the Canadian Auto Workers Union in 1984 are a good case in point (Holmes and Rusonick 1990).

To some extent it may be argued that federal government policy initiatives in the 1970s on either side of the border anticipated these cracks in continentalism. As Watkins (1989: 30) observes, a redefinition of US–Canada relations was signalled, inevitably by the US, in 1971 when 'in the face of a weak American dollar, the United States imposed an across-the-board surcharge on imports and refused to exempt Canada even when asked', a position reinforced by President Nixon in a 1972 speech in Canada which stated: 'Washington would grant to Canada no more exemptions and permit no more special arrangements'. Subsequently in the 1970s, Canadian governments attempted various nationalist initiatives by, for example, introducing controls on foreign investment, creating crown corporations and sponsoring the idea of the Third Option, a strategy of trade diversification from the US. In fact, Canada's dependence on the US actually increased in the 1970s and its so-called Third Option formulation of the early 1970s was never effectively buttressed by effective public or private sector policies. Ineffectual as they were, Canada's flirtation with nationalism profoundly upset engrained continentalist thinking and these criticisms, in association with the onset of severe economic recession in the early 1980s, set the table for the free trade debate and the renewal of commitment to continentalism in the FTA of 1989 and the subsequent creation of NAFTA.

If the cracks in continentalism are nation-wide, it is in Canada's staple industries and regions that these changes are most pronounced. On the one hand, the Auto Pact, which provides the industrial anchor for the central Canadian economy, has defined since 1966 a managed trade-market sharing deal organized within US-controlled firms. There really has been no reason to change the fundamentals of this 'deal' which, from the perspective of trade, anticipated by several decades the US government's shift from a philosophy of 'free trade' to one of managed trade. On the other hand, many of Canada's staples threaten rival US industries and are now perceived not so much as 'complementary' to US needs but as competitive with US sources. In the harsher economic climate of the 1980s and 1990s, this situation has led to a redefinition of the meaning of continentalism. The forest sector is a good example.

In the case of lumber, for example, since 1982 the Canadian industry has been subject to several countervail actions. While Canadian interests have won several rounds in this deeply contentious dispute, after each 'Canadian victory' US lumber interests, the key names of which remain unknown to this day, have nevertheless been able to appeal or successfully change the rules of procedure to have previous decisions overturned (Hayter 1992). In the latest round, following a victory for the Canadian side in the summer of 1994 in the 'final' step of the dispute mechanism, as established under the FTA/NAFTA, US lumber producers appealed to the US courts on the basis that the entire dispute mechanism violates the US constitution since foreign (Canadian) nationals have no right to affect US law, in this case pertaining to import duties. Although the US federal government did not support such an initiative, continuing opposition to Canadian lumber imports, and the expense of prolonged negotiations and court cases, encouraged the Canadian side to agree to a quasi-quota system in 1997.

Essentially, when Canadian imports reach a particular level, tariffs are imposed; an agreement which basically defines its role as a subcontractor, albeit still an important one. As a result of an earlier agreement, the US also has a say in Canadian stumpage formulas, that is taxation levels on trees harvested (Hayter 1992). Thus, in this industry, the free trade system that operated under Fordism has been replaced by a managed trade system and by the extension of US control over resource management, an unprecedented initiative. Moreover, the US is now (1998) insisting that the quota applies to lumber products that have been slightly modified. For the purposes of this study, suffice to say that lumber exports from Canada to the US in the 1990s now occur under a much more complex and uncertain set of regulations than they did from the 1940s to the early 1980s when continentalism was a 'mere' convention. Ironically, for Canada's staple producers the inclusion of a dispute mechanism became the rationale for the FTA as continentalists argued such a mechanism would reduce arbitrary actions by US interests and would at least help secure existing Canadian exports.

The Canadian paper industry has not been targeted by protectionist interests in the US, mainly because the US industry is a lower cost, more efficient competitor and Canadian exports are a declining influence in the US. At the same time, recycling legislation in the US has further enhanced the viability of US locations over Canadian ones, since the US has much greater access to recycled paper. Moreover, one of the legacies of continentalism is that high-value paper production in Canada has been truncated. Consequently, the FTA/NAFTA notwithstanding, Canadian paper producers, along with lumber producers, are now seeking to diversify and develop markets, with a little foresight policies they could have initiated some decades ago.

For most of the twentieth century, for Canada's staple sector as a whole, if not for individual industries and communities, recovery from recession, including the Great Depression of the 1930s, featured a strengthening of continental ties. There are reasons to believe, however, that the present period of restructuring in Canada and the US has more complex implications for continentalism and that particularly for several of Canada's resource industries, including the forest industries, integration with the US does not offer the same hopes for revival. That is, across an important spectrum of Canada's staple industries the recessions of the early 1980s and 1990s are not simply severe downturns in continental relations (and of US demands) but are reflecting more permanent changes in continentalism. In terms of the basic principles of continentalism, the assumption of US hegemony remains unchanged, as does Canada's role within a continental division of labour. A key difference is the shift in US attitude from principles of free trade to principles of managed trade and that this attitude should apply within Fortress North America as well as to 'outsiders'. Under continentalism, nationalists have long interpreted Canada's economic relationship with the US as that of a passive, dependent subcontractor. From the perspective of staple exports, in boom times, or for military support, Canadian resources are absorbed, frequently as tied imports among affiliated plants of international corporations, but in recessions, or if security needs change, purchases can be reduced easily from non-tied sources, and contracts terminated. This relationship seems more firmly entrenched since the FTA than before.

It may be argued from the perspective of Canada's established staple sector that the FTA/NAFTA and the creation of a North American trading bloc is anachronistic. For Canada, the key requirement of FTA/NAFTA was access to the US market, but most of Canada's staples have long had this access. Moreover, the trade dispute mechanism incorporated within the FTA appears to be creating additional uncertainty and reinforcing rather than ameliorating US protectionism. It may well be that, for Canada's staple producers, the signing of the FTA signals a period of diversification away from the US without providing any kind of protection from the broader competitive forces associated with globalization. The implications of FTA/NAFTA, however, are that any diversification of the staple sector's traditional continentalist role depends upon the initiatives of individual firms and communities. Such initiatives may well produce a more variegated economic landscape than the one associated with continentalism. One sector currently in transition from the forces of continentalism to those of globalization is the Canadian paper industry.

Continentalism and the Canadian paper industry

The Canadian paper industry is an example of a staple almost completely developed in the interests of continentalism. Thus, between 1900 and 1920 the industry grew over tenfold from a total output of 181,000 tonnes to 1,902,000 tonnes (Table 8.1). In this twenty-year period the industry changed from a small, diversified, domestically oriented industry to a large-scale export-oriented industry, dominated by newsprint, principally serving the US. Moreover, the basic commodity mix of the industry has remained stable; in 1920 and 1987 about 75% of industry output comprised newsprint and market pulp. The basis for the growth of the Canadian paper (and pulp) industry in the critical decades at the beginning of the century was provided by escalating demands in the US at a time when the US's softwood forests were being rapidly depleted. Given this underlying demand, the 'northwards migration' of the paper (and pulp) industry nevertheless required, first, the introduction of restrictions on raw log exports by Canadian governments. These restrictions, it might be noted, were opposed by American manufacturing interests and by American unions. Indeed, according to Scott, the American Federation of Labour (AFL) strove hard to control Canadian unions in support of its own interests, which closely paralleled those of US business, and when the AFL's first appointed representative in Canada in 1896 began to lobby unexpectedly for Canadian pulpwood to be processed in

Table 8.1 Product mix of the Canadian pulp and paper industry

	1900	*1920*	*1987*
Newsprint	0%	45%	40%
Market pulp	38%	39%	34%
Other	62%	16%	26%
'000 tonnes	181	1,902	16,000

Source: Uhler *et al.* (1991: 106, 108).

Note: In 1987 market pulp refers only to exported pulp.

Canada, to create Canadian jobs at a time of high unemployment in Canada, the AFL fired him 'for having advocated a tax on raw material exports' (Scott 1978: 42). Second, the development of the Canadian newsprint industry was greatly stimulated by the US government's elimination of tariff barriers in 1911 (Table 8.2). In fact, since 1911 there has been no US tariff on imports of Canadian newsprint and by 1913 the tariff on pulp was removed. By contrast, tariffs on value-added paper products were retained and helped constrain the Canadian industry to a commodity orientation (Uhler *et al.* 1991). Canadian governments, for their part, have not tried to stimulate further value added beyond the primary processing of pulpwood.

The subsequent development of the Canadian paper industry is quintessentially continentalist. Several summary points may be made in this regard. First, since 1920 the industry has consistently exported about 90% of its output and only in the Depression years of the 1930s has the US accounted for less than 70% of Canadian production (Table 8.3). Moreover, for several decades after 1911 Canada's share of the US market grew inexorably, reaching a peak share of over 80% of the American newsprint market in 1950. Second, downturns in production during the Depression of the 1930s, in the minor

Table 8.2 US pulp and paper tariffs

Year	*Newsprint*	*Bleached pulp*	*Printing and writing (cut)*	*Envelopes*
1894	15%	10%	20%	20%
1909	17.5%	$5.00	$60.00 + 15%	20%
1911	Free	$5.00	$60.00 + 15%	20%
1930	Free	Free	$60.00 + 22.5%	5%
1947	Free	Free	15%	2.5%
1972	Free	Free	7.5%	8.75%
1987	Free	Free	3%	3.5%

Source: Uhler *et al.* (1991: 120–1).

Note: Dollar amounts indicate dollars per short ton. Also note that the tariff on bleached (and unbleached) pulp was removed in 1913.

Table 8.3 Canadian newsprint production and exports to the US, and US production, 1915–90

Year	*Canadian production, '000 tonnes*	*Canadian exports, %*	*Exports to US, %*	*Share of US market*	*US production, '000 tonnes*
1915	498	77.2	59.9	21.8	1,124
1920	851	89.5	72.4	30.9	1,372
1925	1,469	90.4	81.3	44.5	1,388
1930	2,532	92.7	76.9	60.4	1,163
1935	2,797	92.4	68.8	65.7	827
1940	3,420	96.0	72.7	72.6	919
1945	3,259	93.3	74.2	79.0	657
1950	4,789	93.8	89.9	80.2	921
1955	5,616	93.8	81.9	76.9	1,408
1960	6,114	93.0	78.3	71.5	1,849
1965	7,004	92.7	78.9	71.4	2,037
1970	7,910	91.6	70.7	62.9	3,142
1975	6,966	89.4	71.5	60.4	3,348
1980	8,625	88.6	70.9	59.4	4,238
1985	8,890	88.7	74.2	57.0	4,924
1990	9,068	88.2	70.8	52.8	5,997

Source: Canadian Pulp and Paper Association: Reference Tables 1965 and 1990. All measures are in metric tonnes (= 1.1023 short tons).

recessions of the 1950s and 1960s and in the more severe recessions of the 1980s and 1990s all primarily resulted from declines in American demand. Subsequent recovery from the 1930s Depression, the years of the Second World War and the recessions that punctuated the long boom was also led by American demand and, although by 1950 newsprint was a 'mature' industry, its expansion since then until the last few years has been impressive. Third, Canada's burgeoning newsprint exports to the US were further buttressed by a high level of American equity investment in the Canadian industry. Indeed, Marshall *et al.* (1936) estimate that American-owned mills accounted for 38% of Canadian newsprint production by 1929 and 51% by 1933. In these early decades, American control was initiated in part by acquisition of existing Canadian-owned interests but mostly by investment in new mills, including joint ventures involving American newspaper publishers. At Spruce Falls, Ontario, for example, the US-based Kimberly Clark started up a pulp mill in 1921:

> To obtain a large guaranteed market for prospective newsprint and so that the mill could be expanded into a more profitable size, the company entered into a partnership with the *New York Times*. The *New York Times* not only provided a guaranteed market for future years but also supplied most of the early investment needed to expand the enterprise.
>
> (Dickson 1981: 15)

Since the 1930s, American control of the Canadian industry has remained significant. Overall, foreign control accounted for 40.2–45.8% of Canadian newsprint capacity, depending on whether foreign control is measured by at least 50% or 25% equity (Hayter 1985: 445). There are some large Canadian firms in this industry, such as MacMillan Bloedel, and, while some of these firms have pursued a multinational strategy, most of these foreign investments have been in the US.

Fourth, private sector research and development (R&D) investment in the Canadian pulp and paper industry has traditionally been lower than in other important paper-producing countries, whether these countries are larger or smaller (Table 8.4). In 1986, for example, corporate R&D expenditure in Canada was at the same level as in the much smaller Finnish industry, and as a percentage of sales was less than half Finnish or Japanese levels and less than one-quarter of Swedish and American levels. The technological capability of pulp and paper equipment manufacturers is also very weak and imports of machinery in this sector typically account for over 50% of purchases (Hayter 1988). The low level of private sector R&D results from high levels of foreign ownership, the commodity orientation of the industry and boom and bust cycles. Thus virtually all American-owned forest product firms (and equipment suppliers) in Canada have invested in in-house R&D in the US but only rarely in Canada; more typically existing Canadian R&D has been closed down by American parents. By relying on their parents for R&D, possibilities for similar investments in Canada are necessarily undermined, an observation made about the pulp and paper industry since at least 1936 (Marshall *et al.* 1936). It is also argued within Canada that concentration on standardized bulk commodities utilizing mature technology reduces the need for investment in sophisticated R&D programmes. Of course, securing supplies of bulk commodities for the parent corporation has been an important motivation for foreign investment. In addition, the susceptibility of exporting bulk commodities to cycles of booms and busts has contributed to attitudes within Canada that have militated against R&D investments, as it is argued that during booms R&D is not needed and during busts R&D cannot be afforded.

Table 8.4 Corporate R&D expenditure in the pulp and paper industry in 1986

	R&D expenditure, US$m	*R&D as a percentage of sales*
US	1,224	1.25
Japan	230	0.75
Sweden	86	1.35
Finland	48	0.75
Canada	50	0.30

Source: Hayter (1988).

Fifth, with respect to labour, it might be noted that early attempts at unionization in the first decades of the twentieth century failed and unions were not permanently established until the late 1930s. The American-based International Union of Pulp, Sulphite and Papermill Workers provided important organizational help and this union along with another American-based union, the United Papermakers and Paperworkers, dominated the industry until 1974 when the Canadian locals of these two unions broke away to form the Canadian Paperworkers' Union (CPU). Recently, the CPU merged with the Communication Workers of Canada and the Energy and Chemical Workers to form the Communications, Energy and Papermakers' Union.

In the 1990s the Canadian paper industry is still heavily oriented to serving the US. In 1990, for example, over 88% of production was exported and almost 71% was sent to the US (Table 8.3). In addition, the declines in newsprint production in 1982 and in 1991/92 were almost entirely due to declines in shipments to the US. Yet, apart from the formation of independent Canadian unions, there is evidence that continentalism is a declining force in the Canadian paper industry and that for an increasing number of mills diversification from US markets and a commodity orientation is essential for survival. First, with respect to trade, Canada is a much less important supplier to the US newsprint market than at any time since the 1920s (Table 8.3). In fact, Canada's share of this market has consistently fallen since 1950 and by 1990 Canadian producers accounted for about half of the American newsprint market; the trend is clear. It is true that at least until the late 1980s Canadian newsprint tonnage to the US has increased. However, production within the US, especially the South, has increased much faster and by 1990 the US industry had reached two-thirds the size of the Canadian industry. As previously noted, the US South is now the continent's low-cost location. Moreover, new newsprint mills serving US markets and using recycled paper will most likely locate in the US. Thus the Canadian newsprint industry is becoming increasingly marginal in US markets. At the same time, non-continental markets have become more important and in the 1990s account for about 18% of production.

Second, levels of American ownership in the paper industry declined during the 1980s as several American firms sold their Canadian subsidiaries. The two largest were Crown Zellerbach Canada, which was sold in 1982 by its parent to Fletcher Challenge of New Zealand for approximately $600 million, while International Paper of New York in 1981 sold its Canadian subsidiary (CIP) for $1 billion to Canadian Pacific of Montreal. Both these subsidiaries had been established in the first decades of the twentieth century and, while both subsidiaries historically had been profitable, both companies were sold, during recessionary times when interest rates were also high, to provide their parents with cash to modernize their US-based facilities. All former ties with Canadian operations were severed. A third, recent example is the sale in 1991 of the previously referred to Spruce Falls newsprint mill by the *New York Times* and Kimberly Clark to some of its former employees, which terminated a sixty-year continental link. The story underlying this sale is perhaps particularly revealing of the legacy of continentalism for Canadian producers. Thus in 1980 the *Times* entered a joint venture with Myllykoski, a Finnish firm, to invest in a paper mill in Maine. This mill came on-stream in 1982, one of the first in North America to produce supercalendered uncoated groundwood papers, a high-quality paper developed by the Finns and used in magazine publishing. This mill was the first US source affiliated with the *New York Times,* which had first bought paper from Myllykoski in 1976 because of a strike in its Canadian mills. Because of the superior quality of the paper supplied by Myllykoski, which was much praised by its customers, the *Times* maintained its link with Myllykoski, which soon led to the joint venture in Maine. By 1991, the *Times* had expanded its American supply base to a point where it no longer needed newsprint from Spruce Falls, which is now a much smaller operation and run by former employees. In this case, Finnish innovativeness in paper making (and the lack of any such concern at Spruce Falls), as well as declining cost advantages in Canada, combined to reduce a long-established continental link. This example also illustrates the growing importance of technology-based competitive advantage for the paper industry.

Indeed, technology is the underlying force stimulating fundamental changes in the competitive conditions underlying the Canadian paper industry. Thus developments in pulping technology have progressed rapidly since the 1930s and have reduced and overcome the advantage of the softwood resource regions so that the pulp and paper industry has rapidly expanded in all regions of the world. Other technological changes have featured new paper making machines, new high-yielding pulping processes and computerization, which collectively have significantly increased labour productivity and improved product quality. However, it is the US South that now constitutes the low-cost region for paper manufacture in North America (and possibly the world). Moreover, in many regions of Canada wood fibre supplies (for various reasons) are problematical while mills are having to meet increasingly tough environmental standards. In addition, the fact that many US states have introduced laws requiring recycled paper to be used in newsprint is another development which is placing Canadian mills, located at great distances from used paper supplies, at a disadvantage. In addition, the old mills, such as Powell River, have had to adjust to these changes in the face of competition from entirely new mills employing the latest technology and 'lean and flexible' (and non-union) workforces. By contrast, the long-established paper mills in Canada, including Powell River, by the 1970s had obsolete plant lay-outs and machinery, which were extremely expensive to modernize. Thus, for a variety of reasons, productivity within the Canadian paper industry was deteriorating rapidly in relation to the newer supply regions (Holmes and Hayter 1993). Yet the real impact of these changes in the paper mills seemed only to be felt in the severe recessions of the early 1980s and early 1990s. In fact, the worst effects of the early 1980s recession were largely restricted to British Columbia and in any case the industry boomed in 1990, achieving all-time record high levels of production and exports. The recession of the early 1990s, however, has hammered traditional mills across the country and financial losses, job losses and capacity reductions have been extensive. Job loss and capacity reductions in old mills are expected to continue.

For many established Canadian mills, the mass production of newsprint and reliance on US markets is becoming an increasingly marginal activity. To remain competitive, mills are shifting towards producing a higher value, more differentiated range of papers, even for offshore markets. These product market changes are further interrelated with changes in mill technology and in labour relations that are aimed at developing more 'flexible' operating cultures. The Powell River mill is part of these trends.

Powell River and continentalism

Newsprint production in Canada has traditionally been dominated by very large-scale facilities producing standardized outputs located in small specialized communities. Powell River is a good example (Figure 8.1). Established by US-based entrepreneurs, Powell River began production of newsprint in 1913, the first such mill in western Canada, and its investments and production patterns reflect industry-wide trends. For a while in the 1950s it was the biggest newsprint supplier in the world. Atypically, it became Canadianized in the 1930s when its owners relocated to British Columbia. At this time, the mill also invested in an R&D programme, although this programme was small scale and primarily concerned with relatively short-term research designed to improve the efficiency of existing processes within the mill and with helping to adapt newly purchased machinery to meet Powell River's specific needs. There was no particular concern with developing technology for sale or with product-oriented R&D. In other words, at Powell

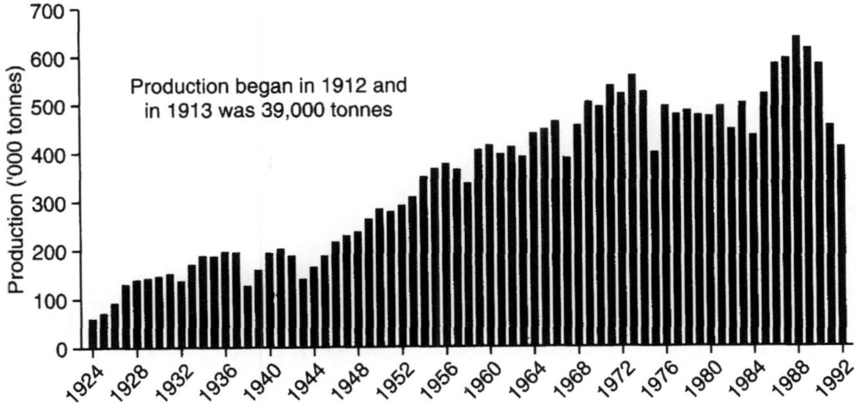

Figure 8.1 Powell River paper mill: production 1924–92

River – as was the case, with very few exceptions, throughout the Canadian industry – R&D was primarily limited to supporting the mill's role of manufacturing and exporting large quantities of standard newsprint to the US. The mill was acquired by MacMillan Bloedel (MB) in 1959 (Hayter 1976), and MB subsequently invested in a more substantial R&D programme located in the Vancouver area.

The Powell River paper mill began production in 1913 to produce newsprint primarily for the US market. The early growth of the mill was arrested by the Great Depression of the 1930s and by the Second World War, but from 1944 to 1974 the mill experienced sustained and substantial expansion (Figure 8.1). During this entire period, the mill's output was sold almost entirely within North America, particularly western North America, 1953 being a typical year in this regard (Table 8.5). Since 1974, the mill's production has been more volatile and sharp reductions in output occurred in 1975, 1981/83 and 1991/92, while in 1988 the mill achieved record levels of production (Figure 8.1). Moreover, in each of these recessions, eight older paper machines have been permanently closed, and while the three remaining machines are relatively large and efficient, production levels are unlikely to recover.

What the recessions of 1975 and the early 1980s and 1990s had underlined was that to maintain, indeed to re-establish, its viability Powell River needed to shift from low-yielding to high-yielding production processes and from a dependence on standard newsprint manufactured for the US market to a

Table 8.5 Estimated geographic distribution of Powell River paper mill's newsprint sales in 1954

Region	*Estimated Powell River sales in 1954, '000 tonnes*	*Region's consumption in 1953, '000 tonnes*	*Powell River's estimated share, %*
Alberta	8,864	14,062	63.0
British Columbia	30,704	41,277	74.4
California	181,921	518,332	35.1
Washington	39,087	80,097	48.8
Texas	28,073	233,711	12.0
Arizona	13,390	20,520	65.3
Colorado	7,516	54,782	13.7
Oregon	4,707	60,689	7.8
New Mexico	3,883	6,296	61.7
Wyoming	1,080	2,368	45.6
Utah	584	22,419	2.6
Arkansas	381	21,223	1.8
Idaho	329	2,723	12.1
Nevada	281	3,142	9.0
Oklahoma	204	52,332	0.4
Total	321,040	1,214,132	26.4

Source: Powell River Company.

wider range of speciality papers produced for more geographically diverse markets. This shift began in 1975 when a new high-yielding, extremely capital-intensive, pulping process known as thermo-mechanical pulp (TMP) was installed, the first such mill in Canada, and by the introduction of new types of speciality (groundwood printing) papers. These new types of papers featured the so-called 'Hi-brite' papers, such as Electratone, which was developed for the rotogravure printing industry for use in newspapers, weekend supplements, advertising flyers and unbound catalogues. In the mid-1970s, Powell River also began to produce a lighter weight newsprint grade paper for use in catalogues, flyers and directories as well as telephone directory paper, which is lighter weight still. These new paper grades, it might be noted, were developed by MB's R&D group and were first manufactured at Powell River.

During the 1980s and 1990s, the production of speciality papers for offshore markets has remained a key element of Powell River's market strategy. In 1993, for example, over 41% of the mill's paper output was delivered to offshore markets and almost 30% of this output was speciality grades (Table 8.6). The mill's reliance on speciality papers actually declined between 1980 and 1993 from 40% to 30% of production. This apparently anomalous shift relates partly to the fact that within the parent company, MB, Powell River pioneered the introduction of speciality papers in the 1970s by converting old and slow paper machines, which were subsequently closed down in the 1980s, while only one of the three remaining newer and much faster paper machines has so far been converted to speciality paper production. The speed and extent of the product shifts at Powell River also need to be placed in conjunction with similar trends occurring at MB's other large paper mill at Port Alberni on nearby Vancouver Island. While initially speciality grade production was concentrated at Powell River, the pressures to diversify paper production at Port Alberni are similar, and a corporate decision was made to transfer and concentrate telephone directory paper production at this location in the early 1980s because this type of paper is very lightweight and Port Alberni's timber supply is good quality but dwindling in size. Indeed, in 1988

Table 8.6 Estimated geographic distribution of Powell River paper mill's sales for 1993

	Standard newsprint, '000 tonnes	*Speciality grades, '000 tonnes*	*Total, '000 tonnes*
Canada	22.4	30.0	52.4
USA	144.8	89.2	234.0
Pacific Asia	90.0	17.9	107.9
Latin America	47.3	2.2	49.5
Europe	39.0	5.0	44.0
Total	343.5	144.3	487.8

Source: MacMillan Bloedel.

Port Alberni manufactured about 200,000 tonnes of telephone directory paper, about half of its output and mainly sold in the US, although Port Alberni has penetrated the Japanese market recently. MB also decided (in 1995) to introduce coated papers at Port Alberni. Powell River's future is clearly dependent on being a high-quality, as well as efficient, producer of large volumes of paper, which will feature speciality grades as well as newsprint. While there are options as to the nature of these speciality grades it is unlikely that Powell River will produce finished paper products such as envelopes and writing paper. These products are typically located near markets and have often been protected for many decades by high tariffs. Within a North American context, as tariffs are eliminated, if these types of paper products are to be relocated out of the US, Mexico may well be a more likely destination than Canada, including Powell River. Nevertheless, the plant now produces over 50 grades of paper, and if a plan to convert one of its existing newsprint machines to speciality papers is realized, speciality paper production will constitute 60–70% of its output. As part of this trend away from continentalism, the mill has sought to modify its preoccupation with cost minimization based on volume to a more quality-conscious operation. Within the plant, this trend was heralded in 1982 by the introduction of its Quality Improvement Programme, which combined slogans with job training schemes, the modernization and computerization of technology and, especially since 1989, encouragement by management of greater employee involvement in the marketing process, including by having groups of employees visit the press and printing processes of customers to enhance employee knowledge of consumer needs and concerns, as well as to encourage consumer loyalty. In addition, as its product has been more differentiated and valuable, the mill has changed its distribution systems to minimize damage as well as to realize savings.

Contemporary market links also differ from traditional continental ties in terms of their volatility. Although Powell River never had the benefit of affiliated sales, in the past it was able to maintain contracts with large customers over many years. Indeed, in 1944 Powell River had 162 contracts with customers of which 107 were 'of a continuing nature subject to cancellation only on two full years' notice' (Powell River 1944: 4). If these war years were unusual for business relations, continuity of links with customers was nevertheless an important feature of Powell River's newsprint sales. Presently, contracts are still signed, often for six months, but the contracts always contain a clause that says that prices must be competitive. As a result, if a customer can find a lower price, they will reduce the contracted tonnage with Powell River or spread deliveries over a longer period of time.

Finally, it might be noted that the restructuring of the Powell River facility has inevitably had enormous implications for labour (Hayter and Holmes 1994). Employment levels among salaried and hourly workers are now less than half what they were in 1974 as a result of technological change, rationalization and, to some extent, the incorporation of more flexible work practices (Table 8.7). Moreover, this downsizing has been associated with contentious and complex shifts towards a more flexible operating culture. Suffice to say, given the context of this paper, these changes represent a marked departure from the standards set under continentalism. Under continentalism, the mass production of resources was associated with a Taylorized work culture with sharp distinctions between management and labour and strong job demarcation and seniority within the latter. The shift towards flexibility has significantly blurred traditional distinctions and has placed more emphasis on formal education before employment as well as after employment. At the same time, while continentalism emphasized industry-wide standards in labour relations the shift towards flexibility is giving more emphasis to creating locally distinct labour relations, a shift symbolized by employer attempts to introduce mill-by-mill bargaining. While the process of increasing labour flexibility at Powell River remains controversial, there is at least tacit agreement between union and management that a more educated workforce and ongoing job training is essential for job security, high wages and the viability of mill operations.

The origins and evolution of paper making at Powell River were predicated on the assumptions of continentalism. By the 1970s, however, the future of exporting large volumes of standard newsprint to the US, the essential imperative of continentalism for the Canadian paper industry, was in question. The recessions of the early 1980s and 1990s highlighted the cracks in continentalism and provided a crisis situation in which Powell River redefined its strategy. This strategy is explicitly based on escaping the constraints of continentalism since it comprises diversification into speciality grades and offshore markets. The US market will doubtless continue to be important to Powell River and to MB as a whole. The fact that MB has already evaluated locations in northern California for a newsprint mill based on recycled paper nevertheless further underscores the fact that Powell River has embarked on a distinct phase in its evolution and that continentalism has a changed meaning for the Canadian paper industry as a whole.

Table 8.7 Powell River paper mill: employment levels 1974–94

	Salaried	*Hourly*	*Relief*	*Total*
1974	339	1,948	240	2,527
1980	330	1,665	315	2,310
1985	265	1,290	272	1,827
1988	306	1,338	346	1,990
1990	303	1,318	285	1,906
1994	182	857	237	1,275

Source: Hayter and Holmes (1994: 16).

Note: The data pertain to the situation at 31 December except in 1994, when the data are for 31 January.

Conclusion

This chapter has provided further confirmation that the economic geography of industrial evolution and industrial restructuring is substantially shaped by international regulations. Moreover, since international regulations are inevitably shaped and dominated by hegemonic powers it is inevitable that regulatory frameworks that shape economic behaviour comprise geopolitical as well as economic motives (Glasmeier *et al.* 1993). Peripheral nations and regions must compete according to rules and values largely set by others. This virtual axiom should not be taken to imply that peripheries are without influence or choice. Moreover, the emergence of international regionalism has helped create a mix of opportunities and constraints facing peripheries. Continentalism (in North America), for example, is a distinct form of regionalism, implying distinct sets of regulations, as in the EC or Pacific Asia. Thus, apart from different histories and cultures, North America is overwhelmingly dominated by the US in a way that does not have parallel in the developed world, either in Europe or in Asia. Even so, for Innisians, Canadian policy making has too often tacitly accepted the 'easy' policy option of relying on US coat-tails. To use a term often used in geography these days, it is a policy that has lacked 'imagination', even if it claims to be realistic. In an increasingly flexible world, however, imagination is not without value. Frankly, whether or not a pragmatic form of imagination can be developed in the Canadian periphery, to allow an alternative to continentalism, remains to be seen.

Acknowledgement

We gratefully thank the Social Sciences and Humanities Research Council of Canada for financial support.

Bibliography

Atkinson, M.M. and Coleman, W.D. (1989) *The State, Business, and Industrial Change in Canada*, Toronto: University of Toronto Press.

Barnes, T. (1987) 'Homo economicus, physical metaphors, and universal models', *Canadian Geographer* 31: 299–308.

—— (1993a) 'Harold A. Innis: a geographical appreciation', *Canadian Geographer* 37: 352–3.

—— (1993b) 'Knowing where you stand: Harold Innis, staple theory, and local models', *Canadian Geographer* 37: 357–9.

Britton, J.N.H. (1976) 'The influence of corporate organization and ownership on the linkages of industrial plants: a Canadian enquiry', *Economic Geography* 52: 311–24.

Britton, J.N.H. and Gilmour, J. (1978) *The Weakest Link: A Technological Perspective on Canadian Industrial Development*, Background Study 43, Ottawa: Science Council of Canada.

Clark-Jones, M. (1987) *A Staple State: Canadian Industrial Resources in Cold War*, Toronto: University of Toronto Press.

Clement, W. (1989) 'Debates and directions: a political economy of resources', in W. Clement and G. Williams (eds) *The New Canadian Political Economy*, Montreal: McGill-Queen's University Press: 36–53.

Clement, W. and Williams, G. (eds) (1989) *The New Canadian Political Economy*, Montreal: McGill-Queen's University Press.

Cox, D. and Harris, R.G. (1992) 'North American free trade and its implications for Canada: results from a CGE model of North American trade', *World Economy* 15: 31–44.

Dickson, T. (1981) 'Spruce Falls modernization scheme is right on schedule in town's anniversary year', *Canadian Pulp and Paper Magazine* 82: 14–17.

Gertler, M. and Schoenberger, E. (1992) 'Commentary: industrial restructuring and continental trading blocs: the European Community and North America', *Environment and Planning A* 24: 2–10.

Gibb, R. (1994) 'Regionalism in the world economy', in R. Gibb and W. Michalak (eds) *Continental Trading Blocs: The Growth of Regionalism in the World Economy*, Chichester: Wiley: 1–31.

Gibb, R. and Michalak, W. (eds) (1994) *Continental Trading Blocs: The Growth of Regionalism in the World Economy*, Chichester: Wiley.

Glasmeier, A., Thompson, J.W. and Kays, A.J. (1993) 'The geography of trade policy: trade regimes and location decisions in the textile and apparel complex', *Transactions of the Institute of British Geographers* 18: 19–35.

Haglund, D.G. (ed.) (1989) *The Geopolitics of Minerals*, Vancouver: University of British Columbia Press.

Hayter, R. (1976) 'Corporate strategies and industrial change in the Canadian forest product industries', *Geographical Review* 66: 209–28.

—— (1982) 'Truncation, the international firm and regional policy', *Area* 14: 277–82.

—— (1985) 'The evolution and structure of the Canadian forest product sector: an assessment of the role of foreign ownership and control', *Fennia* 163: 439–50.

—— (1988) *Technology and the Canadian Forest Product Industries: A Technological Perspective*, Background Study 54, Ottawa: Science Council of Canada.

—— (1992) 'International trade relations and regional industrial adjustment: implications of the 1980s' North American softwood lumber dispute for British Columbia', *Environment and Planning A* 24: 153–70.

—— (1993) 'International trade and the Canadian forest industries: the paradox of the North American free trade arrangements', *Zeitschrift für Kanada-Studien* 23: 81–94.

—— (1996) 'High-performance organizations and employment flexibility: a case study of in situ change at the Powell River paper mill, 1980–1994', *Canadian Geographer* 41: 26–40.

Hayter, R. and Barnes, T. (1990) 'Innis's staples theory, exports and recession: BC 1981–86', *Economic Geography* 66: 156–73.

Hayter, R. and Holmes, J. (1993) *Booms and Busts in the Canadian Paper Industry: The Case of the Powell River Paper Mill*, Discussion Paper No. 27, Department of Geography, Simon Fraser University.

Hayter, R. and Holmes, J. (1994) *Recession and Restructuring at Powell River, 1980–94: Employment and Employment Relations in Transition*, Discussion Paper No. 28, Department of Geography, Simon Fraser University.

Holmes, J. (1997) 'In search of competitive efficiency: labour process flexibility in Canadian newsprint mills', *Canadian Geographer* 41: 7–25.

Holmes, J. and Hayter, R. (1993) *Recent Restructuring in the Canadian Pulp and Paper Industry*, Discussion Paper No. 26, Department of Geography, Simon Fraser University.

Holmes, J. and Rusonick, A. (1990) 'The break-up of an international labour union: uneven development in the North American auto industry and the schism in the UAW', *Environment and Planning A* 24: 95–119.

Innis, H.A. (1930) *The Fur Trade in Canada*, Toronto: University of Toronto Press.

—— (1950) *Empire and Communication*, Toronto: University of Toronto Press.

—— (1956) 'Great Britain, the United States and Canada', in M.Q. Innis (ed.) *Essays in Canadian Economic History*, Toronto: University of Toronto Press: 200–10.

—— (1967) 'The importance of staple products', in M.Q. Innis (ed.) *Essays in Canadian Economic History*, Toronto: University of Toronto Press.

Kierans, E. (1987) 'Forward', in T. Gunton and J. Richards (eds) *Resource Rents and Public Policy in Western Canada*, Halifax: Institute for Research on Public Policy.

Kroker, A. (1985) *Technology and the Canadian Mind*, Montreal: New World Perspectives.

Kumar, P. (1993) *From Uniformity to Divergence: Industrial Relations in Canada and the United States*, Queen's University, Kington: I.R.C. Press.

Laxer, R. (1976) *Canada's Unions*, Toronto: James Lorimer.

McConnell, J. and MacPherson, A. (1994) 'The North American Free Trade Area: an overview of issues and prospects', in R. Gibb and W. Michalak (eds) *Continental Trading Blocs: The Growth of Regionalism in the World Economy*, Chichester: Wiley: 163–87.

McGee, T.M. (1990) 'The changing Pacific economy: challenge to the post-industrial economy', in R. Hayter and P.D. Wilde (eds) *Industrial Transformation and Challenge in Australia and Canada*, Ottawa: Carleton University Press: 9–24.

Mackenzie, S. and Norcliffe, G. (1997) 'Restructuring in the Canadian newsprint industry', *Canadian Geographer* 41: 2–6.

Mackintosh, W.A. (1967) 'Economic factors in Canadian history', in W.T. Easterbrook and M.H. Watkins (eds) *Approaches to Canadian Economic History*, Toronto: McClelland and Stewart: 1–15.

Marchak, P. (1983) *Green Gold: The Forest Industry in British Columbia*, Vancouver: University of British Columbia Press.

Marshall, H., Southard, F.A. and Taylor, K.W. (1936) *Canadian–American Industry: A Study in International Investment*, Toronto: Ryerson Press.

Melody, W.H., Salter, L. and Heyer, P. (eds) (1981) *Culture, Communication and Dependency: The Tradition of H. A. Innis*, Norwood: Ablex Publishing Corporation.

Michalak, W. (1994) 'The political economy of trading blocs', in R. Gibb and W. Michalak (eds) *Continental Trading Blocs: The Growth of Regionalism in the World Economy*, Chichester: Wiley: 37–72.

Neill, R. (1972) *A New Theory of Value*, Toronto: University of Toronto Press.

Norcliffe, G.B. (1996) 'Foreign trade in goods and services', in J.N.H. Britton (ed.) *Canada and the Global Economy*, Montreal: McGill-Queen's University Press: 25–47.

Norcliffe, G.B. and Bates, J. (1997) 'Implementing lean production in an old industrial space: Corner Brook, Newfoundland 1984–94', *Canadian Geographer* 41: 41–60.

Powell River (1944) *Annual Report*, Powell River: Powell River Paper Company.

Preston, V., Holmes, J. and Williams, A. (1997) 'Working with wild rose 1: lean production in a greenfield mill', *Canadian Geographer* 41: 88–104.

Rose, D. and Villemaire, M. (1997) 'Reshuffling paperworkers: technological change and experiences of reorganization at a Quebec newsprint mill', *Canadian Geographer* 41: 61–87.

Rosenbluth, G. (1981) 'Canadian policy on foreign ownership and control of business', in G.C. Ruggeri (ed.) *The Canadian Economy: Problems and Policies*, Toronto: Gage: 342–7.

Rotstein, A. (1977) 'Innis: the alchemy of fur and wheat', *Journal of Canadian Studies* 12: 6–31.

Safarian, A.E. (1966) *The Foreign Ownership of Canadian Industry*, Toronto: McGraw-Hill.

Scott, J. (1978) *Canadian Workers, American Unions*, Vancouver: New Star Books.

Storper, M. (1997) *The Regional World: Territorial Development in a Global Economy*, New York: Guilford Press.

Uhler, R.S., Townsend, G.M. and Constantino, L. (1991) 'Canada–US trade and the product mix of the Canadian pulp and paper industry', in R.S. Uhler (ed.) *Canada–United States Trade in Forest Products*, Vancouver: University of British Columbia Press: 106–22.

Watkins, M. (1963) 'A staple theory of economic growth', *Canadian Journal of Economics and Political Science* 29: 141–8.

—— (1981) 'The Innis tradition in Canadian political economy', *Canadian Journal of Political and Social Theory* 6: 12–34.

—— (1989) 'The political economy of growth', in W. Clement and G. Williams (eds) *The New Canadian Political Economy*, Montreal: McGill-Queen's University Press: 16–35.

Watson, W.G. (1987) 'Canada–US free trade: why now?', *Canadian Public Policy* 13: 337–49.

Weaver, C. and Gunton, T.I. (1982) 'From drought resistance to mega-projects: fifty years of regional theory and policy in Canada', *Canadian Journal of Regional Science* 5: 5–38.

Williams, G. (1983) *Not for Export: Towards a Political Economy of Canada's Arrested Industrialization*, Toronto: McClelland and Stewart.

Part III
Institutions

9 The firm in the region and the region in the firm

Erica Schoenberger

Introduction

In the classic John Ford Western, *Fort Apache*, we watch the US Cavalry go out to do battle against the Apaches, united under the leadership of the great Cochise. But the real struggle in the film lies elsewhere, between the rigid and status-conscious Colonel Thursday, played by Henry Fonda, and his second-in-command, John Wayne's laconic and sceptical Captain Yorke.

Thursday is a West Point-trained martinet, furious at finding himself in this wretched outpost in the desert, and determined to use it as a stepping stone back to the halls of power and prestige in Washington. His plan for doing this is to impose an absolutely by-the-book military discipline on his men, and crushing military defeat on the Apaches, whom he considers to be savages and beneath consideration.

Yorke/Wayne, although a career military man, is essentially an outsider who prefers self-exile on the frontier to the stultifying conventions of life at the centre. But he is a true insider in his own environment who understands his men and knows how to get the best performance from them while being relatively unconcerned with the rules. Most importantly, he understands the Apaches and has a deep respect for their skills as warriors and for their integrity. He has, the film makes plain, learned from watching and speaking with the Apaches, and he and Cochise treat each other as equals and men of honour.

Yorke is in the midst of what look to be promising negotiations with Cochise to end the war when Thursday orders a disastrous attack in which he and his men are massacred. Yorke survives to assume command of the post and we might be left to hope that, under his more insightful leadership, an honourable peace with the Apaches could be achieved. Of course, we, the viewers, know otherwise, as does the film, which ends by showing us how Thursday has been posthumously elevated to the status of hero.

The narrative structure of *Fort Apache*, I think, has some useful lessons for those of us who study firms and the way they shape the social and economic landscape. Its subject is one of the great homogenizing forces of all time, the military, which seeks to impose a unifying discipline from the top down to the lowest and farthest-flung units. Policy is conceived at the centre and executed by the troops wherever (and whoever) they may be.[1] Everyone in the military should be interchangeable with anyone else of the same rank, and each post should be a small exemplar of the military's common values, purposes and methods. In short, we view the military as being much like our conception of the large corporation.

What the film shows is that there are limits to this homogenizing power and that these limits are or could be strategically important. The troops at Fort Apache wear the cavalry uniform, and their purpose is certainly to secure the territory for whites – a purpose from which even Yorke does not fundamentally dissent. But life at the post is different from life at the centre, and these differences are produced through the encounter with the local environment, its particular terrain and its population. The differences are expressed through highly divergent understandings of how things ought to be.

John Ford's military, it turns out, is a very dialectical place, and Yorke is the embodiment of the dialectical process. He alone understands, as though from the inside, both the social forces that face each other eventually on the field of battle, and he has been transformed by that knowledge. Thursday, the agent of the centre who refuses the new understanding, is doomed. The final twist, though, is that the centre doesn't understand what his death represents and persists in its own policies. Unluckily for the Apaches in real life, the centre in this case had the power to impose its vision and understanding in the end.

But it is the dialectical vision that I think needs to be preserved when we try to understand what firms do in the world, and why. For that matter, firms, too, need to think dialectically as they make their way in the world. Or at least they do now, when they no longer have the power to unilaterally impose their own vision and understanding of how the world ought to be.

The argument I want to propose here holds both for the analysts of firm behaviour and for the firms themselves. It involves a reconsideration of the relationship between the centre and the periphery[2] of the firm, organizationally and geographically, which allows for a more creative and transformative role for the periphery than we have been wont to allow. The parallel with *Fort Apache* lies in the suggestion of limits to the very real powers of homogenization that the firm possesses, and the strategic importance of the dialectical process which, as I see it, is inherent in these relations within the firm, and between the firm and its environment.

The firm in the region

Our image of the large, multi-locational firm has for a long time stressed its ability to hive off pieces of itself and locate them in various parts of the landscape, however remote, essentially as smaller, uncontaminated images of itself. The firm operates by its own internal dynamics and imports a set of practices and relations into every territory that it inhabits. The outpost's role and character is determined by the centre, and enforced by lines of power and control linking the periphery to the core.

This view of the firm, it seems to me, is implicit in much of the theorizing about spatial divisions of labour, product cycles and branch plant economies that developed in the 1970s and 1980s, especially with regard to the multinational corporation (Vernon 1966; Hymer 1972; Dicken 1976, 1986; Frobel *et al.* 1980; Massey 1984). The great defect of branch plants, for example, was that they lacked control over resources and, more generally, over their own fates. Headquarters decided how much to invest in the branch, what it would do, how it would do it, what would happen to the profits it generated, where material supplies would come from, where output would go, and whether the plant would, in the end, be closed down.

The branch, then, was integrated into a flow of resources and knowledge that operated within the firm and across regions (Pred 1977). It was also integrated into a division of labour in which the centre conceived and the periphery executed. The parent firm, in this context, presumably had the power to impose its standards, practices and ways of thinking on its affiliates.

This view does not, of course, necessarily imply that firms had the unfettered capability to transform these various localities into little replicas of their own home bases. It was recognized that they would encounter different local circumstances, population and histories that would remain distinctive even as more and more people were drawn into the orbit of the firms' operation (Massey 1984; Storper and Walker 1989). Local practices and regulations concerning labour relations, for example, might have to be respected and local forms of resistance might successfully force certain kinds of compromises that would be unthinkable at the centre (Ong 1987).

In short, not every IBM outpost becomes a little Armonk, New York. But the strong expectation was that the essential policies, technologies, practices, relations and understandings of the centre would manifest themselves largely intact in the firm's various locations. Certainly, there was no expectation that the various permutations that might emerge in particular places would have any effect on the centre. Influence might flow imperfectly, but it flowed only one way. Headquarters do not get transformed by outposts or, to put this another way, the periphery may resist, but it cannot transform the centre.

I should stress that this view of the corporation does not necessarily imply that no thinking or innovation could go on in the firm's various outputs. There may have been any number of Yorkes learning new ways of thinking and trying to work out new ways of doing things in the face of specific local conditions. But it does imply that the centre had the power to override or ignore local ideas and innovations and persist in its own ways so that the Yorkes end up back in regulation uniform. In this sense, the kinds of theories that I am describing were not implausible readings of how large firms worked at the time the theories were developed and may still be applicable today in many cases. But there is reason to believe that firms are less likely to get away with such an approach in contemporary circumstances.

This, of course, raises the question of why firms would ignore or actively suppress local knowledge of a sort that might allow them to respond more effectively to local conditions, whether in supply markets, production relations, production organization, or output markets. That they often do so seems beyond question. US automobile manufacturers, for example, have apparently believed for decades that they ought to to be able to sell large, inefficient, left-hand-drive cars of debatable quality in Japan and can only imagine (at least publicly) that their failure to do so is attributable to protectionism. Yet it is by no means a secret that space and fuel in Japan are expensive, that the local competitors make high-quality cars and that the steering wheel ought to be on the right. How, we might wonder, could anyone overlook such facts and expect to keep his or her job? The answer to that question is necessarily speculative and undoubtedly embraces a multitude of factors. Here I will suggest only two.

The first is that firms acted in this way because they thought they could get away with it, and indeed they did get away with it for quite some time. Why they thought they could get away with it, I would guess, has something to do with the general *weltanschauung* of the times. In the early post-war decades, the discourse of modernization theory was very powerful and encouraged the belief that other places were not so much different as lagging (Rostow 1960). Over time, they would become more like us. Large firms in Western Europe and, especially, the US could see themselves as one of the key agents of this evolution via the mobility of capital in the form of investment, technology transfers and products. In this context, the practices and understandings of the centre are seen to be generalizable – if not now, then soon. They are not recognized as the product of a specific time, place and mode of social organization that may come into conflict with practices and understandings elsewhere. Situated knowledge is mistaken for universal knowledge, with all the errors that this can entail (Rosaldo 1989; Haraway 1991).

In the 1950s and 1960s, however, these errors, though no doubt real enough, were not especially threatening. Many industrial markets were more or less dominated by a stable group of firms that subscribed to similar notions about how the world worked. Competition might have been lively, but it was from known quarters and according to generally accepted rules of the game. Competition from firms representing a radically different conception of production, products and markets was scarce. The dominant firms had the power to impose their practices and understandings on a reasonably large scale, and where they failed utterly to do so the effects, in any case unquantifiable, were substantially mitigated by the profits available elsewhere. Market power, then, helps to explain both why firms thought they could get away with ignoring local conditions and innovations and why they did get away with it for so long. Even quite vigorous signals emanating from the firm's various outposts might, under these conditions, go unread.

A second powerful reason for ignoring or actively suppressing new practices and understandings in the firm's own periphery is that they might well threaten the integrity of the firm's overall production strategy. A commitment to standardized mass production achieved through a division of labour among spatially scattered but functionally interlinked production units cannot easily tolerate a high degree of autonomy and experimentation in the various parts of the periphery. It might be acceptable that an individual unit develop its own style in some respects, but this must still be compatible with certain technical criteria (e.g. parts specifications, materials, quantities, equipment, schedules) that define the standards for the whole. Local variations must be constrained and they must be kept localized, even if they would actually benefit the firm as a whole, because of the high degree of sunk costs involved in setting the whole project in motion to begin with (Collis 1991; Clark and Wrigley 1993; Clark 1994).

Here is an invented example to illustrate how these issues might work themselves out. Imagine an American white goods producer in 1965 that decides to set up a production facility in France to expand its sales of washing machines and dryers. The French plant is responsible for fabricating the metal exterior panels and assembling the machines with locally procured motors. To benefit from the scale economies at its domestic facilities, however, the parent firm will supply the belts, shafts, hoses, pumps, inside baskets and the control panels. Since the metal boxes have to fit around the components, the machines are essentially identical to those produced for the US market.

After a couple of years, sales in France are still lagging and the local management submits a report which argues the following. 'Household space is at a premium in France and French housewives are used to smaller, front-loading machines. If we could narrow the base of our machines and make them front-loading so that we could stack the dryer on top of the washer, we could expand sales by 100%.' This seems like a good idea, not only for France but potentially for many other markets in the world. It may even sell in the US, for apartment dwellers. The problem is that it disrupts the components production base. Parts change size or get reconfigured altogether to fit the different orientation. Everything has to be made to fit into a smaller space, or perhaps one that is taller but less wide. So the costs to the firm are substantial. Still, the benefits may also be large.

What will the firm do? It could overhaul its US production base. Or it could decide to expand the French operation into an integrated design and production facility to serve the French and all similar markets worldwide. Alternatively, it could shelve the report, perhaps arguing that French housewives are, or eventually will be, just like American housewives who, as we all know, prefer huge, top-loading machines. In the short run, the last option is overwhelmingly the cheapest and easiest. Moreover, it is simple to quantify the costs connected with the possible failure of the first two options, while the risks involved in the third, though potentially large, are not so easily calculated.

This does not guarantee that the firm would in fact select the third option, but it does suggest why it might. In this way, the possibility that knowledge developed in the periphery might transform the centre is blocked. As a consequence, the firm might never do so brilliantly in France, but this might not seem much of a defect if firms producing French-style machines are too small and weak to threaten the firm's position in other markets. In 1965, one could imagine that this would be possible.

Times have changed, however. The conditions that allowed or constrained firms to ignore valuable knowledge from their peripheries have eroded. There are now powerful competitors who have successfully developed dramatically different ways of organizing production and relating to their markets. New technologies are available which in theory (if not always in practice) allow firms to produce a more varied range of products while not sacrificing economies of scale. There are even signs that US automakers have finally accepted the fact that the Japanese will continue to drive on the wrong side of the road.

The general scenario is this. In the past, large corporations had the power and sufficient (to them) reason to impose their vision of how things should be on all the outposts of their empires, whatever else might be going on in those places. Corporate headquarters was to branch plant as Washington (in the person of Colonel Thursday) was to Fort Apache. Transformative impulses emanating from the periphery would be refused by the centre. At present, such a refusal is likely to put the entire firm seriously at risk. There is reason to suppose that corporations need increasingly to pay attention to what is going on in their own peripheries in order to prosper.

This also suggests that those of us who study corporations may need to look at branch plants and subsidiaries in a somewhat different light. As suggested above, we have been rather better at asking how the activities and strategies of agents at the centre affect the periphery than vice versa. And we had good reasons for that orientation. Now, though, as well as asking what effects firms have on regions when they implant pieces of themselves in various places, we need more and more to ask what effect these regions have on the firm.

The region in the firm

The argument gets complicated because it is necessary to keep track of what firms do, how they understand what they do and how we analyse them. We may also need to separate the issue of what kinds of changes are going on in the corporate periphery and the effects they may have within that region, and the question of how or whether these changes can be effectively transmitted back to the centre or horizontally among branch plants.

The main argument, however, is that it is probably wrong to conceive of the multi-locational firm, however organizationally centralized, as a unitary agent with a singular and coherent identity. Rather, we should expect that different 'places' within the firm, organizationally and geographically, develop their own identities, ways of doing things and ways of thinking over time (Martin 1992). They do so because they live in different places and must confront and respond to the particularities of these places across a whole range of practices and issues: the nature of the market, local methods and understandings concerning distribution, sales, services, supplier relations, labour relations, government relations and the like. As time goes on, and experiences accumulate, these local corporate cultures may be expected to diverge more and more from that of the centre.

In effect, the large firm is internally regionalized and what goes on its regions is important. The firm's dominant culture, created by and expressed through the activities and understandings of top management at headquarters, necessarily contains multiple subcultures. Some of these may revolve around functions and cut across places (engineers versus sales people, for example), but some will have real geographical locations – they will have grown up in specific plants in particular places. It follows from this that the interesting locus of study and of transformative processes is not only where 'the firm' (conceived as unitary agent) meets the world (competitors, markets, suppliers), but also internally as competing subcultures strive for validation and expression. In short, it's not just the cavalry versus the Indians, but the Thursdays versus the Yorkes, that are centrally at issue.

In this context, we can acknowledge that the body of work that clusters under the rubric of 'locality studies' has shown us a lot about what the presence of particular firms has meant for those places it has examined. But it has been less concerned with looking inside the plant to show us what the transformative encounter between branch and locality has meant for the firm.

Now might be the right time to start following this second line of enquiry since the conditions that allowed firms to get away with ignoring or blocking changes in their peripheries have changed. No one's dominant position in the market is even apparently stable, and the golden age of standardized mass production is definitively over. This creates an opening and an incentive for firms to revise their own expectations concerning the role of the periphery, which also provides an incentive for us to start asking different questions about what goes on there and what it might mean. However, it is still not clear that firms will know exactly what to do with this new opportunity, and that provides, perhaps, an opening for unusual kinds of policy interventions.

Examples, exceptions that prove the rule, and possibilities

Probably the annals of corporate history are full of stories of new operational and strategic models that have emerged at the 'regional' level within firms – or they would be if these models hadn't been thoroughly ignored or even done in by management at the centre. The new models might embrace a set of practices, relations and ways of thinking (about markets, products, competitors, workers, production processes, etc.) that diverge sharply from the corporate norm. In short, they embody a different culture (Schoenberger 1997).

These sub- or countercultures emerge as the people in the corporate region confront their particular situation, which is likely to produce many kinds of problems and opportunities that are not adequately addressed by central norms and standards. Like Captain Yorke, they reflect a dialectical process in which something new is produced through the encounter between the existing firm (a unit of which has been implanted in the new territory) and the particular piece of the world in which it has been established (where piece may be an actual place, as in a certain country or region, but may also imply a particular segment of the market or even a particular role vis-à-vis the firm as a whole).

Xerox

One example that has come down to us, so to speak, concerns the role of Xerox's Japanese joint venture, Fuji-Xerox. According to Jeff Kennard, Assistant to the President of Fuji-Xerox from 1977 to 1982,[4] Fuji-Xerox was explicitly established to be Xerox's 'window on Japan and Japanese competition' and the company's 'primary source of competitive intelligence'. But the offshoot had been thoroughly 'Xeroxised' – that is to say, it followed the strategy and adhered to the cultural norms of the US parent. And, like the parent, it began to lose share to Japanese competitors in the Japanese market during the 1970s.

The Xerox strategy at the time was to concentrate on the high end of the market: larger, higher-volume, expensive machines that, in the US, were sold direct by a very large corporate sales and service operation. The company had consciously abandoned the low end of the market due to its inferior profit margins. Little attention was paid to controlling costs, since these could be passed on to buyers.

Fuji-Xerox, however, found itself in a market in which the demand for smaller, cheaper machines was significant and was being served entirely by its domestic rivals. Moreover, due to their high volumes and associated economies of scale, the competition had an important cost advantage over Fuji-Xerox. At the same time, Fuji-Xerox did not have the internal resources to support a sufficiently large direct sales and services operation to sell large machines at the high end of the market. In any case, in Japan, sales through dealers and stores was the more important avenue to the market. This meant that price, rather than, as in the US, service was a central competitive issue.

According to Kennard, Fuji-Xerox rather rapidly concluded that 'the culture had to change'. The overhaul proceeded on two fronts: strategy towards the market and internal practices and relations. The new strategy entailed developing a line of smaller, lower-cost and lower-margin machines more suited to local market demand. The sales effort was shifted to focus more on dealers and stores, which had the side benefit of being much less costly to the firm. Only large customers were handled through a direct sales and service force.

Internally, Fuji-Xerox instituted a new (to Xerox) approach to doing business which it called, ironically, 'the New Xerox Movement' (Kearns and Nadler 1992). It reflected many of the principles of Japanese business practice that have become increasingly familiar to us, including greater production flexibility, a commitment to total quality and a rather different labour relations style.

As a result, Fuji-Xerox became quite successful at a time when the rest of the company was catastrophically losing market share precisely to Japanese competitors. This should have made Fuji-Xerox a very interesting place to Xerox management. They're being annihilated by the Japanese, but if they want to find out why and what they might do about it, they have a region inside the firm that knows rather a lot about it and was set up to provide just this sort of information. Why not, we might ask, go and look to see if there are any useful lessons that might be taken back to headquarters and considered for their applicability to the rest of the firm.

In fact, as former Xerox CEO David Kearns makes plain in his memoirs, top Xerox management was constantly visiting Fuji-Xerox, so what was going on there was not exactly a secret (Kearns and Nadler 1992). Kennard also reports that a 1978 McKinsey study of Fuji-Xerox validated the offshoot's entire strategy. Still, Xerox didn't use what was presumably learned on site even as its market share continued to decline.

Eventually, of course, Xerox management got the point and succeeded in regaining ground, but not before their share of the market had slid from roughly 90% to less than 15% in the space of ten years. In Kennard's view, Fuji-Xerox in the end became the agent of Xerox's transformation and continues to be so. But for a perilously long period, top Xerox managers refused to make use of the information abundantly available to them. According to Kennard, 'Xerox did not pay sufficient attention either to Japanese companies or to Fuji-Xerox' because they considered them 'just little companies in Japan'. Former Xerox CEO Paul Allaire[5] believes that at the time Xerox was so preoccupied with the anti-trust action underway in the US, and with the potential threat from IBM, that the company wasn't thinking about the Japanese at all. IBM had just entered the mid-volume market, the very heart of Xerox's business, and this was viewed as the company's principal competitive problem. Allaire notes that the fact that many Xerox managers had previously worked at IBM may also account for this focus.

Why Xerox management insisted on ignoring the new ways of doing business that had emerged in its Japanese offshoot until it was almost too late is a complicated issue which I have tried to address elsewhere (Schoenberger 1997). What I want to do here is draw attention to a particularly clear-cut example of regional differentiation within a firm and the way in which the centre can refuse to acknowledge transformations in the periphery. But we should also recall that, in this case, there was something like a happy ending as the acknowledgement was finally made and the lessons from the periphery drawn into the core.

IBM and the VM system

IBM is the favourite target of critics of US industrial performance, and I will not try to review its overall trajectory here (see Ferguson and Morris (1993) for a scathing critique). Instead, I want to look at one rather obscure but revealing story about the troubled development path of the virtual machine (VM) system within IBM. As with Xerox, the story involves a corporate outpost set up as a window on to a very particular market and technical environment whose strong and accurate representations back to the centre are for a long time resisted. The outpost, although staffed by IBM veterans, is transformed by its interaction with this environment, and struggles to marshall resources from within the firm and from the outside to persuade the centre of the validity of its views. As IBM is famous for its pervasive and rigid corporate culture, the analogy with the military of *Fort Apache* seems particularly apt.

My source for this story is something like a samizdat history of VM produced by Melissa Varian, a computer scientist at Princeton (Varian 1991). With Varian being a VM user and enthusiast, the history takes a frankly partisan stance, but given the wealth of detail it provides, including the testimony of many of the IBM personnel involved in the VM development effort, the story as a whole has considerable plausibility. Indeed, the fact that a system user was motivated to compile such a richly detailed account for distribution to a tightly integrated network of VM users (the SHARE group) is itself evidence of the degree to which the mobilization of an entire community, linking a part of the firm to the outside world, was necessary to engage the corporation's commitment to the project.

The VM story originates in Cambridge, Massachusetts, where IBM had established a Liaison Office at MIT. In 1964, this office was upgraded to the Cambridge Scientific Centre (CSC). IBM was particularly concerned to develop good relations with MIT as part of its effort to legitimize its products in the scientific community.

In the early 1960s, MIT researchers, using donated IBM hardware modified to the needs of the project, developed one of the earliest versions of time-sharing software, a system which, according to Varian, 'became the exemplar for time-sharing systems' (Varian 1991: 21). Time-sharing and, eventually, virtual machine systems, would prove to be a crucial avenue for increasing the productivity of enormously expensive machines.

During the same period, IBM's research labs in Poughkeepsie were developing the System/360, on which the company was staking its future. IBM staff from Cambridge, who had excellent relations with their counterparts at MIT (indeed, the CSC would locate its offices in the same building as the time-share research group), lobbied strongly to include the necessary specifications in the S/360 design to support time-sharing. However, as Varian notes, 'inside IBM at that time there was a strong belief that time-sharing would never amount to anything and that what the world needed was faster batch processing' (Varian 1991: 22). System/360 was released without the crucial address relocation hardware.

This early decision had far-reaching consequences, as IBM was never able to position itself as a core supplier for advanced academic computer science research. Both MIT and Bell Labs shifted their time-sharing development work to other hardware, and the systems they developed (Multics and UNIX) would not use IBM processors.

Nevertheless, stung by the loss of such prestigious customers as MIT and Bell Labs, IBM undertook the development of the S/360 Model 67 with a new time-sharing operating system, TSS, which was introduced in 1965. TSS, however, had serious stability and performance problems.

The Cambridge group, meanwhile, unconvinced by TSS, started its own development project for the S/360. The CP-40 project (later, CP-67), funded occultly at CSC, would focus on developing a virtual memory (later, virtual machine) system which would greatly reduce the time spent waiting for exchange of user programs under time-sharing. Also, by allowing programmers to work in virtual mode, it significantly ameliorated the costly memory constraints on system programming. The group also emphasized modular design for system evolution and a user-friendly command language.

Although CP-67 worked better than TSS, it seems likely that IBM would have killed the project, were it not for the fact that CP-67 was now backed by key customers, including MIT's Lincoln Laboratories, several other universities, and Lockheed. In 1968, IBM released the system more generally as a Type III Program that the company expressly refused to warranty or commit to maintain. It was not until 1970 that IBM would offer 'Class A' support for the system.

In that same year, IBM introduced its System/370, again without address translation capabilities. The CSC continued its bootleg project to develop a VM system for the new hardware. Finally, in 1972, IBM brought out an improved S/370 machine which included address relocation hardware and offered a VM system as one of four new operation systems.

It seems, however, that IBM's commitment to VM was still half-hearted at best. Varian writes: 'During this period [the mid-1970s] one noticed geographic pockets of VM activity that corresponded to the presence of a believer inside IBM'. Nevertheless, 'much of the support for new installations had to come from the user community. Most IBM branches were openly hostile to VM, and many used extreme measures to discourage customer managements from installing VM...' (Varian 1991: 62–3). It became apparent to insiders, including Jerry DePass, VM Product Administrator, that IBM had no plans to invest further resources in VM development (Varian 1991: 82).

The user community, during this period, became highly organized. It formed regional VM user groups (including groups in Europe and elsewhere overseas), held annual workshops, and developed an early electronic bulletin board to exchange ideas. Later, user groups would present formal white papers to IBM, arguing in favour of a deeper corporate commitment to VM and outlining the path they thought the company should take. In parallel, VNET, IBM's internal electronic network, helped to strengthen the group of VM supporters inside the company.

These pressures, combined with a stinging front-page critique of IBM's stance towards VM that appeared in *Computerworld* in December 1974, helped save the development effort. However, in 1976, it was moved to Poughkeepsie. Only a quarter of the staffers moved with it. Some 16% moved instead to DEC (Varian 1991: 83). According to Varian, subsequent releases were plagued with an increasing number of defects, and she attributes this to the fact that only a small number of people in the system's development after the move to Poughkeepsie had any experience with it (Varian 1991: 92). The problem was compounded when, in 1982, IBM announced its Object Code Only policy. Without access to the source code, users would be unable to correct problems on their own, and would instead have to await action at the centre.

Despite all of these problems, by 1991 there were more than 200,000 VM licences, considerably more than the 500 that IBM forecasters had predicted in the mid-1970s. Still, this figure pales into insignificance compared with the distribution of UNIX, which Varian describes as 'ugly, cryptic and hard to use' compared with VM/CMS (Varian 1991: 112). In her words: 'Because IBM took so long to make a commitment to VM, VM has been playing catch-up forever' (Varian 1991: 117).

The point of the story, however, is not to demonstrate that VM was a superior technology. Indeed, it had many serious flaws – notably involving its file structure.[6] In this way, we see an innovative, highly capable company refuse to acknowledge the new practices and understandings being formed in its own periphery. It remains loyal to prior commitments (e.g. to hardware rather than software, or to batch processing rather than time-sharing) and marginalizes the new ideas until growing pressures from within the company and, crucially, from without, force it to embrace them, however imperfectly. I don't mean to imply that IBM's difficulties in recent years can be traced to its handling of the VM system. But the story does illustrate the potential richness of experience being developed in peripheral corporate regions and the tremendous difficulty involved in validating the lessons of that experience at the centre.

Perhaps more striking are the exceptions which prove the rule. What I have in mind are those circumstances in which a firm realizes it needs to change and consciously sets out to create a new kind of place within the firm – sometimes as a sort of controlled experiment in which an operational branch will be established as a kind of working laboratory for the new methods and ideas.

I don't have the data to show this, but I suspect that these initiatives nearly always involve organizational and geographical separation from the centre.

Examples would include: the Lockheed Missiles and Space Company, which was moved some four hundred miles from the parent aircraft company's home base in California; IBM's personal computer operation which was set up in Florida; Xerox's Palo Alto Research Centre (PARC), which was created in California; the Digital Equipment Corporation's Palo Alto-based research labs; and two initiatives by GM, its joint venture with Toyota in California, and the Saturn Corporation in Tennessee.

What is sobering about this list is that in each case, the new corporate region did quite well on a variety of indicators (profits, product quality, innovations, market share, etc.), while the parent firm continued to decline. The fact of spatial and organizational separation might account for both these outcomes.

The impulse to separation is a strong one and may be thought to reflect a certain degree of self-knowledge on the part of those high-level managers who make the decision to invest in the new offshoots. But it may also reflect the degree to which the commitments of these managers conflict with the very principles and understandings that the new branch will incorporate. This is the source of a great impasse as the centre both desires and rejects the new creation.

Briefly, the inspiration for separation is that the experiment must be protected from the existing firm and its way of doing business or it will have no chance to emerge and succeed in its own right. At the centre, the infant culture will simply be devoured by the existing culture. At the margin, it has the chance to develop its own identity, uncontaminated by the practices and understandings of the core. Being at the margin, however, means that the new operation can all the more easily be marginalized.

General Motors

NUMMI, the GM–Toyota joint venture, is a striking example. This was really a strong initiative on the part of GM, since it entailed linking up with the perceived enemy with the explicit purpose of learning how to be a different kind of corporation. Toyota provided the operational leadership, and GM dispatched a team of managers to learn from their Japanese mentors, with the idea that they would carry their new knowledge back into GM and disseminate it throughout the firm.

By every standard, NUMMI has been a great success, based on a way of doing business that departs dramatically from the GM model, including low bureaucracy, relatively low technology, and high worker participation and commitment (Brown and Reich 1989; Keller 1989). And by most accounts, the rest of GM remained remarkably immune to the lessons of NUMMI. According to business guru Richard Tanner Pascale, GM central actively prevented the lessons from leaking out by rigorously controlling access to the plant even by GM personnel, and by breaking up and scattering the on-site GM team so that its influence elsewhere in the firm was attenuated (Pascale 1990).

Shortly after NUMMI started up, GM, being a rich firm, started planning its second great experiment, the Saturn Corporation. This experiment entailed a commitment of something on the order of $3 billion, and involved the construction of an entire integrated manufacturing and assembly facility on a greenfield site in rural Tennessee. The labour relations model developed in the plant is, by GM standards, revolutionary.[7] In terms of product design, quality of service, and sales (if not, as yet, profits), Saturn has also been a great success. Yet, though staffed from within GM, there are also serious doubts that much of what makes Saturn a very different kind of place within GM has had any great effect on the rest of the firm (*Financial Times* 1993; Sherman 1994).

In both cases, a new region has been created within the firm with the explicit idea that they can be used to transform the rest of the corporation. The regions are located apart from the centre precisely to allow them the space to develop (although a number of Saturn executives were based in Troy, Michigan). And then this space is used to hold them at arm's length, so that the transformative impulse from the periphery is blocked from reaching the core.

The Digital Equipment Corporation

The Digital Equipment Corporation (DEC) is another good example of a leading-edge firm that grudgingly accepted the fact that it needed to transform its erstwhile market-defining product technology, set up a geographically separate offshoot to accomplish this, and then refused to acknowledge the important lessons emanating from its new corporate region. AnnaLee Saxenian, in her book *Regional Advantage* (Saxenian 1994), offers a penetrating analysis of DEC's trajectory from rapid and tremendous success in the 1960s to multibillion-dollar losses in the 1990s. I rely on her account in the following brief narrative.

DEC, located along Route 128 in Massachusetts, was founded in 1957 by Kenneth Olsen, a graduate of MIT and former IBM researcher. It invented the minicomputer – a smaller, powerful, lower-cost alternative to the mainframe – and beat IBM to market with time-sharing technology that allowed one machine to serve multiple users simultaneously (see also Ferguson and Morris 1993). By 1977, DEC's sales exceeded $1 billion and accounted for 41% of the worldwide market for minicomputers. The VAX 11/780, launched in that year, provided nearly the power of a mainframe at greatly reduced cost. Oriented primarily to sophisticated academic and industrial users, the VAX series carried DEC to $13 billion in sales by 1990 – on which, however, it lost $95 million. By 1992, with quarterly losses approaching $3 billion, Ken Olsen was forced out.

Like Xerox, DEC had created and dominated a new market, which, in the end, proved vulnerable to smaller, cheaper machines originating from an unexpected source. First personal computers, and then more pointedly computer workstations for the same scientific and industrial markets that DEC thought it owned, invaded its terrain. Despite growing evidence that the market preferred high-powered, RISC-based[8] desktop machines with open architectures and operating systems, DEC remained committed to its VAX platform and its proprietary VMS operating system. Unlike Xerox, the new competitive threat was located in the US, in California's Silicon Valley.

Ironically, although the microcomputer makers were essentially replicating DEC's own assault on the mainframe computer market, the company's attitude towards these new products is characterized by Saxenian as dismissive (Saxenian 1994: 100). Ken Olsen is reported to have felt 'that DEC was about VAX-VMS machines' (Ferguson and Morris 1993: 104). In essence, the dominant culture (that is to say, the culture of the dominant: Ken Olsen and DEC's powerful and highly centralized Operations Committee) refused for quite some time to acknowledge the validity of an alternative set of practices and understandings concerning the market for computers, despite the strong signals emanating from that market. When it finally sought to enter into the personal computer and workstation business, it would do so in a confused and contradictory manner that further delayed its progress in an environment in which time-to-market is a crucial competitive variable.

Most relevant to our story, when DEC finally decided (partly at the behest of important customers such as GE and AT&T) to explore the development of its own open-systems workstations, it took care to distance the effort geographically from the centre. Much of the work was done at labs established in Silicon Valley in 1985.

Again, this was both a good and a bad idea. The Silicon Valley location protected the effort from the hostile dominant culture at headquarters, and situated it in the centre of open-systems, RISC-based microcomputer research and development. This strategy worked in the sense that DEC's Palo Alto labs embraced a local culture that was extremely open to the outside, in contrast to DEC's own inward focus, and was, according to Saxenian, 'well-integrated into Silicon Valley's social and technical networks' (Saxenian 1994: 138). Moreover, the labs did produce a series of innovative product and organizational ideas, including a (for DEC) revolutionary initiative to outsource its workstation's microprocessor.

Nevertheless, as Saxenian shows, geographical distance was also used to 'protect' the headquarters from the labs, as the centre, motivated by its continuing loyalty to the VAX system, variously ignored, fought, or dragged its feet on the labs' innovations. As Saxenian notes, 'DEC was ultimately unable to assimilate the lessons of its geographically distant Palo Alto group back to ... headquarters' (Saxenian 1994: 139–40). Or, more precisely, they transferred what was left of the group after its director and several of his colleagues resigned. A year later, the firm reversed course and moved a design team for its promising Alpha chip back to Silicon Valley.

Again we have a portrait of a divided company that contains divergent and incompatible cultures, commitments and identities. The dominant culture is forced by competitive and market changes to deliberately create the new corporate region with its counterculture, as GM did with NUMMI and Saturn, but cannot bring itself to embrace the alternative version of DEC which is the result. Distance allows the new corporate region a protected space in which to develop and also allows the centre to keep the new practices and ways of thinking at arm's length, despite the fact that this puts the entire corporation at serious risk.

John Deere

One intriguing possibility concerns John Deere, which appears (again, in the face of very difficult circumstances) to have adopted an approach which encourages experimentation in its existing corporate regions and actually pays attention to what happens there.[9] Again, the transformations were driven by crisis, so we can't conclude that the firm was especially prescient, and they were by no means speedily accomplished. Still, one gets the impression that the firm was both tolerant of and attentive to changes in the periphery and that news also circulates, to some degree, within the periphery. One may note, however, that although organizationally and geographically distinct, the actual geographical distances involved are quite small.

One part of the story concerns John Deere's Digger Construction Equipment division, located in Dubuque, Iowa. In 1988, following recession, deep layoffs and a major strike, the division adopted 'the New Approach', in which strategic information is shared with employees and decisions decentralized as far as possible. The product development operation was completely overhauled, with most engineers shifted out of functional departments into one of four nearly self-contained businesses within the factory. The aim was to sharply reduce product development and manufacturing cycle times in order to meet the demands of the market and respond to (increasingly Japanese) competition. Along with the new model of labour relations and decision-making, the method was to integrate product and manufacturing engineering, and encourage these to cooperate closely and continuously with welding, tooling, purchasing and quality control. As a result, the 310D backhoe took eighteen months to develop, half the time of its predecessor model, and can be produced in ten hours instead of five days.

Meanwhile, the Harvester division in Moline, Illinois, was pursuing a parallel effort to cut development and manufacturing times in its farm machinery business. Again, this implied considerable devolution of authority within the division, with the number of management layers cut in half. It also involved breaking down functional barriers between product engineering and manufacturing engineering, and between the engineers and purchasing, quality and production. The goal of creating integrated teams was eventually accomplished by co-locating team members at the division's engineering centre, some three miles from the factory. Again, great progress was made. A new rice planter, for example, was developed in eighteen months, against twenty-six months for previous projects.

The difference between Dubuque and Moline, which managers at Harvester appear to be acutely aware of, is that the development operation at Digger is located in the manufacturing plant. The spatial separation at Harvester is a result of a decision made in the late 1970s to remove product engineering from the day-to-day pressures of manufacturing. Though three miles may seem a modest enough distance, Harvester managers consider it to be a serious obstacle to truly integrating engineering with manufacturing. Following the Dubuque model, the plan is to shift engineering back into the manufacturing plant.

This is a small enough story, but it provides a promising hint about what can happen when the centre doesn't make strong assumptions about where in the firm productive new ideas and practices may come from and allows its various branches to experiment with significant changes in their way of operating (granted in this case the outcome may be facilitated by the fact that we're dealing with different lines of business rather than an integrated whole). But these separate units also appear to draw some support from each other. So this may be an example that recognizes its multiple regionalized identities, and uses them to transform itself.

Conclusion

In times of stability and security, firms may succeed in imposing a unified vision of the way things ought to be on all their various parts and branches. Whatever variations exist in the periphery will be contained and ignored, and perhaps no great harm will be done. But in the periods of great uncertainty and turmoil, the large, multi-unit, multi-locational firm is likely to become the site of sharply and actively competing visions of who and what the firm is and how its activities should be ordered. These competing visions are produced through the encounter with a set of highly divergent strategies to deal with their particular part of the world.

This internal competition appears to be highly spatialized – perhaps necessarily so. The likely result is that different regions within the firm become champions of often quite incompatible models of competition and production.

This process of internal regionalization and competition merits analysis in its own right. Increasingly, it may be in the firm's far-flung regions rather than at the centre that the most interesting transformations are taking place. But we are still faced with the worrying prospect that the centre will seek to re-assert its authority by blocking the transformative impulses from the periphery or even by overriding them in the periphery itself.

Is there, in this context, a role for regional development policies that are directed towards strengthening or reviving an existing industrial base? The possibilities would not appear to be abundant, especially as regional development policy has not in the past sought to influence the firm's internal, extra-regional operations. But there might be one or two avenues worth pursuing.

For regions that host branch plants, a first move would be to revise expectations concerning the degree to which the branch is the passive creature of the centre. Local authorities should be alert to the emergence of potentially productive countercultures in the branch, although this implies knowing rather a lot about the centre.

The second step would be figuring out ways to support this emerging corporate region, so that at the least it is less likely to be snuffed out by a recalcitrant headquarters. One possibility might be a kind of outside–inside venture capital: outside because it comes from the region, inside because it supports the corporate region inside to pursue an experiment that the centre has refused to support. If all goes well, the experiment (and the branch) will be successful enough that it can't be closed down by the centre, even if it can be otherwise ignored. The underlying idea here is that the firm itself shouldn't be the only one in charge of the fate of its branches. The region has every interest in identifying and supporting deviants, especially when the dominant culture gives every indication of not being able to respond appropriately to changing circumstances. It may be the case that the centre's collapse will drag the branch down at the end of the day, but this seems one way to give the branch and its host region a fighting chance.

Development authorities in regions that host corporate centres must also be alert to processes going on within the firm but outside their locale. Development assistance should be targeted to supporting the assimilation of lessons from the periphery – perhaps from the firm's own experiments. There is nothing more intrusive than saying, for example to GM: If you really want something from us, we'll help you become more like NUMMI or Saturn but we won't help you become more like the old GM. No more tax breaks which encourage excess investments in unworkable automation, but we'll increase the funding for worker training, etc. If GM refuses, then it's anyway doomed and the region should invest its resources elsewhere.

The key element of the policy departures proposed here are two. They require the region to enter into the life of the firm to a much greater degree than has, I think, been customary. The region has to make it its business to know how things are on the inside and where the most interesting changes are occurring.

The second element follows from the first. In order to know these things, regional development authorities must also be in much closer contact with each other. They need to share what they know in order to develop the knowledge they need. And in order to do something with this knowledge, they need to work together. Rather than seeing themselves in competition with all other regions, they must recognize that they have a common interest in supporting change within the firm as a whole. This, of course, requires regions to also think differently and, dare I say it, dialectically.

Acknowledgements

This chapter benefited greatly from the assistance of Elizabeth Dunn, who organized and carried out the interviews with Xerox personnel. My thanks also to those who generously agreed to participate in the research and to Hugh Ellis, Haydee Salmun, Trevor Barnes and Meric Gertler for their thoughtful comments and suggestions.

Notes

1 As an interesting sidelight, in this film and others, Ford takes great care to show that the post-Civil War cavalry was full of former Confederate troops who assume the uniform and discipline of their erstwhile blood rivals in order to fight the new common foe – Indians. The parallel with the immediate post-World War II environment, in which these films were made and in which the US united with its recent enemies to fight the new Reds, is intriguing.

2 I should note that I am here defining periphery extremely loosely as, essentially, everything organizationally and geographically outside the immediate orbit of a firm's headquarters.

3 Other theoretical frameworks could also be invoked here. Modernization theory supposed that there was a common trajectory to a common version of being modern, which is to say, being as much like the US as possible. Conventional economic theory has its own normative commitments to particular universal categories, whether or not they can be thought to exist in their 'pure' form (e.g. free markets), that are not thought to be marked by historical or geographical circumstances.

4 Interviewed 11 September 1994 by Elizabeth Dunn. For more details on this case see Schoenberger (1997).

5 Interviewed 13 September 1994 by Elizabeth Dunn. Allaire spent much of this period (1970–3 and 1975–83) in Europe with Rank Xerox.

6 My thanks to Hugh Ellis for pointing this out.

7 Of course, GM standards are terrible. Some hint of how far they may still need to go is provided by a quote from Saturn's vice president of communications, Bruce McDonald, who remarks: 'Historically, we never asked people what they thought. Now we empower them to really be an employee.' (Sherman 1994: 16).

8 RISC stands for Reduced Instruction Set Computing; this greatly increases computation speeds.

9 Good news is hard to come by. This account is based on a series of three articles in the *Financial Times*: 'Digger demolishes divisions', 30 September 1991: 12; 'Reaping the harvest on an integrated team approach', 7 October 1991: 11; and 'Different tack up the Mississippi', 7 October 1991: 11.

Bibliography

Brown, C. and Reich, M. (1989) 'When does union-management work? A look at NUMMI and GM–Van Nuys', *California Management Review* 31 (Spring): 26–44.

Clark, G.L. (1994) 'Strategy and structure: corporate restructuring and the scope and characteristics of sunk costs', *Environment and Planning A* 26: 9–32.

Clark, G.L. and Wrigley, N. (1993) 'Sunk costs: a framework for economic geography', paper presented at the Annual Meetings of the Association of American Geographers, Atlanta, GA, 7–9 April.

Collis, D. (1991) 'Organizational capability as a source of profit', Working paper 91-046, Boston, MA: Harvard Business School.

Dicken, P. (1976) 'The multiplant business enterprise and geographic space: some issues in the study of external control and regional development', *Regional Studies* 10: 401–12.

Dicken, P. (1986) *Global Shift: Industrial Change in a Turbulent World*, London: Harper and Row.

Ferguson, C.H. and Morris, C.R. (1993) *Computer Wars: The Fall of IBM and the Future of Global Technology*, New York: Times Books.

Financial Times (1993) 'Saturn profit poses funding dilemma', 24 June: 18.

Frobel, F., Heinrich, J. and Kreye, O. (1980) *The New International Division of Labor*, Cambridge: Cambridge University Press.

Haraway, D. (1991) *Simians, Cyborgs, and Women: The Reinvention of Nature*, New York: Routledge.

Hymer, S. (1972) 'The multinational corporation and the law of uneven development', in J. Bhagwati (ed.) *Economics and World Order*, London: Macmillan.

Kearns, D. and Nadler, D. (1992) *Prophets in the Dark: How Xerox Reinvented Itself and Beat Back the Japanese*, New York: Harper Business.

Keller, M. (1989) *Rude Awakening*, New York: Morrow.

Martin, J. (1992) *Cultures in Organizations*, Oxford: Oxford University Press.

Massey, D. (1984) *Spatial Divisions of Labor*, London: Methuen.

Ong, A. (1987) *Spirits of Resistance and Capitalist Discipline: Factory Women in Malaysia*, Albany, NY: State University of New York Press.

Pascale, R.T. (1990) *Managing on the Edge*, New York: Simon and Schuster.

Pred, A. (1977) *City Systems in Advanced Economics*, London: Hutchinson.

Rosaldo, R. (1989) *Culture & Truth: The Remaking of Social Analysis*, Boston, MA: Beacon Press.

Rostow, W. (1960) *The Stages of Economic Growth*, Cambridge: Cambridge University Press.

Saxenian, A. (1994) *Regional Advantage*, Cambridge, MA: Harvard University Press.

Schoenberger, E. (1997) *The Cultural Crisis of the Firm*, Oxford: Basil Blackwell.

Sherman, J. (1994) *In the Rings of Saturn*, Oxford: Oxford University Press.

Storper, M. and Walker, R. (1989) *The Capitalist Imperative*, Oxford: Basil Blackwell.

Varian, M. (1991) *VM and the VM Community: Past, Present and Future*, Princeton, NJ: Office of Computing and Information Technology, Princeton University.

Vernon, R. (1966) 'International trade and international investment in the product cycle', *Quarterly Journal of Economics* 80: 190–207.

10 The production of industrial processes

Regions, nation states and the foundations of regulation

Meric S. Gertler

Introduction

Interest in the role of regional institutions of the economy has increased dramatically over the past several years. One can discern four key ideas emerging from the literature celebrating the rise of regional institutions. First, especially for technology-intensive products or in sectors where quality and responsiveness to changing market demands are vital, 'social economy' relations are an important source of competitive success (Sayer and Walker 1992). These entail inter-firm co-operation, collaboration, and information-sharing based on the development and maintenance of trust between firms. Second, these social economy relations and the trust between interacting parties on which these relations are based are fostered by spatial proximity between economic actors. Spatial proximity allows or accommodates repeated interaction over time of both a formal and informal nature both planned and unplanned. This interaction is said to promote the trust and mutual understanding necessary to support the easy exchange of proprietary information as part of a socially organized, regionally contained learning process.

Third, these social economy relations are reinforced by (and, themselves, reinforce) a set of institutions, the most important of which are produced and reproduced at the regional (subnational) level. Such institutions include the relatively informal notion of conventions (rules, norms, shared attitudes and values), as well as formal organizations in both the public and private sector (for example, educational and training institutions, industry associations, technology transfer or market analysis centres, supplier clubs) (Storper 1997; Cooke and Morgan 1998). Finally, with the erosion of the economic sovereignty and regulatory power of the nation state, due to fewer restrictions on the geographical mobility of capital and trade flows, this set of regional actors, practices, and institutions is (according to the thesis) becoming ever more important. Hence, the literature has produced concepts such as 'regional innovation systems' (Cooke 1992; Braczyk *et al.* 1997), 'region state' (Ohmae 1995), and the 'learning region' (Florida 1995; Morgan 1995). Most colourfully, in a new twist on the title of Adam Smith's classic tome, several authors have recently celebrated the 'wealth of regions' (Storper and Scott 1993; Wolfe 1993).

There are indeed many important insights, ideas, and policy initiatives which have flowed from this line of argument. Under the right circumstances, it appears that regional institutions do indeed possess the capacity to support and promote innovation-enhancing practices on the part of locally based firms (Saxenian 1994), while in other cases the same institutions hold the potential to discourage or stifle such behaviour (Grabher 1993). Furthermore, the research produced by geographers and planners has triggered something of a 'rediscovery' of economic geography by economists (Tyson 1992; Krugman 1995; Jaffe *et al.* 1993), management theorists (Porter 1990; Kanter 1995), political scientists (Putnam 1993) and others.

However, in this chapter I wish to challenge what is rapidly becoming the mainstream position on the ascendance of regional institutions in contemporary economic dynamics. My objective is to explore the *limits* of this thesis, and to do so by examining the very production of industrial processes themselves. I shall argue, with the help of a transatlantic case study of the development, fabrication, and implementation of advanced manufacturing systems, that other scales of regulation are still crucially important in the shaping of economic processes and outcomes. In doing so, I shall also address some themes which were central to the work of Harold Innis who, decades ago, was equally interested in the mechanisms by which production and control systems extended across international boundaries to shape the developmental paths of regions and nations (Gertler 1993).

The study supporting this analysis was conducted between 1991 and 1996, and focused on the interaction between Canadian users of advanced industrial machinery and those firms, both at home and abroad, which produced this machinery (see Gertler (1995, 1997) and Gertler and DiGiovanna (1997) for a detailed description of the study's structure, rationale, and findings based on analysis of users' experiences). As the large majority of such producers of manufacturing technology were found to be located outside Canada and, particularly, outside North America, the study of user–producer interaction necessarily entailed a strong international dimension.

Since Germany was identified as one of the leading sources of advanced machinery, I conducted a series of interviews with a subset of the German machinery producers found to be supplying North American markets. These interviews began in 1993, and many of the firms were visited more than once between 1993 and 1996. The case study firms were geographically distributed across three regions of Germany (in the Stuttgart region of Baden-Württemberg, around Siegen on the southern fringe of North Rhine-Westphalia, and around the northern cities of Bremen and Hanover, in Lower Saxony). Interviews centred on each firm's experiences with implementing advanced manufacturing systems in North American customers' plants. Much of the discussion explored the firms' relations and interaction with their customers in North America, the extent to which these relations differed from their typical experience interacting with customers in Germany, and the reasons for such differences (for an overview of these findings, see Gertler (1996)).

The transatlantic transfer of advanced manufacturing technology: a case study

The story told in this chapter revolves around the experiences of a large German engineering firm and, in particular, its in-house division producing special machinery and industrial automation systems. At the time of my first visit in June 1993, this division employed roughly 360 people, a small fraction of the firm's worldwide workforce. While 60% of its yearly turnover came from the sale of specialized production equipment to other divisions of the parent firm, the rest of its revenue was earned through sales to customers outside the firm, largely in the automotive, computer, and electronics sectors. Virtually all of the division's work involved the design and production of advanced, highly customized products, in which each system was designed and built to order, according to customers' own production requirements. Consequently, the production of this special machinery was a highly interaction-intensive process, typically involving extensive contact with user firms over an extended period of time.

On this first visit, quite by chance, I found the division to be working on the final production stages of two identical flexible manufacturing systems (FMS) for the assembly and testing of a small automotive part. These two FMS lines had already been fully constructed, and were being fine-tuned, tested, and de-bugged prior to being disassembled and shipped to the 'customer' plants for reassembly. In fact, both lines were being produced for plants within another division of the firm. One of the lines was intended for a plant in another region of Germany where the small automotive part was to be produced. The other line was destined for another of the parent firm's plants, located in the southern United States. This latter plant had been established by the parent in the late 1970s, and made a number of different automotive parts for the North American market.

The FMS lines were complex and technologically sophisticated, dictated in part by the characteristics of the finished product. The auto part being assembled was quite small, with narrow tolerances permitted in order to ensure high performance. Moreover, the quality of this part was crucial to the performance of the vehicle into which it would ultimately be installed. Furthermore, because this part came into contact with fuel during its normal use, testing during the assembly process was to be done with real fuel, introducing stringent requirements for safety. Hence, each of the two FMS systems featured sophisticated robotics, advanced sensor devices, and programmable controls. Although the two lines were identical, the contrasts between the two ends of the plant in which each was being tested were striking. At the 'German' end, all was peaceful. A few engineers wearing white coats could be seen quietly running tests, recording data, and making adjustments. But the 'US' end was a veritable hive of activity. Here, a dozen workers from the US plant were following around the division's German engineers and technical staff, watching them de-bug and break in the new line.

The senior manager in charge of this project indicated that the objective of this exercise was to provide US workers the opportunity to learn how to solve problems occurring on the FMS line by observing the process of problem identification and correction as practised by the firm's German engineers. It was management's hope that when problems arose during normal operation of the FMS lines in the US plant, the problem-solving skills learned through observation in Germany would be applied at home in order to correct difficulties more quickly and easily. Additionally, the firm hoped that its US workers might learn how to avoid many such problems in the first place. In either case, the intent was to reduce down-time or unacceptable variations in product quality due to operational difficulties. Moreover, in order to support this learning process, the parent firm had put the American workers through three months of German language training in the United States before sending them overseas. Furthermore, the length of their stay was a lavish eight weeks, in order to allow sufficient time for the requisite skills to be transferred.

Asked to account for the striking difference between the two ends of the plant, senior management indicated that they were aware of the radically different levels and type of worker training in the southern United States compared with Germany. Their prior experience had taught them that American workers would typically be far less well trained, especially with respect to advanced skills such as the use of electronic controls and the ability to solve production problems on the job. Anticipating future problems at the US plant, the parent firm's management had directed its special machinery division and its US management to do all they could to avoid or minimize their occurrence. Management was confident that they could overcome any difficulties by pursuing this strategy.

Moreover, this approach was supplemented by other measures. In particular, the special machinery/automation division enlisted the support of its North American subsidiary in the US Midwest, which was asked to serve as a closer intermediary during the line's initial set-up and subsequent operation in the US plant. The firm was also taking the further precaution of providing an electronic link-up via modem between the US plant and German headquarters in order to enable engineers at head office to monitor production data in real time and assist with troubleshooting if necessary.

By contrast, the relative calm at the German end of the plant was explained by the firm's confidence in the ability of its domestic workers to solve problems or avoid them altogether, thanks to their lengthier and more extensive training. This training was acquired through both a rigorous technical college programme as well as a three-and-a-half-year apprenticeship period required of all workers as part of the 'dual' training system typical of German manufacturing industries.

A second visit to the division's headquarters in Germany in June 1994 provided an opportunity to monitor the success of the technology implementation process. This second round of discussion with the division's management revealed that they had planned for a six-month period to transfer the lines to the two plants, set them up and break them in. During this time, there were frequent exchanges of engineers and operators across the Atlantic between the two user plants, with the special machinery division and its US subsidiary also heavily involved. The idea was to allow the exchange and sharing of information and experiences in the FMS implementation: in other words, *to create an interplant and international learning process through joint problem-solving*.

The subsequent process did not, however, unfold as expected. The break-in process and time required to reach 'normal' operation were significantly more difficult and longer in the case of the US plant. There were several reasons for these difficulties. Among the more mundane of these, the US line had to operate under conditions of higher average temperature and humidity, producing problems of part recognition, handling, and alignment. Furthermore, this was compounded by what were alleged to be more variable or poorer-quality components from outside suppliers based in the United States. These problems in quality control and materials, while relatively minor, were still significant and – given the parent firm's lengthy experience in the operation of a US plant – it is surprising that they were not anticipated during the design process in Germany.

Other sources of difficulty were more fundamental in nature. It transpired that the training provided for the worker-operatives from the US plant was not sufficient, even with the lengthy eight-week visit to division headquarters. A few months' training was simply not enough to overcome the absence of a basic foundation of background knowledge and skills in the US workforce. Furthermore, the firm found that its US maintenance and support personnel were far less well prepared for the task, through either formal education or experience. Finally, and perhaps most importantly, employee turnover proved to be a very serious source of difficulty for the US plant. Management had indeed anticipated that this might be a problem, but had thought that by investing in the training of their workers, and by trying to build a stronger relation between them, they might inculcate a sense of commitment and loyalty to the firm amongst their American workers. However, such was not to be the case. Indeed, once their workers had received what amounted (in the context of the US South) to such relatively extensive training, they became much sought-after commodities in the regional labour market. In a fashion typical of US-style labour markets, these workers were poached by other manufacturers in the same region and, as a result, the firm's investment in their training yielded very little return for the US plant.

To complete the case study, I visited the US plant in April 1996. Discussions with managers at the plant emphasized the fact that many adjustments to the original design had been implemented to adapt the FMS line to US conditions and respond to the difficulties encountered. Operation of the line had eventually reached the point where disruptions were relatively infrequent and tolerable, although this state had been achieved in a matter of years rather than months. Moreover, another interesting difference was revealed. The line in the US plant was now producing parts more cheaply than its German counterpart, largely due to US management's freedom to work the machinery more intensively – for more hours each week, and with fewer shutdowns for weekends or holidays. By contrast, the German line was producing parts of significantly better quality. Indeed, German managers confirmed that the quality differences were substantial enough to be perceptible to their customers in the automotive industry. This had become the source of some difficulty, since their customers had expected the US-made parts to be cheaper but of equal quality. Given that the firm was hoping to sell its US-made parts not only to American car producers but also to German producers such as BMW and Mercedes-Benz who were in the process of setting up plants in the southeastern United States, this quality gap was highly salient.

Interpreting the case: the influence of macroregulatory frameworks

In the case just described, the two German and American installations had much in common: the two systems' original designs were identical; they were produced by the same division to produce identical products; both were implemented under the umbrella of the same parent firm, and there was also considerable exchange of personnel and information between the two implementation sites; the two projects were undertaken simultaneously. And yet, despite these similarities, the experiences and outcomes at the two sites diverged markedly, and the implementation difficulties at the US plant could not be overcome without years of effort and great expense. That these problems should have been so significant is on one level, at least, quite surprising. After all, the parent firm is a large one with deep financial and technological resources. Furthermore, it had already had many years' experience operating plants outside Germany, and the US plant in question was already fifteen years old when the FMS implementation began. And yet, at another level, the outcomes documented above are not so unexpected.

Examining the differences between the two plants more carefully, it becomes clear that a crucial source of variation is in *the way that labour markets are socially constructed and regulated* in the two countries. The high rates of employee turnover amongst both shopfloor workers and managers at the American plant, which proved to be the source of so many implementation problems, are encouraged by a number of characteristic features of US labour market regulation. Most prominent among these is the extensive reliance by employers on external labour market transactions, that is, a strong tendency to manage their labour force by hiring and firing, leading to relatively shorter employment tenure and more frequent switching of workers between employers (Christopherson 1993; Wever 1995). These prevailing labour market practices, which are frequently celebrated by the business press as a source of competitive advantage under the 'American' (or Anglo-American) model of capitalism, are generally agreed to result from a regulatory system which enshrines employers' flexibility and labour mobility. Under such a system, labour is treated more as a variable cost than as an asset, a feature shared by Canadian, British, and other Anglo-American labour market systems (O'Grady 1994).

Hence, the high rate of employee turnover and instability in the workforce frustrated the firm in its efforts to retain the American workers who had undergone extensive training. This instability was itself heightened by the unwillingness of other employers in the region to invest in training their own workers given the likelihood that these workers, once trained, might be poached by other firms seeking similar skills. As a consequence, they were aggressive in their pursuit of the case study firm's skilled employees. Such behaviour can be understood to have been induced by the systemic influence of flexible employment rules which enhance the ability of firms to deploy labour with few encumbrances, and which fuel the mobility of workers. Moreover, the firm's continuing quality problems are likely to have been exacerbated by a reluctance to spend more funds on training newly hired workers so extensively. Thus, despite the firm's best efforts, their objective of implementing a skill-intensive production process to produce a high-quality product was seriously compromised by the contours of an 'unfriendly' regulatory environment in which their US plant was located.

As for the German plant, the smooth implementation process and high quality achieved reflect the very different prevailing system of labour market regulation in Germany. Instead of enshrining flexibility, this system works to maintain a stable employment relation, minimizing labour force turnover by constraining employers from hiring and firing at will. Without the option to reduce costs in the short term by laying off workers (or reducing their wages), employers instead are induced to compete through other means, especially by achieving technical excellence in products and production processes. Hence, what they may give up to the competition in terms of higher production costs is offset by the higher quality and greater productivity (which helps to keep unit labour costs manageable). Moreover, the stability of the employment relation provides a strong incentive for German employers to invest heavily in training, as they are more or less assured that they will reap the benefit of this expenditure. Further inducements along this trajectory come from the high wages paid to German workers (themselves the result of a strongly centralized industrial relations and wage determination system). Compelled to pay their workers at such relatively high levels, employers see a clear logic in investing in the technological upgrading of their workers in order to ensure productivity levels commensurate with wages paid (see Sengenberger and Campbell 1994).

The role of national and regional institutions

Given the arguments reviewed at the beginning of this chapter concerning the ascendance of regional institutions, it is worth pointing out that the features just described arise largely from *national institutions* in Germany: a nationally defined industrial relations system, national regulation supporting 'co-determination' by workers and managers in the workplace, and other elements of labour market regulation. Furthermore, these regulatory characteristics are *common to both the plant producing the FMS line and the German plant in which it is being used*, while they are very different from the prevailing labour market and industrial relations regime in which the US plant is situated. It is also clear, in hindsight, that many of the technical features of the FMS line itself reflect the German national system of labour market regulation, in that they require and presume a very high level of skill and workplace stability in order for effective implementation to be most easily achieved.

Thus on the basis of this case study it appears that, contrary to the dominant thrust of the contemporary literature on regions, national systems of industrial regulation continue to exert a very strong influence over firms' day-to-day practices in the workplace. They also act to limit the extent to which work practices and technologies can 'travel' internationally in unaltered form (for a more extended discussion of this theme, see Gertler (1997a)).

However, to assert the continuing prominence of national regulatory features is not to deny any role for regional institutions in these processes. Examining our case again, the influence of regional regulation is indeed evident in a number of manifestations. For example, despite strong pressures for inter-regional convergence in wages, work practices, and regulation, there is still significant variation between regions of the United States in the contours of labour market regulation. Clark *et al.* (1986) documented enduring differences in the 1980s between the northern regions of the country, where unions still exert significant influence thanks to features of state-level industrial relations legislation, and the 'right-to-work' states of the South and West, in which anti-union legislative climates afford employers maximum flexibility in their deployment of labour.

Hence the fact that the case study plant was situated in the South probably ensured that implementation difficulties would be especially acute, since employment tenure there is inherently considerably less stable than in other parts of the United States. Furthermore, the poorly developed technical foundation of the workforce in this region is also likely to have been exacerbated by the southerly location, as southern states have typically maintained much lower rates of both personal and corporate income taxation than have their northern counterparts, yielding fewer dollars per capita to put into state education systems.

The significance of regional regulation is also evident in the example of another case study firm whose experiences were examined as part of the same study. This company is based in the same region of Germany as the first case, though as a classic *Mittelstand* firm it is much smaller and far less internationalized. This firm is a producer of highly sophisticated machinery for cutting and shaping metal. Interviews with the firm's senior management revealed that it too had experienced great difficulty penetrating the North American market, and that the principal impediment was that North American workers and managers found its technologically advanced machinery too difficult to use and unnecessarily complex. As a consequence, their manufacturing technology frequently failed to live up to customers' expectations (or the claims of the producer firm's sales personnel).

In response to these difficulties, the firm ultimately decided to redesign their machinery to produce a special model tailored to the North American market. Moreover, in a strategic decision of considerable significance, the firm chose to give the responsibility for this redesign to its US branch office. Since this office had been set up as a service and spare parts operation, the firm was forced to upgrade and expand the engineering capacity of its US branch. This strategy proved to be feasible because the American office was located in New England. Thanks to this region's rich history of manufacturing activity in skill-intensive mechanical engineering industries, the firm was able to draw upon a deep residual pool of skilled engineers and shopfloor workers, and found its skill requirements to be well supported by local educational institutions. Furthermore, the relatively stable employment relation fostered by regionally determined labour relations regulation made it considerably easier for the branch to retain its skilled engineering and technical employees. The redesigned machine, which was considerably simpler to operate (and, since it offered fewer special features, significantly cheaper to buy), proved to be an instant success, enabling the firm to triple its share of the US market in its segment.

Thus, as this example demonstrates, institutions situated at the regional scale continue to play a significant role in the shaping of technological trajectories. And yet, this same episode seems to raise the spectre of a longer-term threat to the vitality of the home region in Germany where the firm is based. After all, having decided to pursue overseas markets more aggressively, the firm ultimately found it necessary to shift responsibility for both design and production of its machinery to the American branch, representing the 'exporting' of highly skilled employment from its headquarter operations at home.

In fact, this study found further evidence that important countervailing forces had begun to emerge in Germany to undermine the integrity and primacy of its regionally focused production systems. Returning again to the first case study: the parent firm was in the process of taking several strategic organizational decisions in order to respond to the serious competitive challenges of the early 1990s. First, in attempting to learn from the unexpectedly difficult FMS implementation at its American plant, the parent firm decided to transfer greater technological capacity to the US subsidiary of its automation/special machinery division in the Midwest. This was achieved by involving the American subsidiary in the design and production of a second FMS for the US plant one year after the first system was installed. This second line was produced jointly by the division in Germany and the subsidiary, with each taking responsibility for the production of one half of the new line. The intent was to enable the subsidiary to perform true design, fabrication, and assembly functions so that it might better serve its North American market (other plants under the same corporate umbrella, as well as outside clients). The hope was that, once its technological capacity was enhanced, the subsidiary would be able to solve production problems as well as head office staff, but more quickly and cheaply since they would be geographically closer to their clients. They would also be able to help their North American clients implement the adjustments to their production equipment necessary to accommodate increasingly frequent modifications to their products.

A second strategic decision taken by the firm entailed a series of reorganizations of its supply chain to reduce its dependence on suppliers in its home region and in other parts of Germany. Head office managers indicated that they had already begun to source certain parts and components in the Eastern European countries of Poland and the Czech Republic. Driven primarily by cost considerations, the inputs involved were generally amongst the least sophisticated or complex, and were typically of lower value added than inputs still obtained at home.

However, even for their more technologically complex inputs, the firm had also chosen to reduce its reliance on outside suppliers in Germany. This decision was prompted not by cost considerations but by concerns about the unwanted diffusion of the firm's proprietary technologies to competitors. Recently, the division had been badly 'burned' by an external supplier who had violated their trust. This supplier had produced some highly specialized production equipment as a subcomponent of a larger manufacturing system they were building. The design of this piece of equipment depended on a detailed knowledge of the firm's product and production process. Although the firm appreciated the risks inherent in such an approach, it had used this strategy many times with other small and medium-sized suppliers in their home region as a way of capitalizing on the technological capabilities of these specialist firms.

Soon after the job was completed, the firm was horrified to learn that the same outside vendor with whom they thought they had established a strong relationship based on trust had turned around and offered the same technology to the firm's biggest competitor in Europe. As a result of this unfortunate experience, based on the uncharacteristically opportunistic behaviour of this supplier, the firm instructed the automation/special machinery division to reduce its outsourcing of specialized inputs and to become more self-sufficient. At the same time, the firm decided that its division should also cease to produce custom machinery and production systems for clients outside its corporate umbrella. In other words, the firm was taking deliberate steps to dismantle what had previously been an intricate, extensive, and highly developed network of relationships with both suppliers and customers in its home region. By internalizing what had previously been a social process of user–producer interaction and inter-firm learning, the firm's actions might well be seen as reducing the beneficial effects which had previously flowed to its partner firms as a result of close interaction and collaboration.

While these strategic decisions to reorganize the firm's production systems both domestically and internationally might have led to greater overall success for the firm, thanks to better implementation experiences abroad, lower production costs, or greater control over the firm's proprietary technology, there can be no doubt that *the changes documented above represent significant losses for the firm's home region and a serious threat to its integrity as a social production system*.

Conclusion

This chapter began with a review of recent arguments supporting the idea of the region's ascendance as a key level of organization and governance in economic systems. Proponents of this thesis contend that the region has come to assume the position formerly occupied by the nation state in this regard, and that (at least in the most successful cases) these new, regionally organized and governed production systems have developed into innovative and robust centres of economic activity, serving as 'anchors' for the global economy.

However, the case studies presented in this chapter raise some significant questions about this thesis, suggesting that the argument concerning the ascendance of regional institutions has serious limits. The difficulties encountered by the firm in the first case study as it sought to transfer its sophisticated production technology to its plant in the southern region of the United States were shown to stem primarily from differences in regulatory frameworks at the national level. Institutional features at the regional scale *did* play a role in shaping outcomes, an influence also demonstrated in the second case study. Moreover, since the firm in the second case (coming from the same country and region as the first) chose to pursue a somewhat different course by electing to locate its US branch in New England instead of the South, we are reminded of the continuing importance of corporate strategy and agency in shaping local outcomes. Nevertheless, the significance of regional context and institutions, and even corporate agency, seems to pale in comparison with the powerful influences exerted by conflicting German and American macroregulatory structures. The role of regional institutions and corporate strategy indicate that technological trajectories and workplace outcomes cannot simply be 'read off' from the national regulatory framework. But by the same token, neither can such outcomes be properly understood without an appreciation of these continuing national influences.

It is also clear from both case studies that the knowledge and production base of the home region in Germany is under siege. The transfer of know-how, design and engineering capability, and actual production to the US plants by the two firms, the first firm's response to the opportunistic behaviour of its former supplier-collaborator, and the retreat from its once-extensive regional network of relationships with outside suppliers and customers all constitute serious threats to the future integrity of the home region as a socially organized production system. Furthermore, these events raise serious questions about the long-term robustness of regional production networks and the ability of region-state institutions to govern economic processes in a way which averts ultimate crisis. In light of these observations, perhaps it is somewhat premature to write the requiem for the nation state.

In retrospect, it seems clear that the success of builders of specialized, advanced manufacturing technologies in Germany and the regionally based industry of which they were a part depended in large measure on an arrangement in which both producers and users were contained in the same region (to foster close interaction leading to innovation), but also in the same nation (so that both production and consumption occurred within a common set of macroregulatory institutions). With the decline of domestic markets in the early 1990s, as recession at home dampened demand and as more and more of this industry's customers stepped up investments abroad at the expense of domestic growth, the geographical integration of production and consumption was seriously weakened (see Gertler (1996) for a more complete development of this argument). When compelled to interact with customers located abroad, especially those in the Anglo-American countries, with user–producer interaction no longer contained by a single regulatory framework, the system of innovation and production could be seen to break down under new strains. While some of the firms involved may well survive and prosper, it is not clear that the region will be as lucky.

Acknowledgement

The author wishes to acknowledge the assistance of the Social Sciences and Humanities Research Council of Canada.

Bibliography

Braczyk, H-J., Cooke, P. and Heidenreich, M. (eds) (1997) *Regional Innovation Systems*, London: UCL Press.

Christopherson, S. (1993) 'Market rules and territorial outcomes: the case of the United States', *International Journal of Urban and Regional Research* 17: 274–88.

Clark, G.L., Gertler, M.S. and Whiteman, J. (1986) *Regional Dynamics*, London: Allen & Unwin.

Cooke, P. (1992) 'Regional innovation systems: competitive regulation in the new Europe', *Geoforum* 23: 365–82.

Cooke, P. and Morgan, K. (1998) *The Associational Economy*, Oxford: Oxford University Press.

Florida, R. (1995) 'Toward the learning region', *Futures* 27: 527–35.

Florida, R. and Kenney, M. "The globalization of Japanese R&D: The economic geography of Japanese R&D investment in the United States", *Economic Geography*, 70, 344–69.

Gertler, M.S. (1993) 'Harold Innis and the new industrial geography', *Canadian Geographer* 37: 360–4.

—— (1995) ' "Being there": proximity, organization and culture in the production and use of advanced manufacturing technologies', *Economic Geography* 71: 1–26.

—— (1996) 'Worlds apart: the changing market geography of the German machinery industry', *Small Business Economics* 8: 87–106.

—— (1997) 'Between the global and the local: the spatial limits to productive capital', in K. Cox (ed.) *Spaces of Globalization: Reasserting the Power of the Local*, New York: Guilford Press: 45–63.

Gertler, M.S. and DiGiovanna, S. (1997) 'In search of the new social economy: collaborative relations between users and producers of advanced manufacturing technologies', *Environment and Planning A* 29: 1585–602.

Grabher, G. (1993) 'The weakness of strong ties', in G. Grabher (ed.) *The Embedded Firm: On the Socioeconomics of Industrial Networks*, London: Routledge.

Jaffe, A.B., Trajtenberg, M. and Henderson, R. (1993) 'Geographic localization of knowledge spillovers as evidenced by patent citations', *Quarterly Journal of Economics* 108: 577–98.

Kanter, R.M. (1995) *World Class: Thriving Locally in the Global Economy*, New York: Simon and Schuster.

Krugman, P. (1995) *Development, Geography and Economic Theory*, Cambridge, MA: MIT Press.

Morgan, K. (1995) 'The learning region: institutions, innovation and regional renewal', Papers in Planning Research No. 157, Cardiff: Department of City and Regional Planning, University of Wales.

O'Grady, J. (1994) 'Case 2 – Province of Ontario, Canada: removing the obstacles to negotiated adjustments', in W. Sengenberger and D. Campbell (eds) *Creating Economic Opportunities: The Role of Labour Standards in Industrial Restructuring*, Geneva: International Institute for Labour Studies: 255–78.

Ohmae, K. (1995) *The End of the Nation State: The Rise of Regional Economies*, New York: The Free Press.

Porter, M. (1990) *The Competitive Advantage of Nations*, New York: The Free Press.

Putnam, R. (1993) *Making Democracy Work*, Princeton, NJ: Princeton University Press.

Saxenian, A. (1994) *Regional Advantage: Culture and Competition in Silicon Valley and Route 128*, Cambridge, MA: Harvard University Press.

Sayer, A. and Walker, R.A. (1992) *The New Social Economy: Reworking the Division of Labor*, Oxford: Blackwell.

Sengenberger, W. and Campbell, D. (eds) (1994) *Creating Economic Opportunities: The Role of Labour Standards in Industrial Restructuring*, Geneva: International Institute for Labour Studies.

Storper, M. (1997) *The Regional World*, New York: Guilford Press.

Storper, M. and Scott, A.J. (1993) 'The wealth of regions: market forces and policy imperatives in local and global contexts', Working Paper No. 7, Lewis Center for Regional Policy Studies, UCLA.

Tyson, L.D. (1992) *Who's Bashing Whom? Trade Conflict in High-Technology Industries*, Washington, DC: Institute for International Economics.

Wever, K.S. (1995) *Negotiating Competitiveness: Employment Relations and Organizational Innovation in Germany and the United States*, Cambridge, MA: Harvard Business School Press.

Wolfe, D.A. (1993) 'The wealth of regions: rethinking industrial policy', paper presented to the Annual Meeting of the Canadian Political Science Association, Ottawa.

11 Does nationality still matter?

The new competition and the foreign ownership question revisited

John N. H. Britton

Introduction

In the late twentieth century the extensive international range of transnational companies (TNCs) has become commonplace. It is a central element, though one of a number of influences, in the process of globalization which suggests the greatly reduced importance of the power of individual nations before the 'combined forces of investment and technology' (Ostry 1997). Flows of foreign direct investment (FDI) are reported as having grown at the rate of 12% per annum between 1991 and 1996, more than twice the rate for global exports. Though TNCs are not new, their enhanced facility to manage the flows of information and finance has been the key to much of this growth. New managerial and communication capabilities permit them to organize the international supply of goods and services for intermediate and end-product use, and to identify and integrate the market needs and production strengths of locations far from head office. The origins of transnationals have also become more diversified as time has passed. In particular, the dominant position held by the United States as the source of investment and technology in the decades immediately following the Second World War has given way to the 'triad' – the US, Europe, and Japan – as the primary origins of FDI.

The twist of irony in the contemporary pattern of TNC investment is that there have been debates in the US about the significance of the level of FDI at home. This is something many other countries began wrestling with much earlier, especially in the 1960s and 1970s. In the 1980s, however, the US was the destination of the largest stream of foreign investment, and experienced visible acquisition of US firms, and this stimulated considerable discussion about the benefits of FDI. The views of the Secretary of Labor in the Clinton administration focused debate by suggesting that the origin of control is unimportant compared with the necessity that the nation's intellectual capital is developed through the availability of needed financial capital (Reich 1991).

At one level, the issue of foreign control of US businesses might appear to be academic since FDI accounts for only a mere 9% of assets in the US, but there is more at stake. In particular, what makes Reich's position interesting is that he appears to be complacent in the face of the acquisition of leading-edge technology companies by foreign interests. On the contrary, he insists that worries about foreigners acquiring the nation's technological assets are usually unfounded, arguing that often further development of intellectual capital already accumulated in the US requires new sources of capital. The possibility that the foreign acquisition of firms responsible for the technological development of the US could have negative consequences is poorly researched in the US. The *Economist* (23 June 1990) specifies the problem but cites work by Graham and Krugman (1989) showing that foreign companies spend more on R&D per worker than domestic firms, information which is material to Reich's position. Nevertheless, when exploring the importance of the allegedly fragmented structure of high-technology industries, Mowery (1992) indicates interest in the possibility that foreign firms can acquire the technological assets of US firms with relatively greater ease than is possible for US firms seeking to obtain technology developed in foreign firms. He implies that in a period characterized 'by intense international competition and technological parity, rather than the U.S. technological hegemony that prevailed through much of the previous postwar era', this is a problematic aspect of the US national system of innovation.

Florida and Kenney (1994: 345) go on to suggest that a portion of Japanese FDI takes the form of R&D facilities which function to 'gain access to pockets of knowledge, skill, and social capability' in regional innovation complexes such as Silicon Valley. These facilities, in turn, are linked to international R&D networks with strong ties to facilities in Japan. Some companies of this type are highly integrated into US sources of knowledge generation, and support cooperative research agreements with major US universities. Whatever implications are drawn from foreign R&D investment, the crucial factor in the US experience is that foreign-owned R&D accounts for only 15% of R&D and for this reason US scholars will not claim to perceive a large problem.

In most ways, however, Canada is the epitome of a 'host' economy. The level of foreign ownership (52% of capital employed in manufacturing) is very high by international standards, and the roots of FDI into the Canadian economy are sufficiently deep to ensure that there is substantial reinvestment of earnings from activities located in Canada. Though quite variable on an annual basis, these contributed 43% of the inflow of funds between 1993 and 1996. The consequence, as McFetridge (1993) points out, is that there is little innovation in Canada that occurs without some form of 'foreign participation'. Under certain circumstances domestic linkages have been substituted for foreign connections but he argues that it 'is virtually impossible to resolve ... whether this is wealth improving'. Others, however, have argued that the negative implications of aspects of FDI should be understood fully.

Benefits that derive from Canada's role as host economy have usually been couched in terms of jobs, capital, and foreign technology. Since the 1960s, however, a contrary stream of thought has developed arguments that attribute weaknesses in Canadian processes of innovation and technological development to FDI.[1] Despite the persistence of technological arguments over the foreign ownership question in Canada, they have not been a theoretically static set of ideas. Rather, they have evolved in response to changes in the characteristics of industry, innovation, international trade and investment, and regional industrial development. An early approach was to attribute weak domestic bonds between both primary industries and primary manufacturing and equipment manufacturers to decisions by foreign firms as they favour imports of capital equipment. More recently, however, the ideas that have driven negative assessments of the implications of FDI have rested on concepts found in innovation theory and are Schumpeterian in origin.

Though it is not immediately apparent, Reich's ideas share some of the same ground since he is concerned with human capital in terms of skills of problem identification, problem-solving, and the work of strategic brokers who can link these skills (Reich 1991). His rethinking of the national issue of foreign ownership effectively privileges knowledge, skills, and technology over the issues of ownership and control, but his argument is specific only about the importance of infrastructure, education, and R&D. It is silent about the organizational structure of industry which will employ and provide opportunities for learning-by-doing in firms. Thus Reich's position is contingent on the prior existence of a well-developed and highly innovative industrial structure within which FDI will in all likelihood have limited impacts, and even then they may be positive or benign. In this respect Reich's argument is vastly more creative than an orthodox economic position. A good example from the *Economist* suggests that even if foreign firms 'merely displace' domestic firms, spin-offs (from R&D) are unlikely to be smaller. In effect, the orthodox position asserts that ownership does not matter and proceeds to ignore the corporate, strategic factors that govern allocative choices about activities, such as R&D and product engineering, within 'hierarchies' and therefore between 'home' and subsidiary locations.

The conditional form of Reich's case opens up the impact of foreign ownership as a research question that may have different answers in different national contexts. The Canadian situation, in particular, presents the case of a country that has industrialized by means of a combination of FDI and domestic sources of capital, and thus it provides an interesting, if difficult, environment in which to assess whether nationality of investment – domestic or foreign – matters.

Models of industrial competition

Traditionally, successful industrial competition is identified with the economic power of large firms, especially their ability to generate economies of scale which allow standard commodities and low- and medium-technology goods to be produced at low unit costs. This is the core concept of the *old competition* as explained by Best (1990). We can add that foreign firms – TNCs – are loosely identified with the large-scale firms that have captured large world markets for these types of products. In some countries, though not Canada, goods are produced by foreign firms because costs (particularly labour costs) are controlled at a low level.[2] While there is innovation in production technology this tends to be directed to reducing costs rather than developing new or improved products.[3] Others have undertaken local manufacture of internationally marketed 'brand name' goods in miniature replica plants, often developed as a response to tariff barriers.

In the world of the *new competition* the effective pursuit of technological innovation by groups of firms comprising industrial systems is a primary element of successful regional and national industrialization. Best's perspective is developed through analysis of internationally competitive performance, i.e. the export success of collections of firms in locations such as the Third Italy and Japan. He indicates the importance of entrepreneurial firms, consultative buyer–seller relations, infrastructural support, and strategic industrial policy as prime elements of the new competition. To generalize his view, firms, especially small and medium-sized enterprises (SMEs), have demonstrated success through their own collective efforts and in partnership with national and regional governments and larger enterprises. Flexible technologies, especially the applications of information technology, have allowed the substitution of economies of scope for economies of scale in many enterprises. Within this paradigm the keywords are exports (rather than foreign investment), innovation (rather than lower unit costs), and collective efforts by firms (rather than large-scale enterprise), many of which may be quite small by international standards.

Best's configuration of the emerging capabilities of constellations of smaller industrial firms is instructive but presents only part of the story. We need to add information on the evolution of larger firms including TNCs. As Martinelli and Schoenberger (1991) point out, flexibility is not a characteristic specific to small firms in locally networked situations, and large firms have proved themselves to be highly adaptable. Anyway, research on large firms including multinationals reveals their success in managing an expanded range of research, production, and distribution activities, and many rely on the types of external production networks outlined for SMEs by Best.

With these considerations in mind, my aim in this chapter is to evaluate how well firms in Canada's foreign sector support the principles of the new competition. The underlying questions are: Does the high degree of FDI in Canada continue to matter? Conversely, does the large proportion of industrial investment under the control of foreign corporations impede Canada's industrial development? Have foreign firms begun to modify their functions during the 1990s?

In constructing this enquiry, the idea of national and regional innovation systems is of considerable value. These are defined as 'the array of public and private institutions and organizations within an economy that fund and perform R&D, translate the results of R&D into commercial innovations, and affect the diffusion of new technologies' (Mowery 1992: 125). Freeman and Oldham (1991) indicate that these systems involve the production system and a continuous process of learning-by-doing. I include the full variety of industrial firms, regardless of ownership, that produce goods and services for domestic and export markets, using domestic and imported inputs, including the movement of intermediate goods and services which constitute the links in various configurations of networks. The broad innovation systems framework supports the three phases of enquiry pursued here. Outcomes of the production system are examined in terms of (international) exports, inputs into the innovation process are examined by recourse to R&D expenditures by firms, and the regionally specific form of these systems prompts a more local analysis of the foreign presence in high-technology activities. In more detail:

- Canada is a net importer of highly manufactured goods and services. Is this because of serious failures by domestic enterprises to penetrate international markets or is a better interpretation that foreign firms have a negative influence on the trade balance? By most measures, Canada's industrial structure has been in a state of flux during the 1990s. Have North American trade agreements had the capacity to modify the competitive conditions under which Canadian and transnational firms operate?
- Export success (one measure of competitiveness) increasingly relies on technological capability. Expenditures on R&D in Canada are used to establish the extent to which foreign firms have the capability to develop technology or improve products and processes. This review is based on the premise that unless foreign manufacturers actually undertake R&D to support Canadian production, Canadian industrial development based strongly on FDI would lack the technological ability to reproduce itself.
- Because foreign ownership in secondary manufacturing is strongly localized, a regional perspective on the development of new technology-based industry is used as a means of discovering whether FDI is contributing to Canadian regional development or whether it consumes emergent indigenous enterprises (see, for example, Acs *et al.* 1996).

The structure of Canadian trade

The contemporary structure of Canada's international trade points to continuity in its traditional comparative advantages associated with raw and semi-processed materials in which scale economies associated with production efficiencies are as important as they are in the auto assembly industry, which has operated under the Canada–US Auto Pact since 1965 (Britton *et al.* 1996). This agreement established the managed structure of trade and the location of jobs. In the areas of production in which there has been comparative growth in world trade over the past three decades – high-technology products such as electronics, telecommunications equipment, computers, aircraft, and pharmaceuticals – Canada records serious trade deficits.

Within technology-intensive manufacturing, Canada's trading strengths are in telecommunications equipment and aircraft and parts, but it is weak in computers, machinery, and electronic equipment. There is also a substantial deficit in the non-merchandise trade account. This is always in deficit because of public and private international debt and the net outflow of dividends associated with FDI in Canada. It also includes royalties and payments for consulting and R&D, that is the net transfer of technology into Canada is reflected in both the merchandise account and the net inflow of services. These technology-intensive components of the trade account are often interpreted in the Canadian economic literature as measures of Canada's technology gap with the rest of the industrial world (Britton 1980; Norcliffe 1996). It will come as no surprise that these net inflows of technology are articulated through intra-corporate flows, alliances, and joint ventures and are, therefore, strongly influenced by corporate strategies.

Competing interpretations of FDI and Canadian trade

In absolute terms, foreign firms are heavily involved in exporting manufactured output from Canada – 75% of the total (Table 11.1). This reflects their substantial participation in primary manufactures and their very large auto industry exports that are part of a managed bilateral flow pattern (transportation equipment). Other secondary manufactures make up a residual component of exports, and foreign firms contribute two-thirds of the Canadian total. But exports by foreign firms pale beside their imports. In imports, there is a massive (reciprocal) flow of auto imports by the foreign-owned assembly plants. Setting this aside, foreign firms in the non-transportation manufacturing industries are responsible for 80% of imports, which is considerably greater than their share of exports.

Table 11.1 Canada: exports by foreign corporations, 1987

		Foreign firms			
Industry	*All firms exports, %*	*Exports/ shipments, %*	*Share of industry exports, %*	*Share of total exports, % (est.)*	
Primary manufacturing	31.2	NA	NA	14.9	
Transportation equipment	53.3	56.0	93.5	49.9	
Other secondary manufacturing*	15.3	NA	NA	10.5	
Total manufacturing	*100.0*	*39.5*	*75.4*	*75.2*	*(est.)*

Source: Corvari and Wisner (1993).

Notes: *not including transportation equipment. NA, not available.

Although it is sometimes thought that TNCs are more outward-oriented than comparable domestic firms (Corvari and Wisner 1993), in non-auto trade the propensity of domestic firms to export (22%) is much greater than for foreign firms (14%). Corvari and Wisner suggest that net export data show that multinationals dominate industries in which Canada has no revealed comparative advantage. An alternative interpretation is that where there is domestic control, industries are stronger exporters, and stronger imports are associated with foreign control. This accords more directly with the close association of foreign ownership with intra-industry and intra-firm trade, the latter of which accounts for 63%[4] of the manufactured imports of foreign firms compared with less than 15% for domestic firms.

Though the implications of intra-firm trade vary according to different forms of corporate organization, its purpose, to provide flexibility for TNCs in their search for minimum costs of production, is a constant. The mechanisms involve the strong possibility of earning returns to scale if intermediate and finished goods (for resale) are imported from other plants. Companies also have access to transfer-cost pricing. One result is the extension of the production and marketing arms of foreign parent corporations into the host economy. These sustain competing interpretations. The positive view of intermediate imports – usually high-value products – made by foreign companies is that they may stimulate local technological, engineering, or design capacity or that there may be transfers of technology into Canadian industry. Positive effects may also result if the manufacture of interrelated components or subassemblies occurs in domestic plants reflecting the technological demands of the foreign firms. Other spillover effects may occur if local producers copy the imported technology, and when labour moves to new work locations with skills learned in the foreign plant.

The alternative argument recognizes that intra-firm imports minimize the need for Canadian R&D and design and engineering functions and there is a weakening of diffusion processes. Intermediate and finished imports already embed new technology ready for assembly or sale in Canada, and it is difficult to see how they can generate significant technology transfer or spillover effects. If Canadian firms were able to bid successfully on the design and production of significant components the interpretation would be different. By their very nature, intra-corporate imports preclude domestic, secondary manufacturing firms from supplying important parts of the intermediate goods required by foreign firms. To complicate matters further, Statistics Canada notes that 'a significant number of subsidiary companies in Canada are not specifically charged for the services supplied to them by their foreign parent companies'; in particular, 'much technology crosses national borders freely without involving monetary payment' (Statistics Canada 1990).

It is difficult to see how there could not be long-run developmental costs for Canada associated with high-value intermediate imports of services and goods on the large scale undertaken by foreign companies. These and the limited market-based exports from secondary manufacturing other than the auto industry provide a sobering indicator of how well Canada is performing.

What is liberalized trade all about?

Although international trade agreements under the General Agreement on Tariffs and Trade (GATT) resulted in progressively lower tariffs, in the 1980s Canadian exporters were worried by rising US protectionism. The arguments for seeking free trade were simple and compelling to advocates of the old competition. Generally, issues of economies of scale and effective competition have had a prime place in their models, the argument being that the protection of a small economy by tariffs encourages national and international producers to crowd the market without due regard to minimum efficient scale. Until recently, a typical, though not universal, result among transnationals serving the Canadian market was to maintain plants whose product lines were miniature replicas of parent corporations. The results were inefficiencies in low- and medium-technology secondary manufacturing where Canada's industrial productivity lagged behind that of the US. The traditional arguments for free trade applied also to resource processing.

Given the limited development of secondary manufacturing exports and the evident disinclination of Canadian industry to diversify its markets, the Canada–US Free Trade Agreement (FTA), and then the North American Free Trade Agreement (NAFTA), had strategic appeal especially to followers of the old competition. Since increased competition and specialization are thought to go hand-in-hand, they argued that plants in Canada surviving the processes of rationalization would be efficient, specialized producers for the North American market.

The trade agreements, however, provide Canada with no leverage to influence firms to produce products with qualities that could establish markets through their performance-maximizing characteristics. There are two reasons: first, products whose markets are defined in terms of product style, design, technology, and performance characteristics have been traded fairly freely in the past. Second, Canada has not integrated the trade agreements into a broader framework of national and regional policy initiatives designed to improve the level of technological innovation by Canadian firms that might stimulate the expansion of exports based on human capital rather than resource-based staples. Rather trade policy has been adopted as an instrument of development, leaving concern with the way a low level of industrial innovation diminishes Canada's potential to develop non-resource-based exports as an issue to be confronted later (e.g. Porter 1991).

New technology-based capability

The structure of Canada's international trade reflects the continuity of its trading specializations and reveals its modest international success in exports of technology-intensive goods, but trade provides only a partial view of the technological capabilities of the economy. A more comprehensive view can be constructed in a variety of ways including the identification of the wide-ranging product mix of firms in Canada that invest in technological innovation, whether they are in scientific instruments, mining, or primary metals (Britton 1996). In many ways this approach is the closest we can come to using an output measure such as recorded innovations; unfortunately, this information is not collected on a regular basis by any agency in Canada (unlike the US – see Feldman and Florida (1994)). In the following account I rely on R&D expenditures because they provide the most accessible information on the activities of foreign and domestic firms that maintain or increase their technological capability. I acknowledge that innovative firms undertake a variety of activities to keep themselves competitive which are not included in R&D measures; design, engineering, and marketing activities are particularly important in this respect. Nevertheless, I have used R&D data as an indicator of the commitment of firms to maintaining and increasing their technological capability.

Although Canada has achieved considerable diversity among the firms that are pursuing technological innovation, Canadian firms collectively have experienced difficulty in keeping up with their counterparts in other small, high-income countries such as Sweden in terms of their contribution to R&D to GDP. The comparison is 0.61% of GDP compared with 1.74% for Sweden (1991). This is an appropriate comparison since it takes account of the possible industrial-mix effect which could derive from the importance of the resource industries in both economies and, as a funding rather than an expenditure statistic, it is not seriously distorted by defence funding of R&D.[5] Canada's performance is substantially weaker than that of larger industrial countries (Table 11.2) and this is especially true of business expenditures on R&D. These were only 54% of the total in 1991 compared with Sweden's 68%, but since then business expenditures have increased at an annual average rate of 6.2% (compared with 2.1% for the previous five years) while the federal government has reduced its funding and performance of R&D.

There have been two interesting changes in the industrial origins of Canadian R&D over the last decade or so, the largest single increases coming from the telecommunications, aircraft and parts, and pharmaceuticals and

Table 11.2 International comparisons R&D/GDP, selected years

	1987	*1989*	*1991*	*1993*	*1995 Total*	*1995 Civil*
Canada	1.40	1.33	1.50	1.50	1.61	1.6
Sweden	2.82	2.76	2.90	3.26	3.02	2.8
US	2.69	2.82	2.75	2.66	2.58	2.1

Sources: Statistics Canada (1995 + 1997, Cat. No. C1-4) and Statistics Canada (1993 + 1991 + 1989, Cat. No. C1-4).

medicine industries and from two industries in the services (Table 11.3). In the latter sector, computer services and other producer services such as engineering and scientific services are the largest performers of R&D and have expanded substantially over the past decade.[6]

Telecommunications equipment and aircraft and parts industries together account for 47% of R&D expenditures in manufacturing. Electronic parts and components, other electronic equipment and business machines add another 16%. As noted, defence production has only limited presence in Canadian R&D and thus the aircraft and electronics industries, though not 'purely' civilian in output, are in this respect unlike most of their counterparts

Table 11.3 R&D expenditures for selected industries[a] in Canada

Sector/industry	*Total R&D (1997 $m)*	*Current R&D/ revenue (1995)*	*Change in R&D 1987–97 (1986 $m)*	*Average annual change 1987–97 (%)*
Agriculture	7	4.2	19	10.0
Manufacturing				
Paper and allied products	113	0.3	5	0.6
Printing and publishing	15	3.5	3	2.9
Primary metals (non-ferrous)	134	1.0	–2	–0.2
Machinery	164	2.9	43	4.2
Aircraft and parts	887	9.2	224	4.0
Motor vehicles, parts, and accessories	154	0.2	20	1.9
Telecommunications equipment	1,573	21.7	423	4.4
Electronic parts and components	85	7.2	33	7.2
Other electronic equipment	400	11.2	15	0.5
Business machines	356	3.0	–80	–2.5
Pharmaceuticals and medicine	547	6.5	179	5.6
Other chemical products	185	1.2	–30	–1.9
Scientific and professional equipment	102	3.8	21	3.1
All manufacturing	*5,252*	*1.8*	*1,268*	*3.8*
Services				
Communication	180	1.1	28	2.3
Finance, insurance, and real estate	476	0.7	NA	NA
Computer and related services	587	14.8	197	5.8
Engineering and scientific	830	10.3	249	5.0
Management consulting	67	10.3	12	2.7
All services	*2,893*	*1.8*	—[b]	—
All sectors	*8,627*	*1.6*	*2,658*	*5.2*

Sources: Statistics Canada (1991, Cat. No. 88-001) and Statistics Canada (1997a, 1997b, Cat. Nos 88-202-XPB and 88-001).

Notes: [a]Industries selected have R&D > $100m or R&D/revenue > 2.5%. [b]The totals for services have not been included because of apparent definitional changes. NA, not available.

in other countries. By contrast with these industries, machinery has a very small base – only 3% of manufacturing R&D – and exhibits less dynamism than might be expected in a period when microelectronics is being applied to capital equipment in the move towards smaller, reprogrammable (flexible) production tools. It is, however, an industry in which engineering and design inputs are very important and, as noted above, these are not included in Canadian data files. The drugs and pharmaceuticals industry, however, may be entering a period of faster growth since a number of international proprietary drug companies have been persuaded to expand their R&D labs as a result of increased patent protection for new drugs afforded by a sequence of federal initiatives.

Foreign firms

Foreign firms have a very strong presence in Canadian industrial R&D, being responsible for 32% of all R&D expenditures (1995) and 40% in manufacturing. Since 1991, however, the foreign share has declined, especially in manufacturing (Table 11.4). On an industry basis, too, foreign firms undertake more than 50% of the R&D in a wide range of manufacturing industries – aircraft and parts, motor vehicles, other electronic equipment, business machines, pharmaceuticals and medicine, and other chemical products. Despite their apparent strength and experience in undertaking R&D elsewhere, foreign firms in manufacturing perform proportionally less R&D in Canada than domestic firms when the R&D/revenue ratio is used to take account of scale (Table 11.4). In the economy as a whole, there is a 67% difference (2.0% R&D/revenue compared with 1.2%) while in the manufacturing sector the difference soars to 1.5 times. In many cases, especially in medium technology manufacturing industries, foreign firms achieve very low rates of expenditures on R&D in relation to revenue. In the chemical industry, for example, the R&D/revenue ratio for foreign firms is 1.2% (cf. 1.5% for domestic firms) and in the auto industry the comparison is 0.2% compared with 2.2%. In the auto and chemicals industries, which are predominantly foreign owned, R&D expenditures exceed $100 million each, but these and other medium technology industries like them, such as rubber and textiles, illustrate the ability of foreign firms to import technology and to undertake adaptive and some developmental work in Canada.

By contrast, in technology-intensive manufacturing industries, where there are also high levels of foreign ownership, reaching 86% of R&D in the pharmaceuticals industry, R&D intensities for foreign firms are often as high as or higher than those of domestic firms. Even among these activities, however, there are sharp differences, often favouring domestically owned firms over foreign. Further discussion is focused on these industries because of their increasing importance in international trade. The R&D/revenue ratio is one way of statistically taking account of the effect of scale but the disparity in relative levels of R&D between the two ownership groups of technology-

Table 11.4 Foreign and domestic R&D for selected industries[a] in Canada

Sector/industry	*R&D, % Canadian-controlled firms* 1991	1993	1995	*R&D/revenue 1995, % Country of control* Canada	Foreign	Total
Agriculture	47	51	59	2.8	12.7	4.2
Manufacturing						
Paper and allied products	95	94	98	0.3	0.1	0.3
Printing and publishing	96	97	100	3.5	0.0	3.5
Primary metals (non-ferrous)	NA	NA	NA	1.0	1.2	1.0
Machinery	71	84	74	3.4	2.1	2.9
Aircraft and parts	45	59	45	7.3	11.9	9.2
Motor vehicles, parts, and accessories	15	12	20	2.2	0.2	0.2
Telecommunications equipment	NA	NA	NA	21.3	27.1	21.7
Electronic parts and components	NA	NA	NA	7.1	7.8	7.2
Other electronic equipment	56	52	44	18.3	8.5	11.2
Business machines	24	29	38	11.5	2.1	3.0
Pharmaceuticals and medicine	11	13	19	6.9	6.4	6.5
Other chemical products	17	21	23	1.5	1.2	1.2
Scientific and professional equipment	66	77	85	7.1	1.2	3.8
All manufacturing	*55*	*60*	*60*	*2.8*	*1.1*	*1.8*
Services						
Communication	NA	NA	NA	1.1	0.8	1.1
Computer and related services	93	85	76	18.1	9.4	14.8
Engineering and scientific	70	80	84	8.9	40.5	10.3
Management consulting	NA	NA	NA	10.3	12.0	10.3
All services	*80*	*82*	*80*	*1.7*	*2.0*	*1.8*
All sectors	*64*	*69*	*68*	*2.0*	*1.2*	*1.6*

Source: Statistics Canada (1997a, Cat. No. 88-202-XPB).

Notes: [a]Industries selected have R&D > $100m or R&D/revenue > 2.5%. NA, not available.

intensive industries tends to be influenced by some very small domestic firms at early positions in their life cycles. In comparison with large international firms, they tend to have very much higher R&D ratios. So to make fair comparisons between the ownership groups it is necessary to hold constant both industry mix and scale. The obvious way of doing this is to use data for large-scale firms in, say, the telecommunications and electronics industries where there is a sufficient number to make the comparison. Even then, the ratio for domestic firms is significantly higher.

A useful way of considering the technological impact of FDI is through the concept of the technological balance of payments, which is a measure of trade in technology acquired through licences, patents, and related means. Though the contribution made by foreign firms to Canada's balance has always been negative, it has improved substantially since the early 1980s.

Income received by these firms has increased and payments made by them have declined. Between 1982 and 1993, the deficit shrank by about a half (to $152 million 1986 dollars). When these data are combined with the 40% increase in R&D expenditures by foreign firms in Canada, the implication seems to be that foreign firms have increasingly taken advantage of the quality of the Canadian labour force for R&D and the lower costs of undertaking R&D.[7] Domestic firms are also technology traders, however, and increased income received for R&D (presumably because of the increased foreign investment of Canadian companies) moved the balance from a deficit position in 1980 to a surplus in 1984, and this has been maintained.[8] While the industrial R&D expenditures of foreign firms have increased, this growth is much smaller than those of domestic firms which have increased by 200% (1980–93).

We can infer that a general characteristic of many foreign enterprises is that they undertake lower levels of R&D than might be expected from their apparent Canadian capacity, and though their expenditures have expanded this has been at a lower rate than in the domestic sector. Nevertheless, they remain competitive by substituting technology imports for which they make substantial net payments, mainly to US affiliates for technological services and for technology embodied in intermediate goods. Calculations by Baldwin and Gorecki (1991) operationalize the idea of technology transfers as substitutes for R&D and technology generation,[9] and in a variety of economic studies technology transfers are viewed as net benefits from FDI (for a summary see Hirshhorn (1997)). As indicated earlier, this approach depends on the assumption that technology transfers to subsidiaries of TNCs generate spillovers to other Canadian firms: learning opportunities are created in domestic firms, lags in the process of technology transfer are shorter, and Canadian managers and other workers obtain training in these firms.

The alternative view interprets the lower level of R&D in many industries, the high propensity of foreign firms to import technology directly or indirectly by means of components (see above), and the limited market-based exports by foreign firms in secondary manufacturing as examples of *truncation*. This term has been used in Canadian research and policy writing to describe the attenuated range of activities that has prevailed among a substantial proportion of foreign subsidiaries (see Gray Report 1972; Britton and Gilmour 1978). Truncation is thought to generate reduced developmental effects within the economy, there being a salient difference in the learning process that domestic firms may enjoy when technology is generated by local firms and in other elements of the Canadian innovation system and when technology is transferred within foreign firms.

Choices by parent corporations that contributed to truncation were much more plausible when tariffs were higher, when the absence of economies of scale in production strongly limited the export base, before it was realized that competitive advantages may be generated by smaller, specialized, flexible production facilities. Changes in the organizational position of foreign plants within their corporations have been made possible by vastly improved communications systems, and FTA/NAFTA have accelerated the pace of more advanced forms of North American integration of Canadian industry. There is, for example, increased North American rationalization of production. One change, in particular, that has been pursued is the acquisition of publicly held shares in Canadian subsidiaries by parent corporations as these operations are absorbed into the parent's North American organization. The programmes of this type undertaken by transnationals can reduce the incidence or intensity of truncation in two ways: one, by increasing the rate at which functionally limited enterprises are closed, or moved out of manufacturing into the trade sector: two, by encouraging the use of their Canadian operations to supply specialized markets within their corporate network of specialized production points.

Inevitably, the choice by firms about their future in Canada reflects some of their history – especially whether core competencies have been developed and sustained in their Canadian branch plants (or subsidiaries). Some corporations allow, or maybe induce, their subsidiaries to develop North American (or world) *product mandates*. In the past, the number has been small and part of the explanation is that the decentralization of related R&D is unattractive to parent companies. This has restricted the application of the convention to niche markets, which tend to be outside the main business of the firm (Young *et al.* 1991). Supporting this interpretation, Birkinshaw (1996), in a sample of US firms in Canada, found that half the companies had some sort of mandate. Nevertheless, most do the majority of their R&D at home despite its importance in the success of mandates. There are reasons, however, to believe that subsidiaries will seek mandates as the new North American trading environment develops. An implication to be drawn from Porter (1991: 372) is that rather than waiting for action by parent corporations, Canadian subsidiaries have the task of defining or at least initiating the task of targeting 'the product segments for which a Canadian home base offers unique advantages'. In effect, he implies that it is timely, in the history of TNCs in Canada, to expect foreign subsidiaries to adopt the 'lead country model' of production (Eden 1991) in which products are tailored to suit dominant markets. This would be consistent with subsidiaries gaining more responsibility in the organizational structure of their parent corporations.

The alternative to the generation of technological capability in Canadian subsidiaries is the acquisition of Canadian firms that have developed attractive technology. This process of purchasing Canadian sources of technology has been made easier under FTA/NAFTA. These agreements liberalized the flow of capital and raised the threshold for review of foreign acquisitions of Canadian companies, and residual impediments to the foreign acquisition of small indigenous companies have been removed. Positive results of takeover (similarly to the US case) could include the improved access of Canadian enterprises to resources that are otherwise in short supply – capital, high-quality management, and access to international markets. The most negative result derives from the technological gutting of the acquired firm and the transfer of the technical workforce to a location abroad. The most common instances where this occurs are in the development of software. Other impacts, however, could well be the stronger development of intra-corporate connections instead of connections within the Canadian innovation system. For that reason, the advice often given to corporations in the business literature – 'think global, act local' – is only that, advice which may further corporate advantage.

A regional perspective on the development of new technology-based industry

Much of the literature on the new competition is concerned with specific regional circumstances involving clusters of innovative small firms, sometimes closely involved with larger enterprises. In the Canadian case it is important to explore the implications of foreign ownership in such a regional context since the concepts of the new competition require adaptation if the impacts of truncation and a very high level of foreign ownership are to be accommodated. Toronto, Canada's largest industrial region, is also the locational concentration of foreign plants which have been attracted to this market location. In this section I discuss trade and acquisition hypotheses that might explain unexpected foreign–domestic differences in the size distribution of plants in technology-intensive manufacturing. The discussion incorporates research that identifies linkage patterns of small firms in Toronto and Canada's difficulties in generating indigenous, medium-sized, growth-oriented – *threshold* – firms.

In large measure Toronto's broad range of functions and its scale[10] reflect its market centrality within a space economy that developed behind a tariff wall for over 100 years. The Toronto labour market has a considerable variety of skills, and Toronto's agglomeration advantages are coupled with easy access to the US through Niagara and Windsor. It has become Canada's largest head-office centre, with employment growth in the services, especially finance and insurance. While building its economic diversity and strength over the past thirty years, other aspects of the economic geography of Toronto have undergone significant changes. Traditional manufacturing industries have declined, especially during the recessions of the early 1980s and 1990s. Imports have replaced domestic products as the need for technological investments in these industries often resulted in closures (Norcliffe *et al.* 1986). As a consequence of these contractions and the generally rising trend in productivity, the share of manufacturing employment has fallen from 26% to 17% and the rise of more technology-intensive industrial activities has not compensated. Despite the shift of jobs to services, Canadian value added in manufacturing has not fared as poorly, and the geography of production in Canada's secondary manufacturing industry continues to reflect the importance of Toronto.

This region represents an enormous range of contrasts in industrial development. It is the location of both firms of considerable innovative strength, and the parent plants of large domestic firms, Nortel for example, that successfully use communications systems to generate multi-locational efficiency (Hepworth 1989). Research has shown also the considerable variation in the extent to which SMEs successfully access the benefits of modern equipment and participate in complex production systems (MacPherson 1988; Britton 1991). Within the Windsor–Quebec City corridor, and nationally, Toronto is the major centre in terms of industrially funded R&D and high-technology manufacturing production. Firms in Toronto spend about $2 billion on R&D (over 26% of Canada's industrial R&D expenditures).

Technology-intensive manufacturing in Toronto

Toronto contributes about half the R&D of the Province of Ontario.[11] Manufacturing is Ontario's main R&D-performing sector activity by a wide margin (69% of expenditures in 1995), with four industries – telecommunications, aircraft and parts, business machines, and pharmaceuticals and medicine, accounting for a very large share of this activity. The recent development of research-intensive services – mainly computer and related services and engineering and scientific services – has also made an impact on the structure of Ontario's R&D and they now account for 10% of expenditures. Although Toronto is acknowledged as Canada's major manufacturing centre, over the period from the mid-1980s to the mid-1990s Toronto's national share of R&D has remained stationary at 26%, unlike that of Montreal, its only rival in terms of scale, which has increased from 19% to 24% (Table 11.5). In Montreal the number of R&D establishments nearly doubled between 1986 and 1995, while in Toronto there has been an increase of less than one-third, which has allowed Montreal to take 22% of the national total and Toronto 15%. This reversed their national positions of 1986. As a consequence, the relative scale of R&D establishments in Toronto has increased absolutely and is now 153% of the average size in Montreal.[12]

To pursue further research, data on technology-intensive manufacturing industries in Toronto have been collected from industrial directories. This has been necessary because the published manufacturing statistical record for the region is out of date and incomplete, and would in any case not provide the opportunity to explore the size distribution of establishments in particular industries or the incidence of foreign and domestic ownership. As is usual for this type of file, employment in each establishment, industry, and location is the only standard information that is available: the major industries indicated in Table 11.4 were selected.

Each of these selected industries employs over 5,000 and contributes to a substantial diversity of technology-intensive industrial jobs: machinery (36.7%), other electronic equipment (18.4%), telecommunications equipment (12.5%), and scientific and professional equipment (12.3%) are the

Table 11.5 Canada: R&D expenditures and R&D establishments, selected regions

	1986	*1990*	*1995*	*Average annual change, %*
R&D expenditures (1986 $m)				
Toronto	1,013	1,127	1,568	4.97
Rest of Ontario	1,298	1,265	1,757	3.42
Montreal	728	1,010	1,438	7.86
Rest of Quebec	144	161	265	7.01
Canada	3,828	4,304	6,007	5.13
Number of R&D establishments				
Toronto	814	733	1,065	3.03
Rest of Ontario	810	751	1,137	3.84
Montreal	520	595	1,499	12.48
Rest of Quebec	333	393	1,076	13.92
Canada	3,689	3,690	6,921	7.24

Sources: Statistics Canada (1986, Cat. No. 88-202) and Statistics Canada (1992, 1997a, Cat. No. 88-202-XPB).

Table 11.6 Technology-intensive manufacturing establishments, Greater Toronto Area, 1995

No. of employees in establishment	*Domestic*	*Foreign*	*Total*
1–4	523	19	542
5–9	559	29	588
10–19	495	43	538
20–49	403	46	449
50–99	177	29	206
100–199	102	17	119
200–499	41	9	50
500–999	10	2	12
1000+	5	4	9
Unspecified	22	5	27
Total no. of establishments	*2,337*	*203*	*2,540*
Total no. of employees	*76,894*	*31,966*	*108,860*

Source: Scott's *Greater Toronto Business Directory* (1995).

employment leaders. Foreign firms dominate jobs in other electronic equipment and aircraft, and domestic firms in all the other activities. Nevertheless, foreign-owned subsidiaries generate about 29% of Toronto's employment in technology-intensive industries. As might be expected, the proportion of foreign plants is highest among large establishments (half the establishments employing 1,000 or more are foreign owned). Most surprising is that they have penetrated the full size range of establishments and are more than 10% of the total for those employing 20 or more and 15% for those employing 200 or more, with greater clustering in the 10–49 employees range than for domestic firms (44% compared with 38%).

Three hypotheses may explain the patterns that have been extracted from the two data sets reviewed above:

- The literature on the new competition suggests that public policy has influenced the growth of regional innovation systems, industrial concentrations, and networked clusters of firms. Unlike Montreal, which has benefited from local, provincial, and federal agencies being well informed about European regional initiatives, Toronto has never developed active policies to nurture and support innovative small firms and their network connections. This may account for the much poorer development of the population of R&D establishments in Toronto.
- The strong presence of foreign firms in all size ranges in Toronto suggests that the acquisition process is highly active in the region's technology-intensive manufacturing.
- It is hypothesized that the survival and growth of new-technology-based firms and their supporting networks in Toronto will be weakened because of the intra-corporate connections that are developed by foreign firms. For this reason, the penetration of foreign firms to even the smallest size range is likely to weaken the advantages of agglomeration for SMEs.

Technology-based firms and weak networks

In the early 1980s Steed reported on his national search for indigenous, medium-sized, growth-oriented – *threshold* – firms which have successfully weathered the crises of new product cycles, demonstrated signs of continuous innovation, and established niche export markets (Steed 1982). He concluded that the growth of Canadian SMEs is limited by their internal resources for effective innovation and marketing, and by implication, for Canada as a whole, inter-firm and other industrial networks are too weak to compensate. This conclusion may still hold true for Toronto, though we need evidence that small firms fail to realize the benefits of functional clustering as described in the new competition.

Evidence of a new competitive geography of strong functional networks of SMEs in Canada is limited, but there is some evidence on the question available for Toronto (see Britton 1991, 1993). We know that innovative SMEs in technology-intensive industries (electrical equipment and scientific equipment) that use technical and other producer service inputs to augment their own R&D and other in-house resources are successful in developing new products and in exporting (MacPherson 1987, 1988). Surprisingly, even in these activities, less than 60% of surveyed SMEs had well-developed input links sustaining innovative behaviour. In mature industries (auto parts, furniture, and metal fabrication) these kinds of network connections were about half as frequent. These data imply that for these selected activities, Toronto does not have SMEs that are strongly connected to regional sources of inputs. In the absence of these commercial links it is unlikely that more informal cooperative activities are developed to any higher level, though at this time systematic research is lacking. On the output side, MacPherson has found that small-scale innovators in the Toronto region are connected to industrial purchasers but these links tend not to be with firms within the Toronto region – predominantly they connect small Toronto firms with industrial markets outside Canada.

It is difficult to tie these results directly to the presence of strong foreign ownership in the Toronto economy. They are more consistent with the characteristics of a regional economy in which the potential for strong local linkages between firms has been diminished by intra-corporate networks operating at the inter-regional scale. There is a sharp contrast with the more highly integrated regional economies used as examples of specialized industrial districts reported by Best and others. In these there are strong local connections between small firms and/or between small firms and larger contractors. Nevertheless, Gertler and DiGiovanna (1997) provide direct evidence that foreign firms in Ontario have little interest in establishing close supply connections within the regional economy. Admittedly, some firms need to seek suppliers abroad for advanced production technology because of the absence of Canadian suppliers. Given this, Canadian firms are much more inclined to use local sources than are foreign firms. Furthermore domestic firms are more likely to develop close collaborative connections with their suppliers. The foreign firms, however, are much more likely to develop a collaborative equipment supply relationship with another part of their corporation.

The industrial characteristics of the Toronto region that I have begun to outline accord with the notion that Canada has weak related and supporting industries (Porter 1991). Porter cites two reasons:

- Leading firms have chosen to vertically integrate and a substantial volume of inputs is acquired from abroad.
- The 'lack of home bases in Canada means that Canada reaps fewer direct and indirect advantages from the presence of these industries than would otherwise be the case' (Porter 1991: 75).

A variety of examples of both is available for the Toronto region from domestically controlled firms. Nortel, Canada's leading telecommunications producer, has several plants in the region but is highly integrated. The STOL aircraft industry obtains its fuel management systems from the US and UK, illustrating participation in an international rather than a regional production system which is supported locally only with some small-scale subcontracting (Hack 1992). There are few industry studies of large foreign firms which have established home bases for products in Canada, though Pratt and Whitney Canada (owned by United Technologies, US), which has the world product mandate for small aircraft engines (turboprop and turbofan), is an exception. Nevertheless, this example is sufficiently rare that the generalized truncation thesis associated with FDI is supported in recent evaluations of Canada's industrial development.

Foreign investment

Foreign manufacturing firms undertake a large proportion of the R&D expenditures in Toronto. As a result, we can expect the imports of R&D, other forms of technology, components, and subassemblies by foreign firms (see above) to depress the formation and growth of SMEs that undertake R&D. By contrast, Montreal, which has received a smaller amount of FDI, has generated many more R&D-performing companies. The limited population of medium-sized Canadian-owned firms in Toronto could result from pre-emptive impacts by foreign firms on the growth of firms in particular product markets. The proposition is that the presence of foreign firms, in particular technological niches (for example, within the industrial groups listed in Table 11.4), reduces the rate of domestic investment in the area. Indigenous firms either find national markets significantly reduced or they are deprived of resources needed for expansion by the venture capital industry. Although this hypothesis has received strong support in Belgium it has not been evaluated in Canada (Corvari and Wisner 1993), though there has been concern over access to risk capital by Canadian firms.

Despite the evidence that Canadian high-technology firms are limited in their growth and development, and despite the alternatives to regional or even Canadian purchasing and subcontracting, Canadian and foreign companies have established mutual interests in other ways. Patel and Pavitt (1991), for example, quote a survey of Canadian high-tech firms by Ernst and Young showing that 41% have strategic alliances – 56% of these are with foreign firms and only 21% are with domestic-and-foreign firms. These proportions, as suggested by Patel and Pavitt, may well reflect the dearth of large Canadian firms to provide access to resources including technology, international markets, and the reputation of their partner (Ahern 1993).

Another possibility is that as medium-sized domestic firms emerge they become attractive to foreign corporations and are acquired by them. The history of this practice is as old as FDI and enquiries verify that the businesses taken over by foreign firms are research-intensive enterprises and in this respect are significantly different from other acquisitions. Subsequent to acquisition and, it is hypothesized, after gaining stronger financial support, the R&D intensity of these firms increases, again contrary to the pattern for other takeover arrangements (McDougall 1995). The effect of acquisitions, like strategic alliances, may be to increase exports from Canada but it is expected that intra-corporate imports will be favoured at the expense of inputs arranged through domestic market processes.

The investment and acquisition hypotheses are attractive because they indicate parts of the process whereby FDI establishes its influence on the size–ownership structure of industry. Still, the most developed hypothesis to explain the problem of threshold firms and SMEs is the process of truncation, specifically that foreign firms are responsible for leakages from the value chain in Canadian production. These leakages effectively limit the quantity and depth of demand to which they are asked to respond. Despite its population of small high-technology firms, Toronto's notable industrial characteristic is that half its technology-intensive industrial economy is tied by branch plants and subsidiaries to foreign parent corporations.[13]

Conclusion

Once the characteristic of smaller economies needing to import capital and technology, foreign direct investment (FDI) is now internationally ubiquitous. Even the US has had to confront the question of whether the origin of capital and the nationality of ownership matters. In this chapter I set out to understand US writing on the question and to develop a perspective that would allow us to examine the issue for other economies, especially one such as Canada that is very much smaller. Implicitly I have sketched a progression of ideas. At one extreme, the neo-classical economic position fails to allow that there can be differences in the incidence of positive externalities, such as spillovers from R&D undertaken by domestic or foreign firms. Neither does Reich, who has argued that the nationality of investing firms is not a matter of policy relevance for the US, even if it is highly innovative firms that are acquired by foreign-based corporations. He suggests that a country's human resources (skills) are what counts, not where firms come from, but he writes in the knowledge that in the US, FDI is of quite limited scale, holding only 9% of assets.

There are, however, other writers who take a less doctrinaire slant, and consequently institutional factors such as the nationality of firms can be evaluated on their merits as influences on technological development. Increasingly, research results verify that the ability of firms to innovate is often deeply enmeshed in their working environment, which is composed of other firms, institutional structures, and infrastructural support. Much of this research is concerned with innovation systems, and the concept of 'techno-nationalism' provides an even more specific recognition of the importance of two core ideas. The technological capabilities of a nation's firms are a vital source of their competitive success, and these capabilities are in some sense national and can be built by national public policies (Nelson 1993). Analytically we can relate national differences in technological progress and industrial growth to different national industrial histories, structures, and policies. While he acknowledges national differences (e.g. Japanese policy model compared with the US), Best places great weight on regionally specific research results that identify new forms of (non-price) competition between firms and the conditions under which they are inclined to collaborate. In particular, he explains the functional importance that clusters of firms may have when they employ flexible technologies to operate as interdependent producers. It is a short step to link this empirical approach to innovation systems identifying the importance of regional or local innovation systems as the locus of 'real worlds of production' (Acs *et al.* 1996).

In the intellectual context of innovation systems, the foreign ownership of firms may be important in two ways. New foreign acquisitions may disrupt national or predominantly regional patterns of interdependence, or potential interdependence, by relocation of key workers or by reorientation of network connections to exploit intra-corporate opportunities. In the case of foreign investments that have a longer history, there are a variety of corporate arrangements that have the potential to limit the production of technology, or product or process innovation, outside the parent plant or the central R&D facility. The technological support of subsidiaries and branch plants by these means may mean that weak patterns of technological development in host economies may be the derivative of FDI.

I set out in this chapter to explore support for this proposition using data for Canada, which has a long history of very strong inbound FDI and which generates technology-intensive firms and resource producers that are interesting acquisition targets for foreign firms. This is an important question, especially as there has been increasing awareness in Canada, over the last three decades, that its rate of technological development has not met international norms for an economy with such a high standard of living. I have put forward the argument that FDI continues to be an important factor in explaining Canada's performance, especially in advanced industries. FDI generates imports, especially intra-firm imports, that have substituted for some goods and services which otherwise might have been supplied by firms in Canadian cities. In this way FDI modifies the stimuli to innovate that might have been experienced by indigenous firms.

Superficially, domestic and foreign firms make about equal shares of Canada's total manufacturing sales and non-auto exports.[14] Also, there is only a small difference between the ownership groups in terms of R&D expenditures in manufacturing, though foreign firms contribute the bulk of expenditures in most technology-intensive industries. When the size of firms and their R&D intensity are considered, however, it becomes apparent that foreign firms collectively contribute very much less than their Canadian counterparts in the way of innovative activity. Ideally, differences in technological intensity of subsidiaries and parents could be explored, the extent of exports of foreign firms to non-affiliate markets could be analysed, and the data on the propensity of foreign firms to import components, high-order services, and goods for resale would be much better than those I have had available. Even if we have these improvements in data it is very unlikely that the conclusion would differ in its general form. Nevertheless, it would be valuable to have more systematic information on those research-intensive Canadian subsidiaries of foreign firms that genuinely use their Canadian operations as a base for innovation and exports. Currently only a modest number of firms such as ICI Explosives Canada (Porter 1991), Pratt and Whitney, IBM, and Mitel visibly fit this description.

The models of regional innovation systems and the new competition point to the need to investigate the extent to which cooperative and collaborative regional production relations are evolving as these might signal emerging new strengths. From what we can gather from existing research, innovation networks in Canada's leading industrial region are not well developed. But Canadian investigators should continue to examine contemporary forms of FDI if only to gauge the impact of foreign capital and international production networks on the regional structure of industry. The international trend is for large enterprises to source more inputs from other businesses, the transaction costs incurred in making these arrangements being less than the gains from trading with technologically specialized firms. In these circumstances industrial research in Canada faces an interesting challenge to establish the regional impacts of this trend.

Canada's very high level of FDI has defined a policy problem of long standing. Its origins probably lie in the geography of North America and the spillover of US industrial development into neighbouring regions in Canada. But the implications of the geographic circumstances were exacerbated by Canadian protection (especially tariffs), which ensured that strong foreign ownership became a corollary of the growth in industrial jobs. In recent years Canada's primary action has been to seek trade agreements that could generate advances in industrial performance by those commodity producers that already have trading advantages. Unfortunately, trade agreements have not provided Canada with any levers other than the market to induce domestic firms to produce performance-maximizing products, and it is in this area that Canada's trade and technological deficits occur.

Even before the recent trade agreements, Canada was not particularly innovative in devising programmes to assist change among domestic firms, for example by transforming the essentially passive delivery of its policies in support of innovation into active initiatives directed to individual firms. Quite possibly Canada has made the characteristics of FDI worse by being lulled into a weak policy position by the number of jobs associated with their production and distribution activities. Until the last decade, federal and provincial policies in Canada tended to constrain or penalize the more innovative and faster-growing regions in the hope of deflecting growth to less fortunate areas. One effect was to limit concern about the generation and support of technology-intensive SMEs in regions such as Toronto, where a large proportion has been generated. Certainly there has been a weak history in Canada of pro-active advisory programmes that might have gone some way towards helping firms prepare for new competitive circumstances. In effect, concerted policy actions have not provided that infrastructural element we associate with many examples of regional success in the new competition. Regional initiatives have been notable in their absence and even the coordination of the access of firms to federal and provincial programmes has been all but ignored in the Toronto region. At no level has Canada positioned trade liberalization within a set of strategic initiatives designed to encourage greater innovation by indigenous firms, and thus from this standpoint the problem of a high level of FDI in technology-intensive industries remains unchallenged.

Notes

1 Some of the salient ideas have been the following: FDI is responsible for capturing indigenous technological know-how; differences in the rates of technological advance made by foreign compared with domestic firms; foreign firms create limited positive spillover effects in the aggregate industrial structure; the downstream development of resource-based products is limited; in resource extraction and primary manufacturing, foreign capital has used foreign technology in the form of capital goods and has not stimulated domestic sources of innovation and supply.
2 For a taxonomy of FDI see Eden (1991).
3 In a minority of cases, foreign subsidiaries have sought corporate 'product mandates' which require the capacity to innovate new generations of products.
4 This figure comes from Corvari and Wisner (1993) and is based on a compilation for manufacturing firms. Eden (1994) uses US data for all exports to Canada and the intra-firm portion for 1990 is 43%.
5 Total Canadian R&D, it should be noted, is not affected to any substantial extent by funding from the defence sector (0.05% GDP; 1991). In this respect it is like Italy, Germany, Holland, and Japan but dissimilar to the US (0.78% GDP) and a group of OECD members which have defence proportions in the 0.30–0.44% GDP range (Sweden, France, and the UK) (Industry Canada 1994).
6 The engineering services industry has developed expertise in a range of activities including urban transit and energy production.
7 The data for this section are drawn from Statistics Canada (1997b). Birkinshaw (1996) estimated that R&D in Canada is up to 50% cheaper than in the US.
8 It was $368 million (1986 dollars) in 1993.
9 Some studies consider the elasticity of R&D with respect to sales, differentiating between foreign and domestic firms. Holbrook and Squires (1996) found that foreign firms' R&D expenditures are less inelastic than those of domestic firms across a wide variety of industries. This is closely related to the higher incidence of larger firms among the foreign-owned ones.
10 The population of the Greater Toronto Area is 4.5 million.
11 Official statistical data put this proportion at 47% but the definition of Toronto is under-bounded.
12 The highest average expenditures are in R&D establishments in Ontario outside

Toronto where the full influence of foreign auto plants is registered: these R&D units are over six times the size of those in Quebec outside Montreal.

13 This occurs through imports of goods and services, product specifications, corporate restraints on expenditures and investments, and limited initiatives to innovate.

14 Auto exports are controlled predominantly by foreign firms.

Bibliography

Acs, Z., de la Mothe, J. and Paquet, G. (1996) 'Local systems of innovation: in search of an enabling strategy', in P. Howitt (ed.) *The Implications of Knowledge-based Growth for Micro-economic Policies*, Calgary: University of Calgary Press, for Industry Canada.

Ahern, R. (1993) 'The role of strategic alliances in the international organization of industry', *Environment and Planning A* 25: 1229–46.

Baldwin, J.R. and Gorecki, P.K. (1991) 'Distinguishing characteristics of foreign high technology acquisitions in Canada's manufacturing sector', Discussion Paper No. 36, Ottawa: Statistics Canada.

Best, M.H. (1990) *The New Competition*, Cambridge, MA: Harvard University Press.

Birkinshaw, J. (1996) 'Mandate strategies for Canadian subsidiaries', Working Paper No. 9, Ottawa: Industry Canada.

Britton, J.N.H. (1980) 'Industrial dependence and technological underdevelopment: Canadian consequences of foreign direct investment', *Regional Studies* 14: 181–99.

—— (1991) 'Reconsidering innovation policy for small and medium sized enterprises: the Canadian case', *Environment and Planning C* 9: 189–206.

—— (1993) 'Canada under free trade: defining the metropolitan agenda for innovation policy', *International Journal of Urban and Regional Research* 17: 559–77.

—— (1996) 'Specialisation versus diversity in Canadian technological development', *Small Business Economics* 8: 121–38.

Britton, J.N.H. and Gilmour, J.M. (1978) 'The weakest link – a technological perspective on Canadian industrial underdevelopment', Background Study No. 43, Science Council of Canada, Ottawa: Minister of Supply and Services.

Britton, J.N.H., Gilmour, J.M., Steed, G.P.F. and Smith, W. (1996) 'Technological change and innovation: the policy agenda', in J.N.H. Britton (ed.) *Canada and the Global Economy*, Montreal: McGill-Queen's University Press.

Corvari, R. and Wisner, R. (1993) 'Foreign multinationals and Canada's international competitiveness', Working Paper No. 16, Ottawa: Investment Canada.

Eden, L. (1991) 'Multinational responses to trade and technology changes: implications for Canada', in D. McFetridge (ed.) *Foreign Investment, Technology, and Economic Growth*, Calgary: University of Calgary Press.

Eden, L. (ed.) (1994). *Multinationals in North America*. Calgary, Alta: University of Calgary Press.

Feldman, M.P. and Florida, R. (1994) 'The geographic sources of innovation: technological infrastructure and product innovation in the United States', *Annals of the Association of American Geographers* 84: 210–29.

Florida, R. and Kenney, M. 'The globalization of Japanese R&D: The economic geography of Japanese R&D investment in the United States', *Economic Geography*, 70, 344–69.

Freeman, C. and Oldham, G. (1991) 'Introduction: Beyond the single market', in C. Freeman, M. Sharp and W. Walker (eds) *Technology and the Future of Europe*, London: Pinter Publishers.

Gertler, M.S. and DiGiovanna, S. (1997) 'In search of the new social economy: collaborative relations between users and producers of advanced manufacturing technologies', *Environment and Planning A* 29: 1585–602.

Graham, E. and Krugman, P. (1989) *Foreign Direct Investment in the United States*, Washington, DC: Institute for International Economics.

Gray Report (1972) *Foreign Direct Investment in Canada*, Ottawa: Government of Canada.

Hack, J. (1992) 'The dawning of flexible production? The changing structure and organisation of the Toronto Region aerospace complex', Research Paper, Department of Geography, University of Toronto.

Hepworth, M.E. (1989) *Geography of the Information Economy*, London: Belhaven Press.

Hirshhorn, R. (1997) 'Industry Canada's foreign investment research: messages and policy implications', Discussion Paper No. 5, Ottawa: Industry Canada.

Holbrook, J.A.D. and Squires, R.J. (1996) 'Canadian R&D', *Science and Public Policy* 23: 369–74.

Industry Canada (1994) *Resource Book for Science and Technology Consultations*, Vol. 1, Ottawa.

McDougall, G. (1995) 'The economic impact of mergers and acquisitions on corporations', Working paper No. 4, Ottawa: Industry Canada.

McFetridge, D. (1993) 'The Canadian system of industrial innovation', in R.R. Nelson (ed.) *National Innovation Systems*, New York: Oxford University Press.

MacPherson, A. (1987) 'Industrial innovation in the small business sector: empirical evidence from metropolitan Toronto', *Environment and Planning A* 20: 953–71.

—— (1988) 'New product development among small Toronto manufacturers: empirical evidence on the role of technical service linkages', *Economic Geography* 64: 62–75.

Martinelli, F. and Schoenberger, E. (1991) 'Oligopoly is alive and well; notes for a broader discussion of flexible accumulation', in G. Benko and M. Dunford (eds) *Industrial Change and Regional Development: The Transformation of New Industrial Spaces*, London: Belhaven Press.

Mowery, D.C. (1992) 'The U.S. national innovation system: origins and prospects for change', *Research Policy* 21: 125–44.

Nelson, R.R. (1993) *National Innovation Systems*, New York: Oxford University Press.

Norcliffe, G. (1996) 'Foreign trade in goods and services', in J.N.H. Britton (ed.) *Canada and the Global Economy*, Montreal: McGill-Queen's University Press.

Norcliffe, G.B., Goldrick, M.D. and Muszinski, L. (1986) 'Cyclical factors, technological change, capital mobility and de-industrialisation in metropolitan Toronto', *Urban Geography* 7: 413–36.

Ostry, S. (1997) 'Canada in the global village', *The Globe and Mail*, 26 May.

Patel, P. and Pavitt, K. (1991) 'The limited importance of large firms in Canadian technological activities', in D. McFetridge (ed.) *Foreign Investment, Technology, and Economic Growth*, Calgary: University of Calgary Press.

Porter, M. (1991) *Canada at the Crossroads*, Canada: Business Council on National Issues and Minister of Supply and Services.

Reich, R.B. (1991) 'The real economy', *The Atlantic Monthly* 267(2): 35–52.

Statistics Canada (1986) 'Industrial research and development statistics', Cat. No. 88-202.

—— (1990) *Indicators of Science and Technology* 2(4), Cat. No. 88-002.
—— (1991) 'Industrial research and development, 1982 to 1991', *Science Statistics* 15(5), Cat. No. 88-001.
—— (1992) 'Industrial research and development – 1992 intentions', Cat. No. 88-202-XPB.
—— (1997a) 'Industrial research and development – 1997 intentions', Cat. No. 88-202-XPB.
—— (1997b) 'The effect of country of control on industrial research and development (R&D) performance in Canada, 1993', *Science Statistics* 21(2), Cat. No. 88-001.
—— (1993 + 1991 + 1989) *Selected Science and Technology Statistics*, Cat. No. C1-4.
—— (1995 + 1997) *Science and Technology Data*, Cat. No. C1-4.
Steed, G.P.F. (1982) *Threshold Firms*, Ottawa: Science Council of Canada.
Young, S., Hood, N. and Peters, E. (1991) 'Multinational enterprises and regional economic development', *Regional Studies* 28: 657–77.

12 Capital and creative destruction

Venture capital and regional growth in US industrialization

Richard Florida and Mark Samber

Introduction

Ever since the transition from feudalism to capitalism, and perhaps even before, the rise of new technologies, new ways of producing goods, and of whole new industries has required capital and credit, or what is more commonly referred to as venture capital. Throughout this industrial history, it has been more common than not for such capital to be mobilized by new providers rather than established institutions of finance. The role of these new institutions of venture finance has been to overcome the risks and other barriers associated with more traditional financial institutions and to make the required investments in those new innovations and business opportunities which are the engines of technological change and economic growth. While at times traditional financial institutions have supplied the ultimate source of capital for these opportunities, the role of these new financiers of innovation has been to mobilize capital from these and other sources and to provide it to those entrepreneurs and risk-takers who have provided much of the impetus for technological progress and economic development.

The classical economists from Adam Smith to Karl Marx outlined the broad relationship between capital and industrial development. But perhaps the clearest statement of capital's role in the processes of innovation and economic development was provided in Schumpeter's classic work *The Theory of Economic Development* (Schumpeter 1934). In Schumpeter's view, capitalism is an inherently dynamic economic and social system; the source of such dynamism lies in the process of innovation. Powering the process of economic development is the phenomenon Schumpeter referred to as *creative destruction*, which 'incessantly revolutionizes the economic structure *from within*, incessantly destroying the old one, incessantly creating a new one' (Schumpeter 1942: 83). The linchpin of this process, Schumpeter observed, was the entrepreneur, whose function is to 'carry out new combinations' of products, markets, supplies, raw materials, and business organizations required for technological innovation and economic growth. Schumpeter further noted that new financial forms at times emerge to assume the risk and uncertainty associated with technological innovations and the rise of new entrepreneurial firms and industries. He emphasized the role of new financiers in supporting entrepreneurs in their quest to carry out these new combinations in the process of creative destruction (Schumpeter 1934). For Schumpeter, the provision of capital and credit to entrepreneurs is a vital element of a dynamic capitalist economy, indeed, 'important enough to serve as its *differentia specifica*' (Schumpeter 1942: 69).

For neoclassical economic theory, the provision of capital and credit is viewed as highly mobile with adjustments occurring relatively quickly over time and space. In Joseph Stiglitz's seminal formulation, capital markets allocate scarce capital among competing users and provide signals to managers making investment decisions (Stiglitz 1982). Many leading economic historians, however, suggest that industrial development is punctuated by periods of market imperfection, or what Lance Davis has referred to as the 'immobility of capital' (Davis 1957). Economic geographers too see finance as characterized by market imperfections and geographic differences which constrain and orient capital flows to particular places.[1] Here, especially, Schumpeter's entrepreneurs provide agency where established institutions of capital fail to pursue opportunity.

Clearly, the field of business and economic history has provided a deep and thorough understanding of the role of new enterprise formations and technological change in American economic history. However, there is surprisingly little systematic research on the role and relationship of financial institutions to technological innovation, and economic growth.[2]

In this chapter, we focus on the role played by venture capital in the processes of technological innovation, new business formation, and economic development. Venture finance differs from more traditional financial intermediaries in two rather fundamental respects. One, venture capitalists exchange equity for an ownership stake instead of providing more traditional forms of debt or fixed income securities which require collateral and a regular repayment schedule. Two, venture capitalists are actively involved in the strategic development and management of the enterprises in which they invest; they are more concerned with growing the cash flows of the business.

In our view, new forms of venture finance are typically required to finance the birth of new technologies and business organizations, and the more general process of technological and industrial development.[3] Thus, the rise of new forms of finance, or venture capital, corresponds to the rise of new industries, e.g. textiles, primary metals, semiconductors, biotechnology, and now the so-called multimedia 'telecosm' defined by the intersection of entertainment, computing, and telecommunications.[4]

We focus explicitly on the role of new forms of venture finance in the various industrial transformations in American economic history.[5] We organize our discussion around the intersection of venture finance and industrial development in particular industrial regions. First, we begin our analysis with the role of early and rather rudimentary forms of venture finance in the growth and development of the textile complex in and around Boston, or what historians such as Lance Davis, Robert Dalzell, and Naomi Lamoreaux have referred to as relationship banking or equity-financed 'insider lending'. Second, we then turn to the role of a new group of venture financiers in the rise of the science-based and/or mass production industries of the late nineteenth and early twentieth centuries. Drawing from original archival research, we focus on the venture capital activities of the Mellon interests in organizing the technology-based industries, particularly in the materials and chemicals sectors, in and around Pittsburgh.[6] Third, we explore the rise of an integrated and increasingly institutionalized venture capital industry to finance the new high-technology industries of semiconductors, computers, and biotechnology in California's Silicon Valley and the Route 128 area surrounding Boston.[7] In doing so, we draw from extensive primary research and personal interviews conducted with venture capitalists in these two regions.[8] This increasingly formal, organized, and institutionalized system of venture capitalists exchanges capital for an equity or ownership stake, participates actively in the development and management of the enterprises in which it invests, and invests in informally organized syndicates, combining the activities of financier, manager, and entrepreneur.[9] Furthermore, this modern brand of venture capital has organized into a formal industry with its own associations (e.g. the National Association of Venture Capitalists), its own research organizations (e.g. Venture Economics and Venture One), and trade publications (e.g. *Venture Capital Journal*).[10]

Early venture finance and the rise of New England textiles

The textile industry, as many have noted, propelled the process of American industrialization. Centered around Boston and Lowell, this industry provided the foundation for subsequent industrial growth and economic development, and according to Brook Hindle and Stephen Lubar, 'set the style of American mechanization, industrialization, and work' (Hindle and Lubar 1986: 185). The factory system accelerated the shift from piece-work to mechanized production, transforming the workplace in fundamental ways. Beyond this, the growth of textiles elicited changes in the structure of industrial financing. With innovative developments in machinery, factory organization, and production, the textile industry required massive amounts of capital; but where would that capital come from? As many scholars of the New England industrial experience have pointed out, the cotton textile industry was one of the first industries organized with the aid of external capital, garnered in large part from the newly formed Boston Stock Exchange in the early 1820s. Merchants and banking institutions supplied the initial source of financing for the rise of the textile industry's factory system, and as the requirements for more capital outstripped the ability of banks and merchants to supply it, many merchant houses reinvented themselves as manufacturing capitalists, with ties to their established trading networks, the new stock exchange, banks, and their own sources of private capital. Out of this melange of financing mechanisms emerged a credit market for Boston's burgeoning manufacturing enterprises.

A primary reason for Boston's rise to manufacturing excellence between 1815 and 1860 was the inventiveness of Francis Cabot Lowell, founder of the Boston Manufacturing Company, a pioneer in the textile industry of New England. The company represented the first successful implementation of the British proprietary technology known as power looms, implementing it on a scale unheard of in existing British or American mills (Dalzell 1987).[11] This not only required innovative approaches to management and organization; it also taxed the conventional methods of entrepreneurism.

Such a high level of capitalization was, according to Lowell, required to adequately equip the factory and provide a safe margin to cover operating expenses. Although capitalized at nearly ten times the amount of competing mills, Lowell and his associates at the Boston Manufacturing Company kept tight reins on the management of the enterprise (Dalzell 1987: 40). In fact, only seven stockholders controlled the entire capital stock of the company. This was rather significant, particularly as increasing scale tended to require new forms of organizational management and control. The Boston Manufacturing Company obtained its capital through an enormous subscription to the company's capital stock by a small group of local investors. The company authorized $400,000 of capital stock, which was issued in three subscriptions. The price was $1,000 per share, which most investors paid in installments over five years (Dalzell 1987: 26–8). The Boston Manufacturing Company became a model for the financing of manufacturing concerns. Furthermore, it enabled traditional mercantile capitalists to invest in new industrial opportunities promising previously unparalleled rates of return (Goldsmith 1955).

The explosive growth in stock subscriptions to local manufacturing mills was facilitated by close-knit relationships between up-start manufacturers and bankers. Naomi Lamoreaux has argued that 'insider lending' played a fundamental role in the industrial development of Boston and the New England region more broadly. According to Lamoreaux, as banks formed in towns and communities throughout the region, they provided more than basic savings and loan functions, figuring in economic development. In a role somewhat similar to that of venture capitalists, banks provided funds to their directors who in turn funneled those funds into manufacturing enterprises. This process of insider lending overcame constraints in the financial markets, providing a much needed spur to entrepreneurial enterprise. As Lamoreaux points out, 'whenever banks maintain an arms-length relationship with their customers, they tend to avoid the risks involved in financing entrepreneurial ventures' (Lamoreaux 1994: 13). The rise of New England's textile industry benefited from close association between bankers and industrialists, enabling capital to be channeled to nascent enterprises.

Rigidities nonetheless began to emerge in this new system of industrial finance. Before 1860, sales-generated equity or retained earnings was the most important source of capital for industrial expansion (Davis *et al.* 1972).[12] As Cochran notes: 'Problems regarding the entrepreneur in capital formation do not differ greatly from those in general economic growth ... In the early phase of industrialization most initial financing was of local origin and there was an intimate relation between entrepreneurs and investors. Expansion of the business was usually financed by reinvesting profits' (Cochran 1955: 339–45). However, the relative importance of equity waned over time. Lance Davis, perhaps the foremost economic historian of capital formation in American industry, argues that American economic and industrial development was punctuated by periods of capital shortage and inflexibility, or what he terms 'capital immobility'. Davis suggests that capital immobility became acute in the post-bellum decades because capitalist firms required external finance (or access to greater resources) as a result of industry's westward migration, and technological innovations in manufacturing ushered in by mass production. While New England's textile industry gave rise to the most advanced capital markets in the nation, little of that capital moved to the South despite the South's intricate involvement in the existence of a textile industry in Boston. Impeded by communications and transportation systems ill equipped to handle continental transactions, New England lenders could not efficiently tap into potential frontier markets, although they actively attempted to establish financial ties to the frontier.[13] Southern and Western industry experienced a widespread shortage of capital, and local pooling of capital was necessary to help these industries finance their expansion. The inflexibility of financial markets comprised a major obstacle to industrial expansion for much of the later nineteenth century.[14]

The role of venture finance in the early textile industry eventually became less important. Gradually, more modern forms of finance began to replace the older, more personal mechanisms. The mobilization of capital through more organized investment and financial markets provided the alternative to self-financed growth and the kind of insider lending Lamoreaux identifies. By the late nineteenth century, new stock and bond markets were beginning to develop outside of traditional financial centers on the East Coast, and during the 1890s long-term sources of capital from banks, trust companies, and life insurance companies began to channel funds into industrial markets (Goldsmith 1958).

But, as we will see, the rise of new, technologically advanced industries would continue to rely on local pooling and the emergence of new regional sources of venture capital similar in many respects to those associated with the growth and development of the textile industry in New England. As the next section will show, the rise of the new science-based industries of the late nineteenth and twentieth centuries would require new forms of venture finance which shared a number of characteristics with those identified immediately above.

Financing the second industrial revolution: Andrew Mellon and the Pittsburgh technology complex

The new form of industrial organization, which most clearly reflected the need for new financial mechanisms, was the modern science-based industrial enterprise. Although eastern capitalists located in colonial centers of merchant finance like New York, Boston, and Philadelphia were by and large the dominant source of new venture capital, the emerging industrial complexes of western Pennsylvania and the Great Lakes region gave rise to their own financial centers. The growth of the modern, *M-form* corporation and the broader economy that it helped to shape and which in turn supported the corporation, are now fairly well understood. Chandler has termed this the managerial revolution and has highlighted the importance of communications and new markets (Chandler 1977). The modern corporation became a propulsive force in the American economy and could not have done so without new forms of finance feeding its insatiable appetite for capital.

Today, we clearly understand the impact of the M-form corporation and mass production on American society. Less well understood, however, is the symbiosis between the new forms of finance that emerged to organize this nascent and dynamic industrial system. The second industrial revolution, like the first, required the development of a series of new financial forms and mechanisms to provide the capital and credit required for technological innovation and industrial expansion. Older, more traditional financial forms were in most cases far too risk-averse to undertake the required investments. Indeed, impeding the emergence of this new technology-intensive industrial system were a series of rigidities or temporary failures in the financial markets (Davis 1963).[15] Throughout the nineteenth century, capital remained a major obstacle to industrial development, as the pace and demand for investment outstripped the ability of lenders to provide it.[16]

Clearly, one of the most important financial innovations of this period was the rise of investment banking activity. As Vincent Carosso's landmark study *Investment Banking in America* outlines, the direct personal ties of the early to mid-nineteenth century became increasingly institutionalized. The railroads, a harbinger of the new corporate form, also best exemplified the growing popularity of securities and bond offerings during the 1870s and 1880s as a form of finance. As Carosso notes: 'Bank representation on railroad directorates ... was an institutionalization of the close personal ties that commonly had existed between bankers and railroad officials' (see Carosso 1970: 32). The structure that emerged to serve the capital needs of the railroad industry provided a model for industrial firms to follow. The new investment banking syndicates emerged because the immense size of industrial capitalization prevented any one firm from bearing the burden of underwriting corporate financing (Carosso 1970: 108–9).[17]

Venture capital was also important to the rise of new science-based industries. As we will see, venture capital would play a central role in the growth and development of an advanced and integrated complex of technology-based industries during the latter part of the nineteenth century. There were two differences between the early and rudimentary forms of venture finance associated with New England textiles and the venture finance of the second industrial revolution. Both of these were evolutionary in nature. First, it required far larger sums of capital to finance the advanced technologies and immense plant and equipment associated with the science-based industries such as electrical power, materials, and chemicals. Second, the venture capitalists of the second industrial revolution played a more central or nodal role in organizing technological capabilities, pulling together business capabilities, and in building the broader infrastructure from which individual enterprises would draw. These venture capitalists thus took on a rather extensive set of non-financial activities – or more appropriately extra-financial activities – in managing the birth and development of new enterprises and industries. They thus evolved the functions of technological gate-keeping, networking, and non-financial resource mobilization associated with modern-day venture capital.

The technological–industrial complex of the greater Pittsburgh region provides a good window from which to illuminate the evolution of these venture capital activities and functions. Pittsburgh was a center for industrial innovation in the materials, electrical power, and chemical industries, and developed as an integrated technological complex. As with American industry more broadly, Pittsburgh industry faced difficulty mobilizing capital during the mid- to late nineteenth century. A common practice in the region at that time was for fledgling entrepreneurs to approach established industrial enterprises that had built up vast equity which could become a source of lending capital. This gave rise to a new form of venture finance, which fuelled the development of the region's increasingly diversified manufacturing complex. Andrew Carnegie's venture into steelmaking, for example, was funded through equity gained in partnerships with the established iron-producing families of Phipps, Kloman, and Shinn, and not coincidentally through his success at the Pennsylvania Railroad. Similarly, George Westinghouse's air brake concern received financial backing from Robert Pitcairn, a Pennsylvania Railroad Vice President, and brother of John Pitcairn who later teamed with John Ford to launch the Pittsburgh Plate Glass Company. Initial backing for H.J. Heinz's 1869 founding was provided by L. Noble, a successful brick manufacturer. That same year, Henry Frick obtained start-up capital for his eponymous coke works from the A.O. Overholt Company distillery.

But it is the venture finance activities of the Mellon interests which best illustrate the emerging functions of venture capital during this period. Indeed, the Mellon interests activities mirror those of contemporary venture capitalists in many respects, by providing both financial resources and management assistance in helping to organize and incubate new industrial enterprises and an entire regional complex of them.

Andrew Mellon's first foray into venture finance involved underwriting Henry Clay Frick's coke business in 1871. In 1874, despite a severe depression in Pittsburgh, T. Mellon & Sons provided H.C. Frick Coal & Coke Company with a $15,000 loan and a $25,000 line of credit, and assumed a $76,000 mortgage on some coal property (see Harvey 1928; Ingham 1989: 124–5). The first of Mellon's venture investments, Frick was anomalous, and in some sense could be considered a learning experience. It was the only investment in which Mellon did not stipulate significant equity participation and managerial control, a practice that would distinguish Mellon-style venture capital from that point on.

The case of the aluminum industry clearly illustrates Mellon-style venture capital. Discouraged by the cool reception to his aluminum reduction process at Cowles Electric Smelting & Aluminum Company, in July 1888 Charles Martin Hall came to Pittsburgh to demonstrate his patented electrolytic process for reducing pure aluminum by dissolving alumina in molten cryolite (see Edwards 1957: 40–1).[18] A company was organized on August 8th of that year by Captain Alfred Hunt and George Clapp of the Pittsburgh Testing Laboratories, and a small shop was established.[19] When Hunt and Charles Martin Hall approached Andrew Mellon for a $20,000 expansion loan, Mellon offered $1 million in venture capital in exchange for a 40% equity participation in the new firm (Bieto 1990: 267–82; see also O'Connor 1932: 79–81). Importantly, Mellon insisted upon naming his own general manager, Arthur Vining Davis, in return for the investment. This case thus represents a critical point in the evolution of Mellon's involvement in venture capital – the exchange of capital for equity and an ownership stake, and an active hand in the organization and management of the new enterprise.[20]

Mellon's growing interest in venture finance convinced him that he needed a formal organization to effectively make venture investments. The vehicle he devised was the Union Trust Company, organized in 1889. After floundering between 1889 and 1895, Union Trust began to aggressively pursue equity investments and syndicated lending to start-up manufacturers. Over the next two decades, Mellon amassed an impressive array of manufacturing investments, ranging from oil exploration and aluminum production to structural steel manufacturing and railroad car companies.[21] Nearly a dozen new enterprises, mergers, and acquisitions were orchestrated by the Union Trust Company, which underwrote and marketed corporate securities such as stocks and first mortgage bonds, including: McClintic-Marshall (1899), Mon River Coal & Coke Company (1899), Pittsburgh Coal Company (1899), Union Steel Company (1899), Standard Steel Car Company (1902), Carborundum Company (1895), Crucible Steel Company of America (1900), Pittsburgh Steel Company (1901), and Gulf Refining Company (1903). Additionally, Mellon reorganized the T. Mellon & Sons bank, acquiring the City Deposit Bank, Pittsburgh National Bank of Commerce, and the Citizens National Bank and rolling them up into one colossal institution, the Mellon National Bank, N.A. in 1902.

Mellon later invested to relocate the byproduct coking industry of the Heinrich Koppers Company to Pittsburgh from Joliet, Illinois.[22] And, of course, Mellon made considerable forays into the steel industry. In a matter of three years, Mellon organized three conglomerates to compete directly in markets that Carnegie's steel empire dominated.[23] The icing on the cake was the sale of Union Steel, in which Mellon had personally invested $100,000, to the U.S. Steel Corporation in 1903 for nearly 300 times that amount (O'Connor 1932: 62).[24]

In his quest to build an integrated complex of finance, manufacturing, and cutting-edge innovation, Mellon sought to create a central source of technological innovation for the firms in which he had invested. In 1909, he read an account of an Applied Chemistry laboratory at the University of Kansas, and spent the next two years convincing the founder, Robert Kennedy Duncan, to relocate to Pittsburgh. Duncan's book, *The Chemistry of Commerce*, outlined the financial rewards that could be realized by marrying scientific research and development and commercial manufacturing. In 1913, the Mellon Institute of Industrial Research was established as a center for metallurgical and chemical research done in collaboration with Mellon's local industrial holdings. In this regard, Mellon-style venture capital sought to build a technological infrastructure off which entrepreneurial ventures could draw.

Our case study of the Mellon interests provides an important window into the relationship between venture capital and industrial development in the late nineteenth and early twentieth centuries. The venture capital and financial activities of the Mellon interests exemplify the concomitant rise of new forms of finance and new industrial enterprises. Mellon's style of venture investing involved a combination of innovative forms of finance and direct managerial control. Furthermore, Mellon's strategy for venture investing reflected a keen sense of the advantages of technological and industrial infrastructure, or what geographers refer to as agglomeration, and the propulsive effect of integrated industrial complexes.[25]

Venture capital and the high-technology revolution

The origins of what is now thought of as the modern, institutional venture capital industry date back to the Great Depression and the World War II period (Reiner 1989: 161; see also Wilson 1985: 44–59). Despite the immediate financial and economic problems of the Depression, the 1930s saw the origin of a proto-venture capital industry organized by a small group of financial elites such as Jock Whitney and Laurence Rockefeller, who created small risk-capital funds. Whitney's own contribution was nearly $10 million, and Rockefeller's venture capital partnership placed roughly $9 million in new ventures.[26] In fact, the phrase 'venture capital' was coined at the 1939 convention of the Investment Bankers Association of America, where in his presidential address Jean Witter highlighted the need for new forms of venture capital to spur economic growth and revitalization.

During this period, it was believed the financial reform and restructuring associated with the New Deal system of financial regulation had led to specialization and segmentation of the US financial system, focused almost exclusively on the needs of large, established industry. Indeed, smaller, start-up enterprises found the investment community rather unreceptive to their needs, in part because debt replaced equity financing and also as formal institutional procedures replaced more personalized forms of finance (see Kuznets 1961).[27]

An important impetus for the modern venture capital system came from a group of influential bankers and industrialists who began to sketch out plans for a new government agency devoted to the problems of small business and small business finance. To lend legitimacy to their designs, they organized their efforts through the influential Committee for Economic Development (CED), a group concerned with the post-war planning and reconversion effort. Many of these elites were concerned with the increasingly conservative outlook of large corporations, and what Schumpeter referred to in his influential book of the period, *Capitalism, Socialism, and Democracy* (Schumpeter 1942), as the increasing bureaucratization of the innovation process. Many also believed that new mechanisms would be required to re-create the entrepreneurial impulse in the American economy – to nurture and support inventive new enterprises.

While the push to develop new sources of capital for entrepreneurial endeavors proceeded on many fronts, the first and perhaps foremost of these efforts involved establishing a new federal program to support small business and provide small business finance. In 1945, Ralph Flanders published an influential manifesto on the subject, 'The Problem of Development Capital', which made the case for the creation of new institutional structures to provide capital for innovative, entrepreneurial enterprises (Flanders 1945). In 1947, a CED study outlined the need for policy initiatives to address the problem of adequate capital for the small business community (see Committee on Economic Development 1947). Five years later, in 1952, *Dun's Review* asked 'Can Small Businesses Get the Capital They Need?', concluding that capital markets were failing to provide required capital to entrepreneurial enterprises (George 1952; see especially p. 141). Furthermore, the study showed that small businesses faced interrelated managerial *and* capital crises, and that both must be addressed.

By the early 1950s, business and financial leaders were beginning to make the case for some sort of government program to bolster small business start-ups. The efforts of bankers and industrialists and the CED led to the establishment of a new federal agency for small business development, the Small Business Administration. The CED's position was outlined in a series of studies and reports that provided much of the background for the establishment of the Small Business Administration (see Committee for

Economic Development 1947; Kaplan 1948). And, by the close of that decade, they succeeded in getting the federal government to initiate a new program to create and to subsidize a new set of institutions, small business investment companies, designed to provide finance capital to start-up companies. In 1958, the Small Business Administration was authorized to establish Small Business Investment Corporations (SBICs), which were private investment companies whose capital was leveraged against asset sources in the federal government. Many of the first venture capital funds actually emerged as SBICs. SBICs also benefited from mandated tax breaks and other investment incentives, which eventually enabled them to become an import source of venture capital, especially in new growth regions such as California and Massachusetts.

Both the federally sponsored SBICs and private investors saw a connection between the new emphasis on scientific research and commercial viability in the marketplace, and sought to capitalize on it. Part of the solution was to forge closer links between entrepreneurship and scientific research and development. Vannevar Bush and others had effectively made the case for the importance of basic research in the war effort, and proposed to tap into the university as a source of new and potentially lucrative technologies. MIT led the way in the commercialization of academic research.[28] Led by Vannevar Bush, Karl Compton, and Horace Ford, MIT envisioned turning the Greater Boston region into an incubator of technology-based economic development. Ironically, they looked to the example of the Mellon Institute in Pittsburgh, sponsored by Andrew Mellon for his industrial investments, as the model of a regional focal point for industrially sponsored research and development projects. To realize this vision, Compton joined forces with a private development agency, the New England Council, to address the decline of New England industries, such as machine tools, by providing capital and managerial support.[29]

Immediately after the war, this group of Boston industrialists and bankers established a formal venture capital vehicle devoted to financing high-technology enterprise – American Research and Development (ARD), the nation's first institutional venture capital firm.[30] They selected Georges Doriot, a Professor of Business at Harvard and former army general, to head their new institution. Although ARD failed to meet its initial subscription goal of $5 million, it played a critical role in the emergence of the region's high-technology complex, providing the initial capital for Digital Equipment Corporation.

The structures of the modern venture capital industry came more fully into form with the rise of the new high-technology industries of the post-World War II period. Most of the early professional venture capital funds were located in large financial centers such as New York, Chicago, and Boston. These funds were tied either to wealthy families or later to large banks and financial institutions. The New York venture capital complex emerged during the Great Depression. Its catalysts were venture capital funds linked to family fortunes, most notably the Rockefellers (Venrock), Whitneys (Jock Whitney and Company), and Phipps (Bessemer Securities). The Rockefeller family made important venture investments in McDonnell Douglass and Eastern Airlines during the late 1930s, while J.H. Whitney and Company provided backing for Minute Maid.[31] The Rockefeller family, for example, transformed its family-run venture interests into a formal venture capital firm, Venrock, during the 1960s. It later provided early stage financing for a host of important high-technology companies such as Intel and Apple Computers.[32] Other wealthy families did the same. Being close to large financial institutions, venture capital in New York grew very rapidly, giving rise to some 50 New York funds tied to banks or investment houses and another 40 or so linked to financial institutions such as large commercial and investment banks.[33] During the 1960s and 1970s, New York City was the nation's largest center of venture capital. New York venture capitalists tended to invest their funds on a national basis, funneling their capital to the burgeoning high-technology industries of Silicon Valley and the Boston Route 128 area.

Chicago was another important source of venture capital for high technology. Allstate Insurance was very important to the rise of Chicago venture capital. In 1960, it became one of the first financial institutions to set up a venture capital fund.[34] Allstate's director, Ned Heizer, made very successful investments in young high-tech companies such as Control Data, Memorex, Scientific Data Systems, Teledyne, and others (see Bylinsky 1976: 29). In 1969, Heizer spun off from Allstate and formed what was then the largest venture capital fund in the country, Heizer Corporation. Heizer Corporation became a training ground for venture capitalists and was in turn responsible for spinning off a number of important venture capital funds. Chicago banks became active in venture capital during the late 1960s and early 1970s with the First National Bank of Chicago spawning two venture capital affiliates and Continental Illinois also creating two venture capital units.

The modern institutional system of venture capital emerged during the 1970s and 1980s. During this period, the amount of funds devoted to venture capital skyrocketed from an average of $3.5 billion to more than $30 billion. There were four basic reasons for massive expansion in the amount of venture capital and more importantly for the institutionalization of that segment of the financial markets. First, sharp declines in the overall rate of profit during the mid-1960s prompted an investment shift from basic industry toward new industries and more speculative investment opportunities. As a result, some small portion of the leftover capital from declining investment in old line industries spilled over into venture capital-related activities. Second, by the mid-1970s it became obvious that venture capital investments produced huge returns far exceeding those on corporate stocks and bonds. This exerted a powerful pull on outside capital sources, drawing external capital into venture investments. Third, success itself was reinforcing, encouraging more entrepreneurs to form companies and opening up additional investment opportunities for venture capitalists. Fourth, two major changes in federal government policy, a series of reductions in the capital gains tax rate, and the loosening of restrictions governing pension fund investments increased the attractiveness of venture capital and caused a variety of institutions to increase their venture capital investments.

Perhaps most significantly, it was only during the 1960s and 1970s that a new form of venture capital institution, the venture capital limited partnership, emerged to finance high-technology companies. Under this new form, professional venture capitalists (the general partners of the fund) were able to raise money from limited partners, i.e. banks, corporations, pension funds, and wealthy families. Venture capital funds could now be established right in the heart of emerging technology centers by personnel familiar with the most current technologies and business opportunities. During the period stretching from the mid-1960s through the 1980s, a huge number of limited partnerships were formed.

The venture capital industry in Silicon Valley, which represents the largest concentration of venture capital in the US, emerged during the 1960s and 1970s alongside the development of high-technology enterprises in that region.[35] Before then, entrepreneurs had to rely on industrial corporations or financial firms in more established financial centers for early-stage funding. For example, Shockley Transistor Corporation was started with backing from Beckman Industries, while financing for Fairchild Semiconductor was provided by Fairchild Camera.

The early venture groups in the San Francisco Bay Area took on a variety of forms. The first venture capital firm in California, Draper, Gaither and Anderson, was founded in 1958 as a limited partnership. The following year saw the establishment of two federally leveraged SBICs, Continental Capital Corporation and Small Business Enterprises. Another SBIC, Draper and Johnson, was set up in 1962. The venture capital firm Sutter Hill was founded as the venture capital arm of a successful real estate development firm. Bank of America and a number of other commercial banks also provided venture financing for expanding businesses. In 1961, New York investment banker Arthur Rock formed a model limited partnership with Tommy Davis of Kern County Land Company. Of even greater significance was the revolving syndicate of independent investors centered around John Bryan and Bill Edwards which later came to be known as 'the Group'. One intermittent partner of 'the Group', Reid Dennis, was able to persuade his employer, Firemen's Fund Insurance, to invest in a number of new ventures. The San Francisco Bay Area venture capital industry thus emerged from a period of active experimentation with different types of organizations for providing venture capital. Faced with acute difficulties mobilizing funds and the need to share information and expertise, these early venture capitalists gradually evolved into an interactive community, trading information and participating together in rudimentary co-investments.

The late 1960s and early 1970s saw the dramatic growth and reorganization of the Silicon Valley venture complex. Much of this expansion came from the original group of venture capitalists launching new venture capital funds.[36] Former entrepreneurs also became involved in venture capital. Eugene Kleiner of Fairchild Semiconductor was a co-founder of the important firm Kleiner Perkins in 1974, while Donald Valentine, an alumnus of both Fairchild and National Semiconductor, established Capital Management Services, Inc. (later Sequoia Capital) around the same time. A variety of other actors and institutions entered the Silicon Valley venture industry during this period. In 1968, Bessemer Securities became the first East Coast venture capital firm to open a California branch. Citicorp opened a West Coast office in 1973. The growth of Silicon Valley as an entrepreneurial center resulted in a shift in the locus of venture capital activity from San Francisco to Silicon Valley. By the 1970s, many of Silicon Valley's leading venture capital funds clustered in a new office complex at 3000 Sand Hill Road, Menlo Park, which became the largest single enclave for venture capital in the United States.

This period saw the emergence of the limited partnership, with professional venture capitalists managing capital provided by passive outside investors, as the dominant model for venture capital. University endowments, financial institutions, and pension funds initially bet on venture capitalists with proven track records. Over time, a growing group of former entrepreneurs, past employees of venture firms, and outside personnel were able to attract financial resources and launch limited partnerships. The reduction in the tax rate on capital gains and the liberalization of restrictions on pension fund investments were two reasons for this. The remarkable returns generated by the dozen or so original Silicon Valley venture funds sparked a massive surge of funds to venture capital partnerships. In contrast to venture capital in financial centers like New York and Chicago, the great bulk of Silicon Valley venture capital is invested in local companies. Furthermore, Silicon Valley's venture capital community grew up right alongside high-technology industry in a mutually reinforcing and symbiotic way, similar to what occurred in the Boston textile industry or heavy manufacturing around Pittsburgh. Silicon Valley venture capitalists gradually insinuated themselves into developing entrepreneurial networks, bringing important financial resources and business development skills to those networks and hiring successful entrepreneurs.

As we have already seen, Boston was perhaps the nation's original source of venture capital.[37] As early as 1911, the Boston Chamber of Commerce generated a small pool of risk capital and began providing managerial assistance to new enterprises.[38] Later, in the 1930s, Boston retail magnate Edward Filene and a group of New England businessmen launched the New England Industrial Corporation to provide organized assistance to new industries (see Leavitt 1940). Boston was the home of American Research and Development (1946), the nation's first institutional venture fund, which had been created by a prominent group of bankers and industrialists who saw such an entity as a way to more effectively finance technology-oriented enterprise (see Liles 1977: 28–36). In addition, a significant number of early venture capital investments in the Boston area were made by private individuals and wealthy families both from the Boston area and from New York City.

By the early 1960s, large Boston financial institutions also became involved in venture capital. In the early 1960s the major bank in the region, the First National Bank of Boston, 'the Bank', established a program for providing loans to high-technology businesses and formed an SBIC affiliate. Other large banks established SBICs to invest in the technology-oriented businesses that were springing up in the region. Federal Street SBIC was established by a consortium of Boston banks.

Both ARD and 'the Bank' became important sources of spin-off funds. In 1963, for example, ARD alumnus Joseph Powell founded Boston Capital Corporation. By the 1970s, ARD alumni were instrumental in launching a host of top-level partnerships including Palmer, Greylock, Charles River Partnership, and Morgan Holland.[39] Another important development was the rise of TA Associates, currently the nation's largest venture capital fund with assets of $1 billion-plus dollars. In 1968, Peter Brooke left his position as director of 'the Bank's' high-technology loan program to launch TA Associates. And as TA Associates grew it begat a number of other partnerships such as Burr Egan and Deleage and Claflan Capital Management.

Boston, like Silicon Valley, thus witnessed the development of a technology-oriented venture community parallel to the emergence of the Route 128 entrepreneurial complex.[40] ARD's enormously successful investment in Digital Equipment Corporation (DEC) in the late 1950s provided a vital impetus to the climate for high-technology entrepreneurship in Boston.[41] DEC played a significant role in the evolution of the Route 128 high-technology center; it became an incubator for more than 30 spin-offs, most notably Data General (see Dorfman 1983). As the technology base of the Boston region developed, a host of partnerships were organized by veteran venture capitalists. The late 1970s and early 1980s also saw the formation of new funds such as Eastech and Zerostage and the movement of branch offices of funds headquartered elsewhere, such as Bessemer Venture Capital, to the Boston area.

The role of the Route 128 venture capital community in financing new innovation is similar to that in Silicon Valley, but the evolution of venture capital in the Boston area has been much more closely tied to large local financial institutions and wealthy families. In fact, venture capital in the Route 128 area was largely orchestrated by large business and financial interests, a far cry from the organic model of venture capital that grew up in and around Silicon Valley. Yet, like their counterparts in Silicon Valley, Boston venture capitalists also invest heavily in local high technology, bolstering that region's capacity to engender important new innovations.

Venture capital in the Silicon Valley and Route 128 evolved gradually alongside the high-technology industrial complexes that grew up there. Venture capital thus became an integral part of the regional technology infrastructure, or what has been elsewhere termed the social structure of innovation – an interactive system comprising technology-intensive enterprises, highly skilled human capital, high-caliber universities, substantial public/private R&D expenditures, specialized networks of suppliers, support services such as law firms and consultants, strong entrepreneurial networks, and informal mechanisms for information exchange and technology transfer (see Florida and Kenney 1987). The synergies among the various elements of this infrastructure created a unique window of opportunity for the emergence of technology-oriented investing apart from traditional financial institutions. The growth of venture finance then proceeded along a learning curve characterized by the gradual accumulation of investment and management skills on the part of venture capitalists and entrepreneurs alike. This in turn facilitated the development of extended entrepreneurial networks that became conduits for sharing information, making deals, and mobilizing resources. As a central component of such networks, venture capital thus played an important role in incubating entrepreneurial activity, attracting entrepreneurs, and accelerating rates of new business formation.

Conclusion and discussion

The very phrase 'venture capital' calls forth the image of new financiers of innovation who back cutting-edge high-technology concerns. These industrial enterprises are usually linked to some cutting-edge, industry-defining technology – biotechnology, advanced materials, computer software and the like. Popular conventions aside, we tend to associate venture capitalism with the sweeping technological and economic revolution of the past two or three decades. But venture capital has a much deeper and richer history than that. Indeed, the rise of new forms of finance to channel capital to new enterprise and new industries is a defining feature of America's technological, industrial, and economic development.

We started from the premise that new forms of finance, or more appropriately venture capital, are typically required to finance the birth of new technologies and business organizations, and the more general process of technological and industrial development. In other words, we suggested that the rise of new forms of finance, or venture capital, corresponds to the rise of new industries and technologies. We aimed to essentially draw upon, expand, and test Schumpeter's seminal insights on the role of innovation in capitalist development. In Schumpeter's eyes, economic development is a process of discontinuous evolution which is driven by technological change. Major innovations or clusters of innovations set in motion strong 'gales of creative destruction' which revolutionize industrial production and industrial organization. However, the risks associated with these major innovations are sufficient to deter average firms, so 'exceptional entrepreneurs' are required to set such gales in motion. In our view, Schumpeter's risk-taking entrepreneurs require a symmetric counterpart in the financial system.

We believe that the historical record, at least for the American case, lends considerable support for this hypothesis. America's first industrial revolution of textile production in and around Boston both required and reinforced the rise of a new set of financial institutions that economic historians such as Lance Davis, Robert Dalzell, and Naomi Lamoreaux have variously referred to as relationship banking or equity-financed insider lending. New financiers of innovation similarly arose to finance the technology-based corporations and corporate complexes of the second industrial revolution: the activities of Andrew Mellon in financing Pittsburgh's industrial complex are illustrative of this process. During this epoch, a new and more complex system for banking and investment thus emerged as a vehicle for technological change and industrial development. The high-technology revolution of the mid- to late twentieth century required yet another round of financial innovation and a new set of venture capitalists to bring it to fruition. These new venture capitalists grew up alongside the high-technology innovation complexes of Silicon Valley and Route 128. By the 1980s, a new and highly institutionalized national system for venture capital had emerged to finance the latest wave of entrepreneurial, technology-based enterprise. Simply put, venture capital is a defining element of the American pattern of technological change and industrial development.

The venture capital system itself evolved alongside American industrialism, becoming increasingly formal and institutional in character over time. The early venture capital or 'insider lending' of the New England textile industry was largely a regional system, built upon close personal ties between the region's financiers and industrialists. The new forms of venture capital that emerged to finance America's second industrial revolution took shape as more formal institutions, such as Andrew Mellon's Union Trust Company. The high-technology venture capital of the mid- to late twentieth century evolved into a more fully blown institutional system of formal (indeed legal) organizations such as the limited partnership with its own set of trade associations and research organizations. Furthermore, this institutional system of venture capital evolved into a well-articulated national system for mobilizing capital via co-investment syndicates and other mechanisms.

Our historical excursus thus lends considerable support to the view that the processes of finance or capital formation, technological change, and industrialization occur in tandem over time. They can be seen as different 'faces' of an overall development process which grow up together, influence and shape one another, and are to some degree inseparable. This can be thought of as a cumulative process as industrial growth generates new sources of capital, which are in turn invested into subsequent rounds of industrial expansion and growth. With every major technological step forward, corollary shifts in finance occur and new forms of venture finance are created. These new financial forms emerge in response to the mismatch of capital and industrial needs, as older, more traditional forms of capital remain tied to older paradigms of industrial organization and growth. New mechanisms for providing capital – and new financiers of innovation – are required to support the rise of new technologies, new enterprises, and new industries.

Furthermore, our findings suggest that place matters in the co-evolution of finance and industrial development. Here, we simply suggest that Schumpeter's fundamental insights have a considerable spatial or geographic dimension. As we have seen, major technological changes or shifts in the organization of production tend to occur in specific places and diffuse unevenly across the industrial landscape. The growth and development of local industrial complexes in turn creates the expanding economic base, a vibrant investment climate, and new opportunities for capital accumulation. The initial opportunities may well be filled by traditional financiers and investors in established financial centers, especially given the well-developed financial structure of contemporary capitalism. Yet over time, the developmental trajectory of the new growth complex creates a momentum of its own, helping to create and indeed generate new sources of indigenous capital, finance, and investment articulated to the needs of its local industries. The new complex is now able to finance itself and embarks on a period of self-reinforcing growth while, at the same time, retaining connections to outside sources of capital and investment.

Our review of the historical record leads us to conclude that venture capital has played a rather fundamental role in innovation, industrial transformation, and economic development. Capital and creative destruction thus go hand in hand in the process of technological change and industrial growth in American economic history.

Acknowledgements

The authors acknowledge the financial support for this research provided by the Ford Foundation and the US Economic Development Administration, and the Center for Economic Development. David Hounshell, Martin Kenney, and Joel Tarr provided important comments and discussions and contributed to aspects of this research in numerous ways. Portions of this paper were presented at the Social Science History Association 1993 Annual Conference in Baltimore, MD. Special thanks are due to the venture capitalists and entrepreneurs who participated in interviews, which comprise an important source of information in our discussions of the role of venture capital in the mid- to late twentieth century. We of course assume full responsibility for our argument, analysis, and text.

Notes

1 Gunnar Myrdal's theory of cumulative causation, for example, views investment as a cumulative process governed by the existing distribution of productive activity and past investments – one which is characterized by small, incremental changes over time and space (see Myrdal 1957). More recent historical

scholarship documents the growing specialization of industrial and financial functions under capitalism and the rise of specialized financial centers in places like London and New York. In their classic account of the growth and development of the metropolitan New York region, Hoover and Vernon noted that the New York City financial district emerged as a series of specialized financial service centers tied to specific forms of industrial and merchant capital (Hoover and Vernon 1962: 88–94). See also Pred (1966, 1973) for a documented history of the rise of a small group of financial centers (e.g. New York, Philadelphia, and Boston) tied to specialized mercantile functions in the late eighteenth and early nineteenth centuries. Pred noted the role of large financial centers, such as New York and Boston, in performing such nodal functions in the US financial system and documented the evolution of a spatially dispersed but well-integrated national financial system with New York at its center. See also Conzen (1977). More recent research on 'corporate complexes' includes Stanback and Noyelle (1982) and Noyelle and Stanback (1984). Furthermore see also Wheeler (1986) and Gertler (1984, 1987).

2 Trescott (1963) is a seminal work on the credit side of banking and its role in the economic development of the United States. Additionally, Sylla (1975) and Lamoreaux (1985) are quintessential studies of the role of financing in economic growth.

3 On venture capital as a form of investment see Bean *et al.* (1975).

4 We suggest that finance, capital formation, and industrialization are not the product of abstract economic theories; rather they are informed by historical events and social institutions. Following Alexander Gershenkron and James Kurth on the comparative institutional structures of finance in the process of national economic development, we suggest that there are no single or optimal mechanisms for providing finance. The relationship between the political structure and the industrial sector essentially plays itself out in the various stages of product cycle development. Who performs the financial functions varies from country to country and even within some countries. Banks, the state, industrial corporations, and even decentralized financial systems composed of complex multiple subsystems all provide capital. Simply put, there are multiple forms, or functional alternatives, which are formed by the actual process of historical and institutional development. In formal terms, the relationship between capital formation and industrial development is 'path-dependent' – that is, informed by the particular historical path taken. See Kurth (1979), David (1975), and Arthur (1988).

5 To some degree, we follow Lazonick and others who characterize American economic history as comprising three relatively distinct periods: (1) proprietary capitalism, (2) managerial capitalism alongside the vertically integrated corporation and Fordist mass production; and (3) the rise of the new high-technology industries, knowledge-based production, and/or collective capitalism. In periodizing the growth of US industry we have drawn from Lazonick (1987). Lazonick lays out these three stages of industrial and entrepreneurial growth, labeling them proprietary, managerial, and collective. Proprietary capitalism took root in England as it became the world's workshop and spread to the United States during the mid-nineteenth century. See also Lazonick (1990, 1991).

6 See Chandler (1977). In Chandler's words: 'The Visible Hand of management replaced the invisible hand of market forces where and when new technology and expanded markets permitted a historically unprecedented high volume and speed of materials through the processes of production and distribution' (Chandler 1977: 12). See also Hounshell (1984).

7 An increasing number of scholars have argued that the United States and international economies are in the midst of a third major period of technological,

economic, and institutional restructuring. This has been variously termed flexible production, post-Fordism, lean production, and/or collective capitalism. See Lazonick (1990, 1991) and Piore and Sabel (1983). Generally speaking, the contours of this new production system are shifts in the main source of value creation from physical skill to intellectual capability, increasing importance of collective knowledge, accelerated innovation cycles, and greater reliance on continuous improvement on the shopfloor which serves to blur the lines of distinction between R&D and the factory. See also Drucker (1993). As management theorist Peter Drucker has argued, the foundation of capitalism is experiencing a fundamental restructuring, which will have significant effects on economic and social organization. See also Florida and Kenney (1991).

8 This research was conducted jointly by Richard Florida and Martin Kenney, and is summarized in Florida and Kenney (1987, 1988).

9 There is a vast literature on the modern-day venture capital industry: see, for example, Bygrave and Timmons (1990), Doerflinger and Rivkin (1987), Wilson (1985), Sahlman (1991), Florida and Kenney (1988), and Janeway (1986).

10 Indeed Venture Economics defines venture capitalists as 'participating investors seeking to add value through long-term involvement with continuing business development'. See *Venture Capital Journal*, March 1987.

11 See Dalzell (1987), pp. 8–9 for a discussion of how Francis Cabot Lowell surreptitiously obtained the designs for the Cartwright power loom while on vacation in England and Scotland. See also Ware (1931) and McGouldrick (1968). Scranton (1983) presents an excellent commentary on the Lowell system in Chapter 2.

12 See especially pp. 301–30 of Davis *et al.* (1972).

13 See North (1956), Davis (1963), and Hunter (1930). For a thorough account of Boston elite financing the western railroads see Johnson and Supple (1967).

14 In addition, public trust in the banking system evaporated in the wake of the bank panic of 1857. The National Currency Act of 1863, which assured a national currency of private bank notes backed by treasury bonds, restored a modicum of public confidence, and bank participation in financing enterprises through collateral notes increased significantly.

15 See also Porter and Livesay (1971: 65–8) and Hunter (1930).

16 See Davis *et al.* (1972) for a discussion of the many ways industrialists sought to obtain capital to finance expansion. For an important account of the capital flow into and out of a nineteenth century industrial city see Cronon (1991). Cronon gives an intricate account of the flow of capital between Chicago and the eastern financial centers. Significantly, Pittsburgh was an important creditor in the expansion of the Chicago manufacturing community. See also Hyde (1984), who presents the argument that places like Pittsburgh speculated in the mining commodities of frontier regions.

17 Sophistication on the part of investment bankers was necessary to accommodate the investment needs of these new firms, thus existing brokerage firms diversified and new niche markets developed in the financial services industry. See also Supple (1957) for a discussion of the importance of foreign investment, which even more heavily depended on personal relationships and close-knit groups. Foreign capital became a widespread option for cash-starved manufacturers in the mid-nineteenth century and remained so into the twentieth century. Participation by financiers such as Cornelius Vanderbilt, John Jacob Astor, or John Murray Forbes was a sufficient guarantee to attract foreign investors. This bred familiarity of the older established European financial institutions like the Rothschilds and Lloyds with American financiers such as J.P. Morgan, William Vanderbilt, Henry Villard, and Nathaniel Thayer. In addition, enclaves of immigrant groups in Boston, New York, and Philadelphia maintained close ties

with their home countries in Europe, gaining access to capital in the old country.

18 Hall was unable to attract investors because the expense for generating enough electric current to produce merely a pound of commercially viable aluminum was too high. Thus in small-scale demonstrations Hall could not achieve the reduction he needed.

19 Four other men were also part of the original company. Two were from Carbon Steel Company, one was from Carnegie Steel Company, and one from the Pittsburgh Testing Laboratories. Hunt and Clapp both worked for the Park Brothers' Black Diamond Steel Works as metallurgical engineers. In 1882, Black Diamond hired two college graduate engineers, William Kent and William Zimmerman, who formed a department in the company known as the Pittsburgh Testing Laboratory for the Testing of Materials and Engineering Inspections. Hunt and Clapp worked in that division of Black Diamond. In 1886, Hunt and Clapp spun off the company, gained full title to it, and renamed it the Pittsburgh Testing Laboratory.

20 Mellon also tried to take a considerable equity in Westinghouse. When Mellon was approached by George Westinghouse in late 1891 to provide $500,000 to finance a new air brake plant, Mellon demanded a high level of equity in his air brake and electrical equipment divisions, as well as latitude to name his own general manager. Westinghouse found this untenable and turned toward the New York financial community for help (Hersh 1978). Westinghouse came away from the deal empty handed, and with a bitter distaste for the baronial Mellons and the whole Pittsburgh capital financing scene. Westinghouse had been given a similar ultimatum in 1869 by Robert Pitcairn when he sought to start up the air brake company. Andrew Mellon vowed never to allow a Pittsburgh manufacturing firm slip away from his financial control, and to one day control the Westinghouse company.

21 Although Union Trust proved to be lucrative beyond anyone's imagination, Andrew's initial wealth was built up from his father's real estate and banking activities, and his brothers' construction and lumber company (Koskoff 1978). It seems the Judge had a reputation for being a prudent and difficult lender who rarely dirtied his hands with disreputable businessmen. The fact that Judge Mellon ensured that 'investments covered almost every phase of commercial activity' was not lost on Andrew and Richard during their forty-year reign over investment capitalism in Pittsburgh. See also Mellon and Sparkes (1948). When Andrew Mellon assumed the Secretary of the Treasury in 1919, his longtime friend and legal advisor Philander Knox advised him to relinquish all formal ties to his financial and industrial empire. As a result he resigned from the boards of more than 50 national corporations, including Gulf Oil, Mellon Bank, Alcoa, Standard Steel Car, American Locomotive Company, and the Crucible Steel Company of America. His brother Richard B. Mellon remained at the helm of the Mellon empire. Eventually there were Congressional hearings in 1925 to determine what if any undue influence Andrew Mellon had over his former investments. For an account of these hearings see the muckraking story by O'Connor (1932).

22 In 1915, the Koppers Company became another part of the Mellon family of firms, and enjoyed extensive interlocks with other giant enterprises like McClintic-Marshall Construction Company and Crucible Steel Company. Two years later, after American involvement in the war became inevitable, the Alien Property Act was applied to Heinrich Koppers' investments in the company. His shares were sold at auction in the Mellon-controlled Pittsburgh Stock Exchange on 13 September 1918. Andrew Mellon paid $300,000 for Koppers' 3,000 shares, which represented their 1914 value plus interest. On the day he gained title, the market value of the stock exceeded $3,000,000. Andrew W. Mellon not only pulled

off a managerial coup in gaining nearly complete voting control of the Koppers Company, but realized a phenomenal profit as well.

23 McClintic-Marshall set its sights on the lucrative Ambridge unit of Carnegie Steel, Union Steel competed directly with finished steel products such as those manufactured by American Steel and Wire, and Standard Steel Car competed with Pressed Steel Car after Carnegie forced Henry Oliver and Charles T. Schoen out of that company in 1901. The Crucible Steel Company endeavor and the organization of Union and Donner Steel to produce wire and finished steel products at Donora, PA, permanently changed the concentration of power in the steel industry. Crucible Steel pulled together the loosely held alliance of independent steel producers. The Union Steel Company recruited Henry C. Frick, just ousted from Carnegie Steel (Wall 1971; see the detailed account on pp. 724–37). See also Ingham (1990: 140–7) and O'Connor (1932: 64–78).

24 Capital of the company had been increased from $1,000,000 to $45,000,000 after Mellon negotiated to purchase the Sharon Steel Corporation and announced plans to build a new mill at Donora on the Monongahela River. Rather than compete head on with Union Steel, which would have 'disturbed industrial conditions which the Steel Corporation sought to establish', the directors of U.S. Steel authorized the purchase of Union Steel from Mellon.

25 Despite all their dealings outside of the metalworking sectors of Pittsburgh's industry, Mellon's eventual investments in the Crucible Steel Company of America, McClintic-Marshall Construction Company, and the Standard Steel Car Company indicate his attempt to benefit from the agglomerative advantages of steel production in Pittsburgh. Mellon came to control McClintic-Marshall in a manner similar to his ownership of the Pittsburgh Reduction Company. In 1899 two engineer–inventors, Howard McClintic and Charles Marshall, approached the Mellons looking for a loan to start a new business. Both gained experience in structural steelmaking and bridge construction at the region's leading bridge firms (Ambridge, Fort Pitt Bridge Works, and Keystone Bridge). Interestingly, the Ambridge and Keystone Bridge firms were part of the Carnegie Steel empire. Aware of the skyscraper building boom, and recognizing the potential to compete with industry leaders, Mellon offered his financial resources in exchange for equity participation and management control. He (and three other partners) retained ownership of the company until 1932 when it was sold to the Bethlehem Steel Company.

26 Wilson devotes considerable attention to some of the new industries financed by J.H. Whitney & Company and other new venture capital syndicates that emerged in the 1930s and took off after World War II. See Wilson (1985: 19–29).

27 These segmentations included: Federal Reserve banks, commercial banks, savings banks, savings and loan associations, credit unions, postal savings systems, personal finance companies, life insurance companies, private pension funds, federal pension funds, land banks, mortgage companies, investment companies, investment bankers, securities brokerage houses, government lending institutions, and trust funds. See also Galbraith (1954) for perhaps the most insightful account of the 1929 stock market crash and its aftermath.

28 This should come as little surprise given its historical commitment to industrial–academic partnerships, dating back to the vision of MIT benefactor William Barton Rogers. During the 1930s, MIT began to look into direct industrial partnerships with companies like Raytheon.

29 On MIT's interaction and involvement with high-technology industry see Leslie (1992) and Etzkowitz (1990).

30 On the history of ARD see Liles (1977).

31 *Venture Capital Journal*, November 1974 and *Venture Capital Journal*, June 1979.

32 *Venture Capital Journal*, June 1979.

33 Our discussion of New York venture capital is based upon oral interviews and back issues of *Venture Capital Journal*.
34 *Venture Capital Journal*, June 1975.
35 There is a substantial body of literature which addresses the development and organization of high-technology industry in Silicon Valley: see, for example, Saxenian (1994), Rogers and Larsen (1984), Malone (1985), Frieberger and Swaine (1984) and Hanson (1982). For a historical perspective, see Leslie (1992), Norberg (1976), and Sturgeon (1992). A suitable antidote to the boosterish quality which is typical of much of this genre of literature can be found in Hayes (1990).
36 In 1968, for example, Bryan and Edwards was established and George Quist of Bank America set up Hambrecht and Quist. In 1974, Reid Dennis founded Institutional Venture Associates with Burton McMurtry of Palo Alto Investment. Two years later, Institutional Venture Associates split into two partnerships, McMurtry's Technology Venture Associates and Dennis' Institutional Venture Partners. Tommy Davis launched the important Mayfield Fund in 1974.
37 Our discussion of Boston venture capital draws mostly from personal interviews with venture capitalists in the Boston area conducted by Richard Florida and Martin Kenney. See Adams (1977) for a discussion of early efforts. The early history of ARD is chronicled in Liles (1977). Back issues of *Venture Capital Journal* (especially March 1974, August 1975, November 1976) describe the formation of a number of funds.
38 For the early history of venture finance in Boston see Adams (1977).
39 *Venture Capital Journal*, March 1974, August 1975 and November 1976.
40 The Route 128 technology complex has been the subject of a considerable literature: see, for example, Rosegrant and Lampe (1992), Roberts (1991), Lampe (1988), and Dorfman (1982, 1983).
41 On DEC see Rifkin and Harrar (1990).

Bibliography

Adams, R. (1977) *The Boston Money Tree*, New York: Thomas Crowell.

Arthur, W.B. (1988) 'Urban systems and historical path dependence', in J. Ausubel and R. Herman (eds) *Cities and Their Vital Systems*, Washington, DC: National Academy Press: 85–97.

Bean, A., Schiffel, D. and Mogee, M. (1975) 'The venture capital market and technological innovation', *Research Policy* 4: 380–408.

Bieto, D.T. (1990) 'Andrew Mellon', in Larry Schweikart (ed.) *Banking and Finance, 1913–1989*, New York: Facts on File: 267–82.

Bygrave, W. and Timmons, J. (1990) *Venture Capital at the Crossroads*, Boston, MA: Harvard Business School Press.

Bylinsky, G. (1976) *The Innovation Millionaires*, New York: Charles Scribner & Sons.

Carosso, V. (1970) *Investment Banking in America: A History*, Cambridge, MA: Harvard University Press.

Chandler, A. (1977) *The Visible Hand: The Managerial Revolution in American Business*, Cambridge, MA: Belknap Press.

Cochran, T. (1955) 'The Entrepreneur in American capital formation', in *Capital Formation and Economic Growth*, National Bureau of Economic Research Service, Princeton, NJ: Princeton University Press.

Committee on Economic Development (1947) *Meeting the Special Problems of Small Business*, New York: McGraw-Hill Co.

Conzen, M. (1977) 'The maturing urban system in the United States, 1840–1910', *Annals of the Association of American Geographers* 67: 88–108.

Cronon, W. (1991) *Nature's Metropolis: Chicago and the Great West*, New York: Norton.

Dalzell, R. (1987) *Enterprising Elite: The Boston Associates and the World They Made*, Cambridge, MA: Harvard University Press.

David, P. (1975) *Technical Choice, Innovation, and Economic Growth*, New York: Cambridge University Press.

Davis, L. (1957) 'Sources of industrial finance: the American textile industry', *Explorations in Entrepreneurial History* 9 (April): 189–203.

Davis, L.E. (1963) 'Capital immobilities and finance capitalism: a study of economic evolution in the United States, 1820–1920', in *Explorations in Entrepreneurial History* 1 (Fall): 88–105.

Davis, L.E., Easterlin, R. and Parker, W.N. (1972) *American Economic Growth*, New York: Harper and Row.

Doerflinger, T. and Rivkin, J. (1987) *Risk and Reward: Venture Capital and the Making of America's Great Industries*, New York: Random House.

Dorfman, N. (1982) *Massachusetts' High-technology Boom in Perspective: An Investigation of its Dimensions, Causes and the Role of New Firms*, Cambridge, MA: MIT, Center for Policy Alternatives.

—— (1983) 'Route 128: the development of a high-technology region', *Research Policy* 12(6): 299–316.

Drucker, P.F. (1993) *Postcapitalist Society*, New York: Harper Business.

Edwards, J. (1957) *A Captain in Industry*, New York.

Etzkowitz, H. (1990) 'MIT's relations with industry: origins of the venture capital firm', Working Paper, SUNY-Purchase.

Flanders, R. (1945) 'The problem of development capital', *Commercial and Financial Chronicle*, 29 November.

Florida, R. and Kenney, M. (1987) 'Venture capital, high technology and regional development', *Regional Studies* 22(1): 33–48.

—— (1988) 'Venture capital-financed innovation in the USA', *Research Policy* 17: 119–37.

—— (1991) *The Breakthrough Illusion*, New York: Basic Books.

Frieberger, P. and Swaine, M. (1984) *Fire in the Valley: The Making of the Personal Computer*, Berkeley, CA: Osborne–McGraw-Hill.

Galbraith, J.K. (1954) *The Great Crash, 1929*, Boston, MA: Houghton Mifflin Co.

George, G. (1952) 'Can small business get the capital they need?', *Dun's Review*, October.

Gertler, M. (1984) 'Regional capital theory', *Progress in Human Geography* 8(1): 50–81.

—— (1987) 'Capital, technology and industry dynamics in regional development', *Urban Geography* 8(3): 251–63.

Goldsmith, R. (1955) *A Study of Savings in the United States*, National Bureau of Economic Research Service, three volumes, Princeton, NJ: Princeton University Press.

—— (1958) *Financial Intermediaries in the American Economy Since 1900*, National Bureau of Economic Research Service, Princeton, NJ: Princeton University Press.

Hanson, D. (1982) *The New Alchemists: Silicon Valley and the Microelectronics Revolution*, Boston, MA: Little Brown.

Harvey, G. (1928) *Henry Clay Frick: The Man*, New York: Charles Scribner & Sons.

Hayes, D. (1990) *Behind the Silicon Curtain*, Montreal: Black Rose Books.

Hersh, B. (1978) *The Mellon Family: A Fortune in History*, New York: William Morrow & Company.

Hindle, B. and Lubar, S. (1986) *Engines of Change: The American Industrial Revolution, 1790–1860*, Washington, DC: Smithsonian Press.

Hoover, E. and Vernon, R. (1962) *Anatomy of a Metropolis*, New York: Anchor Books.

Hounshell, D. (1984) *From the American System to Mass Production*, Baltimore, MD: Johns Hopkins University Press.

Hunter, L. (1930) 'Financial problems of early pittsburgh iron manufacturers', *Journal of Economic and Business History* May: 520–44.

Hyde, C.K. (1984) 'From "subterranean lotteries" to orderly investment: Michigan copper and eastern dollars, 1841–1865', *Mid-America* 66(1): 3–20.

Ingham, J. (1989) 'Henry Clay Frick', in P.F. Paskoff (ed.) *Iron and Steel in the Nineteenth Century*, New York: Facts on File, 124–5.

—— (1990) *Making Iron and Steel: Independent Mills in Pittsburgh, 1820–1920*, Pittsburgh, PA: University of Pittsburgh Press.

Janeway, W. (1986) 'Doing capitalism', *Journal of Economic Issues* 20: 431–41.

Johnson, A. and Supple, B. (1967) *Boston Capitalists and Western Railroads*, Cambridge, MA: Harvard University Press.

Kaplan, A.D.H. (1948) *Small Business: Its Place and Problems*, Committee for Economic Development Research Study, New York: McGraw-Hill.

Koskoff, D.E. (1978) *The Mellons: The Chronicle of America's Richest Family*, New York: Thomas E. Crowell Publishers.

Kurth, J. (1979) 'The political consequences of the product cycle: industrial history and political outcomes', *International Organization* 33(1): 1–34.

Kuznets, S. (1961) *Capital in the American Economy: Its Formation and Financing*, National Bureau of Economic Research Service, Princeton, NJ: Princeton University Press.

Lamoreaux, N.R. (1985) *The Great Merger Movement in American Business, 1895–1904*, New York: Cambridge University Press.

—— (1994) *Insider Lending: Banks, Personal Connections, and Economic Development in Industrial New England*, Cambridge: Cambridge University Press.

Lampe, D. (ed.) (1988) *The Massachusetts Miracle: High Technology and Economic Revitalization*, Cambridge, MA: MIT Press.

Lazonick, W. (1987) 'Business organization and competitive advantage: capital transformations in the twentieth century', paper presented to the Second International Conference on the History of Enterprise, Terni, Italy, 1–4 October.

—— (1990) *Competitive Advantage on the Shop Floor*, Cambridge, MA: Harvard University Press.

—— (1991) *Business Organization and the Myth of the Market Economy*, New York: Cambridge University Press.

Leavitt, W. (1940) 'Small business wants capital', *Harvard Business Review* 18 (Spring): 265–74.

Leslie, S. (1992) *The Cold War and American Science*, New York: Columbia University Press.

Liles, P. (1977) *Sustaining the Venture Capital Firm*, Cambridge, MA: Harvard University, Management Analysis Center.

McGouldrick, P.F. (1968) *New England Textiles in the Nineteenth Century: Profits and Investment*. Cambridge, MA: Harvard University Press.

Malone, M. (1985) *The Big Score*, New York: Doubleday.

Mellon, W.L. and Sparkes, B. (1948) *Judge Mellon's Sons* (privately printed).

Myrdal, G. (1957) *Economic Theory and Underdeveloped Regions*, New York: Harper and Row.

Norberg, A. (1976) 'The origins of the electronics industry on the Pacific Coast', *Proceedings of the Institute of Electrical and Electronics Engineers* 64(9): 1314–22.

North, D.C. (1956) 'International capital flows and the development of the American West', *Journal of Economic History* XVI (December): 493–505.

Noyelle, T. and Stanback, T. (1984) *The Economic Transformation of American Cities*, Totowa, NJ: Allandheld, Osmun and Co. Publishers.

O'Connor, H. (1932) *Mellon's Millions: The Life and Times of Andrew W. Mellon*, New York: John Day.

Piore, M. and Sabel, C. (1983) *The Second Industrial Divide: Possibilities for Prosperity*, New York: Basic Books.

Porter, G. and Livesay, H. (1971) *Merchants and Manufacturers: Business in the Nineteenth Century*, Baltimore, MD: Johns Hopkins University Press.

Pred, A. (1966) *The Spatial Dynamics of U.S. Urban–Industrial Growth, 1800–1914*, Cambridge, MA: MIT Press.

—— (1973) *Urban Growth and the Circulation of Information: The United States System of Cities, 1790–1840*, Cambridge, MA: Harvard University Press.

Reiner, M.L. (1989) 'The transformation of venture capital: a history of venture capital organizations in the United States', PhD dissertation, University of California, Berkeley.

Rifkin, G. and Harrar, G. (1990) *The Ultimate Entrepreneur: The Story of Ken Olsen and Digital Equipment Corporation*, Rocklin, CA: Prima Publishing.

Roberts, E. (1991) *Entrepreneurs in High Technology: MIT and Beyond*, New York: Oxford University Press.

Rogers, E. and Larsen, J. (1984) *Silicon Valley Fever: Growth of a High-technology Culture*, New York: Basic Books.

Rosegrant, S. and Lampe, D. (1992) *Route 128: Lessons from Boston's High-tech Community*, New York: Basic Books.

Sahlman, W. (1991) 'Insights from the American venture capital organization', paper prepared for the Council on Competitiveness and Harvard Business School Time Horizons Project.

Saxenian, A. (1994) *Regional Advantage: Culture and Competition in Silicon Valley and Route 128*, Cambridge, MA: Harvard University Press.

Schumpeter, J. (1934) *The Theory of Economic Development*, Cambridge, MA: Harvard University Press.

—— (1942) *Capitalism, Socialism, and Democracy*, New York: Harper and Row.

Scranton, P. (1983) *Proprietary Capitalism: The Textile Manufacture at Philadelphia, 1800–1885*, New York: Cambridge University Press.

Stanback, T. and Noyelle, T. (1982) *Cities in Transition*, Totowa, NJ: Allandheld, Osmun and Co. Publishers.

Stiglitz, J. (1982) 'Information and capital markets', in W. Sharpe and C. Cootner (eds) *Financial Economics: Essays in Honor of Paul Cootner*, Englewood Cliffs, NJ: Prentice Hall.

Sturgeon, T. (1992) 'Origins of Silicon Valley: the development of the electronics industry in the San Francisco Bay area', Master's thesis, Department of City and Regional Planning, University of California, Berkeley.

Supple, B. (1957) 'A business elite: German-Jewish financiers in nineteenth-century New York', *Business History Review* 31 (Spring): 143–78.

Sylla, R. (1975) *The American Capital Market, 1846–1914*, New York: Arno Press.

Trescott, P.B. (1963) *Financing American Enterprise: The Story of Commercial Banking*, New York: Harper and Row.

Wall, J.F. (1971) *Andrew Carnegie*, Pittsburgh, PA: University of Pittsburgh Press.

Ware, C. (1931) *The Early New England Cotton Manufacture*, Boston: Houghton Mifflin, 1931. New York: Johnston Reprint Corp. [1966]

Wheeler, J.O. (1986) 'Corporate spatial links with financial institutions: the role of metropolitan hierarchy', *Annals of the Association of American Geographers* 76(2): 262–74.

Wilson, J.W. (1985) *The New Venturers: Inside the High-stakes World of Venture Capital*, Reading, MA: Addison-Wesley Publishing.

13 Institutional issues for the European regions

From markets and plans to socioeconomics and powers of association

Ash Amin and Nigel Thrift

Introduction

These are times of major economic and institutional transformation in Europe, with uncertain regional implications. One possibility is that structural processes such as globalization and European integration, under the auspices of neo-liberal policies, might undermine regional cohesion in Europe by rewarding only the richest or most dynamic regions. A very different possibility is the rise of a 'Europe of the regions' as the outcome of a structural shift towards a decentred economy and decentralized institutions within Europe.

This paper, which is in four main parts, sides with the first of these interpretations. The first part outlines some of the policy alternatives which might help to counteract the centralizing tendencies encouraged by the pursuit of a neo-liberal agenda within the European Union. It explores the limitations of models of the managed economy which draw on a combination of neo-Keynesian and neo-Schumpeterian thought. The second part of the paper explores the significance of an emerging, third, model of regional development which stresses the powers of 'associationist' networking (Amin and Thrift 1994; Storper 1997; Cooke and Morgan 1998). It is a model rooted in new theorizations of the socioeconomy within institutional and evolutionary economics and economic sociology. But it is also clear that this model has its own problems. The third part of the paper identifies these problems with a too ready acceptance that the economic efficiencies generated by networking automatically translate into a gain in equity and democracy. We argue that, at best, this contribution is unproven and that, at worst, such networks may simply constitute a new weapon in the armouries of the powerful. In other words, the task of formulating strategies to counter the worst depredations of state and capitalism (even in their new, 'flatter', form) remains a pressing one. Finally, the conclusions to the paper offer some brief thoughts on ways of reworking what is to be defined as the economic, which is, we believe, the logical next step beyond 'socioeconomics'.

The growing regional divide in Europe

Current policy reference to concepts such as 'cohesion' and 'Europe of the regions', to defend the possibility of regional economic convergence within the European Union, tends to hide the reality that the gap between the rich and the poor regions continues to widen. The 1980s reversed the trend of the 1960s towards convergence reflecting a decisive shift in the European economy from an era of full employment to one of structural mass unemployment. Since the early 1980s there has been a steady increase in productivity and unemployment disparities between prosperous and less favoured regions. Rates of unemployment well above 20% in Southern Italy and regions of Spain contrast sharply with much lower figures of below 5% in Southern Germany and Northern Italy. Similarly, against productivity levels of around 60% of the EU average in the least developed regions such as Greece and Portugal, a small group of regions in Europe's arch of prosperity that stretches from London through the Netherlands, Northern France and Western Germany to Northern Italy enjoy a per capita GDP of over 125% of the EU average.

The major economic and institutional forces driving European integration are likely to exacerbate this gap (Amin and Tomaney 1995). There are a number of challenges with particularly stark implications for Europe's less favoured regions (LFRs) which include old industrial areas in the 'North' and lagging industrial regions in the 'South'. The first is the slowdown of growth, rising mass unemployment and growing fiscal pressure on Keynesian income redistribution policies. This process threatens to restrict the economic reconversion of the LFRs and to cut off vital transfer payments for the survival of their communities. Like the pressure of structural adjustment in the Third World and in the Eastern European economies more recently, the LFRs face the dual prospect of reduced growth opportunities and reduced welfare expenditure to guard rising poverty and unemployment (Michie and Grieve Smith 1994).

Compounding this problem is the pursuit of neo-liberal economic policies by both the European Commission and many member states. This is serving to strengthen the competitive position of the Union's strongest firms and most capable regions at the expense of the LFRs. For the latter, the 'market shock' represents exposure to stronger competition in markets, the harsh consequences of capacity rationalization as firms reconsider their geographical division of labour in the light of European integration, and heightened competition between similar regions for investment as barriers to the mobility of capital are progressively removed. There is ample evidence to suggest that against such a background, current regional policy expenditure and its orientation towards infrastructural upgrading and indigenous entrepreneurship falls far short of compensating for the centralizing tendencies unleashed by the 'market shock' (Amin and Tomaney 1995).

Another 'structural' transformation tending to disadvantage the LFRs is the growing salience of knowledge, information and innovation as key conditions for competitive advantage in the emerging information economy (Castells 1996). This is likely to work in favour of the advanced metropolitan areas of the European arch of prosperity owing to their established monopoly over the ideas, expertise, know-how and information circuits which pervade the global industrial networks they represent (Fast/Monitor 1992). These new factors of competitive advantage are not the ready properties of Europe's LFRs. Their ability to anticipate or respond to the driving forces of the 'information age' is severely hampered by problems of 'lock-in' and 'path dependency' associated with their specialization in the industries or activities of an earlier age.

An added challenge is the accentuation, as a result of the rules of the Single European Market and the 'opening up' of Eastern Europe, of longer-term processes of Europeanization and globalization affecting enterprises, institutions, industrial standards, communications networks, labour markets and consumption norms. These forces represent the construction of a genuinely European economic space straddling across local and national communities, but one which continues to discriminate between regions. Globalization is likely to force a sharp division between regions which can secure top functions (e.g. HQs, R&D, advanced services, advanced skills, etc.) to remain at centre-stage, and those which attract only lower order activities or are bypassed by international investors. It can be argued that Europe is in the middle of a transition from a system of inter-regional hierarchies of power and opportunity to a trans-regional hierarchy of unevenly distributed economic possibilities.

Finally, an institutional challenge facing the LFRs relates to the purported 'hollowing out' of the nation state, as a consequence of European integration and longer-term processes of globalization, as well as increasing pressures from below for regional autonomy. This twin process could lead to the transfer of certain functions to the higher level of Europe (e.g. security, competition, industrial and regional innovation policies) and others to the subnational level (e.g. infrastructural improvements, supply-side support for entrepreneurship, etc.). Associated with this process is said to be a shift in the nature of national state policy. Jessop (1994), for example, writes of the transition from a Keynesian welfare state to a Schumpeterian workfare state, in which economic policy will turn from growth strategies through planned industrial intervention and demand management, towards broad supply-side interventions (innovation, training, infrastructure, technological upgrading, etc.) in order to encourage Schumpeterian entrepreneurialism and global competitiveness. He also argues that welfare policies, owing to fiscal pressures and the declining need to prop up mass consumption, will become less concerned with the needs of the unemployed and the marginalized, and more focused towards securing the needs of the economically most active groups (hence 'workfarism').

Such a change in state form and function has particular implications for the LFRs. First, it means a reduction in the level of direct state support for industry, that is, loss of the mainstay of economic activity and employment in many LFRs. Second, it decisively shifts policy priority in favour of only those sections of the local economy and society capable of securing a foothold in the global economy, thus abandoning any commitment to the idea of a local community of interests and obligations. Third, for LFRs with weak institutional capacity and capability, the prospect of inheriting new local powers is not likely to translate into a new local Schumpeterian growth trajectory, thus widening the distance with advanced regions endowed with the appropriate institutional arrangements.

All of the above challenges represent not only a fundamental shift in the terms for regional prosperity in the new Europe, but also a considerable raising of the stakes for successful economic regeneration within the less favoured regions against a background of powerful centripetal forces.

The managed economy as an alternative to neo-liberalism

Part of the problem of the LFRs, as already implied above, stems from the politics and policies of neo-liberalism which, for the moment, continues to dominate the European project. The vivid examples are the European Union's commitment to monetary union and market economics as the basis for economic integration and growth (e.g. liberalization, curbs on state aids and public procurement, relaxation of controls on mergers, acquisitions and joint ventures, and free trade within a unified market). In the fields of regional policy, technology policy and social policy, however, there remains commitment to active intervention through schemes such as regional entrepreneurship incentives, innovation and technology transfer programmes, and directives to upgrade and harmonize working conditions and industrial relations. These are actions which go against the neo-liberal grain, but the salient point is that such intervention remains embedded within an overall framework of market-led integration policies for Europe.

It is widely accepted that a market-led political project claiming to reduce regional disparities through the allocative powers of the market mechanism is pure fiction. Liberalization, the rolling back of the welfare state, deregulation and the unification of markets on a European scale will serve only to transfer and consolidate resources from capital and investment through to skills, knowledge and entrepreneurship towards the core regions which offer the highest returns (Dunford 1992; Thompson 1993; Collier 1994; Amin and Tomaney 1995). It would be disingenuous to think that markets, and the institutions of neo-liberalism, will meet the interests of regions which do not offer immediate economic rewards. In addition, there should be no doubt that the politics and policies of neo-liberalism are designed to support the interests of the most powerful economic and social groups, and to end the traditional 'Keynesian' commitment to income redistribution towards LFRs via tax and welfare transfers (Dunford and Perrons 1994; Peck and Tickell 1994). Both these developments will reinforce the hand of the advanced regions.

Against this design for Europe which is defended most ardently by neo-classical economists, big business and the New Right, there stands an alternative design which imagines a reduction in regional disparities through the renewal of Euro-federalist social democracy and the policies of a managed economy. This is a design supported by the broad European Left and draws upon the economics of supply-side Schumpeterianism and Keynesian demand management. It lays much of the blame for regional polarization in Europe at the feet of neo-liberalism, and in so doing it assumes the possibility of a better deal for the regions in a managed European economy.

What does the managed solution amount to? First, and echoed by Jacques Delors' White Paper against unemployment, is the strong recommendation for expansionist policies designed to stimulate growth in the macroeconomy. It is argued that the pursuit of initiatives such as public expenditure programmes, fiscal policies to encourage investment, and monetary and credit measures to stimulate demand will generate the higher level of sustained growth necessary 'for narrowing regional disparities in job creation and unemployment' (Cripps and Ward 1994: 242). While the mechanisms for securing the regional spread of growth opportunities tend to be ill specified, it is assumed that, without overall expansion, even the possibility of 'trickle-down' is removed. Much of the work of the Cambridge economists has been concerned to show that, with sound and stable monetary and fiscal management at the European level, an expansionary programme is possible without harmful inflationary or budgetary implications (Michie and Grieve Smith 1994).

The alternative model also argues for 'federal fiscalism' (Thompson 1993; Dunford and Perrons 1994) as a key financial mechanism for the regions. Greater fiscal powers at the European level are proposed so as to secure the pooling of revenue across the Union, and through this process the redistribution of income and welfare benefits to the LFRs through automatic alignment between incomes and needs. Such a transfer mechanism through the fiscal system mechanism, it is claimed, would simultaneously remove the funding of regions from the political and ideological manipulations of different national governments, and provide a relatively secure financial base to fund local development schemes. Federal fiscalism, thus, implies a partnership between regional and European authorities as regards the governance and expenditure of tax revenue.

The managed solution to regional polarization concedes that neo-Keynesian measures to manage demand and the monetary system are not sufficient to secure competitiveness at the regional or national level. Thus, a case is made for an active industrial strategy designed to promote and support 'Schumpeterian' entrepreneurship. Such a strategy should seek, on the one hand, to strengthen competition policy so as to mitigate against the unfavourable (regional) consequences of mergers, takeovers and alliances in unregulated markets (Cowling and Sugden 1993; Sawyer 1994) and, on the other hand, to promote best practice in industrial innovation and organization. Suggestions regarding the latter range from advocacy for inter-firm networking and targeted support for small firms and indigenous industry

(O'Donnell 1993), encouraging the development of clusters of local competitive advantage (Porter 1994), through to suggestions for institutional upgrading to underpin flexible specialization (Murray 1992). Thus, this arm of the managed solution prescribes different forms of state support for local industrial innovation and upgrading. It should be noted, however, that rarely is the case made for simultaneous action on all the above recommendations within the framework of one broadly conceived industrial strategy.

Finally, and in recognition of the implicit centralism of national Keynesian solutions of the past, the managed solution argues for federal institutional and political structures. At one level, this amounts to a defence of the need for close co-ordination across the functional areas of policy intervention in the arena of economic development (from technology policy to competition policy and training policy) as well as across the spatial tiers of policy action (EC, national, regional) in order to minimize conflicting policy outcomes (Thompson 1993; Amin and Tomaney 1994). At another level, it amounts to a strengthening of the political alliance between the regions and the institutions of the European Union, a Euro-federalism in which local democracy and institutional strategies are allowed to flourish in a supra-national political setting of open but watchful governance of the European economy (Day and Rees 1991; Kellas 1991; Marquand 1994). The argument here is that in order to secure a 'Europe of the regions', the political horse has to be placed before the economic cart, but on the basis of devolution of state authority downwards to the region and upwards to the level of Europe.

These strands of the managed solution amount to a strategy which is unquestionably different from, and more open than, orthodox definitions of the managed economy. The stress on the guided nature of economic success makes it quite clear that without state intervention (at local and European level) explicitly in favour of the LFRs the regional gap in Europe will not be narrowed. In contrast to the Keynesian orthodoxy, it is also argued that the new regionalism has to go beyond the instrument of redistribution of income and investment, through its active support for local supply-side improvements and local institution-building.

From the perspective of the regions the managed economy alternative is a welcome corrective to the centralizing biases of the neo-liberal solution. Yet there is something too easy about it (Amin and Hausner 1997). The economics of this design shares with the neo-liberal solution a formula-based approach, a certain prescriptive rationality that does not square easily with the way in which historical processes operate in reality. There is nothing wrong with some of the universal principles, such as the recommendation that a steady flow of funds towards the LFRs be guaranteed or that regional institutions be strengthened. Other 'universals', however, such as the assumption that national or Europe-wide growth resulting from expansionary policies will spread to the LFRs, remain unconvincing. Equally, the supply-side solutions, despite their novelty in relation to past regional industrial policy (e.g. networking or clustering), tend to be offered as a formula for all regions.

This is to forget that the real economy, unlike the controlled experiment, normally works on the basis of distorting or defying universalistic solutions, and that its spatial differentiation amounts to something more than the degree to which individual regions possess specified growth factors. Regions are historically constructed entities, and, as such, the product of unique development trajectories, rather than the more or less imperfect reflections of any 'ideal' growth model. Hence their defiance of prescriptive formulae, and hence the insufficiency of formal rules of regional development.

The managed economy framework, in summary, is probably most useful as a reminder of the continuing need for state action, rather than as an imperative or a set of universally applicable prescriptions for regional development.

A third way

In this section, we want to suggest that a 'third way' is now developing. It draws in part on the managed economy framework, but is also a conscious attempt to go beyond it. The impetus for trying to construct a third way lies in the situation that we have already considered: the pessimistic outlook for many LFRs in Europe, which does not appear to be capable of solution by managed economy means alone even if these were politically feasible. Some of the reason for this pessimism lies in the power of the networks of large corporations and dominant institutions (including the state) to influence regional development, simply through a few arbitrary decisions made without recourse to regional development issues, or through forms of behaviour which serve to consolidate the strength of core regions.

In part, the third way is an attempt to set up networks of intermediate institutions in between market and state that can act as a counter to such decisions and outcomes. But the third way is also an attempt to build networks of institutions *democratically*, at local, national and international levels, so that they can be used to give a region 'voice'. Crucially, this cannot be done by dictat. Thus, in part, the third way is also an attempt to change the position of the politician and the policymaker. Because more emphasis is placed on the *process* of institution-building, the latter can no longer prescribe goals. The commitment in the third way to including the whole community means that more attention is paid to the process of evolution and learning. Finally, then, in part, the third way is an attempt to avoid simply reproducing local statism. Its emphasis on forms of governance which integrally involve institutions in civil society, especially those without hegemonic power, is not only a theoretical but also a political statement.

The theoretical 'glue' of this third way is what might be described as 'socioeconomics' (Grabher 1993). Socioeconomics has been derived from a number of different strands of work in the social sciences, of which five stand out. The first and second of these strands come from sociology and anthropology. One strand of work (see Granovetter and Swedberg 1992;

Smelser and Swedberg 1994; Ingham 1996) has its roots in the rediscovery of Polanyi's vision of the economy as an instituted process and Granovetter's seminal publication of 1985 which argues that economic behaviour is 'clearly embedded in networks of interpersonal relations' (Granovetter 1985: 506). Another strand of work from sociology and anthropology has also become increasingly influential. This is the actor-network theory of Latour (1986), Callon (1986), Law (1994) and others which combines the insights of economics, that it is *things* that draw actors into relationships, with the insights of sociology, that actors come to define themselves, and others, through *interaction*. When these insights are combined, then it becomes clear that 'actors define one another in interaction – in the intermediaries that they put into circulation' (Callon 1991: 135), where intermediaries are usually considered to be embodied subjects, texts, machines and money. These different types of intermediaries, which are far from passive, can be used to build networks in which, and through which, it is possible for actors to exert power. Actors constantly strive to enrol (human and non-human) entities in a network by channelling and stabilizing their behaviour in the desired direction, such that they gain new and stable identities or attributes within the network. Thus, power is seen as depending on the strength of the associations between actors, which, in turn, will depend on the ability to use a network to enrol the force of others and speak for them. In other words, power is the action of others. If actors are successful they will be able to build, maintain and expand these networks so that they can act at considerable distances.

A third strand of work comes from economics. The rise of institutional economics has been rapid and still continues (see Hodgson 1988, 1993, 1994; Samuels 1988; Hodgson *et al.* 1993; Witt 1993). The new economics takes the view that economics must be about the study of institutions. Thus the older form of institutional economics associated with Veblen, Commons and Mitchell has been rediscovered in the work of North and Olson and latterly, Scholte and Hodgson. In the more interesting heterodox institutional economic approach, in which notions of rationality and rational choice between preferences do not figure, institutions are usually broadly defined. Hamilton's (1963: 84) definition is perhaps the best known:

> It connotes a way of thought or action of some prevalence and permanence, which is embedded in the habits of a group or the customs of a people. … Institutions fix the confines of and impose form upon the activities of human beings.

Most particularly, institutional economists tend to distinguish between habits, which involve individuals; routines, which involve groups; and institutions which are composed of habits and routines (Hodgson 1997). Again, as in actor-network theory, institutions are viewed as able to stabilize over a certain period, against a background of uncertainty, characteristics which, most importantly, will include skills, tacit knowledge and formalized information. Thus significantly institutional economists stress the evolutionary nature of economic change, against the rational abstractions of neo-classical economics as well as the structural teleologies of certain strands of Marxist economics.

A fourth strand of work comes from politics. The new subdiscipline of international political economy, pioneered by writers such as Strange (1988), has, in trying to seek a rapprochement between international economics and international politics, had to consider in some detail the evolution of the global economy as an instituted process in which the presence of hegemonic states, markets, firms and political cliques cannot be taken for granted but have to be built and maintained. In particular, a number of authors in international political economy (e.g. Cox 1987; Gill 1993) have drawn on Gramscian notions of hegemony and the integral economy to extend the orbit of what is conventionally regarded as 'economic'. Gramscian international political economy draws attention to the role of dominant institutions including state, ideology and culture in securing economic reproduction and to the idea of the economy as a network of powerful and subordinated actors serving to underwrite particular dominant imperatives.

The fifth and final strand of work can be found within organization theory. A new organizational theory is currently being built up which relies, to a much greater extent, on the notion of organizational cultures, on the notion of organizations as 'many different things at once' (Morgan 1986: 339), and on the notion that organizations are modes of representation, rather like texts (Cooper 1987, 1992, 1993; Cooper and Burrell 1988; Hassard and Parker 1993). Here, too, the definition of 'the economic' is extended to include the salience of institutionalized cultural and cognitive forces in explaining economic behaviour as well as success or failure in economic competition.

These are strands of work with diverse origins and objectives, some of which intersect while others clash with each other. However, they have many elements in common. Of these commonalities, a number seem particularly important. First, there is an emphasis on the portrayal of institutions, as 'artful arrangements of bits and pieces' (Law 1994: 33) which are 'more or less long and more or less connected' (Latour 1993: 122). Networks are modes of transaction which presume some form of *mutual orientation* and usually *obligation*. They infer a *process* of ordering, usually over some length of time, that will involve intermediaries like embodied subjects, texts, machines and money.

In addition, the binding agent of networks is usually held to be *information*. This information can be tacit and informal (like certain kinds of skill) or explicit and formal (like many kinds of management procedures). It can be in the form of habits, or routines, or conventions, or narratives (Storper 1997). It can be held in embodied subjects, in texts, in machines, or in signals like price. The emphasis on information means that representation, and the technologies of representation, are constantly stressed.

As a direct corollary of the emphasis on information, the socioeconomic approach also tends to emphasize the *learning* abilities of networks (Nonaka and Takeuchi 1995). Considerable effort has gone into investigating the degree to which certain networks, for a variety of reasons, are able to both store information and reflect on it rather better than others (Dosi 1988). This is in line with a much greater emphasis in the socioeconomic approach on *innovation*, understood as the construction of networks which are able to cope with the uncertainty that is produced in capitalist economies, as a result of constant innovation, by themselves promoting constant innovation. Storper (1997) adds to the work of Lundvall (1992) on national systems of learning to stress the role of localized 'untraded interdependencies' in securing learning and innovation advantage in inter-regional competition. Similarly, Sabel (1994), observing the strength of the Japanese economy, stresses the power of networks based on goal monitoring learning, which simultaneously fix rules to enable widespread diffusion of standards at any given time, but are also open to new forms of learning.

A further commonality is a tendency to focus on *'intermediate' forms of governance*, which best illustrate the power of networks and the information they carry. These intermediate forms of governance are relatively purposeful and participatory forms of arrangement which emphasize reciprocity and which allow the rapid transfer and build-up of information. They can be of many varieties, and can be in the sphere either of the firm (Table 13.1) or of civil society (Hirst 1994).

The socioeconomic approach also tends to consider in some depth the importance of the *thickness* and openness or closure of networks. That is, the approach is concerned with the degree to which networks of governance can interweave and the ways in which this interweaving can be beneficial or

Table 13.1 Examples of intermediate forms of governance

High degree of formal integration	• Equity agreements • Joint ventures • Non-equity agreements: Controlled franchising Technology financing Consortia – e.g. joint research institutions, databanks, marketing institutions Co-operative accounts • Co-operative territorial complexes: Non-contract co-operative production system
Low degree of formal integration	Industrial district

Source: Christensen *et al.* (1990: 21).

detrimental to economic 'performance' (howsoever defined) by allowing transfers of appropriate knowledge and information, thereby allowing other networks to learn similar lessons (Arthur 1989; Sabel 1994; Grabher and Stark 1997).

Another commonality is the tendency to emphasize *path-dependent evolutionary change*, that is, the degree to which networks constructed in particular contexts for particular purposes are sedimented over time (North 1990). Networks are thereby relatively invariant but they are still subject to change because networks remain *context dependent*. Most especially, there is a somewhat intractable geography of *places* into which the ordering arrangements of the network can only extend so far: 'since there are discontinuities in place and discontinuities in ordering, it follows that the largest part of the action is always being generated elsewhere' (Law 1994: 47).

Critical socioeconomics recognizes also the *asymmetry of power* between networks. The recognition of the networked nature of economic behaviour thus is not necessarily only an acknowledgement of relations of co-operation, trust and mutual reward, but also a recognition of interdependencies, which are underpinned by inequalities within and between networks. Indeed, for some close to Foucault or Gramsci, an important rationale behind networks and the institutions which dominate them is to act as a means by which webs of power cutting across state economy and civil society are retained (Cox 1987; Strange 1992; Watts 1993; Van der Pilj 1994). They are a means by which power is institutionalized, mobilized effectively and exercised over other, weaker, networks of association.

Finally, the socioeconomic approach tends to assume that the category of the economic is a diachronic rather than a synchronic one. That is, what can be termed 'the economic' is assumed to change over time. In other words, each and every one of the socioeconomic approaches is trying to change current definitions of what counts as economic in recognition of the fact that what we can regard as the economy has constantly changed through history, and also that current economic discourse moves in much too confined a space. In a sense, much of the force of socioeconomics comes in its search for new metaphors that will allow us to see 'the economic' in new ways (Barnes 1995; Thrift and Olds 1996).

No doubt there are other insights that can be gleaned from this literature but these eight seem to be the most salient. What is clear is that much of the impetus behind socioeconomics comes from practical demonstrations of economic success which, however ambiguously, seem to suggest the importance of networks of association, whether at the global scale (for example networks of overseas Chinese capital), at a national scale (for example parts of Japanese industry) or at an urban and regional scale (for example in certain European industrial districts). In turn, these demonstrations of 'success' provide a pressing practical agenda which is how associationism and economic success are, or more importantly, could be linked.

Building powers of association

The practical agenda consists of attempts to produce regional and national economic success in Europe in the less than propitious conditions already outlined above. This agenda assumes a set of four '*orientations*' to economic success. The first of these is that attempts to produce associative economies must be based in the construction of institutional capacity which cannot be brought into existence by command of the state or assumed to be formed by the market. In other words, these attempts must be based in a negotiated 'interactive' rather than an 'imperative' approach which fosters rather than enforces (Hausner 1995; Amin and Hausner 1997). This interactive approach consists of:

> ... eliciting the desired changes by generating a process of social innovation resulting from social interaction. In this method, the central authority, initiating and directing the changes, takes on the role of participant and treats the other participants as independent agents, whose behaviour can only change as a consequence of mutual interaction. The task of the central authority initiating the transformation process does not involve establishing certain new systemic rules, forcing the participants to respect them; rather, it is to stimulate the process of defining and formulating these rules, thus allowing the participants to satisfy their needs and realise their interests. In this process, the role of the 'central authority' is also subject to definition and formation by society.
>
> (Hausner 1995: 1)

The second orientation is that the practical agenda that is produced must, in line with the theoretical precepts already suggested, be context dependent. That is, it must reject *binary thinking* (for example assuming certain institutional arrangements as necessarily in opposition to one another as in plan versus market, public versus private, or state versus society); reject an approach which assumes a *linear trajectory* from one system to another (for example from a planned to a market economy); and reject the idea of a *uniform progression* which assumes that regions need to embark on the same programme and then follow the same path (Miliband 1993).

The third orientation of the associative approach is the overall goal. This is to give a community (local or otherwise) sufficient potential for strategic action (by a process of institutional 'filling in' rather than 'hollowing out') through a process of *negotiation*, in which *the process of negotiation is itself a vital part of the institution-building process* (Healey 1997; Douglass and Friedmann 1998). Thus the social consciousness of a community is changed, and not just its institutional framework and, in this process, the community is endowed with agency.

The fourth and final orientation is towards intermediate forms of governance as the main instruments of the construction of institutional thickness:

> An industrial policy oriented towards structural changes in the economy and promotion of producers' adaptability to the conditions of domestic and international competition must focus on the intermediate-level structures. Its efficiency depends on the nature of the meso-structures in the given economy and its social environment. Therefore, the creation of intermediate-level structures that would facilitate economic restructuring is the top priority of industrial policy and the goal of the economic strategy.
>
> (Hausner 1995: 22)

These intermediate forms refer to formal institutions over and above those of Europe and the nation state, to a process of collective governance of the socioeconomy. In short, it represents a process of broadening the arena of institutions at diverse spatial scales involved in guiding economic outcomes (see below).

Based around these four orientations, it is possible to identify a number of closely related supply-side measures which are often regarded as opportune for an associationist agenda. The most general of these is a need to gear up the supply side, most especially as this relates to the circulation of information and skill formation (training). Following from this is the need to ensure the accumulation of knowledge-transfer networks. These networks are intended to produce not just knowledge transfer but also a more general disposition to collaborate, a disposition which is most needed in less favoured regions which are more likely to harbour unresponsive or undemanding firms. The focus on information and knowledge has to be seen, in addition, as part of a wider aim of encouraging learning and adaptation across the industrial and institutional base, so that local path dependencies can be built upon or challenged through strategic goal monitoring actions and rationalities of behaviour.

All this, in turn, produces a need to more fully integrate supply chains between firms, not just as a way of producing inter-firm complementarities and economies of association, but also as a means of obtaining rudimentary knowledge-transfer networks (transferring knowledge from winners) which can subsequently be built upon. The integration of supply chains may or may not centre around selected clusters of industries with deep enough roots in the local context to secure competitive advantage.

Another measure is a need for enterprise support systems which can keep networks of firms innovative. These might be modelled on the example of the Sternlieb centres in Baden-Württemberg or the sector-specific and 'lateral' service centres in Emilia-Romagna. Finally, the associationist agenda would endorse the need in many regions to build up regional governance capacity. Above all, this means measures designed to increase a region's institutional thickness, in such a way that a region's ability to orchestrate becomes greater. This implies that a network of institutions can be built up of a quality and in such a way that the sum is greater than the parts. Civic assemblies, integrated regional offices and the like can all, in concert, produce governance capacity. But, as has been stated before, it is often the acts of building these institutions in an open, inclusive way which are more important for a region's governance capacity than the actual institutions themselves.

Local associationist solutions for global problems?

The policy measures which follow from the associationist model are all attempts to develop and strengthen local institutional networks. The third way is also quite clearly an attempt to provide a region with 'voice', with agency, with orchestrating capacities which cannot be reduced to arbitrary statist forms invented by an elite of policymakers on the lookout for a quick fix, or for a way of pursuing narrow sectarian interests. As such, it is necessarily tentative, because it has no endpoint in the conventional sense and because it is an attempt to broaden out the policy community, so that it includes the community!

Building local associationism is clearly not sufficient on its own. For, as suggested in the earlier accounts of the global challenges which confront the European regions, their problems are the product of processes beyond the reach of individual regions (e.g. globalization, the vested power of states, transnational corporations and core regions, etc.). These are not challenges which will wait for a region to build up its local powers of association.

Local associationist strategies thus have to be part of a wider programme of anti-neo-liberal policies at national and European level, which can help to maintain a flow of resources towards the least favoured regions as well as minimize the damaging effects of wider economic forces. Some solutions may well fall within the framework of the managed economy model, and therefore, at a practical level, a certain degree of complementarity between the two models cannot be denied. Active intervention in favour of the LFRs might indeed necessitate rules, sanctions, incentives, perhaps even quick fixes. One example is the guarantee of automatic fiscal transfers to underwrite basic income and basic welfare rights within the LFRs. Another might be long-term commitment to the range of supply-side improvements identified by the managed economy model. Also necessary might be a tightening of both EU and national competition policies through the introduction of sanctions against corporate actions such as mergers and alliances which have damaging consequences on dynamic or innovative firms in the LFRs. Equally important is the need for whatever practicable co-ordination between policy communities so as to minimize conflict or duplication of effort between regional development initiatives taken at local, national or European level.

We accept that in Europe, in which so much is stacked in favour of the dominant and most powerful interests, it would be naive to think of genuine development prospects within the LFRs in the absence of such 'statist' solutions. However, we would also contend that to take seriously the argument that building powers of association is indispensable for economic success means to recognize that practical action has to enter into areas beyond the reach of orthodox policies, and it has to involve new social actors and new ways of doing things based on the dialectic between diverse communities (Lipietz 1993).

It is important, therefore, not to blur the differences between the associationist and the managed economy model. There remain fundamental differences in the assumptions and expectations of the two models. The key distinction lies between the open and evolutionary nature of the associationist model and the narrowly defined prescriptions of the managed economy model, between the possibilism of the former and the formulaic imperatives of the latter. Against the readily operationalized universal policies of the managed economy model, the associationist model stresses the role of institution-building, interactive governance and civic empowerment in formulating and implementing development goals. It is an approach of broad overall aims and interactive procedures, standing in sharp relief against the abstract rationalist and anti-holistic epistemology that has dominated policy action for so many years. Any defence of the third way, therefore, is a defence of a fundamental shift in the meaning, scope and procedures of public policy at every level.

From associationism to radical democracy

Socioeconomics stresses collective practice, consensus and co-operation. This stress follows from the emphasis placed on the associationist foundations of economic success. In contrast to the focus on individuals by the neo-classical orthodoxy, socioeconomics privileges alliances and collective agency as a source of economic learning, innovation and adaptability. There is more than a hint that socioeconomics has positive lessons for issues of democracy, since economic success is so often coupled with a commitment to participatory democracy and equity of outcome. For example, in the writing of those who promote firm-networks it is often implied that these networks minimize hierarchy, are managed by multiple actors, and are generous towards workers and managers alike. Similarly, associationist thought in regional development studies tends never to be far from the Marshallian industrial district as an ideal type because it is believed to combine economic efficiency with social equity.

Our view is that this slippage from economics to equity is potentially problematic, since the powers of association alone do not resolve the two problems of, first, equitable distribution of the benefits of growth and, second, democratic governance of the socioeconomy. For a start, networks of collaboration have their own political economy, that is, inequalities and irreconcilable interests. For example, even the 'flattest' of contemporary corporate networks are not openly constructed spheres of action, but carefully crafted 'heterarchies' of power which unevenly distribute tasks, competencies and rewards between their members. They are not democratic institutions, nor do they see it as their mission to put social goals before profit-based goals.

It can also be argued that networking is a means by which the powerful, however defined, maintain or extend their sphere of influence (Allen 1997). For example, the efflorescence in the 1980s of urban 'growth machines' composed of local rentiers, developers, financiers, planners, media, utilities companies and so on, can be seen as a network drawing together strands of the local elite, serving to *dominate* rather than empower the local patch. In a similar vein, Susan Strange (1992) has hinted that 'structural' power in the global political economy increasingly is becoming a matter of alliances among the elites of different interest coalitions, in order to exercise corporate control in an age in which it has become difficult to identify power with any single hegemon:

> I am not alone in seeing the present order as approximating more to that of medieval Europe in which markets functioned under systems of rules in which authority was widely dispersed between princes – but princes with very unequal command of resources – the Church, professional guilds, and local lords of the manor ... what we do not know, or perceive only vaguely, is where the locus of authority in world society and economy now resides, and over what issues, if not with the governments of each territorial state.
>
> (Strange 1992: 20)

In a world of increasing fragmentation, complexity and interpenetration, associationism can be a powerful and effective means by which relations of dominance and embedded power are retained across disparate interest groupings.

It is essential, therefore, to distinguish between progressive and regressive coalitions, or more grandiosely, between hegemonic and counter-hegemonic associationist projects. Examples of the latter include social movements ranging from protests against a new road, to networks of small producer co-operatives and alternative housing projects for the young and the unemployed, established specifically for reasons of social justice or for developing a more inclusive way of doing things. This is an associationism which is quite different from that of the dominant networks of power. One of its explicit purposes is to represent the interests of those who are excluded by the established networks of dominance, and in a way which enables the latter to develop governance capability.

For these reasons alone, it cannot be assumed that the associationist institutions of socioeconomics are a guarantor of social and political democracy. The socialized economy is neither communitarian nor interested in equity of reward. It continues to exclude, exercise power unequally and represent corporatized interests. Thus the tacit assumption within socioeconomics that economic association combines efficiency with social equity is not one which we share. Instead, we would stress that democracy has to be defended consciously as a political project regardless of the sources of economic prosperity.

In this final section we wish to propose that any discussion of the interests of those excluded by the networks of the powerful (weaker regions, the socially excluded, minority groups, the economically weak, the unemployed) has to look beyond the institutions of socioeconomics. As a corollary, any discussion of new or alternative trajectories of economic development must go beyond socioeconomics, into the terrain of 'oppositional' politics and political organization. This is because their construction depends crucially on the ability of their protagonists to create a space for themselves, and to curb the influence of the powerful. It requires, therefore, *political* action in favour of counter-hegemonic forces, as much as it requires the alternative networks to be well resourced. In addition, the distinction between 'progressive' and 'regressive' coalitions becomes immediately a matter of politics, in the sense that a defining feature of 'progressive' coalitions is that they represent participatory governance, that is, a different, more active and more inclusive way of doing things.

The practical agenda for the regions therefore cannot avoid the question of regional *political* empowerment and regional political *practice*. But what does this involve? What we are sure of is that a strategy which stops at facilitating the efflorescence of associations within civil society is not enough because it fails to confront the issue of how the practices of the powerful are to be changed (Kumar 1993). Equally unconvincing is the frame of action put forward recently by Geoff Mulgan (1994), who calls for greater civic responsibility and active citizenship. It too fails to confront the issue of embedded power, and it places too heavy a burden on individual and social morality. Finally, the model of liberal democracy alone is also weak as a solution, since its institutions (representative bodies such as parliament) serve to deny the participatory politics embraced by heterodox networks of association.

The kind of model we subscribe to is best represented by Table 13.2, which constitutes a radical democratic agenda (Amin 1996). The table shows that a project of building networks of association must simultaneously democratize the economy and the state (by giving more voice to those least well represented) and civil society (by building voice among the excluded). Such a model is intended to build on the institution of networks of association in the economy by concerted action in the state and in civil society, which can compensate for the democratic deficit that will otherwise be experienced. In other words, our aim is to boost levels of active participation across economy, state and civil society, so that each provides a check on the other, and, as importantly, so that the disempowered are able to be given a voice (Mouffe 1992). Without such a radical democratic agenda, an approach based in socioeconomics will simply slip back into a neo-liberal or liberal orthodoxy.

Table 13.2 Radicalizing socioeconomics

Economy/state	*Civil society*
Main activity	
Giving voice by democratizing existing networks	*Building voice* by building alternative networks
Main objectives	
1 Equitable economic success	1 Giving the excluded an economic stake
2 Producing more democratic processes	2 Extending democratic procedures
3 Democratizing the public sphere	3 Creating a public sphere
4 Dampening hegemonic cultures	4 Disputing monocultural hegemonies
Examples of forms of association	
Works councils	Credit unions
Worker co-operatives	Local banks
State–labour–business partnerships	Women's co-operatives
Producer/consumer co-operatives	LETS
Regional assemblies	Housing co-operatives
Decentralized and decentred state bureaucracy	Neighbourhood associations
	Campaign for civil liberties, constitutional reform, Bill of Rights
'Open' government charters	
Political lobbies	Consumer groups
Industrial tribunals	Civil disobedience and protest campaigns
	Issue coalitions

State and politics

Clearly, the role of the state and politics is rather different in this agenda from those previously espoused. Unlike other commentators (e.g. Mulgan 1994) we are not necessarily arguing that the role of the state must be radically reduced. Rather our aim is to forge a flatter, more diffuse and more permeable state. This is a state for which it is much more difficult to draw a clear dividing line between state institutions and the institutions of civil society. If the result is fewer state institutions, there will probably be more quasi-governmental organizations (ironically, of the kind that have now become much more common because of 'market testing' programmes being carried out in a number of European nations, but overhauled to make them more democratic and accountable) and more non-governmental organizations.

Such a system is not simply a paper exercise. In Latin America, a new balance between state, market and civil organizations has been struck as the state has been 'descaled' as a result of widespread programmes of austerity. At first widely criticized, this descaling is now believed to have had positive effects since it has led to the construction and mobilization of new decentralized associations on the boundaries between state and civil society. The list of such associations (de Janvry and Sadoulet 1993; Nash 1994) is quite bewildering in its diversity – neighbourhood associations (e.g.

neighbourhood committees in Mexico City), Christian-based communities, parents associations, producer organizations (e.g. the federation of coffee growers in Colombia), youth clubs, community movements, new social movements, non-governmental organizations and grass roots organizations. Many of these forms of association have moved from being 'organizations used for self-help and voicing of demands for social justice ... [to] become institutionalised channels for influencing national public policy, thus providing the instruments for social incorporation and participatory democracy' (de Janvry and Sadoulet 1993: 670). In other words, these associations, over time, have been able to muster voice and deploy bargaining power.

As the boundaries between state and civil society become more fluid, and as institutions of state and civil society mix to a hitherto unknown degree, so the role of the state must clearly be redefined. We can identify three main redefinitions. First, the chief functions of the state as a provider of public goods are highlighted. The state maintains a role as a purchaser of services (and most especially, in economic terms, as the chief purchaser of training), as a provider of resources, as a regulator (equally enforcing rules and sanctions in areas like competition law) and as a forum for new ideas. Second, and related, the state becomes involved in fostering the new transboundary organizations, via funding, regulation and transmitting new ideas. Third, the state is forced to redefine its own practices, so that they come to mimic more closely the new forms of association (Arato and Cohen 1992) by demands from newly formed decentralized associations, many of which were formerly in the state sector. For example, the state might begin to promote new forms of regional government (including regional assemblies that provide a voice for all local institutions, perhaps, through a second chamber made up of the representatives of associations), regional courts with some degree of localized jurisdiction over economic rules and arbitrage, and various forms of civic forum.

One final point is in order. The politics of a 'radical democracy' as defined above should not be seen as simply a local politics. Although in most cases associations will start as local enterprises, the aim of the associationist approach must be to build actor networks that are able to rival the networks of the powerful. Thus the intent is always to build 'outwards and upwards', for example from a local foundation to regional, national and even European-wide coalitions (as has happened in the case of Britain where credit unions, local banks and Local Economic Trading Systems (LETS) have formed the Social Investment Forum, which, in turn, is now part of a European-wide 'Bankwatch' organization). In other words, we do not believe that it is necessary to counterpose a local grass roots politics with a centralized state politics (e.g. Harvey 1989), as though the two were mutually exclusive, or to suggest that the first is more 'authentic' than the second. A politics of association would more easily travel across these dualistic boundaries, not least because one of the aims of the radical democratic project is to rework the state, making it more democratically accountable by producing a political process which is more locally responsive.

Conclusion

In this paper, we have tried to outline a socioeconomic approach which can form the basis of a new kind of European regional strategy. However, we have also tried to warn against the implicit assumption made in much of the literature that espouses one or other variant of associationism, that the kind of economic efficiencies produced by the application of socioeconomics will automatically produce outcomes which are more equitable and/or more democratic. We have suggested that the application of a socioeconomic approach will still leave a deficit of equity and/or democracy which cannot be gainsaid. This points to the need for much more work on social infrastructures which can 'turn' socioeconomics from one more weapon in the armouries of the powerful into a weapon that the disempowered can equally use.

In conclusion, it may be that one of the reasons for the kinds of problems we have encountered with the socioeconomic approach is that it is a literature that is now reaching its theoretical limits. In some ways, it might be argued that socioeconomics is only a halfway house in the general reformulation of economics which is now under way. Most particularly, it might be argued that its definition of what is an 'economy' remains essentially conservative. For example, the idea of an economy 'embedded' in a society, which is at the root of the socioeconomic approach, simply restates the dualism between economy and society, which is perhaps the main problem in economics nowadays. In turn, such problems of definition suggest that new 'cultural' approaches to what constitutes 'the economic' and economic governance may offer a potential way forward. The debate over socioeconomics and the politics of association is clearly only just beginning.

Acknowledgements

An earlier version of this chapter appeared as 'Institutional issues for the European regions: from markets and plans to socioeconomics and the powers of association' in *Economy and Society* (1995, 24: 41–66).

Bibliography

Allen, J. (1997) 'Economies of power and space', in R. Lee and J. Wills (eds) *Geographies of Economies*, London: Arnold.

Amin, A. (1996) 'Beyond associative democracy', *New Political Economy* 1(3): 309–33.

Amin, A. and Hausner, J. (eds) (1997) *Beyond Market and Hierarchy: Interactive Governance and Social Complexity*, Aldershot: Edward Elgar.

Amin, A. and Thrift, N. (1994) 'Living in the global', in A. Amin and N. Thrift (eds) *Globalisation, Institutions and Regional Development in Europe*, Oxford: Oxford University Press.

Amin, A. and Tomaney, J. (1995) (eds) *Behind the Myth of European Union: Prospects for Social Cohesion*, London: Routledge.

Arato, J. and Cohen, A. (1992) *Civil Society and Political Theory*, Cambridge, MA: MIT Press.

Arthur, W.B. (1989) 'Competing technologies, increasing returns, and lock-in by historical events', *Economic Journal* 99(1): 116–31.

Barnes, T. (1995) 'Political economy I: "the culture, stupid" ', *Progress in Human Geography* 19(3): 423–31.

Callon, M. (1986) 'Some elements of a sociology of translation', in J. Law (ed.) *Power, Action and Belief*, London: Routledge and Kegan Paul: 196–233.

—— (1991) 'Techno-economic networks and irreversibility', in J. Law (ed.) *A Sociology of Monsters*, London: Routledge: 132–61.

Castells, M. (1996) *The Rise of Network Society*, Oxford: Blackwell.

Christensen, P.R., Eskelinen, H., Forsstrom, B., Lindmark, L. and Vatne, E. (1990) 'Firms in networks: concepts, spatial impacts and policy implications', in S. Illeris and L. Jakobsen (eds) *Networks and Regional Development*, Copenhagen: Nordrefo: 11–58.

Collier, J. (1994) 'Regional disparities, the single market and European monetary union', in J. Michie and J. Grieve Smith (eds) *Unemployment in Europe*, London: Academic Press.

Cooke, P. and Morgan, K. (1998) *The Associational Economy: Firms, Regions and Innovation*, Oxford: Oxford University Press.

Cooper, R. (1987) 'Information, communication and organisation: a post-structural revision', *Journal of Mind and Behaviour* 8: 395–416.

—— (1992) 'Formal organisations as representations: remote control, displacement and abbreviation', in M. Reed and H. Hughes (eds) *Rethinking Organisation*, London: Sage: 254–72.

—— (1993) 'Technologies of representation', in P. Ahoven (ed.) *Tracing the Semiotic Boundaries of Politics*, Berlin: de Gruyter.

Cooper, R. and Burrell, G. (1988) 'Modernism, postmodernism and organisational analysis: an introduction', *Organisation Studies* 9: 91–112.

Cowling, K. and Sugden, R. (1993) 'Industrial strategy: a missing link in British economic policy', *Oxford Review of Economic Policy* 9: 1–18.

Cox, R. (1987) *Production, Power and World Order: Social Forces in the Making of History*, New York: Columbia University Press.

Cripps, F. and Ward, T. (1994) 'Strategies for growth and employment in the European Community', in J. Michie and J. Grieve Smith (eds) *Unemployment in Europe*, London: Academic Press.

Day, G. and Rees, G. (1991) *Regions, Nations and Europe: Remaking the Celtic Periphery*, Cardiff: University of Wales Press.

Dosi, G. (1988) 'Institutions and markets in a dynamic world', *The Manchester School* 56: 119–46.

Douglass, M. and Friedmann, J. (eds) (1998) *Cities for Citizens*, Chichester: Wiley.

Dunford, M. (1992) 'Socio-economic trajectories. European integration and regional development in the EC', in D. Dyker (ed.) *The European Economy*, London: Longman.

Dunford, M. and Perrons, D. (1994) 'Regional inequality, regimes of accumulation and economic integration in contemporary Europe', *mimeo*, Department of European Studies, University of Sussex.

Fast/Monitor (1992) *Archipelago Europe – Islands of Innovation*, Brussels: Commission of the European Communities.

Gill, S. (ed.) (1993) *Gramsci, Historical Materialism and International Relations*, Cambridge: Cambridge University Press.

Grabher, G. (ed.) (1993) *The Embedded Firm*, London: Routledge.

Grabher, G. and Stark, D. (1997) 'Organising diversity: evolutionary theory, network analysis, and postsocialist transformations', in G. Grabher and D. Stark (eds) *Restructuring Networks in Postsocialism: Linkages and Localities*, Oxford: Oxford University Press.

Granovetter, M. (1985) 'Economic action and social structure: the problem of embeddedness', *American Journal of Sociology* 91: 481–510.

Granovetter, M. and Swedberg, R. (eds) (1992) *The Sociology of Economic Life*, Boulder, CO: Westview Press.

Hamilton, W.R. (1963) 'Institution', in E.R.S. Seligman and A. Johnson (eds) *Encyclopaedia of the Social Sciences* 7: 84–9.

Harvey, D. (1989) *The Urban Experience*, Oxford: Blackwell.

Hassard, J. and Parker, M. (eds) (1993) *Postmodernism and Organisations*, London: Sage.

Hausner, J. (1995) 'Imperative vs. interactive strategy of systematic change in Central and Eastern Europe', *Review of International Political Economy* 1: forthcoming.

Healey, P. (1997) *Collaborative Planning: Shaping Places in Fragmented Societies*, London: Macmillan.

Hirst, P. (1994) *Associative Democracy*, Cambridge: Polity Press.

Hodgson, G.M. (1988) *Economics and Institutions*, Cambridge: Polity Press.

—— (1993) *Economics and Evolution*, Cambridge: Polity Press.

—— (ed.) (1994) *The Economics of Institutions*, Aldershot: Edward Elgar.

—— (1997) 'The ubiquity of habits and rules', *Cambridge Journal of Economics* 21: 663–84.

Hodgson, G.M., Samuels, W.J. and Tool, M.R. (eds) (1993) *The Elgar Companion to Institutional and Evolutionary Economics*, Aldershot: Edward Elgar.

Ingham, G. (1996) 'Some recent changes in the relationship between economics and sociology', *Cambridge Journal of Economics* 20: 243–75.

de Janvry, A. and Sadoulet, T. (1993) 'Market, state and civil organisations in Latin America beyond the debt crisis. The context for rural development', *World Development* 21: 659–74.

Jessop, B. (1994) 'Post-Fordism and the state', in A. Amin (ed.) *Post-Fordism: A Reader*, Oxford: Blackwell.

Kellas, J.G. (1991) 'European integration and the regions', *Parliamentary Affairs* 44(2): 226–39.

Kumar, K. (1993) 'Civil society: an inquiry into the usefulness of an historical term', *British Journal of Sociology* 44(3): 375–95.

Latour, B. (1986) 'The powers of association', in J. Law (ed.) *Power, Action and Belief*, London: Routledge and Kegan Paul: 264–80.

—— (1993) *We Have Never Been Modern*, Hemel Hempstead: Harvester Wheatsheaf.

Law, J. (1994) *Organising Modernity*, Oxford: Blackwell.

Lipietz, A. (1993) 'The local and the global: regional individuality or interregionalism?', *Transactions of the Institute of British Geographers* NS 18: 8–18.

Lundvall, B.-A. (ed.) (1992) *National Systems of Innovation*, London: Pinter.
Marquand, D. (1994) 'Reinventing federalism: Europe and the Left', *New Left Review* 203: 17–26.
Michie, J. and Grieve Smith, J. (eds) (1994) *Unemployment in Europe*, London: Academic Press.
Miliband, D. (1993) 'The new politics of economics', in C. Crouch and D. Marquand (eds) *Ethics and Markets: Co-operation and Competition within Capitalist Economies*, Oxford: Blackwell.
Morgan, G. (1986) *Images of Organisation*, Beverly Hills, CA: Sage.
Mouffe, C. (ed.) (1992) *Dimensions of Radical Democracy*, London: Verso.
Mulgan, G. (1994) *Politics in an Antipolitical Age*, Cambridge: Polity Press.
Murray, R. (1992) 'Europe and the new regionalism', in M. Dunford and G. Kafkalas (eds) *Cities and Regions in the New Europe*, London: Belhaven.
Nash, J. (1994) 'Global integration and subsistence insecurity', *American Anthropologist* 96: 7–30.
Nonaka, I. and Takeuchi, H. (1995) *The Knowledge-creating Company*, Oxford: Oxford University Press.
North, D. (1990) *Institutions, Institutional Change and Economic Performance*, Cambridge: Cambridge University Press.
O'Donnell, R. (1993) *Ireland and Europe: Challenges for a New Century*, Dublin: Economic and Social Research Institute.
Peck, J. and Tickell, A. (1994) 'The search for a new institutional fix in *after*-Fordism', in A. Amin (ed.) *Post-Fordism: A Reader*, Oxford: Blackwell.
Porter, M. (1994) 'The role of location in competition', *Journal of the Economics of Business* 1(1): 35–9.
Sabel, C.F. (1994) 'Learning by monitoring: the institutions of economic development', in N. Smelser and R. Swedberg (eds) *Handbook of Economic Sociology*, Princeton, NJ: Princeton University Press.
Samuels, W.J. (ed.) (1988) *Institutional Economics* (three volumes), Aldershot: Edward Elgar.
Sawyer, M. (1994) 'Industrial strategy and unemployment in Europe', in J. Michie and J. Grieve Smith (eds) *Unemployment in Europe*, London: Academic Press.
Smelser, N. and Swedberg, R. (1994) *Handbook of Economic Sociology*, Princeton, NJ: Princeton University Press.
Storper, M. (1997) *The Regional World: Territorial Development in a Global Economy*, New York: Guilford Press.
Strange, S. (1988) *States and Markets*, London: Pinter.
—— (1992) 'Territory, state, authority and economy. A new realist ontology of global political economy', *mimeo*, Department of Politics, London School of Economics.
Thompson, G. (1993) *The Economic Emergence of a New Europe? The Political Economy of Co-operation and Competition in the 1990s*, Aldershot: Edward Elgar.
Thrift, N. and Olds, K. (1996) 'Refiguring the economic in economic geography', *Progress in Human Geography* 20(3): 311–37.
Van der Pilj, K. (1994) *The Making of an Atlantic Ruling Class*, London: Verso.
Watts, M.J. (1993) 'Development 1: power, knowledge and discursive practice', *Progress in Human Geography* 17(2): 257–72.
Witt, U. (1993) *Evolutionary Economics*, Aldershot: Edward Elgar.

Index

absolute advantage 38, 39
accumulation 3, 4, 54
actor-network theory 299, 310
actors: 157, 158, 299, 300, 306; and associationism 299; interdependent 38, 42; policy 54, 171; and power 299; *see also* rationality
advanced: manufacturing systems 226; research and development 33; technology *see* high technology
agency 303, 305, 306; *see also* actors
agglomeration 28–34, 36, 39, 41, 44, 45, 47n, 100, 108, 117, 273; economies 109, 110
allocational competition 38
American: firms 38, 190; institutional economics 1; school of high-tech regional development 33, 35; unions 180, 181, 184, 187
American Research and Development (ARD) 275, 278, 279
Amin, A. 11, 12, 14–15, 59–60
Anglo-American: countries 236; governance 157, 169; labour market 231; model 230–1; ownership structure 159
Antonelli, C. 40
Arthur, B. 36, 37
ASEAN (Association of South-East Asian Nations) 54
assets: material 24; national 169; (non)specific 43, 45, 47n, 162
associationism 15, 292; 303–11; economics 303; local 305–6; networks 292, 299, 302, 308–9; and radical democracy 306–11
asymmetric: information 158; power 302
'atmosphere' *see* Marshallian
Audi 82, 83
automotive industry: in Baden-Württemberg 65–6, 75, 78–83, 88, 89, 92; in Canada 181, 184; in Detroit 112; in Germany 75, 79, 82, 83, 89, 92, 168; in Japan 23, 56, 67, 75–8, 81–9, 110, 112–17, 165; in Wales 67
Auto Pact (Canada–US) 181, 185

Baden-Württemberg: 23, 57, 62–3, 68, 69, 75–95, 226, 304; automotive cluster in 65–6, 75, 78–83, 88, 89, 92; Future Commission report 62, 91, 92
Bagnasco A. 25
Becattini G. 25, 58; Florentine group 25; and industrial districts 25
Benton, L. 69
Bernstein R.J. 7, 9
Best, M. 101
'best practice' 26, 63, 70, 296
biotechnology 34, 62, 65
BMW 62, 63, 83–85, 230
Boekholt, P. 58, 59
Boeing 110, 112
'borderless world' 55
Bosch 62, 67, 80, 82, 86–8, 92
Boston 267, 268, 278
branch plants 57, 135, 177, 181, 182, 184, 207, 210, 222
Brazil 100, 113, 115, 117; São José des Campos 110, 115; Campinas 110, 115
British Columbia forest industry 184, 192, 193; *see also* Powell River
Brusco, S. 58, 60
business: economics 27, 29, 39, 47n; organization 15; practice 27, 67; strategy 156, 164; unionism 184

California: cases in 30, 33, 34 (*see also* .

Silicon Valley); southern 34, and military-industrial complex 34
California School: critique of 30–2; and external economies 28–32; and input-output models 34, 36; and transactions-cost theory 41, 44
Callon, M. 299
Canada 1, 226, 239–62; and continentalism 176–98; firms 14; foreign direct investment 238–40, 243–45, 257–8; economics 1; economy 3, 179, 182; foreign firms in 248–52; firms 190; forest industry 184, 185, 192, 193; industrial policy 179, 245, 261; industrial structure 182, 253–8; paper industry 4, 184, 186–97; political economy 6; regional policy 179, 198, 260–1; research and development 239–40, 246–52; staples 176–81, 183–7; technology 182, 183, 190, 192, 193, 196; technology gap 243; trade 242–45; truncation 183, 250–1, 258; unions 184, 191, 192; *see also* British Columbia, Ontario, Powell River, Spruce Falls, Toronto
capital: 4, 295; allocation 158, 160; American 180, 182; cost 160; international 184; labour relations 158, 163; market 160; mobility 157, 164, 166, 171, 173n, 266, 269, 293; overseas Chinese 302; patient 108, 111, 114; regulation 14
capitalism 23, 24, 30, 36, 38, 42, 46, 47n, 158, 159, 292, 301; 'casino' 168; contemporary 25, 32
capitalist development 25, 26, 27, 45
Carey, J.W. 1, 5
Carosso, V. 270
central planning 15
centralization 4, 292, 293, 297
centre (*see also* core) 206–208, 210, 211, 213, 217–220, 222
Centres of Excellence 138, 143, 146, 147
centrifugal regimes: 157, 161, 162, 165–8, 170; defined 157; and industrial policy 168; and investment 169; in the US 157, 161, 165, 169;
centripetal regimes 157, 161, 162, 164–7, 170, 295; defined 157; in Germany 157, 161, 162, 164–5, 169; and investment 169; in Japan 157, 161, 162, 164–5; and private governance 170
Christopherson, S. 28, 99
Chrysler 62, 86
Clark, G.L. 232
class 12, 15, 157
cluster(ing) 57, 58, 59, 62, 63–70, 297, 304; and production 64
Cochran, T. 269
co-determination 232
collaboration (*see also* co-operation): 60, 62, 235; inter-firm 225; networks 306
collective: agency 306; entrepreneur 76, 77, 95; governance 304
colonialism 1, 2, 6
commodity chain 166–7; buyer-driven 167; producer-driven 167; *see also* supply chain, value chain
communication 2, 4, 5–6, 39, 44, 45, 57, 296; media 5; rules 30; and staples 5–6; studies 3, 5–6; types 5
communities: and agency 303; of interest 55, 295; supranational 55
comparative: advantage 3, 38, 39, 56, 169, 177, 182, 293; statics 36
competition 11, 26, 55, 57, 59, 62, 71, 158, 162, 164, 168, 183, 293; allocational 38; and co-operation 58, 63, 167; imperfect 16; industrial 240–1, 245; new 24; non-price 58; policy 296, 297, 305; price 79; technological 38
competitive advantage 11, 24, 57, 58, 59, 169, 170, 171, 192, 294, 297, 304
consumer preferences 10
context 36, 302, 303; cultural 13, 17; historical 25; local 13, 304; national 157; and networks 302; social 17
contextual: explanation 9, 12; position 13
continentalism 176–98
contingency 17; cultural 9
'continuous improvement' 162 (*see also* quality)
conventions 1, 10, 13, 15–16, 40, 42, 44, 45, 47n, 58, 177, 186, 225, 300
co-operation (*see also* collaboration) 15, 58–60, 64, 66, 70, 162, 301, 302, 306, 307, 309; and competition 58, 63, 167; strategy 71
co-operative advantage 58–63, 71; and Baden-Württemberg 62–3; and Emilia-Romagna 60–1
co-ordination 157, 167; policy 305; and power 156; structures 155; *see also* economic, firm hierarchy, market

core (*see also* centre) 206–208, 210, 211, 213, 217–220, 222; firm 156, 162, 166–7, 172n; regions 295, 298
corporate: decision making 171; headquarters 207, 210, 211, 219, 220, 222; networks 306; restructuring 16, 27; strategy 13
corporations *see* large, transnational; M-form 270
Courchene, T. 149
craft production 30
'creative destruction' 266, 280, 282
crisis 183, 197
critical realism 17, 158
cultural: context 13, 17; contingency 9; economics 7; norms 13; system 6; 'turn' 13
culture 300; economic 16; institutionalized 300; organizational 300; of Silicon Valley 44
cumulative causation 7, 11, 17
Czech Republic 234

Daimler-Benz 80, 83, 85, 86, 94, 166
David, P.A. 11, 37
Davis, L. 266, 267, 269, 281
decentralization 44, 292, 309, 310
democracy: deficit 308, 311; and governance 306; liberal 308; radical 306–11
deregulation 55
Dei Ottari, G. 58
Detroit 109, 110, 111, 112, 118
Dicken, P. 155
Digital Equipment Corporation (DEC) 218–220, 279
differentiation 39, 171, 193, 196; *see also* spatial
diffusion 44, 166, 301
disintegration *see* vertical disintegration
diversification 3, 64–9, 70, 191, 195, 197; in North-Rhine Westphalia 64–7; in Wales 67–9
division of labour 25, 26, 28, 33, 40, 46, 164–6, 180, 186, 293
Dosi, G. 36, 40, 47n
dualism 303, 310, 311
dual training system (in Germany) 93, 94, 228
Dunning, J.H. 31, 40

economic geography 1–2, 12–17, 23, 45, 155, 198
economic: base 33; co-ordination 58, 60, 71; cultures 16; discourse 302; integration (*see also* European) 295; liberalism 179; metaphors 302; organization 56; policy 54, 61; rationality (*see also homo economicus*, rationality) 7, 10, 12, 179; spaces 32; sociology 2, 11–12, 29, 35; sovereignty 54, 55, 180; value 10
economics: diachronic 302; of the firm 31; international 300; nationalist 3; *see also* business, cultural, evolutionary, external, neoclassical, institutional, orthodox, socioeconomies: associative 303, 304; urbanization 31, 32; *see also* external, scale
economy: domestic 156; global 295; of organizations 31; as instituted process 58, 299; as a network of actors 300; *see also* European, managed, social
efficiency 8, 12, 26, 62, 182, 292, 306, 307, 311
electronic data interchange (EDI) 87
embeddedness 11, 12, 13, 15, 35, 57, 155, 156, 159, 295, 299, 311; institutional 2, 12; of power 307, 308
Emilia-Romagna (Italy) 57, 78, 98, 304; and co-operative advantage 60–1
empire 2, 3, 4, 5, 6, 8, 179
empowerment 306
England 25
enterprise geography 14
entrepreneur 33, 60, 70, 193, 293–6; incentives 295
Europe 29, 39, 74, 77, 82, 89, 95, 108; Eastern 234, 293, 294; 'of the regions' 292, 297
European: economy 293–7; FTA 166; industrial districts 32, 302; integration 292–5; neoclassical theory 7; regional policy 25, 311; school of high-tech development 35 (see also GREMI); Union 54, 55, 75, 292–5, 297
evolutionary economics 2, 7, 10–11, 12, 16, 30, 36–42, 47n, 300, 302
exchange rate mechanism 60
external economies 25, 28–30, 34, 37, 38; of scale 43

financial: controls 54; deregulation 54; markets 156–7, 159, 161; services 30, 171

firms 31; hierarchy *see* network, organizational; post-Fordist 31; *see also* large corporations, small firms, theory of the firm
fiscal policy 55, 59, 296, 305
Fletcher Challenge 191
flexible: agglomerations 36; employment rules 231; manufacturing systems (FMS) 227–230; 232–3; production 13, 16, 23, 31, 32; specialisation 25–7, 29, 30, 33, 75, 297; workforce 192, 196, 197
flexibility 25, 26, 28, 29, 32, 33, 38, 39, 71, 171, 177, 193, 197, 198, 241; of networks 31
Florence school 25, 26; and industrial districts 25
Fordism 56, 127, 177, 183, 184, 186; *see also* post-Fordism
foreign: direct investment (FDI) 56, 62, 67, 68, 156, 169, 170, 190, 238–40, 243–5, 257–8, 294; investment in Canada 180–3, 185; ownership 181, 183, 190; trade 56
frameworks: political-legal 156; industrial policy 142–3, 149; *see also* institutional, regulatory, organizational
France 28, 32
Franchi, M. 61
free trade 177, 180, 183, 185, 186, 295; agreement/area (FTA) 54, 137, 140, 176–7, 179, 183, 186, 187; *see also* NAFTA, European Union, ASEAN
Freeman, C. 128, 130
Fuji-Xerox 212–13
Fukao, M. 161, 163

GATT (General Agreement on Tariffs and Trade) 60, 176
gender 12, 15
General Motors (GM) 217–18, 219, 222
geography *see* economic, enterprise, industrial
Gereffi, G. 167
Germany 81–94, 168, 226–36; cases in 25, 39, 165–6, 171; industrial relations 231–2; machinery 14; southern 26, 65; *see also* Lower Saxony, Mittelstand, North Rhine Westphalia, Ruhrgebiet, Stuttgart
Gertler, M. 14
Glasmeier, A. 176
globalization 41, 44, 45, 55–57, 62, 65, 71, 74, 79, 127, 156, 159, 166, 171, 177, 178, 187, 292, 294, 305
'glocalization' 164–7
golden age 135
governance 296, 298, 301, 306–8, 311; Anglo-American 157; democratic 306; institutions 159; intermediate forms 301, 303; local 171; market 155–7, 160, 162, 171; networks 301; private 170; regional 304, 305; systems 156–7, 159, 172n, 304; *see also* centrifugal, centripetal
Gramsci, A. 300, 302
Granovetter, M. 11, 15, 35, 298
GREMI (Groupe de Recherche Européen sur les Milieux Innovateurs) 35, 36
grounded 15; *see also* situated, embedded
'gunbelt' 34

Hamilton, W.R. 299
Harrison, B. 61, 101
Harvie, C. 55
Hausner, J. 303–4
hegemony, US 180, 183, 186, 298, 300, 307–9
Heizer Corporation 276
'heterarchy' 306
heterodox: economics 298; networks 308
Hodgson, G. 9, 10, 12, 298
Holmes, J. 28
high technology 30, 31, 33–6, 44, 70, 227–30; centres 40; development 33, 35; and American school 33, 35; industries in 'Route 128' 267, 278–280; industries in Silicon Valley 267, 277, 278–80; and R&D 33; revolution 273–80; sector 15, 17; and venture capital 267, 273–80
hinterland 3, 8
'hollowing out' 294, 303
homo economicus 7 *see also* rationality
hub-and-spoke industrial district 102, 103, 105, 110–12, 113, 115, 117, 118, 120
Hutton, W. 54, 56

IBM 26, 27, 31, 214–17
idiographic analysis 46
IG Metall 94, 95
imperfect competition 16
increasing returns to scale 16

indigenous firms 67, 69, 138, 182, 296
industrial: adjustment 27; atmosphere *see* Marshallian; communities 30; competition 240–1, 245; development 273, 280–2; divide 25–7, 40; organization 24, 25, 28–32, 57, 71, 296; region 293; relations *see* labour; restructuring 138; revolution 270–3, 281; new spaces 29, 183; specialization 57; strategy 297; structure 178; systems 26
industrial district 25, 26, 43, 57, 58, 60–1, 69–70, 77, 101, 106, 118–20, 155, 301; European 32, 302; Italian 101–2, 106–9, 111, 117; Marshallian 25, 57, 101–2, 105, 106–9, 112, 116–18, 306; military 116; model 74, 75, 77; new (NID) 98–101, 106, 119–20; state-anchored 102, 104, 115–18; *see also* hub-and-spoke, satellite
industrial geography 1–2; and conventions 15–16; and embeddedness 15; new 12–17; and reflexivity 12–14; and untraded interdependencies 17
industrial policy 25, 54, 56, 62, 63, 135, 140, 147, 150, 158, 167, 168, 170, 297, 304; in Canada 179, 245, 261; in Europe 56; framework 142–3, 149; in Germany 168; in the US 168
Industrie- und Handelskammern (IHK, German chambers of commerce) 80, 92, 93, 94
infant industry 34
information: 'age' 294; asymmetric 158; economy 293; imperfect 158; technology 62, 127, 133
infrastructure 4, 34, 157, 167, 168, 169, 180, 293, 294, 311; 'soft' 58
Innis, H. 1–9, 11–14, 16–17, 178, 179, 183, 198, 226; on communications, knowledge and power 4–6; on continentalism 183; and institutional economics 6–8; on staples 3–6; on technology 8; and Veblen 6–8
innovation: 8, 17, 31, 33–6, 42, 62, 67, 70; 75–9, 90, 108–9, 157, 165, 207, 226, 236, 293, 296, 297, 301, 305, 306; centres 61, 68–9; methodological 17; and milieu 35, 68; network 68, 304; organizational 24; policy 67; social 303; systems 156, 241, 258–61; national systems of 128–30, 131; regional systems of 134, 138, 146, 225, 294; technological 24, 30, 68, 75, 93, 162, 165, 226, 265, 270
input-output (I-O): chains 32, 43; linkages 34, 44; models 36; relations 25, 28, 29, 31, 32, 37, 40, 41, 43, 45; system 30, 35, 44; transactions 47n
inside: information 161; lending 268
institutional economics: 1, 3, 6–12, 299–300; contemporary 8–12; context 29; and economic sociology 11–12, 292; and evolutionary economics 10–11, 292; and Innis 6–8; new 9–10; and Veblen 6–8
institutional: embeddedness 2, 12; framework 33, 303; networks 10, 11, 27, 298, 305, 308; reflexivity 134, 140–6, 150; power 8, 12, 14, 302; situatedness 7, 9, 17; specificity 23; structure 1, 4, 5, 14, 15, 32, 158, 297; thickness 12, 15, 29, 301, 303, 304; transformation 292
institutionalism 2, 5, 6, 9–14, 17, 29, 33, 58; American 1, 6
institutions 1, 3, 6–10, 14, 24, 25–7, 30, 32, 67, 155, 156, 159, 162, 171, 177, 293, 295, 298–300, 304, 308; agglomerations and 30; building 297, 303, 306; defined 299; federal 297; intermediate 298; market 157; national 14, 231–5, 309; public 37; regional institutions 35, 225, 226, 231–5, 236, 297; regulatory 158, 160; of socioeconomics 308
integration (*see also* vertical integration) 179, 186, 304; in Europe 292, 293; and governance 301
interdependence: 28, 29, 42, 302; and actors 38, 42
inter-firm interaction 25, 28, 30, 70, 155, 156, 162, 171, 296
intermediaries 298–9, 301, 304
international: investment *see* foreign direct investment; politics 300; relations 179; trade (*see also* trade) 24, 39, 40, 41, 156, 176
inter-personal: networks 11; relations 58, 299
intervention 295, 297, 305; state 164, 179, 297; supply-side 294
investment (*see also* foreign direct investment, venture capital) 4, 24, 34, 40, 54, 66, 155, 160–3, 167, 171,

176, 180, 184, 189, 293–6; rules 159, 164; orientation 160, 162, 167; strategies 157, 166; and trade 24, 177, 178, 182
'invisible hand' 10
Italy: cases in 25, 28, 39, 40, 171; Emilia-Romagna 78, 98; Florence 25, 26; industrial districts 101–2, 106, 108–9, 111, 117; Northeast-central 23, 25; Prato 26; Third 25, 26, 29, 77, 99, 100, 117; Tuscany 26
Italian school 26

Jaffe, A. 40
Japan 26, 29, 32, 301, 302, cases in 39, 56, 67, 75–8, 81, 82, 84, 85, 87, 89, 100, 112–17, 196, 212; Toyota City 23, 110; satellite industrial platform 114
Japanese: firms 67, 75–7, 190; production systems/methods 27
Jessop, B. 294
John Deere 220–1

Kennard, J. 212–13
Kester, W.C. 166, 172n
Keynes 8; Keynesianism 46, 55, 56 141, 292–7
knowledge 4, 8, 12, 34, 44, 57, 63, 71, 182, 196, 293–5, 300, 302; (non)codifiable 28, 37, 39, 43; creation 36; development 30, 38, 39; intensity 31; local 2, 13; monopolies 5; politics 5; and power 3–5; reflexive 13; spillovers 37; transfer 304
Krugman, P. 16

labour: –capital relations; intensity 30; practices 156; relations 176, 193, 197, 295; *see also* division of
labour market 14, 30, 32, 37, 40, 43, 45, 157, 169, 294; external 230; US 229, 230; in Germany 163; segmented 14; social construction 230–2; regulation 230–2; in the US 163
large corporations 4, 31, 32, 298
Lamoreaux, N.R. 267, 268, 281
Langlois, R. 58
Latin America 309–10
Latour, B. 299
lean production 46, 56, 71, 75, 283; in Japan 77
learning 23, 24, 27, 42, 47n, 162, 225, 228, 229, 298, 304, 306; economy 39, 46; inter-firm 234; and networks 301, 302; -based production systems 23; region 149, 225; *see also* organizational, technological
least favoured regions 56, 57, 59, 60, 63–70, 293–8, 304, 305
liberalization 55, 295; of trade 245
linkages 31, backward 180; and transactions-cost model 30; *see also* inter-firm, local, input–output
local: associationism 305–6; context 13, 304; economy 169, 294; institutions 297; knowledge 2, 13; linkages; learning 41; networks 57; politics 310; scale 177; statism 298
localization 23, 27, 30, 36, 74; economies 32
location: analysis 155; process 171; theory 17
'lock-in' 11, 13, 16, 17, 28, 81, 294
Los Alamos 116, 117
Los Angeles 34, 99, 115; clothing industry in 23, 28, 29; Hollywood 28, 29
Lowell, F.C. 268
Lower Saxony 226
lumber 4
Lundvall, B.A. 39, 47n, 128, 130, 131, 301

McDowell, L. 12, 15
Mackintosh, W.A. 179
McLuhan, M. 6
MacMillan Bloedel 190, 194–7
microeconomics 27
managed economy 292, 295–8, 305, 306
management literature 27
market: co-ordination 58; global 159; governance 155–7, 160, 162, 171; institutions 157, 160, 170, 298; rules 157, 158, 164, 167, 171; regulation 158, 171; share 161, 170; 'shock' 293
markets 59, 155, 183, 300; domestic 157; goods and services 10, 12, 26, 42; factor *see* labour market; social nature 155
Marshall, A. 25, 43, 57–8, 106, 108
Marshallian: 'atmosphere' 30, 58, 60; industrial districts 25, 57, 101–2, 105, 106, 108–9, 112, 116–18; school 35
Marshall, H. 180
Marxism 1, 9, 12, 13, 17, 36, 300

Massachusetts: cases in 33, 34; *see also* New England and 'Route 128'
Massey, D. 13
mass production 16, 23, 25–7, 29, 38, 39, 47n, 56, 193, 197, 209, 211
material assets 24
Mellon, A. 270–3, 275, 281, 285
Mercedes-Benz 62, 82–7, 89, 92, 230; see also Daimler-Benz and Chrysler
Metcalfe, S. 131
metropole 3, 8, 177, 179, 183
Michalak, W. 178
microelectronics revolution 129
milieu: defined 35–6; and innovation 35
military–industrial complex 34
Mirowski, P. 10, 12
MIT (Massachusetts Institute of Technology) 33
Mitchell, K. 15
Mittelstand (Germany) 88, 90, 91, 93, 94, 95, 232
modernization theory 208, 223
monetarism 54, 296; global 54, 56, 60; policy 55, 56, 59
Mulgan, G. 308
multilateralism 178
multi-locational firm 113, 206, 220, 221; *see also* transnational corporations
multinational corporations (MNCs) 156, 183, 184, 207; *see also* transnational corporations

NAFTA (North America Free Trade Agreement) 54, 176–7, 179, 183–7, 245
nation state 4, 40, 54, 55, 56, 57, 60, 159, 171, 225, 236, 292, 294, 298, 304, 307
national identity 156
nationalism 180, 182, 183, 185
Nelson, R. 10, 11, 36
neoclassical economics 1, 3, 9, 13, 36, 59, 295, 300, 306; European 7
neo-liberal: economic policy 292, 293, 295–8, 305; ideology 76
network: form 155; horizontal 166; metaphor 35; organization 166; paradigm 27, 29; relations 40, 56, 166; vertical 166
networking 15, 63, 67, 70, 75, 296, 297, 307
networks 13, 15, 31, 37, 64, 70, 71, 155–158, 164, 171, 241, 255–7; associationist 292, 299, 302, 308–9; collaborative 306; cohesive vs. strategic 167; defined 300; of firms 304, 306; of governance 301; and hierarchy 166, 306; and information 300; of institutions 10, 11, 27, 298, 305, 308; interpersonal 11; knowledge 304; learning 301, 302; of power 298, 301, 307, 308; of social relations 12, 234, 236, 299; trade 167
New England 118, 233, 235, 267–9; and military-industrial complex 34; textile industry 267–9, 271; *see also* 'Route 128'
new industrial spaces 183
new institutional economics 9–10, 299
North America 55, 74, 77, 194, 198, 226; market 226, 233, 234; free trade agreement *see* NAFTA; regional policy in 25
North Rhine Westphalia 64–7, 71, 226; and internal diversification 64–7
NUMMI 217, 219, 222

OECD (Organization for Economic Co-operation and Development) 56
Ohmae, K. 55, 56 133
Olsen, K. 218–19
Ontario 127, 135–50, 189; *see also* Spruce Falls, Toronto
opportunistic behaviour 234, 235
Orange County 23, 99, 108, 109
organizational: change 24, 25; creation 36; culture 300; economy 31; form 26; framework 33; hierarchy 10, 58; innovation 24; learning 42, 44, 45; paradigm 56; rationality 42, 45; reflexivity 14; spaces 43; theory 300; trajectory 43
orthodox: economics model/theory (*see also* neoclassical economics) 3, 6, 12, 26, 36, 37, 38, 306, 308; Keynesian 297; new 27
out-sourcing 56, 62, 167
ownership structure 159; Anglo-American 159; in Germany 159–60; in Japan 159–60; network 160

Pacific Rim 15
paper industry 4, 66, 178, 184, 186, 187
Patel, P. 31, 40
'path dependence' 11, 13, 16, 30, 36–41, 294, 302, 304
pathways of development 30; *see also* trajectories

Pavitt, K. 31, 40
periphery 4, 181, 198, 206–11, 213, 218, 220, 221
Perrin, J.C. 36, 47n
Perroux, F. 32, 37, 47n
Piore, M. 25, 26, 28, 43, 99, 101
Pittsburgh 109, 267, 270–3, 281
Poland 234
Polanyi, K. 11, 299
policy: interventionist 56; neo-liberal 61; public 306; *see also* actors, fiscal, monetary
political economy: 6, 155, 162, 171, 176, 183, 300, 307; Canadian 6
Porsche 62, 82, 83
Porter, M. 47n, 57–9, 132, 143; diamond 59, 62; *see also* competitive advantage
post-Fordism 23, 27, 30, 36, 38, 43, 75, 177, 183, 283; *see also* flexibility; flexible production, Fordism
post-industrial society 129
Powell River mill (British Columbia) 178, 192, 193–7
power: 5, 6, 155, 292, 294, 299, 302, 311; bargaining 168, 169, 310; embedded 307, 308; institutional 8, 12, 14, 302; networks 298, 301, 307, 308; and knowledge 3–5; relations 158
pragmatism (philosophical) 13
Prato district 58; *see also* Emilia-Romagna
Premier's Council 137–40, 142, 147, 149
price competition 79
primary resources 3; *see also* staples
primate urban system 32
principal–agent relations 158, 160–1
privatization 55, 61
problem-solving 228, 229
producer–user: interaction 37, 226, 234, 236; relations 30, 45
product: differentiation 47n; mandates 251
production: craft 30; paradigm 28, 33 (*see also* flexibility, Fordism, post-Fordism); organization of 157; strategies 157; system of 6, 23, 24, 25, 27, 28, 42, 44, 178, 242; worlds of 16, 42; *see also* flexible, mass
productivity 62, 162, 163, 192, 293
property: ownership 162–3; and control 159, 163; rights 158–9, 164, 166, 172n; in Germany 158–9; in the US 159, 172n
protectionism 169, 177, 184, 186, 187
proximity *see* spatial proximity
Pyke, F. 71

quality: institutional 304; of life 34; product 58, 68, 162, 192, 196

radical democracy 306–11
Rastatt 84, 85, 89
rationality (*see also* economic, *homo economicus*) 10, 12, 36, 58, 297, 299, 300, 304, 306; and actors 36, 37; *economic*; organizational 42
reciprocity 157, 158, 301
reflexivity 2, 12–14, 15; individual 14; and knowledge 13; organizational 14; theoretical 14
region(s) 8, 23, 28, 39, 45, 71; core 295, 298; dynamic 292; less-favoured (LFR) 56, 57, 59, 60, 63–70, 293–8, 304, 305; learning 149, 225; 'motor' 25; role for 24, 46; states 55, 133, 149, 150, 225; status of 25
regional: assets; autonomy 294; cohesion 292; co-operation 71; convergence 293; development 14, 33–6, 40, 46, 61, 66, 67, 69, 70, 74, 75, 79, 155, 222–3, 292, 298, 305, 306; divide 292–7; disparities 33, 46, 56, 293, 295–7; dynamics 131–3; economics 23, 25; economic structure 23; economy 32, 36, 38, 43, 45, 46, 56, 57, 62, 64, 169, 171; governance 304, 305, 310; growth 57, 70–1; hierarchy 294; institutions 35, 225, 226, 232, 235, 236, 297; networking 70; politics 34, 308; restructuring defined 64; science 36, 60; specialisation 16, 57, 64 (*see also* territorial); trade 16, 39; 'voice' 298, 305
regional policy 24, 25, 56; in Baden-Württemberg 62, 63; in Canada 260–1; in Europe 295
regionalism 4, 23, 27, 43, 176; international 178, 198; new 297
regionalization 23–4, 26, 41, 44, 45, 56; debate 24–5; importance 24; schools of thought 24–5
regulation 13, 29, 59, 157–8, 160, 170, 183, 310, anti-trust 161; of capital 14; environmental 168; international 159, 198; private 170; 'spaces' 171, 172n; of trade 185; wage 56
Regulationist school 47n

regulatory framework: 1, 10, 157–9, 171, 176, 178, 183, 198; macro- 230–1, 235, 236; national 159, 235; 'thick' 157; 'thin' 157
Reich, S. 168, 170
relational assets 17
representation 300
Research and Development (R&D) 33, 34, 66, 70, 139, 147, 156, 161, 165, 167, 239–40, 246–50, 294; in Canada 181–3, 190, 193, 195
Research Triangle Park 113, 114
resource industries 4, 176, 182, 186
restructuring 186, 304; corporate 16, 27, 63, 66, 71, 196, 198; industrial 64, 178, 183, 184; regional 64; and regionalism 178
robotics 227
Rockefeller, L. 273, 275
Rorty, R. 9
Rosenbluth, G. 183
'Route 128' (Massachusetts) 14, 23, 33–4, 218, 278–80; and MIT 33
Ruhrgebiet (*see also* North Rhine Westphalia) 64–7, 81, 89
Ruigrok, W. 156, 162, 164
Russo, M. 30

Sabel, C. 25, 26, 28, 99, 101, 128, 301
Salais, R. 16, 47n
satellite industrial platform 102, 103, 105, 112–15, 117, 118, 120; in Japan 114; *see also* industrial districts
Saxenian, A.L. 14, 33, 99, 101, 172n, 218–19
Sayer, A. 76
scale: geographical 15, 26, 31, 169, 302; economies of 43, 164, 167, 187; increasing returns to 16; local 177
Schoenberger, E. 16
Schumpeter, J. 76, 128, 265, 266, 274, 280, 282; Schumpeterian 33, 36, 292, 294, 295, 296
Scott, A. 9, 28, 33, 40, 47n, 99, 117
Seattle 110, 115, 117
second industrial revolution 270–3, 281
sectoral: policy 167; 'voice' 167–71, 172n
segmented labour markets 14
semiconductors 34, 43, 44, 165; *see also* 'Route 128', Silicon Valley
Silicon Valley 14, 23, 29, 31, 33–34, 43, 44, 99, 108, 109, 115, 117, 118, 218–20, 277–80, 287; culture 44; and Stanford 33, 34
situatedness: institutional 7, 9, 17; space-time 12
small- and medium-sized enterprises (SMEs): 61, 62, 68, 71, 166, 274, 275, 277, 279, 296; debate 25–27; networks 69, 70; suppliers 57, 234
social: capital 78, 80, 90, 132; economy 225; relations 11, 12, 15, 155; power 17; system 6
socioeconomics 2, 11–12, 158, 292, 298–302, 304, 306–11; critical 302; debate 311; institutions 308
South Korea 100, 110, 113, 115, 117
spaces *see* economic, organizational, technological
space–time 4, 5, 6, 16, 40; situatedness 12; specificity 13
Spaeth, L. 90, 91
spatial: differentiation 171, 297; pattern 69, 297, 156; proximity 15, 17, 32, 47n; scale 15, 304; science 1, 3, 17;
specialization 3, 17, 24, 25, 28, 29, 56, 57, 66, 177, 182, 294; and trade 41; *see also* industrial, regional; territorial
specificity 47n; *see also* assets, institutional, space-time, territorial
spillovers *see* knowledge, technological
Spruce Falls mill (Ontario) 189, 191–2
stakeholders 157, 163, 164
standardization 177
Stanford University 33, 34
staples 2–4, 5, 6, 8; in Canada 176–81, 183–7; economy 3; thesis defined 3–4; 'trap' 3, 17
state (*see also* nation state): intervention 164, 179, 297; institutions 309, 310; -firm relations 166; policy 167, 168; politics 310
'sticky places' 98–102, 106, 109, 117–20
Stiglitz, J. 266
Storper, M. 11, 14, 15, 16, 17, 33, 99, 101, 102, 132, 177, 301
Strange, S. 168, 300, 307
Stuttgart region 80, 82, 84, 89, 94
strategic alliance 156, 164, 165, 172n
structural: adjustment 293, 304; unemployment 293
subsidy 55, 59, 60, 64, 168–170, 172n, 180
sunk costs 157, 169, 170
sub-contracting 56, 57, 60, 186
suppliers 14, 31; 'clubs' 67, 68, 162;

relationships 166, 170; resource 177
supply: and demand 10; chain 59, 68, 304; -side 60, 294, 296, 297, 304, 305

tariffs 179, 181, 186, 188
Taylorism 63, 197
Techno-: economic paradigm 129, 130, 150; nationalism 258–9
technology 1, 3, 4, 6, 8, 10–13, 16, 17, 23–7, 36–46, 62, 67, 70, 156, 162; accumulation 46; in Canada 182, 183, 190, 192, 193, 196; centres 67–9; development 16, 167, 294; districts 41; fund 138, 139; gap 243; importance for Innis 4, 8; parks 67; policy 295, 297; strategy 68; transfer 61, 166, 227–36, 295; and Veblen 8; *see also* high
technological: branching point 29; change 24, 25, 33, 37, 40, 41, 70, 183, 192, 196; dependency 181; learning 24, 39, 41, 44, 45; choice 10; innovation 24, 30, 68, 75, 93, 162, 165, 226, 265, 270; paradigm 39; revolution 64; spaces 32, 43; spillovers 37, 39, 40, 43; trajectory 28, 41
technopole 68
telecommunications 32; *see also* communications
terms of trade 183; *see also* trade
territorial specialization 27, 36, 39, 45
territorialization 36, 39, 40, 132
theory of the firm 26, 32
threshold firms 252, 255
Third Italy 25, 26, 29, 77, 99, 100, 117
Thrift, N. 11, 12, 14–15
time–space: *see* space–time
Toronto: industrial structure 253–8; University of 3
Toyota 56, 67, 83, 85, 110, 112; City 23, 110
trade 27, 39, 46, 60, 169, 170, 184; in Canada 176, 178, 181, 185, 242–5; conflict 184; and investment 24, 177, 178, 182; liberalization 245; managed 185, 186; in US 177, 185; *see also* free, international, regional, regulation
traded interdependencies 32
trading blocs 177, 178, 187
training 157, 161, 163, 170, 196, 197, 297, 304; with advanced manufacturing technologies 228, 229, 231; 'dual' system 228; incentive 231;
trajectories: of conventions 42; development 295, 298, 308; linear 303; of unionism 184; of worlds of production 42; *see also* organizational, technology
transactions: 16, 24, 28–32; costs 28, 30, 32, 44, 45; external 9; theory 41
transnational corporations (TNCs) 156, 170, 238–41, 305; *see also* multinational corporations
'trickle down' 296, 297
truncation 183, 250–1, 258
trust 15, 28, 58, 155, 157, 162, 225, 234

Uhler, R.S. 188
unions: American 180, 181, 184, 187, 191; anti 232; Canadian 184, 191; influence of 232; international 181–2; *see also* IG Metall
Union Trust Company 272, 281
United Kingdom (UK) 82, 89; Wales 88, 89
United States: 39, 40, 83, 85, 89; 98–100, 106, 108, 113, 115, 117, 118, 120, 169, 187, 212, 227–33, 235; economy 179; institutionalist school 6; Midwest 117, 118, 228, 233; South 228, 229–30, 232, 235; West 232; *see also* hegemony, Los Angeles, Orange County, New England, 'Route 128', Seattle, Silicon Valley
university-production link 34; *see also* MIT, Route 128, Silicon Valley, Stanford
untraded interdependencies 11, 17, 24–5, 36–46, 47n, 301; and the region 24
urbanization economies 31, 32
user–producer *see* producer–user

Valencia 64, 69–70; and Baden-Württemberg 70; and Emilia-Romagna 69, 70
value chain 164; *see also* supply chain
van Tulder, R. 156, 162, 164
Varian, M. 214–16
Veblen, T. 1–3, 6–17, 299; and Innis 6–8; on technology 8
venture capital 160, 265–82; limited partnerships 277–78; and textile industry in New England 267–9; and the second industrial revolution 270–3; and the high-technology

revolution 273–80; and industrial development 280–1; in Boston 278; in Chicago 276; in New York 276; in San Francisco 277; in 'Route 128' 278–80; in Silicon Valley 277–80
de Vet, J. 56
virtual machine (VM) system 214–17
vertical: disintegration 28, 29, 31, 32; integration 61, 162
voice 308–310; *see also* regional, sectoral
Volkswagen (VW) 168

Wales 58, 64, 67–9, 88, 89; and Baden-Württemberg 68–9; and external diversification 67–9; Welsh Development Agency (WDA) 67–9
Walker, R.102
Watkins, M.H. 4, 177, 181, 185
Watson, A.J. 5, 6
welfare policies 294; state 295; and workfare 294
Whitney, J. 273, 276
Williamson, O. 9, 47n
Winter, S. 10, 11, 36
works councils 163
worlds of production 16, 42; trajectories 42
World Trade Organization (WTO) 120

Xerox 212–13, 218

Young, A. 40

Ziegler, N. 165